POWER WITHOUT
RESPONSIBILITY

D1099077

POWER WITHOUT RESPONSIBILITY

The press and broadcasting in Britain

James Curran and *Jean Seaton*

Routledge
London and New York

First published in 1981 by Fontana
Second edition published in 1985 by Methuen & Co. Ltd
Third edition published in 1988 by
Routledge
11 New Fetter Lane, London EC4P 4EE

Reprinted 1989 (twice)

Printed and bound in Great Britain by
Biddles Ltd, Guildford and King's Lynn

British Library Cataloguing in Publication Data

Curran, James
Power without responsibility: the
press and broadcasting in Britain.
——3rd ed.
1. Mass media——Great Britain
I. Title   II. Seaton, Jean
302.2' 34' 0941   P92.G7

ISBN 0–415–00653–8

*To Albert and Joan Seaton,
Doodles Curran, and the
memory of Geoffrey Curran*

Contents

About the authors

James Curran is Principal Lecturer in communications at Goldsmiths' College, University of London. He has written extensively on the mass media and is the editor or joint editor of *Mass Communication and Society*; *The British Press: A Manifesto*; *Newspaper History*; *Culture, Society and the Media*; *British Cinema History*; *Media, Culture and Society: A Critical Reader*; *Bending Reality: The State of the Media*; and *Impacts and Influences: Essays on Media Power in the 20th Century*. He was an academic consultant to the Royal Commission on the Press 1974–7, a political columnist for *The Times*, and the founding editor of *New Socialist*.

Jean Seaton is a Senior Lecturer in sociology at the Polytechnic of the South Bank. She has written on the history and theory of broadcasting, the role of the media during the Portuguese Revolution, in the reporting of atrocities, unemployment, politics, the publicity given to child abuse, and on pornography. She has been awarded a British Academy *Thank Offering to Britain* Research Fellowship.

Preface to the third edition

Part I has been revised throughout, and chapter 7 has been rewritten in response to major changes in Fleet Street (which will soon become the home of financial institutions rather than of newspapers). Parts II and III have been modified with additional material concerning the social and political impact of recent technological change on broadcasting, and with a new chapter on recent developments in video, satellite, and cable added. Part IV has been reorganized as a new section, including a completely new chapter 19 surveying alternative proposals for reforming the media. The select bibliography at the end of the book has been pruned and brought up to date.

Acknowledgements

Although this book is very much a joint effort there has been some division of labour. Thus Jean Seaton has concentrated on broadcasting and the sociology of the mass media (chapters 8–15 and 16), and James Curran on the history and political theory of the press (chapters 1–7, 16). However in some parts of the book it is impossible to say where the work of one author ends and that of the other begins.

We would like to thank the BBC Written Archive Centre for the help of its staff and the use of copyright material, the IBA for information on audiences, and the British Library of Economic and Political Science for permission to quote from the unpublished diary of Hugh Dalton. We are also obliged to J. Walter Thompson Ltd, Leo Burnett Ltd (incorporating the London Press Exchange), the Mirror Group, Associated Newspapers, the Thomson Organization, Express Newspapers, the *Daily Telegraph*, and the *Guardian* for access to company archives and research reports.

We are very grateful to Herminio Martins, Anthony Smith, Colin Seymour-Ure, Malory Wober, Simon Clarke, Simon Frith, Keith McLelland, Nick Hartley, Alan Lovell, and Angela Smith for making many useful comments on draft chapters. James Curran would also like to thank Andrew Goodwin for his invaluable contribution to chapter 6, as well as Angus Douglas and Garry Whannel for skilfully preparing the content analysis summarized in chapter 7, and Brendon Wall and Gill Bucknall for help in compiling Table 3.

We owe a great debt to Mies Rule, Janet Sandell, and Angela Smith for typing successive drafts of this book with their usual speed, accuracy, and good humour.

We would like to express our appreciation to Lynn Blowers who greatly added to the first edition of the book by her careful editing.

Jean Seaton would like to thank Annette Zakary for looking after her son Daniel, and then Rebecca Holmes for looking after her sons Daniel and Nathaniel, with such affection and thoughtfulness, while work was being done on the second and third editions of this book.

James Curran would like to thank his wife, Margaret Hung, for urging him to write his part of the book and for sustaining him – with her laughter, zaniness, intelligence, and good sense – in the writing of it.

Finally we are especially grateful for the great care with which Ben Pimlott read the manuscript. His detailed criticisms and suggestions immensely improved the final version of the book. We are also particularly indebted to him for giving us the title. Jean Seaton depended on his enthusiasm throughout.

Introduction

This book is about the press, broadcasting, and politics. It argues that the influence of the media has been immense – on institutions, the conduct of affairs, and the way in which people think and act politically. It also argues that the mass media and mass politics have inspired, reflected, and shaped each other more than has commonly been realized.

The power of the press and broadcasting has often been obscured. Thus, for example, the view that the British Press is one of the great instruments of liberty, an independent fourth estate, the vital defender of public interests, is a central part of our political culture. Yet, as will be shown, this is a very modern theory which has more than an element of special pleading. The theory was produced to justify those who created the press and whose interests it largely served. This does not mean that newspapers, television, and radio have generally been instruments of crude propaganda: rather that the media are political actors in their own right.

It is equally mistaken to believe that the press and broadcasting simply reflect contemporary political forces. In the first place, some groups – stronger, richer, and with better access – are always able to secure more attention than others. Secondly, the media do have some political autonomy. Thus the radical press was relatively strong in 1860, when the labour movement was divided and defeated. Just before the First World War, on the other hand, a comparatively militant working class had few radical newspapers to support it. In contrast, there have been other times when developments in the media have been more closely related to social moods. During the 1960s a new boldness in television seemed to be connected with a rapid change in public mores. Thus the relationship between the media and society has varied. Indeed this variety is the source of the power which the press and broadcasting may wield. If the media merely mirrored events then they would have little effect on them.

Yet the media are not a force in themselves. Editors and producers – in

Britain as elsewhere – are blamed for many things: from race riots to dress fashions, from teenage delinquency to the fall of governments. But this scapegoating generally mistakes a catalyst, or even a symptom, for a cause: investing the media with a magical importance they do not possess.

With the extension of the franchise the role of the press changed. Arguably the popular press, together with the mass membership party, helped to produce a predictable electorate. Much more recently television has brought political information to a new section of the population. Yet broadcasting has been obliged to balance political views. It has also developed a style and a rhetoric which are in themselves anti-partisan, and indeed anti-party. As broadcasting became the dominant source of political knowledge, these constraints must have affected popular understanding and involvement in politics.

Now, with the growth of video, cable, and satellite technologies, the conventions of scheduling programmes built up over sixty years are becoming redundant. The capacity of broadcasting to attract a mass, nation-wide audience regularly for any particular programme, or indeed any kind of programme, is fast disappearing. Every previous change in the pattern of communications has had important political consequences. So will this revolution, even though its effects are still a matter for speculation.

The press was the arena of a major political struggle during the nineteenth century. Different classes contended not only for the right to express their own causes and interests but also to suppress other views. The newspapers we have today, and their way of dealing with politics, are a product of that competition. The battle was political. Yet in the end economic pressures were far more effective in limiting the variety of expression than any direct censorship. The market promoted some interests, but at the expense of others.

The control of broadcasting in Britain was not decided by the same kind of political confrontation which had marked the history of newspapers. Although in all countries the state has determined who can broadcast, the conditions of this right have varied enormously. In some liberal democracies broadcasting has been directly controlled, either by government or by a coalition of political parties. In others, private enterprise and the profit motive have been dominating forces. In Britain broadcasting has had some protection from market pressures, and has claimed political independence.

The first objective of the media has always been to attract an audience. Hence press and broadcasting have sought to provide instantly appreciable material that is loosely described as 'entertainment'. Some people have regarded entertainment as of little social or political importance. Others have accorded it a sinister role: as a device to numb the public into political acquiescence. It is argued here that such views need to be reconsidered.

The assumptions which underlie the conduct of the press and broadcasting also need to be reassessed. Thus it is widely believed that press freedom exists because anyone who does not find his views expressed has the right to start his own newspaper. In practice very few can exercise this right. It might be argued that the same is true of political parties. However, while it may not be practical for an individual or minority group to start a new mass political organization, it is possible to enter and influence existing parties to a far greater extent than is the case with newspapers.

In the same way broadcasting authorities today are less confident than in the past of asserting their omniscient appreciation of the public good. Rather they argue that they attempt to reflect competing interests, interpreting attacks from both left and right as evidence that they are arriving at a proper balance of views. But many of the interests and groups which are now excluded from access to broadcasting fall outside such conventional political definitions. Indeed it will be argued that accuracy, precision, and veracity should not be confused with independence. It is rarely indicated to the public that objectivity is different from the equality of competition between selected opponents.

There is one common view that the role of the media has always been the same. The press and broadcasting have always exaggerated, distorted, and suppressed. Thus, it has been suggested, they have had little overall effect on political life. The trouble with this view, however, is that the role of the press and broadcasting has changed. Arguably the power of the media has increased remarkably in the last forty years. There are fewer alternative sources of information, while the control of the media has become concentrated in fewer hands.

At the same time the press and broadcasting have become less accountable. The public means of monitoring performance is wholly incapable of coping with growth and technological change in increasingly complex industries. The press and broadcasting exercise a massive power, but it is more than ever a power without responsibility.

Part I

Press history

1

Whig press history as political myth

The orthodox interpretation of the development of the British press has remained unchanged for over a century. 'The British press', writes David Chaney, 'is generally agreed to have attained its freedom around the middle of the nineteenth century.'[1] This view, first advanced in the pioneering Victorian histories of journalism, has been repeated uncritically ever since in histories of modern Britain and historical studies of the British press.

This watershed in the history of the press is frequently portrayed as the culmination of a heroic struggle against the state. The key landmarks in this struggle are generally said to be the abolition of the Court of Star Chamber in 1641, the ending of press licensing in 1694, Fox's Libel Act, 1792, and the repeal of press taxation – the so-called 'taxes on knowledge' – in the period 1853–61. Only when the last of these reforms was secured, it is claimed, did the forces of liberty and progress finally triumph by establishing a press fully independent of state regulation.

This political struggle was accompanied by a development which is widely held to be of even greater significance for the emergence of a free press – the *economic* emancipation of the press from political control. 'The true censorship', Professor Roach writes of the late Georgian press, 'lay in the fact that the newspaper had not yet reached financial independence, and consequently depended on the administration or the parties.' The growth of newspaper profits, largely from advertising, is said to have rescued the press from economic dependence on the state. This view has been succinctly restated by Ivon Asquith in a scholarly study of the early-nineteenth-century press. 'Since sales were inadequate to cover the costs of producing a paper', he writes,

> it was the growing income from advertising which provided the material base for the change of attitude from subservience to independence .... It is perhaps no exaggeration to say that the growth

of advertising revenue was the most important single factor in enabling the press to emerge as the Fourth Estate of the realm.

This view of the triumphant rise of a free press as a product of capitalist evolution provides a persuasive interpretation of press history which legitimizes the market-based system of the press. It has frequently been invoked by popular historians of journalism, both on the left or the right, to justify the role of advertising in the press. 'The dangerous dependence of newspapers on advertising', wrote Francis Williams, a former editor of the Labour *Daily Herald*,

> has often been the theme of newspaper reformers – usually from outside its ranks. But the daily press would never have come into existence as a force in public and social life if it had not been for the need of men of commerce to advertise. Only through the growth of advertising did the press achieve independence.

Similarly some popular commentators have sought to extract a contemporary moral from their accounts of the struggle against state control of the press. John Whale concluded his historical survey, for instance, with the warning that politicians are still seeking 'indirect ways of bringing state power to bear on unsympathetic journalism'. The principal way this is being manifested, he cautions, is in proposals to limit concentration of media ownership.

A number of commentators have also discerned a link between the historic struggle to free the press from state control and the current assault on public service broadcasting. Indeed the recent Peacock Committee on *Financing the BBC* was so impressed by the parallel that its report contained a potted history of print censorship from the sixteenth to the nineteenth centuries as a prelude to recommending the phasing out of most public regulation of broadcasting.[2]

Conventional interpretations of press history thus have a powerful ideological resonance. This is reinforced by the inspirational way in which the press is generally portrayed in the period after it broke free from state tutelage. According to the New Cambridge Modern History, financially independent newspapers became 'great organs of the public mind', amplifying the voice of the people and exposing governments to the full blast of public opinion. The press is also said to have become more balanced and objective in the second half of the nineteenth century, which enabled people to make more informed political judgements in Britain's maturing democracy. Even a Marxist like Raymond Williams notes with approval that after 1855 'most newspapers were able to drop their frantic pamphleteering',[3] while the radical historian, Alan

Lee, portrays the late Victorian period as a 'golden age' of British journalism.

There is not, of course, total unanimity among historians. Differences persist about when newspapers became financially independent of political parties. Some historians also express misgivings about the growing 'commercialization' of the press, and are sharply critical of the first generation of press barons. But few contest the conventional wisdom, embalmed in a much acclaimed two-volume study by Stephen Koss, that there has been 'a transition from official to popular control' of the press during the modern period. Fewer still contest the central thesis of Whig press history that this 'progress of the press' was central to 'the broadening of political liberty'.

What follows is a long overdue attempt to reappraise the standard interpretation of press history.[4] It will indicate the need not merely to re-examine critically the accepted view of the historical emergence of a 'free' press but to stand it on its head. The period around the middle of the nineteenth century, it will be argued, did not inaugurate a new era of press freedom and liberty: it introduced a new system of press censorship more effective than anything that had gone before. Market forces succeeded where legal repression had failed in conscripting the press to the social order.

Notes

1. References have been kept to a minimum throughout the book but a select bibliography is provided at the end.
2. The Peacock Report's account is derived largely from Macaulay and conveniently ignores modern, revisionist interpretations of the reduction of publishing controls in the seventeenth century.
3. R. Williams, *The Long Revolution* (Harmondsworth, Pelican, 1965), p.218. For a later more critical assessment, see R. Williams, 'The press and popular culture: an historical perspective' in G. Boyce, J. Curran, and P. Wingate (eds), *Newspaper History* (London, Constable, 1978).
4. A number of important studies of early-nineteenth-century working-class politics – notably by the Thompsons, Hollis, Wiener, and Epstein – provide evidence that, by implication at least, casts doubt on the conventional Whig thesis of the triumphant rise of a free press in mid-Victorian Britain. The wider implications of these studies for reinterpreting press history have been buried, however, because their focus is on early working-class struggles rather than the long-term development of journalism.

2

The struggle for a free press

The remarkably resilient Whig interpretation of press history has been sustained by focusing attention upon mainstream commercial newspapers, while ignoring or downplaying the development of the radical press. Only if this selective perspective is maintained does the conventional view of advertising as a midwife of press independence appear plausible.

During the second half of the eighteenth century and in the early nineteenth century, a section of the commercial press became more politically independent largely as a consequence of the growth of advertising. This additional revenue reduced dependence on political subsidies; encouraged papers to reject covert secret service grants (the last English newspaper to receive a clandestine government grant was the *Observer* in 1840); improved the wages and security of employment of journalists so that they became less susceptible to government bribes; and, above all, financed greater expenditure on news-gathering so that newspapers became less reliant on official sources and more reluctant to trade their independence in return for obtaining 'prior intelligence' from the government. This shift was symbolized by *The Times*'s ma isterial declaration in 1834 that it would no longer accept early informati n from government offices since this was inconsistent with 'the pride and independence of our journal' and anyway its 'own information was earlier and surer' (*The Times*, 26 December 1834).

However, the growth of advertising did not transform the commercial press into an 'independent fourth estate'. On the contrary, the development of modern political parties from the 1860s onwards encouraged a closer interpenetration of party politics and commercial journalism. A number of leading proprietors in Victorian and Edwardian Britain were members of parliament, while some national newspapers were subsidized by party loyalists or from party funds until well into the twentieth century. This continuing involvement with government or opposition parties belied the often repeated claim that the press was an *independent* check on parliament and the executive: in reality, newspapers long remained an extension of the party system.[1]

The conventional portrayal of advertising as the midwife of press independence is also directly contradicted by the emergence of the radical press as a political force in the late eighteenth century. As we shall see, early radical papers did not obtain significant advertising support. Yet they were wholly independent both of government and of all political groupings in parliament. Their rise plainly demonstrated that newspapers could become autonomous from the state through financial support other than advertising.

Due to its outspoken independence, the radical press was confronted not by the subtle arts of news management but by the full force of legal repression. Successive administrations in the late 18th and early 19th centuries sought to suppress dissident journalism by prosecuting journalists for legal or blasphemous libel. But although this was a catch-all law that made illegal fundamental criticism of the social order, it was sometimes difficult to enforce. Juries, empowered by Fox's Libel Act to determine guilt or innocence, were often reluctant to convict. This was brought home to the authorities by the sensational acquittals of Eaton, Hardy, and Tooke in the 1790s, Wooler and Hone in 1817, and Cobbett in 1831. The sharp edge of the law was further blunted in 1843, when Lord Campbell's Libel Act made the statement of truth in the public interest a legitimate defence in seditious libel suits.

Even before the 1843 Act was passed, the authorities had come round reluctantly to the view that libel prosecutions were often counter-productive. When the editor of *The Republican* was prosecuted in 1819, the paper's circulation rose by over 50 per cent. Similarly disillusioning experiences prompted the Attorney General to conclude in 1843 that 'a libeller thirsted for nothing more than the valuable advertisement of a public trial in a Court of Justice'. This disenchantment was reflected in a shift of government policy: there were only 16 prosecutions for seditious and blasphemous libel in the period 1825–34, compared with 167 prosecutions during the preceding eight years.

Instead the government came to rely increasingly on the newspaper stamp duty and taxes on paper and advertisements as a way of curbing the radical press. The purpose of these 'taxes on knowledge' was to force up publishing costs and thereby restrict the ownership of newspapers to people who, in the words of Cresset Pelham, 'would conduct them in a more respectable manner than was likely to be the result of pauper management',[2] and also to restrict the readership of newspapers to the well-to-do by increasing cover prices.

The stamp duty was increased by 266 per cent between 1789 and 1815. Publications subject to the stamp duty were redefined in 1819 to include political periodicals. In addition, a security system was introduced which required publishers of weeklies to register their papers and place financial bonds of between £200 and £300 with the authorities. Although the ostensible purpose of this requirement was to guarantee payment of libel fines, its real objective was to force up further the cost of publishing and thus ensure, as Lord Castlereagh explained to the Commons, that 'persons exercising the power of the press should be men of some respectability and property'.[3] Ironically in view of the way in which publishing costs were subsequently to soar, the government was persuaded by the parliamentary opposition that its original intention of insisting on a bond of £500 represented an unacceptable limitation on press freedom.

The authorities were relatively successful during the 1820s in curbing the radical press. However, they faced a more formidable challenge in the early 1830s – the systematic evasion of the stamp duty by a highly organized radical press with a well-developed distribution network and well-endowed 'victim funds' to help the families of people imprisoned by the authorities.

The government responded by prosecuting publishers and printers, seizing supplies and smashing, wherever possible, networks of distributors. At least 1,130 cases of selling unstamped newspapers were prosecuted in London alone during the period 1830–6. But the reserve army of the unemployed provided a steady supply of street sellers. Radical publishers, printers, and journalists continued their activities despite continuous harassment. 'Prosecutions, fines and imprisonments were alike failures,' the minister in charge of the fight against the unstamped press later recalled.[4] By the summer of 1836 the government was forced to concede defeat. The Commons was informed on 20 June that the government 'had resorted to all means afforded by the existing law for preventing the publication of unstamped papers', but that 'the existing law was altogether ineffectual to the purpose of putting an end to the unstamped papers.'

A crisis had been reached. By 1836 the unstamped press published in London had an aggregate readership of at least 2 million. Even the government admitted that its circulation exceeded that of the respectable, stamped press. Indeed the whole system of press control seemed on the point of final collapse, since leading publishers of stamped papers warned the government that they would also evade the stamp duty unless more effective steps were taken to enforce it.

The Whig government responded to the crisis with a well-planned counter-offensive. New measures were passed which strengthened the government's search and confiscation powers. Penalties were increased for being found in possession of an unstamped newspaper, and the stamp duty was reduced by 75 per cent in order to make 'smuggling' less attractive. Thus what has been seen as a landmark in the advance of press freedom was manifestly repressive in both intention and effect. As Spring Rice, the Chancellor of the Exchequer, explained to the Commons, a strategic concession, combined with increased coercive powers, was necessary in order to enforce a system that had broken down. The aim of these new measures, he stated candidly, was to 'put down the unstamped papers'.[5]

The government's new strategy succeeded in its immediate objective. 'No unstamped papers can be attempted with success,' declared Hetherington, a leading radical publisher, shortly after being released from prison, unless 'some means can be devised either to print the newspaper without types and presses, or render the premises ... inaccessible to armed force.'[6] By 1837 the clandestine radical press had disappeared.

Compliance with the law forced radical newspapers to raise their prices, even though the stamp duty was much reduced. Whereas most unstamped papers had sold at 1d in the early 1830s, most of their successors in the 1840s sold at 4d or 5d – a sum that was well beyond the means of individual working-class consumers. But the government's aim of destroying the radical press was nevertheless frustrated by organized consumer resistance. Informal groups of working people pooled their resources to purchase a radical paper each week. Union branches, clubs, and political associations financed the collective purchase of newspapers. Even taverns were threatened with the withdrawal of custom unless they bought radical papers. Partly as a consequence of this concerted resistance, new radical papers emerged which gained even larger circulations than those reached by their best-selling unstamped predecessors selling at a quarter the price.

The radical press was not as strong in relation to the respectable press as it had been during the mid-1830s. Between 1836 and 1855 there was a substantial growth in the number and circulation of commercial local weekly papers as well as in the readership of religious publications and of family and 'useful knowledge' magazines. But since much of the expansion of the commercial press appears to have taken place amongst the middle and lower-middle classes,[7] this did not greatly diminish the radical press's influence within the working class.

The principal rivals to the radical press within the working class (of whom well over half were literate or semi-literate by the 1830s) were almanacs, printed ballads, gallowsheets, and chapbooks. But the radical press remained dominant as far as political papers read by the working class were concerned. Due to the relative size of this market, radical papers were also the pacesetters in terms of circulation for the newspaper press as a whole during the first half of the nineteenth century.

Cobbett's radical *Twopenny Trash* broke all circulation records in 1816–17, achieving a circulation several times that of most respectable papers. This record was probably beaten by the left-wing *Weekly Police Gazette* which, to judge from a government raid on its premises, had a circulation of over 40,000 in 1836 – well over double that of conservative weeklies such as the *Sunday Times* and *Bell's Life in London*. In 1838 the militant *Northern Star* gained the largest circulation of any newspaper published in the provinces and, in 1839, the largest national circulation of any paper apart from the liberal radical *Weekly Dispatch*. Its success was followed by the still larger circulation secured by the radical *Reynolds News*, the paper with the second-largest circulation in Britain after the liberal radical *Lloyds Weekly* in the early 1850s. Both publications were the first newspapers to break through the 100,000 circulation barrier in 1856.[8]

Newspaper circulations during the first half of the nineteenth century seem very small by modern standards. But circulation statistics provide a misleading historical index of newspaper consumption, since the average number of readers per copy has declined markedly since the mid-nineteenth century. A copy of a leading radical paper such as the *Northern Star*, selling at 4½d in 1840, cost (if taken as a proportion of the contemporary average male manual worker's wage) the equivalent of well over a pound today. Sharing of high-cost papers, together with the widespread practice of reading papers aloud for the benefit of the semi-literate and illiterate, resulted in a very high number of 'readers' for each newspaper sold. Hollis and Epstein estimate, for instance, that radical papers in the 1830s and 1840s reached upwards of twenty readers per copy. This compares with an average of only two to three readers per copy of contemporary daily papers. Yet even if a cautious estimate of ten readers per copy is taken as the norm for radical papers in the early Victorian period, it still means that leading militant papers such as the *Northern Star* and its successor, *Reynolds News*, each reached at their peak, before the repeal of the stamp duty, half a million readers when the population of England and Wales over the age of 14 was little over 10 million. The emergent radical press was thus a genuinely popular force, reaching a mass public.

The economic structure of the radical press

The rise of radical journalism can be understood only in the context of the prevailing economic structure of the press industry. Since this is an important aspect of the central argument that follows, it is worth examining in some detail the finances of the early radical press.

The initial capital required to set up a radical paper in the early part of the nineteenth century was extremely small. Most radical unstamped papers were printed not on a steam press, but on hand presses, which cost as little as £10 to acquire. Metal type was often hired by the hour and print workers paid on a piecework basis.

After 1836 leading stamped radical papers were printed on more sophisticated machinery. The *London Dispatch*, for instance, was printed on a Napier machine, bought with the help of a wealthy well-wisher and the profits from Hetherington's other publications. The *Northern Star* had a steam press specially constructed for it in London. Even so, launch costs were extremely small in comparison with the subsequent period. The *Northern Star*, for instance, was launched in 1837 with a total capital of £690, mostly raised by public subscription.

Financing a paper during its initial establishment period could often cost more than setting it up. Even so, early trading losses were minimized by low operating costs. Radical unstamped papers paid no tax, relied heavily upon news reports filed by their readers on a voluntary basis, and had small newsprint costs because of their high readership per copy. Consequently radical unstamped newspapers needed to attain only a small circulation in order to be economically viable. For instance the *Poor Man's Guardian*, a leading newspaper of the early 1830s, broke even as soon as its circulation reached 2,500.

Even after 1836, when a penny stamp duty had to be paid on each copy sold, the running costs of the radical press remained relatively low. The influential *London Dispatch* reported, for example (17 September 1836), that 'the whole expense allowed for editing, reporting, reviewing, literary contributions etc., in fact, the entire cost of what is technically called "making up" the paper, is only six pounds per week'. In the same issue it reported that, at its selling price of 3½d, it could break even with a circulation of 16,000. Similarly the *Northern Star* which, unlike its predecessors, developed a substantial network of paid correspondents, claimed to be spending little more than £9 10s a week on its reporting establishment in 1841. Selling at 4½d, it was able to break even with a weekly circulation of about 6,200. This low break-even point meant that its run-in costs were very small. Indeed the *Northern Star* almost certainly moved into profit within its first month of publication.

Because publishing costs were low the ownership and control of newspapers could be in the hands of people committed, in the words of Joshua Hobson, an ex-handloom weaver and publisher of the *Voice of West Riding*, 'to support the rights and interests of the order and class to which it is my pride to belong'. Some newspapers, like the *Voice of the People*, the *Northern Star*, the *Liberator*, and the *Trades Newspaper*, were owned principally by working men and trade union organizations. Others were owned by individual proprietors like Cleave, Watson, and Hetherington, many of them people of humble origins who had risen to prominence through the working-class movement. While not lacking in ruthlessness or business acumen, the people they entrusted with the editing of their newspapers were all former manual workers like William Hill and Joshua Hobson, or middle-class activists like O'Brien and Lorymer, whose attitudes had been shaped by long involvement in working-class politics. A substantial section of the popular newspaper press reaching a working-class audience was thus controlled by those who were committed to the working-class movement.

This pattern of ownership influenced the way in which journalists working for the radical press perceived their role. Unlike the institutionalized journalists of the later period, they tended to see themselves as activists rather than as professionals. Indeed many of the paid correspondents of the *Poor Man's Guardian*, *Northern Star*, and the early *Reynolds News* were also political organizers for the National Union of the Working Classes or the Chartist Movement. They sought to understand and expose the dynamics of power and inequality rather than to report 'hard news' as a series of disconnected events. They saw themselves as class representatives rather than as disinterested intermediaries and attempted to establish a relationship of real reciprocity with their readers. As the editor of the *Northern Star* wrote in its fifth anniversary issue,

> I have ever sought to make it [the paper] rather a reflex of your minds than a medium through which to exhibit any supposed talent or intelligence of my own. This is precisely my conception of what a people's organ should be.

The second important feature of the economic structure of the radical press in the first half of the nineteenth century was that it was self-sufficient on the proceeds of sales alone. The radical unstamped press carried very little commercial advertising and the stamped radical press fared little better. The *London Dispatch* (17 September 1836) complained bitterly, for instance, of the 'prosecutions, fines and the like et ceteras with which a paper of our principles is sure to be more largely honoured than by the lucrative patronage of advertisers'. The grudge held by the *London Dispatch* and other radical newspapers against advertisers was fully justified. An examination of the official advertisement duty returns reveals a marked disparity in the amount of advertising duty per 1,000 copies (an index of comparison that takes into account differences in circulation) paid by the radical press compared with its more respectable rivals. For example in 1840 two middle-class papers published in Leeds (the *Leeds Mercury* and *Leeds Intelligence*) and the four leading national daily papers (*The Times, Morning Post, Morning Chronicle*, and *Morning Advertiser*) all paid over fifty times more advertisement duty per 1,000 copies than the radical *Northern Star*, a Leeds-based paper with a national circulation.

A similar pattern emerges in the case of other leading radical papers for which returns are available. In 1817, for instance, Cobbett's *Political Register* received only three advertisements: its advertisement duty per 1,000 copies was less than one-hundredth of that of respectable rival periodicals, although this disparity was somewhat reduced by the 1830s. The *London Dispatch* in 1837 was only marginally better off: it paid per 1,000 copies less than one twenty-fifth of the advertisement duty collected from each of its main respectable rivals in London, also with a national circulation.

This lack of support placed radical stamped newspapers at a serious disadvantage. They were deprived of the advertising which enabled respectable publishers to spend more on editorial outlay. Some radical papers were forced to close down with circulations larger than those of commercial papers, buoyed up by advertising. This retarded the growth of the radical stamped press at a time when the high price of newspapers, inflated by the stamp duty, was a major deterrent against buying papers amongst the working class.

Yet despite these substantial disadvantages, the absence of advertising did not prevent the radical press from flourishing. While fortunes were not easily made, radical newspapers – both stamped and unstamped – could be highly profitable. Hetherington, the publisher of the stamped *London Dispatch*, was reported to be making £1,000 a year from his business in 1837. Similarly the stamped *Northern Star* was estimated to have produced a remarkable profit of £13,000 in 1839 and £6,500 in 1840, which was generated very largely from sales revenue.

This independence from advertising was itself a liberating force. Radical papers were, by the 1830s, increasingly oriented towards a working-class audience, and became more uncompromising in their attacks on capitalism. They had no advertising clients to pander to, and they were under no pressure to court the well-to-do readers favoured by advertisers. They were free because they were financed by the pennies of their readers.

The impact of the radical press

The radical press grew out of the working-class movement. But it did not merely reflect the growth of working-class organizations: it also deepened and extended radical consciousness, thereby building support for them.

One of the most important, and least remarked, aspects of the development of the radical press in the first half of the nineteenth century was that its leading publications developed a nationwide circulation. Even as early as the second decade, leading radical papers like the *Twopenny Trash*, *Political Register*, and *Republican* were read as far afield as Yorkshire, Lancashire, the Midlands, and East Anglia, as well as in the south of England. By the early 1830s the principal circulation newspapers like the *Weekly Police Gazette*, the *Poor Man's Guardian*, and *Dispatch* had a distribution network extending on a north-south axis from Glasgow to Land's End, and on an east-west axis from Carmarthen to Norwich. Part of the impact of the radical press stemmed from this central fact – the extent of its geographical distribution.

The radical press was effective in reinforcing a growing consciousness of class and in unifying disparate elements of the working community, partly because its leading publications provided national coverage and reached a national working-class audience. It helped to extend the often highly exclusive occupational solidarity of 'the new unionism' to other sectors of the labour community by demonstrating the common predicament of unionists in different trades throughout the country. Workers attempting to set up an extra-legal union read in the radical press in 1833–4, for instance, of similar struggles by glove workers in Yeovil, cabinet-makers and joiners in Glasgow and Carlisle, shoemakers and smiths in Northampton, and bricklayers and masons in London, as well as of working-class struggles in Belgium and Germany. Similarly the radical press helped to reduce geographical isolation by showing that local agitation – whether against Poor Law Commissioners, new machinery, long working hours, or wage cutting – conformed to a common pattern throughout the country. The radical press further expanded its readers' field of social vision by publishing, particularly in the later phase from the 1830s onwards, news that none of the respectable papers carried, and by interpreting this news within a radical framework of analysis. It was, in the words of the Chartist leader, Feargus O'Connor, 'the link that binds the industrious classes together'.[9]

The radical press also helped to promote working-class organizations.

Movements ranging from early trade unions to political organizations, like the National Union of the Working Classes and the Chartist Movement, partly depended for their success on the publicity they obtained from the radical press. O'Connor recalled that before the emergence of Chartist newspapers, 'I found that the press was entirely mute, while I was working myself to death, and that a meeting in one town did nothing for another.' Press publicity stimulated people to attend meetings and to become involved in political and industrial organizations; it also brought the activist vanguard of the working-class movement into national prominence helping, for example, to turn farm workers victimized for joining a trade union in the remote village of Tolpuddle into national working-class heroes. No less important, it helped to sustain the morale of activists in the working-class movement confronted by what must have seemed, at times, insuperable odds. Without the *Northern Star*, declared one speaker at a local Chartist meeting, 'their own sounds might echo through the wilderness'.[10]

Above all, the radical press contributed to a major political reorientation within a section of the working class. We have become so accustomed to the individualized pattern of newspaper consumption amidst a steady flow of information from a variety of media that it is difficult to understand the political significance of newspapers in the early nineteenth century. Newspapers were often the only readily available source of information about what was happening outside the local community and, in some cases, generated passionate loyalty amongst their readers. 'On the day', recalls Fielden, for instance, 'the newspaper, the *Northern Star*, O'Connor's paper, was due, the people used to line the roadside waiting for its arrival, which was paramount to everything else for the time being.' The impact of the radical press was further reinforced by the discussions that followed the reading aloud of articles from newspapers in taverns, workshops, homes, and public meetings, vividly described in numerous memoirs and reminiscences.[11] This social pattern of consumption (which continued on a diminished scale late into the nineteenth century) resulted in political newspapers having a greater agitational effect than those of today.

The first wave of radical papers from the 1790s through to the late 1820s played an important part in the psychological reorientation that preceded the political mobilization of a section of the working class. They raised expectations both by proclaiming a mythical past in which affluence and natural justice had prevailed, and by promising a bright future in which poverty could be relieved through political means. It was this raising of hopes, combined with a direct assault on the Anglican 'morality' which sanctioned the social order, that most alarmed parliamentarians at the time. As Dr Philimore, MP, warned the Commons following official reports that servants and common soldiers had been seen reading radical newspapers,

> Those infamous publications ... inflame [working people's] passions and awaken their selfishness, contrasting their present condition with what they contend to be their future condition – a condition incompatible with human nature, and with those immutable laws which Providence has established for the regulation of civil society.[12]

The radical press not only helped to erode political passivity, based on fatalistic acceptance of the social structure as 'natural' and 'providential', but also began to dispel the collective lack of confidence that had inhibited working-class resistance. The least valued section of the community was able to obtain a new understanding of its role in society through its own press. 'The real strength and all the resources of the country', characteristically proclaimed Cobbett's *Political Register*, for instance, 'ever have sprung from the *labour* of its people.' This novel view of the world, popularized through the more radical journals, provided a means of reordering the entire ranking of status and moral worth in society. The highest in the land were degraded to the lowest place in society as unproductive parasites: working people, in contrast, were elevated to the top as the productive and useful section of the community. The early militant press thus fostered an alternative value system that symbolically turned the world upside down. It also repeatedly emphasized the potential power of working people to effect social change through the force of 'combination' and organized action.

The radical press also played a part in radicalizing the emergent working-class movement by developing a more sophisticated political analysis. The first generation of radical papers that developed during the Napoleonic War was trapped inside the political and social categories of the eighteenth-century liberal attack on the aristocratic constitution. Conflict was generally portrayed in political terms as a struggle between the aristocracy and the 'productive classes' (usually defined to include working capitalists as well as the working classes); criticism was mainly focused upon corruption in high places and repressive direct taxation that allegedly impoverished the productive community. The main thrust of this early radical criticism was thus largely in terms defined by middle-class critics that would leave the reward structure of society fundamentally unchanged.

By the 1830s the more militant papers had shifted their focus of attack from 'old corruption' to the economic process which enabled the capitalist class to appropriate in profits the wealth created by labour.

Conflict was redefined as a class struggle between labour and capital, between the working classes and a coalition of aristocrats, 'millocrats', and 'shopocrats'. This more militant analysis signposted the way forward towards a far-reaching programme of reconstruction in which, in the words of the *Poor Man's Guardian* (19 October 1833) workers will 'be at the top instead of at the bottom of society – or rather that there should be no bottom or top at all'.

This new analysis was often conflated with the old liberal analysis in an uncertain synthesis. There was, moreover, a basic continuity in the perspectives offered by the less militant wing of the radical press, which grew in influence during the 1840s. But such continuity should come as no surprise. It was only natural that the political complexion of the broad left press should reflect the ebb and flow of militancy within the radical movement. Nor is it at all surprising that traditional political beliefs should have persisted over a time-span as brief as twenty-five years. But so long as the activist working class controlled its own popular press, it collectively possessed a means of arriving at a more radical understanding of society. It also possessed the institutional means of defining, expressing, and maintaining a radical public opinion different from that proclaimed by the capitalist press, and of resisting the ideological assault mounted on the working class through schools, mechanics' institutes, and useful knowledge magazines.

The militant press sustained a radical sub-culture, which represented a potential threat to the social order. Indeed in 1842, a General Strike was called to secure universal suffrage through the force of industrial action. It received extensive support in industrial Lancashire, much of Yorkshire, and parts of the Midlands. While the strike was crushed, and some 1,500 labour leaders were imprisoned, it was a sign of an increasingly unsettled society in which the radical press had become a destabilizing element.

In short, the control system administered through the state had failed. Neither prosecutions for seditious libel nor a tax system designed to ration newspapers had succeeded in preventing the rise of the radical press. As we shall see, this prompted thoughtful parliamentarians to consider whether there might be a better way of dealing with insurgent journalism.

Notes

1 In the last ten years, five researchers – George Boyce, Alan Lee, Stephen Koss, Colin Seymour-Ure, and Lucy Brown – have documented in general surveys the press's continuing involvement in party politics long after the press is supposed to have blossomed as an

'independent fourth estate'. Their studies have thus modified one aspect of the traditional Whig interpretation of press history. For more about this, see chapter 5.

2. Pelham, *Parliamentary Debates*, 11 (1832), cols 491–2.
3. Castlereagh, *Parliamentary Debates*, 91 (1819), cols 1,177 ff.
4. Spring Rice, *Parliamentary Debates*, 138 (1855), col. 966.
5. Spring Rice, *Parliamentary Debates*, 34 (1836), cols 627–34; 37 (1837), col. 1,165.
6. *London Dispatch* (17 September 1836).
7. Report of the Select Committee on Newspaper Stamps (SCNS), *Parliamentary Papers*, 17 (1851); Milner-Gibson, *Parliamentary Debates*, 135 (1853), col. 1,136, amongst others.
8. P. Hollis, *The Pauper Press* (London, Oxford University Press, 1970), p. 95; *Parliamentary Debates*, 34 (1836), col. 627; SCNS Appendix 4; V. Berridge, 'Popular Sunday papers and mid-Victorian society' in G. Boyce, J. Curran, and P. Wingate (eds), *Newspaper History* (London, Constable, 1978), p.249.
9. *Northern Star* (16 January 1841).
10. *Northern Star* (26 August 1848).
11. For instance W. E. Adams, *Memoirs of a Social Atom*, vol. 1 (London, Hutchinson, 1903), pp. 164–6; interview with Wesley Perrins, *Bulletin of the Society for the Study of Labour History* (1970), pp. 16–24.
12. Dr Philimore, *Parliamentary Debates*, 91 (1819), col. 1,363.

3

The ugly face of reform

The parliamentary campaign against 'the taxes on knowledge' is generally portrayed as a triumphant campaign for a free press, sustained by an amalgam of special interests but motivated largely by libertarian ideals in opposition to the authoritarian legacy of the past.[1] The only discordant note in this inspiring account comes from the parliamentary campaigners for a free press celebrated in this historical legend. Their aims and, indeed, their public utterances are difficult to reconcile with the historic role assigned to them in liberal ideology.

Widespread evasion of the stamp duty in the early 1830s caused press regulation to become a major political issue. Traditionalists argued that the government should enforce the stamp duty with tougher measures, while a relatively small group of reformers in parliament argued that the stamp duty had become unenforceable in the face of mass resistance and should be repealed. The two sides to the debate did not disagree over objectives so much as over tactics. As the Lord Chancellor succinctly put it in 1834,

> the only question to answer, and the only problem to solve, is, how they [the people] shall read in the best manner; how they shall be instructed politically, and have political habits formed the most safe for the constitution of the country.

Traditionalists alleged that abolition of the stamp duty would result in the country being flooded with 'atrocious publications'. Reformers countered by arguing that the stamp duty merely suppressed 'the cheap reply' to seditious publications from responsible quarters. Radical publishers were not being stopped by inefficient controls. Instead they were being given a clear field in which to indoctrinate the people with 'the most pernicious doctrines' without encountering any competition.[2]

Underlying this difference over tactics were divergent approaches to social control. Supporters of press regulation tended to favour coercion. Reformers, on the other hand, generally stressed the importance of engineering social consent. As Bulwer Lytton argued when proposing the repeal of the stamp duty in 1832:

> At this moment when throughout so many nations we see the people at war with their institutions, the world presents to us two great, may they be impressive examples. In Denmark, a despotism without discontent – in America, a republic without change. The cause is the same in both: in both the people are universally educated.

The parliamentary repeal lobby argued that the lifting of the stamp duty would encourage men of capital to invest in an expanding market and consequently enrol 'more temperate and disinterested friends of the people who would lend themselves to their real instruction'. In particular, many of the parliamentary campaigners of the 1830s believed that cheap newspapers, owned by capitalists, would become an educational weapon in the fight against trade unionism. Francis Place, the organizing secretary of the repeal campaign, even told a parliamentary Select Committee in 1832 that 'there would not have been a single trades union either in England or Scotland' if the stamp duty had been repealed some years earlier. Similarly Roebuck informed the Commons that if the stamp duty had been lifted the agricultural workers at Tolpuddle would probably not have been so ignorant as to have joined a trade union. Another leading campaigner, Grote, was even more sanguine about the benefits of an expanded, capitalist press: 'a great deal of the bad feeling that was at present abroad amongst the labouring classes on the subject of wages' was due, he believed, to 'the want of proper instruction and correct information as to their real interests' caused by taxes on the press.[3]

What these parliamentary campaigners for a 'free press' emphasized was not libertarian principle but the need for a more positive approach to political indoctrination. Their speeches occasionally betrayed anxiety, however, that the time might not be ripe to lift controls on the press. It was this ambivalence which perhaps explains why so few amongst the repeal lobby of MPs voted consistently against the government's counter-offensive in 1836 designed, as we have seen, to restore the stamp duty and destroy the radical press. In the revealing words of Collet, who was later to co-ordinate the campaign for a free press in Westminster, the government's attack on radical journalism was 'not a liberal, but it was in some respects, a statesman-like measure'.[4]

The new campaign

A new parliamentary lobby against 'the taxes on knowledge' was organized in 1848. Although it posed as a broadly based organization, it had a narrow social base. As Cobden confided privately, 'Exclusively almost, we comprise steady, sober middle-class reformers.' The driving force behind the campaign was a group of liberal industrialist MPs who saw in the repeal of press taxation a means of propagating the principles of free trade and competitive capitalism. In particular, they hoped that a reduction of newspaper prices, following the abolition of press taxes, would assist the growth of the local commercial press with which many of them were closely connected and undermine the dominant position of the 'unreliable' *Times* by exposing it to increased competition.

They skilfully involved a variety of different interest groups in the campaign – all of whom had something to gain from the expansion of a cheap press – such as temperance campaigners, adult educationalists, publishers (though these were deeply divided over the stamp duty), and proselytizing politicians of varying persuasions. The differences between them merely reflected, for the most part, competition between rival élites for the attention and support of the subordinate classes. However, the common concern of most leading supporters of the campaign was to secure the loyalty of the working classes to the social order through the expansion of the capitalist press. 'The larger we open the field of general instruction,' declared Palmerston when speaking for the repeal of the stamp duty in the Commons, 'the firmer the foundations on which the order, the loyalty and good conduct of the lower classes will rest.' Repeal the taxes on knowledge, proclaimed the Irish politician, Maguire, and 'You render the people better citizens, more obedient to the laws, more faithful and loyal subjects, and more determined to stand up for the honour of the country.' 'The freedom of the press', argued Gladstone, 'was not merely to be permitted and tolerated, but to be highly prized, for it tended to bring closer together all the national interests and preserve the institutions of the country.' The new market-based press, they were agreed, would be an effective instrument of social control.[5]

But while the fundamental objectives of the campaign against press taxes were the same as before, its rhetoric was modified. Whig history was invoked more often to stigmatize supporters of press taxes as enemies of liberty and the heirs of court censorship of the press. Opposition to press taxation was more frequently voiced in the form of abstract and elevated principle. Freedom of expression should not be taxed; truth would confound error in open debate; good publications would drive out bad ones in fair competition; and even that truth would emerge only through the interplay of the free market-place of ideas.

Reformers' apposition of libertarian and authoritarian arguments may seem a little incongruous to contemporary ears. But most respectable campaigners against the 'taxes on knowledge' appear not to have perceived any tension to exist between the concepts of press freedom and social control. As Alexander Andrews, editor of the first journalists' trade journal, eloquently argued, for instance, the great mission of a free press was to 'educate and enlighten those classes whose political knowledge has been hitherto so little, and by consequence so dangerous'. This theme of political indoctrination fused naturally and unself-consciously with that of liberty. 'The list of our public journals,' Andrews continued, 'is a proud and noble list – the roll call of an army of liberty, with a rallying point in every town. It is a police of safety, and a sentinel of public morals.'[6] The very facility with which these dissonant themes could be conflated reveals the ideological universe within which the press freedom campaign was constructed. A tacit model of society which admitted no conflict of class interest, only a conflict between ignorance and enlightenment and between the individual and the state, provided the mental framework in which a free press could be perceived as both a watch-dog of government and guard-dog of the people.

However, commitment to the principle of free competition was not entirely disinterested. The arguments for a free market press were part of a wider set of arguments that had been deployed in middle-class-dominated campaigns against the aristocratic state across a broad front. Open competition in the free market-place of talent had become the rallying cry behind the campaigns to reform the armed forces, the civil service, and the universities during the 1850s, which opened up new avenues of influential and well-remunerated employment to the professional middle class. The material blessings of competition in the free market had also been extensively invoked in the attacks on the Corn Law and aristocratic protectionism during the 1840s and 1850s. In the context of the press, enthusiasm for reform reflected a growing confidence amongst middle-class reformers that their views would prevail at a time when their intellectual ascendancy seemed increasingly assured.

The key members of the press freedom campaign were also under no illusion that a free market would be neutral. More sophisticated than their predecessors in the 1830s, they had a better understanding of how the press industry worked. The repeal of press taxes, declared Milner-Gibson, president of the Association for the Promotion of the Repeal of the Taxes on Knowledge (APRTK), would create 'a cheap press in the hands of men of good moral character, of respectability, and of capital'. Aware of the rise of capital and operating costs in popular newspaper publishing in the USA, he believed that free market processes would favour entrepreneurs with large financial resources. Free trade, he stressed, in common with other leading campaigners, would 'give to men of capital and respectability the power of gaining access by newspapers, by faithful record of the facts, to the minds of the working classes'. The free market, argued Sir George Lewis, the Liberal Chancellor of the Exchequer, would promote papers 'enjoying the preference of the advertising public'. Furthermore, reformers argued, responsible control over a cheap press would educate public demand. As one campaigner put it, 'The appetite grows by what it feeds on.'[7]

Most reformers also assumed that journalists would be unresponsive to radical ideas because of their background and social position. The establishment of a cheap press, explained Hickson, a leading campaigner, would create a new hierarchical system of communication in which journalists 'two or three degrees' above the labouring classes would enlighten them. To Gladstone, the principal attraction of repeal was that it would lead to more men of 'quality' working in the press, and consequently educating the people. 'A perfectly free press', wryly commented the journalist, J. F. Stephen, 'is one of the greatest safeguards of peace and order' since successful journalists belong to 'the comfortable part of society' and will 'err rather on the side of making too much of their (comfortable) interests than on that of neglecting them.'[8]

Reinforcing this commitment to creating a cheap, unrestricted press was a growing conviction that it was now safe to lift controls. The radical working-class movement was on the retreat in the 1850s. There was, proclaimed reformers, 'a great increase of intelligence among the people'.[9] Even those who were uncertain whether the working class would 'become the glory, or might prove greatly dangerous, to the peace of the country', agreed that it was a good time to attempt an experiment. Significantly only those who were convinced that the lower classes were wedded to radical prejudices (and this group included not only entrenched traditionalists but also some distinguished liberals committed to free market competition in other spheres)[10] remained resolutely opposed to the repeal of the stamp duty.

The campaign against press taxes was conducted with remarkable skill and tenacity. Reformers packed the Parliamentary Select Committee on the Stamp Duty and largely determined the contents of its report. They attacked poorly briefed ministers and won the support of officials in the Board of Inland Revenue. They harassed the government through the law courts, exposed the inconsistencies in the way the stamp duty was enforced, organized public meetings, petitions, and deputations, and attacked press taxes in sympathetic newspapers. Their political virtuosity was finally rewarded with the abolition of the advertisement duty in

1853, the stamp duty in 1855, the paper duty in 1861, and the security system in 1869.

But the parliamentary campaign for a free press was never inspired by a modern libertarian commitment to diversity of expression. Indeed the ruthless repression of the unstamped press in the mid-1830s had much the same objective as the campaign which set the press 'free' twenty years later: the subordination of the press to the social order. All that had changed was a growing commitment to positive indoctrination of the lower orders through a cheap press, and a growing conviction that free trade and normative controls were a morally preferable and more efficient control system than direct controls administered by the state. Underlying this shift was the growing power and confidence of the Victorian middle class, which dominated the parliamentary campaign for repeal of press taxes and recognized in the expanding press a powerful agency for the advancement of their interests.

The confidence of reformers in the 'free' market-place of opinion proved to be justified. The radical press was eclipsed in the period after the repeal of press taxes. Why this happened has never been adequately explained.

Notes

1. For instance G. A. Cranfield, *The Press and Society* (Harlow, Longman, 1978), p. 205. This view is contested in relation to the 1830s by P. Hollis, *The Pauper Press* (London, Oxford University Press, 1970), and by J. Wiener, *The War of the Unstamped* (New York, Cornell University Press, 1969).

2. *Parliamentary Debates*, 13 (1832), cols 619–48; 23 (1834), cols 1,193–1,222; 30 (1835), cols 835–62; 34 (1836), cols 627 ff.; 35 (1836), cols 566 ff., 46 (1837), cols 1,164–84. In actual fact the radical unstamped press did not have a 'clear field'. The authorities harassed radical unstamped papers, while regularly turning a blind eye to 'moderate' unstamped papers in the early 1830s.

3. Place, Select Committee on Drunkenness, *Parliamentary Papers*, 8 (1834), question 2,054; Roebuck, *Parliamentary Debates*, 23 (1834), cols 1,208–9; Grote, ibid., col. 1,221.

4. C. D. Collet, *History of the Taxes on Knowledge: Their Origin and Repeal*, vol. 1 (London, T. Fisher Unwin, 1899).

5. Palmerston, *Parliamentary Debates*, 127 (1854), col. 459; Maguire, *Parliamentary Debates*, 157 (1860), col. 383; Gladstone, cit. J. Grant, *The Newspaper Press: Its Origins, Progress and Present Position* (London, Tinsley Brothers, 1871–2).

6. A. Andrews, *The History of British Journalism to 1855* (London, Richard Bentley, 1859), ii, p.347.

7. Milner-Gibson, *Parliamentary Debates*, 137 (1855), col. 434, and *Parliamentary Debates*, 110 (1850), col. 378; Lewis, *Parliamentary Debates*, 137 (1855), col. 786; Whitty, Report of the Select Committee on Newspaper Stamps (SCNS), *Parliamentary Papers*, 17 (1851), para. 600.

8. Hickson, SCNS (1851), para. 3,169; Gladstone, *Parliamentary Debates*, 137 (1855), col. 794; J. F. Stephen, 'Journalism', *Cornhill Magazine*, 6 (1862);

9. Bulwer Lytton, *Parliamentary Debates*, 137 (1855), col. 1,118; Ingram, *Parliamentary Debates*, 151 (1858), col. 112; Digby Seymour, *Parliamentary Debates*, 125 (1853), col. 1,166.

10. For instance J. R. McCulloch, *Dictionary of Commerce and Commercial Navigation* (London, Longman, Brown, & Green, 1854), p. 893.

4

The industrialization of the press

During the half century following the repeal of the 'taxes on knowledge', a number of radical newspapers closed down or were eventually incorporated, like the *Reynolds News*, into the mainstream of popular Liberal journalism. Militant journalism survived only in the etiolated form of small circulation national periodicals and struggling local weeklies. Yet this decline occurred during a period of rapid press expansion, when local daily papers were established in all the major urban centres of Britain and a new generation of predominantly right-wing national newspapers came into being. These included newspapers such as the *People* (1881), *Daily Mail* (1896), *Daily Express* (1900), and *Daily Mirror* (1903), which have played a prominent role in British journalism ever since they were founded.

Most historians, on the left as well as the right, attribute the decline of radical journalism to a shift of public attitudes. The collapse of Chartism in the early 1850s produced a wave of disillusion. Many radical activists were absorbed into the Liberal Party, particularly after the upper strata of the working class gained the vote in 1867. Trade unions also became more inward looking, seeking to improve wages and working conditions rather than to change the structure of society. These changes were reinforced by the relative success of the British economy: most workers in employment became substantially better off during the second half of the nineteenth century. Intensive proselytization of the working class through schools, churches, youth clubs, and other socializing agencies like the Volunteer Force also contributed to the spread of anti-socialist views.

These developments diminished the potential market for radical journalism. They also had another consequence which has tended to be overlooked. The reduction of support for the left made it more difficult to raise money within the working-class movement for new publishing ventures. As the TUC Congress debates in the early part of the twentieth century make clear, many Liberal and Lib-Lab trade unionists were reluctant to invest their members' money in setting up new socialist publications because they had become reconciled to the commercial press.

However, this '*Zeitgeist*' interpretation provides an insufficient explanation for the fall of the radical press. It is based on the misleading *laissez-faire* model of the press which assumes that newspapers must respond to the public mood if they are to stay in business in a competitive environment.

In fact the evidence clearly shows that there was no close correspondence between the climate of opinion in the country and the political character of the press. What may be broadly defined as the radical press was still a powerful force in popular journalism in 1860 when the working-class movement was divided and defeated. In sharp contrast, the radical press was dwarfed by its rivals fifty years later, when the radical movement was gathering momentum.[1] The steady growth of general trade unionism, the radicalization of skilled workers, the spread of socialist and Labourist ideas, and the revival of industrial militancy did not give rise to an efflorescence of radical journalism, although it produced a few notable publications before 1914. The absence of a close correlation between press and public opinion is further underlined by voting figures. In the 1918 general election, for instance, the Labour Party gained 22 per cent of the vote but did not obtain the unreserved support of a single national daily or Sunday newspaper.

Lucy Brown has recently suggested a supplementary explanation for the decline of 'critical vigour' in the Victorian press. She shows that the political élite devoted more time and skill to cultivating the press, and became increasingly dominant as sources and definers of news. But while this helps to explain the rightward drift of part of the commercial press, it still does not account for the eclipse of radical journalism. The militant press's adversarial style effectively inoculated it against the gentler arts of press management described by Brown. Its weakness was more fundamental: its share of circulation steadily declined during the later Victorian period.

Virginia Berridge has advanced a more plausible explanation of the decline of committed journalism. This was due, she argues, to the 'commercialization' of the popular press. New popular papers came into being which were primarily business ventures. They concentrated on entertainment rather than taxing political analysis, and consequently secured a much larger audience than politically committed radical papers.

This analysis focuses attention upon a significant change within part of the radical press. Its circulation during the 1840s was swollen by the emergence of the *News of the World* and *Lloyds Weekly*, both commercial papers whose radicalism was the product more of commercial expediency than of political commitment. As the *News of the World* frankly stated in its first issue (1 October 1843), 'It is only by a very extensive circulation that the proprietors can be compensated for the outlay of a large capital in this novel and original undertaking.' Although the same issue contained an impassioned attack upon conditions in some poor-houses, where inmates were forced to wear prison clothes, the paper also made clear that its general orientation was to please as many people as possible by serving 'the general utility of all classes'. This led to the adoption of consensual views and the growth of entertainment at the expense of political news. Yet, not very surprisingly, Sunday papers in the *News of the World* mould, with a professionally processed combination of news, sport, human interest stories, and political commentary, proved more appealing than the didactic journals that were the principal organs of the left in late Victorian Britain.

This explanation is persuasive as far as it goes. But it glosses over one striking feature of the development of the radical press. During the first half of the nineteenth century left-wing papers evolved from being journals of opinion, based on a quarto format, into broadsheet newspapers carrying news as well as commentary. This change was particularly marked during the 1830s, and was accompanied by a significant broadening of news content. Some of these radical papers began to develop a wide audience appeal by drawing upon the popular street literature tradition of chapbooks, broadsheets, gallowsheets, and almanacs. Indeed Cleave's *Weekly Police Gazette*, the *London Dispatch*, and the early militant *Reynolds News* were important partly because they started to rework this popular tradition in ways that projected a radical ideology through human interest news and entertainment as well as through political coverage.

Why, then, did the committed radical press increasingly retreat in the second half of the nineteenth century into the ghetto of narrowly politicized journalism? Why did it leave the field of popular news coverage and entertainment to the commercial press? Thus the question that needs to be asked is not why Victorian working people should have preferred the *News of the World* to rather arid socialist journals such as *Justice* and *Commonweal*, but why the radical press should have failed to live up to its early promise.

Berridge's analysis is an historical version of a standard critique of mass culture. This assumes that material commercially processed as a commodity for the mass market is inevitably 'debased' because it relies on the manipulation of public tastes and attitudes for profit. This is based on assumptions that are open to question. In the context of Victorian Britain, it also obscures under the general heading of 'commercialization' the complex system of controls institutionalized by the industrialization of the Victorian press.

The freedom of capital

One of the central objectives of state economic controls on the press – to exclude pauper management – was attained only by their repeal. The lifting of press taxes resulted in an enormous expansion of market demand for cheaper newspapers, and this led in turn to the development of expensive new print technology. Rotary presses, fed by hand, were introduced in the 1860s and 1870s and were gradually replaced by web rotary machines of increasing size and sophistication in late Victorian and Edwardian England. 'Craft' composing was mechanized by Hattersley's machine in the 1860s, and this was later replaced by the linotype machine in the 1880s and 1890s. Numerous innovations were also made in graphic reproduction. These developments led to a sharp rise in fixed capital costs. Northcliffe estimated half a million pounds as 'the initial cost of machinery, buildings, ink factories and the like, and this was altogether apart from the capital required for daily working expenses' in setting up the *Daily Mail* in 1896 – although this figure almost certainly includes the cost of establishing the paper as a property around which other publications were grouped.[2]

This enormous increase in capital investment made it much more difficult for people with limited funds to break into mass publishing. It also gave considerable economic advantages to newspaper groups which printed more than one paper at the same plant. The profits from the vertical integration of publishing – Edward Lloyd led the way in the 1870s and 1880s by establishing paper mills and growing esparto grass as raw material for paper – were also reinvested in the development of newspaper enterprises. Nevertheless, the rising fixed capital costs of newspaper publishing did not constitute an insuperable obstacle to the launch of new publications with limited capital resources even in the national market. Newspapers like the *Daily Herald*, launched in 1912, could be started with only limited capital by being printed on a contract basis by an independent printer.

A more important financial consequence of the repeal of press taxes was to force up the running costs of newspaper publishing. National newspapers became substantial enterprises with large staffs and long print runs. They also cut their cover prices. The combination of rising expenditure and lower cover prices forced up the circulation level that newspapers had to achieve in order to be profitable. This raised, in turn, the run-in costs of new papers before they built their circulations to break-even point. New newspapers could be launched with limited funds and derelict newspapers could be bought relatively cheaply. It was increasingly the establishment of newspapers that required large capital resources.

Thus in 1855 Disraeli was advised by D. C. Coulton that a capital of about £20,000 was needed to start a London daily paper. In 1867 W. H. Smith estimated that about £50,000 was needed to fund a new London morning paper. By the 1870s Edward Lloyd needed to spend £150,000 to establish the *Daily Chronicle* (after buying it for £30,000). During the period 1906–8 Thomasson spent about £300,000 attempting to establish the liberal daily, *Tribune*. By the 1920s, however, Lord Cowdray spent about £750,000 attempting to convert the *Westminster Gazette* into a quality daily. Even more was spent on developing mass-circulation papers during the same period.

Indeed the full extent of the material transformation of the press is perhaps most clearly revealed by comparing the launch and establishment costs of newspapers before and after the industrialization of the press. As we have seen, the total cost of establishing the *Northern Star*, a national weekly newspaper, on a profitable basis in 1837 was well under £1,000. It was able to break even with a circulation of about 6,200 copies, which was probably achieved within the first month. In contrast the *Sunday Express*, launched in 1918, had over £2 million spent on it before it broke even, with a circulation of well over 250,000. Thus while a public subscription in northern towns was sufficient to launch a national weekly in the 1830s, it required the resources of an international conglomerate controlled by Beaverbrook to do the same thing nearly a century later.[3]

These statistics illustrate the privileged position of capital in the creation of the modern press. Even when the costs of launching and establishing a popular paper were relatively low in the 1850s and 1860s, they still exceeded the resources readily available to the working class. The *Beehive*, for instance, was started in 1862 with a capital of less than £250 raised by trade union organizations and a well-to-do sympathizer. Its inadequate funding crippled it. Although it set out to be a paper with a broad audience appeal, it lacked the finances to be anything other than a weekly journal of opinion. Despite a small amount of additional capital put up by unions and other contributors, it was also forced to sell at double the price of the large-circulation weeklies it had been intended to compete against. In effect, its under-capitalization condemned it to the margins of national publishing as a specialist, if influential, weekly paper.

As the resources of organized labour increased, so did the costs of establishing a national paper. It was not until 1912 that papers financed and controlled from within the working class made their first appearance in national daily journalism – long after most national daily papers had become well established. The brief career of the *Daily Citizen*, and the early history of the *Daily Herald*, illustrate the economic obstacles to setting up papers under working-class control. The *Daily Citizen*, launched in 1912 with a capital of only £30,000 (subscribed mainly by trade unions), reached a circulation of 250,000 at its peak within two years and was only 50,000 short of overhauling the *Daily Express*. Although the *Daily Citizen* almost certainly acquired more working-class readers than any other daily, it still closed three years after its launch.

The more left-wing *Daily Herald*, started with only £300 and sustained by public donations (notably from two wealthy socialists, the Countess de la Warr and H. D. Harben, the son of the chairman of Prudential Insurance), lurched from one crisis to another despite reaching a circulation of over 250,000 at its meridian before 1914. On one occasion it came out in pages of different sizes and shapes because someone 'found' old discarded paper supplies when the *Daily Herald* could no longer afford to pay for paper. On other occasions it bought small quantities of paper under fictitious names from suppliers all over the country; the directors of the *Daily Herald* even threatened to organize industrial action against paper manufacturers, a stratagem that secured paper supplies without a guarantee. While the *Daily Citizen* closed, the *Daily Herald* survived by switching from being a daily to becoming a weekly during the period 1914–19. Lack of sufficient capital prevented its continuation in any other form.

The rise in publishing costs helps to explain why the committed left press in the late nineteenth century existed only as under-capitalized, low-budget, high-price specialist periodicals and as local community papers, an important but as yet relatively undocumented aspect of the residual survival of the radical press. The operation of the free market had raised the cost of press ownership beyond the readily available resources of the working class.

Market forces thus accomplished more than the most repressive measures of an aristocratic state. The security system introduced in 1819 to ensure that the press was controlled by 'men of some respectability and capital' had fixed the financial qualifications of press ownership at a mere

£200–300. This financial hurdle was raised a hundredfold in the period celebrated for the rise of a free press.[4]

But although the heavy capitalization of the British press was an important factor inhibiting the launch of new radical papers, it still does not explain the ideological absorption of radical papers already in existence before the repeal of the press taxes. Nor does it fully explain why small-circulation radical papers could not develop into profitable mass-circulation papers and accumulate enough capital, through retained profits, to finance new publications. For an answer to these questions we need to look elsewhere.

The new licensing system: advertising

The crucial element of the new control system was the role of advertising after the repeal of the advertisement duty. The reduction of this from 3s to 1s 6d in 1833 led to a 35 per cent growth of London and a 27 per cent growth of provincial press advertising in the space of one year. Between 1836 and 1848 the total volume of press advertising in Britain, as measured by the number of advertisements, increased by 36 per cent. Examination of the distribution of this increase shows, however, that a disproportionate amount went to established middle-class newspapers. It did not transform popular newspaper publishing.

It was only with the repeal of the advertisement duty in 1853 that it became profitable to advertise goods in papers aimed at the popular market. Previously, as John Cassell, the publisher of popular useful knowledge publications, complained to the Parliamentary Select Committee on Newspaper Stamps, 'It [the advertisement duty] entirely prevents a certain class of advertisements from appearing: it is only such as costly books and property sales by auction that really afford an opportunity of advertising and for paying the duty.' The end of the advertisement tax led to cheap press advertising.

Popular newspapers consequently attracted more advertising; in the four years between 1854 and 1858 *Reynolds News* increased its volume of advertising by over 50 per cent. This growth, together with the repeal of the stamp and paper duty, resulted in the modal price of popular newspapers being halved in the 1850s and halved again in the early 1860s. This transformed the economic structure of popular publishing. In the 1840s it had still been possible for working-class newspapers to be profitable, with only marginal advertising support, because of their high retail price. But with these massive reductions in price, all competitively priced newspapers – including those with very large circulations – became dependent on advertising. Advertisers thus acquired a *de facto* licensing authority since, without their support, newspapers ceased to be economically viable.

Reducing print unit costs and the sharp fall in the price of newsprint between 1875 and 1895 did not diminish the central role of advertising in the press. Advertising expenditure steadily increased in the Victorian and Edwardian period, rising to an estimated £20 million in 1907. This financed increased press expenditure on bigger papers, more staff, and the introduction of sale-or-return arrangements with distributors. It also helped to underwrite a further halving of the price of most popular papers to ½d in the late Victorian period.

The political implications of newspapers' economic dependence on advertising have been ignored largely because it is assumed that advertisers bought space in newspapers on the basis of market rather than political criteria. But political considerations played a significant part in some advertisers' calculations during the Victorian period. In 1856 the principal advertising handbook detailed the political views of most London and local newspapers with the proud boast that 'Till this Directory was published, the advertiser had no means of accurately determining which journal *might be best adapted to his views*, and most likely to forward his interests.'[5] (emphasis added). Even non-socialist news-papers found that controversial editorial policies led to the loss of commercial advertising. The *Pall Mall Gazette*'s advertising revenue dropped sharply in response to its 'Maiden Tribute' crusade in 1885 in which the editor 'procured' a 15-year-old girl as part of his paper's campaign to raise the age of consent. The *Daily News* was boycotted by some advertisers in 1886 when it campaigned for Home Rule. Govern-ment advertising long continued to be allocated on a partisan basis. As late as 1893 the incoming Home Secretary, Herbert Asquith, was told that generally 'it is the custom to transfer advertisements according to the politics of governments'.

Political prejudice in advertising selection almost certainly declined during the latter part of the nineteenth and early twentieth centuries. The rise of advertising agencies, the emergence of major, national advertisers, and the increasing availability of circulation statistics en-couraged the adoption of a more professional approach. Even so, the frequent remonstrations against 'mixing politics with business' in advertising manuals published between 1850 and 1930 suggest that political prejudice continued to influence some advertisers.

But even when political prejudice played no part in advertising selection, left-wing publications still faced discrimination on commercial grounds. As the head of a well-known advertising agency wrote in 1856, 'Some of the most widely circulated journals in the Empire are the worst possible to advertise in. Their readers are not purchasers, and any money thrown upon them is so much thrown away.' In contrast, select newspapers read by affluent readers were rated favourably. 'Character is of more importance than number,' advised an advertising handbook in 1851, adding that 'a journal that circulates a thousand among the upper or middle classes is a better medium than would be one circulating a hundred thousand among the lower classes.' Similar, though usually less extreme, advice continued to be given for a long time. For example Sir Charles Higham, the head of a large advertising agency, wrote in 1925, 'A very limited circulation, but entirely among the wealthy ... may be more valuable than if the circulation were quadrupled.'[6]

Many advertisers also made a distinction between the skilled and poor working class. Indeed the latter were often excluded from the early market research surveys in the 1920s on the grounds that they were not worth bothering about. Once newspapers became identified with the poor, they found it difficult to attract advertising. As an advertising handbook cautioned in 1921, 'You cannot afford to place your advertisements in a paper which is read by the down-at-heels who buy it to see the "Situations Vacant" column.'[7]

The main problem encountered by radical newspapers was that they were generally associated with a working class, and sometimes with a 'down-at-heels' readership. This was because, in the absence of readership research, advertisers relied very heavily on the general appearance and editorial policies of papers to gauge the social class of their readers.

This combination of economic and political discrimination by advertisers crucially influenced the development of left-wing journalism. In the first place, it exerted pressure on the radical press to move up-market in order to survive. A number of radical newspapers redefined their target audience, and moderated their radicalism in an attempt to attract the more affluent readers that advertisers wanted to reach.

This process is well illustrated by the career of *Reynolds News*. It was founded in 1850 by George Reynolds, a member of the left-wing faction of the Chartist National Executive. Reynolds had urged a 'physical force' strategy in 1848 and opposed middle-class collaboration in the early 1850s. His paper was initially in the *Northern Star* tradition of class-conscious radicalism, and had close links with the working-class movement.

Yet despite its radical origins, *Reynolds News* changed under the impact of the new economic imperatives of newspaper publishing. The fact that it never provided, even at the outset, a consistent theoretical perspective doubtless made it vulnerable to ideological incorporation. Inevitably it was influenced by the decline of radicalism in the country during the 1850s and early 1860s. But an important factor in its absorption was the need to attract advertising revenue. The change was symbolized by the inclusion of regular features on friendly societies in the year after the repeal of the advertisement duty, as a ploy to attract advertising. Thus enterprises which had been regularly attacked in militant newspapers as 'a hoax' to persuade working-class people to identify with capitalism became a much-needed source of revenue for *Reynolds News*.

The paper continued to take a radical stand on most major events of the day, but it increasingly expressed the individualistic values of the more affluent readers it needed to attract. It adopted many of the tenets of political economy that it had so virulently attacked during the 1850s, even to the extent of accepting the palliatives of 'prudent marriage' (that is sexual restraint) and emigration as solutions to unemployment. It reverted to those common denominators of radicalism that united the lower-middle and working classes – attacks on 'the vices' of the aristocracy, privilege, corruption in high places, the monarchy, place-men, and the Church. Attacks on industrial capital were modulated to attacks on monopoly and speculators, while criticism of shopkeepers as the exploitive agents of capital gave way to articles that celebrated the expansion of the Victorian economy. *Reynolds News* became a populist paper catering for the coalition of lower middle-class and working-class readers necessary for its survival, with occasional bursts of radicalism as a reminder of its past. Acquired by the Dicks family in 1879 and later by J. H. Dalziel, it gradually evolved into a conventional Liberal paper.

Reynolds was accused of commercial opportunism by contemporary critics (including Karl Marx). Yet it is difficult to see what else he could have done if the paper was to survive the transition to an advertising-based system. Even the radical *People's Paper* boasted in 1857 of its appeal to 'high paid trades and shopkeepers' in its promotion to advertisers. Failing to attract affluent readers in sufficient numbers, the *People's Paper* was forced to close down with a circulation far larger than middle-class weeklies like the *Spectator* and *John Bull*.

Radical newspapers could survive in the new economic environment only if they moved up-market to attract an audience desired by advertisers or remained in a small working-class ghetto, with manageable losses that could be met from donations. Once they moved out of that ghetto and acquired a large working-class audience, they courted disaster. If they sold at the competitive prices charged by their rivals, their sales revenue after distributors' discounts did not cover their costs. Any increase in their circulation, without a corresponding growth in advertising, merely increased their losses, and brought them closer to folding.

This fate befell the London *Evening Echo*, which was taken over by wealthy radicals in 1901 and relaunched as a socialist paper. A special number was issued, firmly committing the paper to 'the interests of labour as against the tyranny of organized capital'. In the period 1902–4 its circulation rose by a phenomenal 60 per cent, leading to its abrupt closure in 1905. The growth of advertising had failed to keep pace with the growth of circulation, making the continuance of the paper impossible.[8]

The same thing almost happened to the *Daily Herald* when it was relaunched as a daily in 1919. It spent £10,000 on promotion – a small amount by comparison with its main rivals, but sufficient to ensure that it sharply increased its circulation. 'Our success in circulation', recalled George Lansbury, 'was our undoing. The more copies we sold, the more money we lost.' The situation became increasingly desperate when, partly aided by the unexpected publicity of attacks on the *Daily Herald* by leading members of the government alleging that it was financed from Moscow, the *Daily Herald*'s circulation continued to rise in 1920. 'Every copy we sold was sold at a loss,' mourned Lansbury. 'The rise in circulation, following the government's attacks, brought us nearer and nearer to disaster.'[9] The money raised from whist drives, dances, draws, and collections was not enough to offset the shortfall of advertising. Even the expedient of doubling the paper's price in 1920 did not compensate for lack of advertising. Money from the miners and the railwaymen stopped the paper from closing. But the only way the paper could be saved, in the long term, was by being taken over as the official organ of the Labour Party and TUC in 1922. A paper that had been a free-wheeling vehicle of the left, an important channel for the dissemination of syndicalist ideas in the early part of the twentieth century, became the official mouthpiece of the moderate leadership of the labour movement. Lack of advertising forced it to become subservient to a new form of control.

In short, one of four things happened to national radical papers that failed to meet the requirements of advertisers. They either closed down; accommodated to advertising pressure by moving up-market; stayed in a small audience ghetto with manageable losses; or accepted an alternative source of institutional patronage.

Yet publications which conformed to the marketing requirements of advertisers obtained what were, in effect, large external subsidies which they could spend on increased editorial outlay and promotion in order to attract new readers. Rising advertising expenditure also provided a powerful inducement to entrepreneurs to launch publications directed at markets that advertisers particularly wanted to reach. Between 1866 and 1896 the number of magazines increased from an estimated 557 to 2,097, many of which were trade, technical, and professional journals aimed at specialized groups attractive to advertisers. The number of local dailies grew from only 2 in 1850 to 196 in 1900, falling to 169 by 1920 due mainly to the casualties caused by intense competition. There was also a substantial expansion in the number of local weekly papers from fewer than 400 in 1856 to an estimated 2,072 in 1900, declining to an estimated 1,700 by 1921. Above all, there was a substantial increase in the number of national daily and Sunday papers, mostly founded between 1880 and 1918, which catered either for mass, middle-market audiences or small élite audiences.[10]

This growth in the number of publications was accompanied by an enormous expansion in newspaper consumption. Annual newspaper sales rose from 85 million in 1851 to 5,604 million in 1920. Only part of this increase was due to rapid population growth: the number of newspapers purchased *per capita* over the age of 14 rose from 6 copies in 1850 to 182 copies in 1920. Even allowing for a reduction in the number of readers per copy, due to a marked decline in the collective purchase and reading aloud of newspapers, this still constitutes a remarkable increase in the audience reached by the press. Sunday and local daily papers achieved aggregate circulations of 13.5 million and 9.2 million respectively by 1920. In contrast the national daily press with a predominantly middle-class public had a circulation of only 5.4 million in 1920, while the local weekly press (which was particularly strong in rural areas) had a 9.2 million circulation.[11]

This growth was not simply the consequence of the sharp reductions in newspaper prices. Adult literacy (as measured very imperfectly by the ability to sign one's name) rose from 69 per cent in 1850 to 97 per cent in 1900. The normal number of hours worked in many industries fell from 60 hours a week to 54 hours or less between 1850 and 1890, and average real wages rose by an estimated 84 per cent between 1850 and 1900. These important social changes provided the essential background for the expansion of the capitalist press with important consequences for the political development of modern Britain.

Impact of the industrialized press

Traditional educationalists like Hannah More and Andrew Bell taught working-class children to read but not to write. They were thus able to read what was good for them but not write what might be bad for them. Something very close to this division was achieved through the industrialization of the press: working-class consumption of newspapers was separated from control over its production.

Many of the new local dailies were started or bought by leading local industrialists. Both the *Northern Daily Express* and the *Northern Leader* were bought by colliery owners; the *South Shields Gazette* was acquired by Stevenson, a member of a local chemical manufacturing family; the *Bolton Evening News* belonged to local industrialists, the Tillotsons; the *Yorkshire Post*'s principal shareholder was the Leeds banker, Beckett-Denison; the *Ipswich Express* was owned by Colman, the mustard manufacturer, and so on. These papers offered a very different view of the world from that of the early radical press they supplanted. Papers like the *Northern Star* had amplified class conflicts in the local community ('to talk of reconciliation between the middle and working class will, henceforth, be a farce' was a typical lead-in to one of its news reports). In contrast the new local commercial press tended to block out conflict, minimize differences, and encourage positive identification with the local community and its middle-class leadership. Characteristic of this style of consensual journalism was a report in the *Leeds Mercury* (printed in the same city as the *Northern Star*) of a local dignitary addressing the annual public soirée of the Leeds Mechanics Institute on the subject of 'these popular institutions, sustained by the united efforts of all classes ... thereby to promote the virtue, happiness and peace of the community'.

The early militant press had fuelled suspicion of middle-class reformists with a barrage of criticism against 'sham-radical humbugs' and 'the merciful middle-class converts to half Chartism at half past the eleventh hour'. In contrast the new local daily press encouraged its readers to identify with the political parties controlled by the ruling class. Ten of the new local dailies that emerged between 1855 and 1860 were affiliated to the Liberal Party; eighteen created between 1860 and 1870 were affiliated to the Tory or Liberal Party, and forty-one of the local dailies created in the following decade were similarly linked to the two great parties. The new party press played a central role in transforming what had been essentially aristocratic factions in parliament into mass political movements by mobilizing popular support behind them. It thus reinforced the division of the working-class movement through its absorption into rival parliamentary parties.

The new liberal press diluted the ideology of the early militant press to such an extent that it acquired a new, therapeutic meaning for the functioning of the social system. The co-operative ethos that would inform the new social order, proclaimed by some militant papers, became transmuted into the spirit of partnership between masters and men that would make the British economy prosper. The early radical stress on moral regeneration through social reconstruction became a celebration of moral improvement through the spread of middle-class enlightenment and prosperity. And the value formerly attached to self-education as a means of ideological resistance to class domination gave way to a stress on the undifferentiated acquisition of 'knowledge' as the means of individual self-advancement and economic progress. Admittedly these transformations drew upon a radical tradition that contained contradictory elements within it. But by emphasizing the liberal rather than more radical lineaments of this tradition, the new press contributed to the disorganization of the working-class movement.

There were important differences between individual newspapers, particularly in relation to their coverage of trade unions. But notwithstanding these differences, all national newspapers launched between 1855 and 1910, and the overwhelming majority of new local daily papers, encouraged positive identification with the social system. The shift in the press that this represented is perhaps best illustrated by the way in which Queen Victoria was portrayed. Most radical papers in the period 1837–55 were aggressively republican: the Queen was vilified as politically partisan and reactionary, the head of a system of organized corruption, the mother of a brood of royal cadgers, and the friend and relative of European tyrants. In contrast the new press portrayed the Queen particularly from the mid-1870s onwards as a dutiful and benign matriarch, who symbolized in an almost talismanic way the moral and material progress of her reign. Projecting her as a living embodiment of national unity, they also played a key role in converting the jubilee celebrations of 1887 and 1897 into popular, mobilizing rites of national communion.

Above all, the new popular press fostered the wave of imperialism that swept through all levels of society. It tended to portray Britain's colonial role as a civilizing mission to the heathen, undeveloped world, and as an extended adventure story in which military triumphs were achieved through individual acts of courage rather than through superior technology. Common to both themes was pride in Britain's ascendancy: as the *Daily Mail* (23 June 1897), the most popular daily of late Victorian Britain, enthused:

We send out a boy here and a boy there, and the boy takes hold of the savages of the part he comes to and teaches them to march and shoot as he tells them, to obey him and believe in him and die for him and the Queen. A plain, stupid, uninspired people they call us, and yet we are doing this with every kind of savage man there is.

This celebration of Britain's dominion sometimes struck a more atavistic note as in this report of the 1898 Sudan expedition in the *Westminster Gazette*:

A large number of the Tommies had never been under fire before...
and there was a curious look of suppressed excitement in some of the
faces. .... Now and then I caught in a man's eye the curious gleam
which comes from the joy of shedding blood – that mysterious impulse
which, despite all the veneer of civilization, still holds its own in man's
nature, whether he is killing rats with a terrier, rejoicing in a prize
fight, playing a salmon or potting Dervishes. It was a fine day and we
were out to kill something. Call it what you like, the experience is a big
factor in the joy of living.

The paper which celebrated 'potting Dervishes' was, in terms of the
political spectrum represented by the contemporary national press, on
'the left'. It was, for example, one of the few liberal papers not to join the
press campaign for vengeance during the Boer War. However, it joined
all other daily papers of note in providing uncritical, Hun-hating
support for Britain's involvement in the First World War.

To summarize, the shift of public attitudes following the defeat of the
Chartist Movement partly explains the decline of the radical press. But it
does not account for why the press, taken as a whole, moved further to
the right than public opinion; nor does it explain why the subsequent
revival of the radical movement did not give rise to a stronger revival of
radical journalism. Both the extent and permanence of the eclipse of
radical journalism as the dominant force in the national popular press
can be properly understood only in terms of structural changes in the
press industry.

Notes

1. For the relative weakness of the radical press in 1910, see A. J. Lee,
   'The radical press' in A. Morris (ed.), *Edwardian Radicalism 1900–
   1914* (London, Routledge & Kegan Paul, 1974).
2. R. Pound and G. Harmsworth, *Northcliffe* (London, Cassell, 1959), p.
   206.
3. A. J. P. Taylor, *Beaverbrook* (London, Hamish Hamilton, 1972), p.
   175.
4. The costs of market entry for mass publishing were particularly high
   in Britain due to the dominating role of the national press. This
   partly explains why the radical press in Britain was much weaker
   than in many other European countries, where the press remained
   decentralized and entry costs were lower.
5. *Mitchell's Newspaper Press Directory* (Mitchell, 1856). It should be
   noted, however, that Mitchell himself cautioned advertisers against
   political bias.

6. *Mitchell's Newspaper Press Directory* (Mitchell, 1856); Anon., *Guide to Advertisers* (1851); C. Higham, *Advertising* (London, Williams & Norgate, 1925), p. 166.

7. C. Freer, *The Inner Side of Advertising: A Practical Handbook for Advertisers* (London, Library Press, 1921), p. 203.

8. F. W. Pethick-Lawrence, *Fate Has Been Kind* (London, Hutchinson, 1943), pp. 65 ff.

9. G. Lansbury, *The Miracle of Fleet Street* (London, Victoria House, 1925), pp. 160 ff.

10. The figures for regional dailies relate to Britain and for other categories of publications to the UK, as reported in *Mitchell's Newspaper Press Directory* (Mitchell, 1856).

11. N. Kaldor and R. Silverman, *A Statistical Analysis of Advertising Expenditure and of the Revenue of the Press* (Cambridge, Cambridge University Press, 1948), p. 84.

5

The era of the press barons

The era of the press barons is often seen as a maverick interlude in the development of the press when newspapers became subject to the whims and caprices of their owners. According to this view, the press barons built vast press empires and ruled them like personal fiefdoms. In the hands of men like Beaverbrook and Rothermere, newspapers became mere 'engines of propaganda' manipulated in order to further their political ambitions. As Baldwin said in a memorable sentence (suggested to him by his cousin, Rudyard Kipling), 'What proprietorship of these papers is aiming at is power, and power without responsibility – the prerogative of the harlot throughout the ages.'

The despotic rule of the press barons is usually compared unfavourably with a preceding 'golden age' when proprietors played an inactive role and 'sovereign' editors conducted their papers in a responsible manner. In some accounts, too, the era of Northcliffe and Rothermere is contrasted with the period after the Second World War when journalists became more educated, independent, and professional. The press barons have thus become favourite bogeymen: their indictment has become a way of celebrating other periods of press history.

But in reality the reign of the press barons did not constitute an exceptional pathology in the evolution of the press, but merely a continuation of tendencies already present before. Indeed in so far as the barons can be said to be innovators, it is not for the reasons that are generally given. They did not break with tradition by using their papers for political propaganda; their distinctive contribution was rather that they downgraded propaganda in favour of entertainment. Nor did they subvert the role of the press as a fourth estate: on the contrary it was they who detached the commercial press from the political parties and, consequently, from government. What actually happened is, in some ways, the exact opposite of the myth.

The creation of press empires

The press chains created by the press barons in the late nineteenth and early twentieth centuries were not a new phenomenon. Multiple owner-ship of weekly newspapers had developed as early as the eighteenth century largely because it enabled costs to be reduced through shared services. Local daily chains had also emerged shortly after the local daily press was established. By 1884, for instance, a syndicate headed by the Scots-American steel magnate, Carnegie, controlled eight dailies and ten weeklies. During the same period major groups were also being formed in London, most notably by Edward Lloyd who controlled two mass-circulation papers – *Lloyds Weekly* and the *Daily Chronicle* – along with other publications.

Although some of the papers controlled by the press barons also gained a dominant market position, this, too, had been a traditional feature of the development of the press. Papers which secured an initial circulation lead over their rivals generally enjoyed lower unit costs (due to their ability to spread the high costs of the 'first copy' over a larger print run), as well as more sales and advertising revenue. This helped them to increase their circulation lead by spending more on editorial outlay, promotion, and, sometimes, price-cutting.

The press barons' empires were also swollen by the rapid growth of circulation that took place during their lifetimes. But a sustained increase of demand for newspapers had characterized the development of the press ever since the eighteenth century and had been particularly pronounced, as we have seen, in the period after the repeal of press taxes.

These three traditional features of the press – chain ownership, an expanding market, and a tendency for a few papers to become dominant – merely became more accentuated under the press barons. Between 1890 and 1920 there was a rapid acceleration of newspaper chains incorporating national as well as local papers. By 1921 Lord Northcliffe controlled *The Times*, the *Daily Mail*, the *Weekly* (later *Sunday*) *Dispatch*, and the *London Evening News*; his brother, Lord Rothermere, controlled the *Daily Mirror*, the *Sunday Pictorial*, the *Daily Record*, the *Glasgow Evening News*, and the *Sunday Mail*. Jointly they owned the large magazine group Amalgamated Press and their brother, Sir Lester Harmsworth, had a chain of newspapers in the south-west of England. Together they owned newspapers with an aggregate circulation of over 6 million – probably the press grouping with the largest sale in the western world at the time.[1] In addition the Hulton chain controlled three Sunday and four daily papers and the Pearson chain included nine daily and twenty-one local weekly papers.

Between the wars, concentration of press ownership entered a new phase, with the spectacular consolidation of the regional chains. The percentage of provincial evening titles controlled by the big five chains rose from 8 to 40 per cent between 1921 and 1939; their ownership of the provincial morning titles also increased, from 12 to 44 per cent during the same period. The power of the chains was further extended by the elimination of local competition. Between 1921 and 1937, the number of towns with a choice of evening paper fell from twenty-four to ten, while towns with a choice of local morning paper declined from fifteen to seven.

The principal pacesetters in the expansion of the regional chains were the Berry brothers, Lords Camrose and Kemsley. Their group grew from four daily and Sunday papers in 1921 to twenty daily and Sunday papers in 1939. This was achieved only after a long-drawn-out and costly 'war' with Lord Rothermere, which was eventually resolved in a series of local treaties in which the three lords divided up different parts of the country between them.

During the inter-war period there was also an enormous increase in the sales of national dailies which overtook for the first time that of local dailies. Between 1920 and 1939 the combined circulation of the national daily press rose from 5.4 million to 10.6 million, while that of the local daily and weekly press remained relatively static. This major expansion of the London-based press meant that some proprietors commanded very large audiences, even when they owned relatively few papers. This was particularly true of Lord Beaverbrook whose small empire of only four papers included one market leader which pushed up the total circulation under his control to 4.1 million by 1937.

These changes in the ownership and readership of the press meant that, after the death of Lord Northcliffe in 1922, four men – Lords Beaverbrook, Rothermere, Camrose, and Kemsley – established a dominant position during the inter-war period. In 1937, for instance, they owned nearly one in every two national and local daily papers sold in Britain, as well as one in every three Sunday papers that were sold. The combined circulation of all their newspapers amounted to over 13 million.

However, there was a shift away from proprietorial domination of the press during the later part of the inter-war period. In 1937 the three leading Sunday papers' owners (Kemsley, Beaverbrook, and Camrose) controlled 59 per cent of National Sunday newspaper circulation – significantly less than the 69 per cent share of national Sunday circulation controlled by three relatively obscure proprietors (Dalziel, Riddell, and Lloyd) in 1910. Similarly in 1937 Rothermere, Beaverbrook, and Cadbury controlled 50 per cent of national daily circulation – again, much less than the 67 per cent share controlled by Pearson, Cadbury, and Northcliffe in 1910.

Underlying this shift was a decline in individual proprietorship and a successful assault on the major press groups. There was a revival of corporate press ownership during the inter-war period with the relaunch of the *Daily Herald*, the acquisition of *Reynolds News* by the Co-operative Movement, and the launch of the *Daily Worker* in 1930. The rise in publishing costs also resulted in a dispersal of newspaper ownership through the sale of shares so that three important papers – the *Daily Mirror*, *Sunday Pictorial*, and the *People* – ceased to have a dominant share-holder. The press magnates' hegemony over the press was, in fact, waning during the period celebrated for their ascendancy.

Press barons and proprietorial control

Not all proprietors attempted to use their papers for political purposes. For instance Astor, joint owner of *The Times* after 1922, was teased by his friends for not reading his own paper. Indeed even proprietors like Northcliffe, Rothermere, Beaverbrook, and Kemsley, who saw their papers as an extension of their own political views, did not exercise a uniform degree of control over all their papers.

Thus in the late 1930s Beaverbrook deluged the *Daily Express* with instructions to support appeasement ('No War Talk. NO WAR TALK', read one telegram of that period), but did not seem to mind that its sister paper, the *Sunday Express*, adopted a traditional patriotic hostility towards Germany, or that another of his papers, the *Evening Standard*, under the socialist editor Percy Cudlipp, urged a popular front against fascism. Similarly Northcliffe was mainly concerned in his later years with the *Daily Mail*, a preoccupation that his brother Rothermere later shared.

The two archetypal press barons, Northcliffe and Beaverbrook, had very different personal styles. While Northcliffe was notorious for personally harassing his staff, Beaverbrook's remoteness was legendary. In *Scoop*, Evelyn Waugh satirized a visit to him:

> The carpets were thicker [as one approached Lord Copper's private office], the lights softer, the expressions of the inhabitants more careworn. The typewriters were of a special kind: their keys made no more sound than the drumming of a bishop's finger-tips on an upholstered prie-dieu. The telephone buzzers were muffled and purred like warm cats. The personal private secretaries padded

through the ante-chambers and led them nearer and nearer to the presence.

Yet despite their differences of personality, both men exercised detailed control over their favourite papers through a constant barrage of instructions. Beaverbrook sent 147 separate instructions to the *Express* in one day. Northcliffe would sometimes phone his staff at 6 in the morning: 'Wake up! Wake up! Have you seen the papers yet?' he would demand. One editor, who replied that you could not get the *Mail* in Northlake at 6 am, was woken up at 5 the next morning by a pantechnicon backing into his garden, delivering a copy.

The press barons maintained their personal domination with extreme ruthlessness. Northcliffe, in particular, had a brisk way of dismissing employees. 'Who is that?' Northcliffe said on the phone. 'Editor, *Weekly Dispatch*, Chief,' came the reply. 'You were the editor,' responded Northcliffe. When a luckless sub-editor filled a lull in conversation over lunch with the information that he had been shipwrecked three times, Northcliffe abruptly said, 'Four times'. Beaverbrook also had a fearsome reputation. 'Fleet Street', recalled one of his employees, 'was strewn with the corpses of *Express* editors.'[2]

The barons combined terror with generosity. Journalists' memories and official histories are full of anecdotes about the sudden gifts, holidays, and salary rises which were showered on staff. As a genre these stories could be called 'Courageous underling gets his reward'. They usually take the form of the plucky journalist standing up for himself (or, more rarely, for what he believes) in the face of the baron's fury. They are clearly intended to enhance both the baron, who is revealed as discriminating and fundamentally right-minded in his judgments, and the journalist, whose independence is demonstrated by his courage. But what they actually reveal is an almost continuous process of humiliation. Bernard Falk, usually rewarded with a cigar when he took down Northcliffe's dictated social column for the *Mail*, was once allowed to choose the one he wanted. 'What!' said Northcliffe, 'You have the nerve to pick on those cigars! Don't you know, young man, that they cost 3/6 each?' 'Yes,' said the intrepid reporter, 'but they're worth every penny.' Another editor who dared to disagree with Northcliffe recorded gratefully the telegram he received: 'My dear Blackwood, you are grossly impertinent to your affectionate Chief.'

Losing a battle with a baron hardly made such a good story. Buckle, the editor of *The Times* (whose editorial independence Northcliffe had promised to uphold), was eased out of the editorship when he failed to adapt to the political views and managerial strategy of the Chief. Lewis

Macleod, literary editor of the *Mail*, received a communiqué from Northcliffe: 'This is the last occasion on which I can tolerate Macleod's gross neglect and carelessness. He will read this message out to the editorial conference on Monday.' When Northcliffe was angered by what he thought were defects on the *Daily Mail*'s picture page, he lined up all involved in its production and put the tallest man in charge. Feeling dissatisfied with the *Mail*'s advertising department, he appointed the commissionaire to act as censor of advertisements. Beaverbrook was also unpredictable though not on the scale of Northcliffe.[3] Yet behind both men's seemingly random acts of ferocity and generosity, there was a consistent purpose. Beaverbrook ensured that many of his best journalists wrote under pseudonyms so that, if they left the *Express*, they could not take the goodwill of their copy with them.

Northcliffe and Beaverbrook shaped the entire content of their favourite papers, including their layout. Thus Northcliffe raged at an employee at *The Times*, 'What have you done with the moon? I said the moon – the *Moon*. Someone has moved the moon! ... Well, if it's moved again, whoever does it is fired!' (The position of the weather report had been changed.) Beaverbrook and Northcliffe constantly pestered journalists about the language and phrasing of their reports. 'To Eastbourne's balding, myopic, Edinburgh-trained physiotherapist, William John Snooks, 53, came the news that ...' parodied Tom Driberg, a former *Express* journalist, in the approved Beaverbrook style. Both press barons even interfered in the choice of pictures. 'Alfonso' (the King of Spain), complained Northcliffe, 'is always smiling. This smile is not news. If you get a picture of Alfonso weeping, *that* would be news!'

The barons' personal foibles influenced the selection of news stories, thereby helping to form what are now the news values of Fleet Street. Northcliffe had a lifelong obsession with torture and death: he even kept an aquarium containing a goldfish and a pike, with a dividing partition, which he would lift up when he was in need of diversion. His obsession was reflected in his first magazine, *Answers*, which dealt with such enquiries as, 'How long is a severed head conscious after decapitation?' The first feature article Northcliffe wrote for his first evening newspaper described the day he spent with a condemned murderer in Chelmsford jail. He later briefed *Daily Mail* staff to find 'one murder a day'. Similarly Beaverbrook, a hypochondriac, told the editor of the *Daily Express* that 'The public like to know ... what diseases men die of – and women too.'

Proprietors' perceptions of their readers set the tone of their papers. The *Daily Express* aimed, in Beaverbrook's words, at 'the character and temperament which was bent on moving upward and outward', reflecting Beaverbrook's own New World ethic, with its celebration of the self-made. The *Daily Mail*, on the other hand, projected a more static, hierarchical world in keeping with Northcliffe's more traditional brand of conservatism and catered, as Northcliffe patronizingly put it, for 'people who would like to think they earned £1,000 a year'.

The proprietorial control exercised by the press magnates did not represent, however, a decisive break with the past. Indeed Lucy Brown's recent revisionist account of the Victorian commercial press even argues that 'what is an important and unvarying generalization is that the sovereign powers of decision were exercised by the proprietors and not by the editors'. Many of the Victorian editors celebrated for their independence, such as C. P. Scott of the *Manchester Guardian* (1877–1929), were either the owners of the papers they edited or members of the proprietorial family. Other leading editors prove, on close examination, to have been less autonomous than has usually been believed. Even Delane of *The Times*, often seen as a model of the sovereign editor, was repeatedly excluded from key planning decisions affecting the development of his paper. Indeed he was so convinced that he was going to be sacked, at one stage, that he started 'taking dinners' in order to be eligible to practise as a barrister. Others were less fortunate: Cook, Gardiner, Massingham, Greenwood, Annand, Watson, and Donald were only some of the distinguished editors who were compelled to resign between 1880 and 1918 as a result of political disagreements with their proprietors.

The tradition of editorial sovereignty which the press magnates allegedly destroyed was, to a large extent, a myth. It has been inspired by journalists like Sir Robert Ensor and Michael Foot to legitimize the political argument that editors rather than proprietors should be in charge of newspapers' editorial columns. Only in a very limited sense can the proprietorial style of the press barons be said to differ from that of their predecessors, most of whom were mainly interested in shaping their papers' political line. The press barons, by contrast, exercised personal control over the general content and administration of their key papers on an almost daily basis. They were business managers as much as political entrepreneurs. Yet even this difference should not be overstated since some of the Victorian pioneers of 'popular' journalism, notably Edward Lawson of the *Daily Telegraph* and Edward Lloyd, were active business as well as editorial managers of their papers.

Profits and politics

The press barons have been portrayed by historians primarily as ˇrnalist-politicians – a view of themselves which they publicly cultivated. ˇrook, for instance, told the first Royal Commission on the Press that he ran the *Daily Express* 'merely for the purpose of making propaganda and with no other motive'. Yet this simple image has tended to obscure another, more important aspect of their dominion over the press.

The press barons were forced by economic pressures to seek increasingly large circulations. Intense competition resulted in rising levels of paging, bigger editorial staffs, and, above all, massive promotion. Northcliffe and Rothermere led the way by spending up to 1928 approximately £1 million on the *Daily Mail*'s readers' insurance scheme in order to attract more readers. Rival press magnates fought back with competitions offering lavish prizes and their own readers' insurance schemes. After a legal judgment in 1928 outlawed newspaper competitions as lotteries, promotion shifted towards free gifts. Teams of canvassers moved through the countryside offering surprised housewives anything from cameras and wristwatches to silk stockings and tea-kettles, in return for taking out a newspaper subscription. The promotion for the *Daily Herald* alone is estimated to have amounted to £1 per new reader between 1930 and 1932. Even in 1937, when the 'circulation war' had abated, a typical national daily newspaper employed five times as many canvassers as editorial staff.[4] The effect of this heavy promotion and rising editorial outlay was to force up costs and, therefore, the circulations that popular newspapers needed to achieve in order to stay profitable.

Publishers were consequently under increasing pressure to give more space to material with a universal appeal to less differentiated audiences. The editorial implications of this were spelt out in market research, which most leading publishers commissioned during the 1930s, into what people read in newspapers. A major survey, based on a national quota sample of over 20,000 people and commissioned by the *News Chronicle* in 1933, revealed, for instance, that the most-read news in popular daily papers were stories about accidents, crime, divorce, and human interest. They had a near-universal appeal. In contrast most categories of public affairs news had only an average or below-average readership rating. This was because, although some aspects of public affairs had an above-average readership among men and people over the age of 35, they had a weak appeal among women and the young. Public affairs content was thus, in marketing terms, a commodity with a sectional appeal. It lacked, moreover, the passionate following amongst a large minority commanded by sport, and it also lacked the appeal to advertisers possessed by some minority consumer features.

Pressure to maximize audiences consequently resulted in the progressive downgrading of political coverage. By 1936 six out of a sample of seven papers devoted more space to human interest content than to public affairs – indeed, in some cases three or four times as much.[5] The one exception was the *Daily Herald*, which allocated 33 per cent of its editorial content to public affairs – substantially more even than in the *Daily Telegraph*. The *Daily Herald*'s commitment to political coverage reflected the concerns of its TUC-nominated directors. For the press barons, profits mattered more than politics.

This shift away from the traditional concept of a *news*paper to a magazine miscellany was part of a long-term trend dating back to the mid-nineteenth century. It accelerated, however, during the inter-war period. Thus between 1927 and 1937 the *Daily Mail*'s sports coverage rose from 27 to 36 per cent of its total news, while home political, social, and economic news fell from 10 to 6 per cent of total news content.[6]

The quality press remained more faithful to the traditional concept of the newspaper, despite the fact that market research showed that the most-read news items in quality dailies were very similar to those in popular papers.[7] However, quality newspapers were protected from the economic pressure to build large circulations because over two-thirds of their revenue came from advertising secured by reaching small, élite audiences. Advertising thus discouraged quality papers from adopting popular editorial strategies by making it financially disadvantageous for them to dilute the class composition of their readership.

The rise of the 'fourth estate'

The press barons are usually accused of using their papers as instruments of political power. But they were hardly unique in this. What made the press magnates different is that they sought to use their papers, not as levers of power within the political parties, but as instruments of power against the political parties. The basis of the Establishment's objection to men like Rothermere and Beaverbrook was not that they were politically ambitious, but that they were politically independent.

In the early twentieth century the majority of London-based daily papers were owned by wealthy individuals, families, or syndicates closely linked to a political party. Between 1911 and 1915, for instance, funds from the Unionist Central Office were secretly paid through respectable nominees to the *Standard*, *Globe*, *Observer*, and *Pall Mall Gazette*. A wealthy Conservative syndicate, headed by the Duke of Northumberland, bought the Tory *Morning Post* in 1924. Similarly Lloyd George engineered the purchase of the *Daily News* in 1901 by the Cadbury family in the Liberal interest, and arranged the purchase of the *Daily Chronicle* in 1918 through a syndicate headed by Dalziel with money accumulated through the sale of honours and laundered through the Lloyd George Fund.

This pattern of political control was undermined by the growth of advertising expenditure (mostly on the press) which nearly trebled from £20 million in 1907 to £59 million in 1938. This funded an escalating rise in press expenditure, and increasingly made papers too expensive for political parties and their supporters to sustain. Pearson refused to dig deeper into his pocket to keep the *Westminster Gazette* going in the party interest after 1928; Lloyd George and his associates were forced to sell the *Daily Chronicle* in 1928 to the Inveresk chain; the TUC gave up financial control of the *Daily Herald* to the Odhams Group in 1929; no Tory syndicate could be found to prevent the *Daily Graphic* closing in 1926 or the *Morning Post* disappearing in 1937.

The enormous expansion of advertising also weaned the national press from dependence on the political parties. Although the major press barons were Tories, they were first and foremost newspapermen. With the exception of papers controlled by Beaverbrook in his early days, all their publications were subsidized solely by advertising, and consequently were free to operate entirely independently of political patronage. An independent 'fourth estate', prematurely announced in the mid-nineteenth century, came much closer to reality during the inter-war period, under the aegis of the press barons.

Beaverbrook and Northcliffe played an important part in the political revolt that unseated Asquith as premier in 1916, and established Lloyd George in his place. The press barons played a more unconventional role after the war by directly confronting the political parties. Between 1919 and 1922 Rothermere, aided by Northcliffe, unleashed a violent propaganda campaign against 'squandermania', urging extensive cuts in public spending, the abandonment of wartime planning controls, and the sale of publicly owned enterprises. When the Coalition government partially rejected these policies, Rothermere appealed directly to the country by backing the Anti-Waste League in parliamentary by-elections in 1921. Three Anti-Waste League candidates succeeded in winning at Dover, Westminster St George's, and Hertford. Although these victories were not matched by by-election gains elsewhere, Rothermere had demonstrated the strength of grass-roots Conservative opposition to government policies. Partly in response to this pressure, the Ministries of Shipping, Munitions, and Food were abolished, a wide range of public controls was lifted, and publicly owned factories and shipyards were sold to private enterprise.

The Anti-Waste Campaign petered out with the break-up of the Coalition government in 1922, and its replacement by a Conservative administration backed by the press barons. But Beaverbrook and Rothermere later became persuaded that Britain's economic problems could be solved by converting the Empire into a free trade zone protected by a high tariff wall. Unable to convince the Conservative Party leadership, they made a direct appeal to the country by forming the United Empire Party (UEP) and campaigning for its candidate, Vice-Admiral Taylor, in a by-election in the safe Tory seat of Paddington South on 30 October 1930. The press barons' candidate won an unexpected victory. This was followed by another by-election in the safe Labour seat of East Islington in 1931, where the UEP candidate came second, beating the official Conservative candidate into an ignominious third place. These defeats destabilized the position of the Conservative leader, Stanley Baldwin. Sir Robert Topping, the chief Conservative agent, wrote a memorandum saying that Baldwin must go, which was subsequently endorsed by most leading Conservatives consulted by Neville Chamberlain, the party chairman. Baldwin, for a time, agreed to go quietly, telling the chairman bitterly that 'the sooner, the better' suited him.

Stanley Baldwin decided in the end to stay and fight, staking his political career on the outcome of the parliamentary by-election at Westminster St George's. Mounting a brilliant political campaign in which he shifted attention from Empire free trade to the unaccountable power of the press barons, he helped the official Conservative candidate, Duff Cooper, to win the by-election with a comfortable majority. Thereafter Baldwin's personal position was safe, though he was sufficiently shaken to make what was, in effect, a peace treaty with Beaverbrook shortly after the by-election.

The impetus behind the Empire free trade campaign was broken by the 1931 crisis, the collapse of the Labour government, and the landslide election victory won by the Coalition administration headed by Ramsay MacDonald. It was also weakened by lack of enthusiasm in the Dominions for the press barons' grand design. Nevertheless, Beaverbrook and Rothermere succeeded in strengthening the imperialist wing within the Conservative Party and some imperial preference policies were implemented during the 1930s. This was more than Joseph Chamberlain, the great apostle of Empire free trade, achieved during the nineteenth century despite his explosive impact on late Victorian politics.

Rothermere subsequently came out in support of the British Union of Fascists (BUF) in 1934. His papers pumped out stirring calls like 'Give the Blackshirts a Helping Hand' (*Daily Mirror*, 22 January 1934) and 'Hurrah for the Blackshirts' (*Daily Mail*, 15 January 1934). The *Evening News*, under his control, even ran a competition for the best letter on the theme of 'Why I like the Blackshirts'. This support from a mass-circulation press thrust a relatively obscure organization into the limelight and contributed to an increase in its membership. But Rothermere withdrew his support after little more than five months, thereby helping to deny the BUF the legitimacy which it needed in order to attract substantial right-wing 'respectable' support.

The press barons and the social order

Some historians have interpreted the relative failure of the press barons to persuade people to vote for the new political parties they backed and support some of the causes they championed as evidence that they exercised no significant political power. Thus A. J. P. Taylor writes, 'Though people bought Northcliffe's papers for their news, they were no more impressed by his political sense than that of any other successful businessman.' But to define the impact of the press barons in terms appropriate to pressure groups is to misunderstand the nature of their influence. Their main significance lies in the way in which their papers provided cumulative support for conservative values and reinforced opposition, particularly among the middle class, to progressive change.

The papers controlled by the press barons conjured up imaginary folk devils that served to strengthen commitment to dominant political norms and to unite the centre and the right against a common enemy. The most prominent of these public enemies were British Marxists controlled from Moscow. The first ineffectual Labour coalition administration formed in 1924 was branded as a Marxist-dominated regime by the press barons' papers, even though it showed little signs of pursuing radical policies during its short period in office. In the subsequent general election campaign, the 'red peril' campaign reached new heights. 'Civil War plot by Socialists' Masters,' screamed the *Daily Mail*'s (25 October 1924) front page banner headline, heading a report of a letter supposedly sent by Zinoviev (president of the Third Communist International in Moscow) to the British Communist Party. Although the letter was patently a forgery, it was given massive, largely uncritical publicity by all the press barons' papers, and was shamelessly exploited to define the choice before the electorate as a simple one between moderates and Marxists, British civilization or alien domination. 'Vote British, not Bolshie,' urged the *Daily Mirror* (29 October) in its front page headline. Underneath it printed the simple question in heavy type, 'Do You Wish to Vote for the Leaders of Law, Order, Peace and Prosperity?' (with reassuring pictures of Lloyd George, Baldwin, Asquith, and Austen Chamberlain), 'or to Vote for the Overthrow of Society and Pave the Way to Bolshevism?' (with sinister pictures of Russian leaders).

It is doubtful whether such crude propaganda deterred many would-be Labour voters – not least because the majority of working people did not read a daily paper in 1924 (unlike ten years later). Although the Labour Party lost forty seats, its share of the vote increased by 3.2 per cent largely because it fielded sixty-four more candidates. But the effect of the sustained red scare in the press was to polarize the election between left and right. The centre vote collapsed, with the Liberal Party being reduced from 158 to 40 seats. The hysteria whipped up by the press also contributed to a massive increase in turn-out, which rose by over 2 million compared with the previous general election held less than a year before. Thus the principal effect of the red scare was not to reduce the Labour vote but to inflate the Conservative vote, thereby contributing to a landslide Tory victory.

The press also tended to select and interpret the news within a framework that supported conservative views. Most national newspapers, for instance, portrayed the 1926 General Strike not as a class struggle, but as a conflict between the majority and a militant minority. 'Trade unionists in this country', declared the *Observer* (16 May 1926), 'are and always will be a minority, and if they seriously try to break the majority, they make it quite certain that the majority, if further provoked, will break them.' This simple characterization of strikers as a minority detached them from a class interest and provided a tacit explanation of the causes of the conflict – it was the work of unrepresentative militants. This enabled, in turn, the strike to be characterized as an attempt by subversives to overthrow democracy. 'The defeat of the General Strike', concluded the *Daily Mail* (14 May 1926), 'will end the danger of communist tyranny in Europe.' In a similar vein, the economic depression was widely reported in the press as if it was a 'natural catastrophe', comparable to a hurricane or flood. In this way, the appropriate response was defined as national unity in the face of a common calamity rather than radical new policies.

The press controlled by the barons helped to maintain the dominant consensus by stigmatizing radical opponents of the political order. The Communist-dominated Unemployed Workers' Movement, for instance, received hostile coverage when it organized marches of unemployed workers from Scotland, Wales, and the north of England all converging on London early in 1929. The *Daily Mail* (24 February 1929) called it 'a weary tramp to advertise Reds', while *The Times* (11 January 1929) called it 'heartless, cruel and unnecessary'. In common with most other papers, they deflected attention from the issue of unemployment by defining the protest mainly in terms of the threat it posed to law and order. Significantly the press provided much more sympathetic coverage of the

1936 Jarrow March, which had the support of both Conservative and Labour councillors and a much more limited political goal. The press thus helped to police the boundaries of legitimate dissent.

The central core of the conservatism expressed by papers under the barons' control was a deep and emotional attachment to Britain and her Empire. This intense patriotism sometimes shaded off into open racism and, particularly in the case of the papers controlled by Northcliffe and Rothermere, aggressive anti-semitism. The *Daily Mail* (10 July 1933) explained, for instance, the background to Hitler's rise in this way:

> The German nation was rapidly falling under the control of its alien elements. In the last days of the pre-Hitler regime there were twenty times as many Jewish government officials in Germany as had existed before the war. Israelites of international attachments were insinuating themselves into key positions in the German administrative machine.

Such interpretations of the rise of fascism in Europe served to reinforce popular anti-semitism in Britain and contributed to the maintenance of Britain's immigration policy which prevented many Jews from finding refuge in Britain.

Modification of economic controls

Although the press became more independent of political parties and of government, it operated within an economic framework which limited the range of voices that could be heard. The rise in publishing costs during the inter-war period, largely funded by advertising, sealed off entry into the national newspaper market. With one exception, no new national daily or Sunday newspaper was successfully established between 1919 and 1939, largely because of the prohibitive cost of establishing new papers. The one exception – the Communist *Sunday Worker*, launched in 1925 and converted into the *Daily Worker* in 1930 – was boycotted by distributors, and was so under-financed that it existed only on the margins of publishing with a circulation of well under 100,000.

The easiest way to break into national newspaper publishing was to buy an established newspaper. But even this still required massive expenditure to develop and promote the title that had been acquired. The level of investment needed was beyond the readily available resources of the Co-op when it took over *Reynolds News*. Indeed the triumphant rise of the *Daily Herald* would never have happened on such a spectacular scale if Odhams had not acquired a 51 per cent interest in the paper in 1929 and spent £3 million on its relaunch. Carrying twice as many pages as before, equipped with a northern as well as a London printing plant, and very heavily promoted, the *Daily Herald* increased its circulation from a little over 300,000 in 1929 to 2 million in 1933. Without this backing by one of the country's largest publishing conglomerates (based on a serious commercial miscalculation since, though the *Daily Herald* was a popular success, it was a financial failure) even Labour's official voice would have been muzzled by the capital requirements of mass publishing.

The persistence of advertising discrimination against left publications acted as a further brake upon their development. *Reynolds News*, for instance, received only 0.82d per copy in gross advertising revenue in 1936, less than half that obtained by the *Sunday Express* (1.9d per copy) and less than one-eighth of that bestowed on the *Sunday Times* (6.4d per copy).[8] Left publications were also forced to close down with circulations far higher than those of their respectable rivals. Thus the *Clarion* closed in 1933 with a circulation of over 80,000 copies – more than four times that of the *Spectator* and ten times that of the *Economist*. Even massive circulations were not enough to attract some mass-market advertisers. In 1936 the *Daily Herald* obtained less than half the gross advertising revenue per copy of the smaller-circulation *Daily Mail*.

But advertising hostility to the radical press was not as great during the inter-war period as it had been before. The standard advertising textbook of the 1930s advised that 'The first test that must always be applied to a press advertising medium is the cost of placing an advertisement of a given size before a given number of suitable readers.' While this precept was not new, the ability to put it into effect was. Circulation figures became more reliable during the 1920s and this trend was consolidated by the establishment of the Audit Bureau of Circulation in 1931. Survey research into the size and social composition of newspaper readership was introduced on a commercial basis in 1924 and obtained official endorsement from the advertising industry in 1930.

The provision of reliable statistical data encouraged a more impersonal approach to advertising selection, based on quantifiable cost criteria, in which political value-judgments played a less important part. Readership research also caused advertisers to reassess stereotyped images of the readers of left publications as being 'down at heel'. For instance the 1934 official readership survey showed that the *Daily Herald* was read by more middle-class people than *The Times* (even though the *Herald*'s readership was predominantly working class).

The development of market research in the 1920s also helped radical publications by underlining the importance of the working-class market. Typical of the shift of orientation among many advertisers during this period was Sun-Maid Raisins, which changed its advertising from high-class women's magazines to mass market media in 1929 because research 'shows that 91.2 per cent of the families of Great Britain have incomes of under £400'.[9] The adoption of more sophisticated methods of analysis reinforced this more positive valorization of the working-class market. 'Inequalities of consumption', concluded the principal marketing manual of the mid-1930s, 'are less than inequalities of income, and inequalities of income are less than inequalities of wealth'.[10] A similar message was put rather less abstractly in the trade promotion of Odhams, the publisher of the *Daily Herald, John Bull*, and other working-class publications. As one of their advertisements proclaimed, 'If the housewives who read *John Bull* put their purses together next year, they could buy the Giaconda diamond or Da Vinci's "Mona Lisa" hundreds of times over, then they could spend the change on the richest treasures of Bond Street or the Rue de la Paix.'

Selling the working class to advertisers was made easier by the growth of working-class purchasing power, and the related growth of large-scale production of mass market goods. *Per capita* annual consumer expenditure at constant (1913) prices rose from £42 in 1921 to £54 in 1938, a large increase that reflected the rise of real wages among working people in employment during the Depression. This contributed to an enormous increase in the purchase of branded products like cosmetics, medicines, bicycles, and electrical appliances.

These cumulative changes were of crucial importance in enabling the *Daily Herald* to gain in influence and circulation. Although it obtained only a fraction of the advertising revenue per copy of its main rivals, it was still able to pick up over £1.5 million in gross advertising receipts by 1936. Without this backing, the *Daily Herald* would have been forced to double its price and so lose circulation. Even this might not have been enough to cover the losses incurred by its very heavy promotion and expanding circulation. Indeed despite its increased advertising, the *Daily Herald* was still trading at a loss when it became the western world's largest circulation newspaper in 1933.

Changes in the orientation of advertisers contributed to another important development in the press – the relaunch of the *Daily Mirror* and *Sunday Pictorial*. In the early 1930s the *Daily Mirror* seemed to be a dying paper. Although it had a disproportionately middle-class readership, it was denied the usual benefits of reaching an affluent audience because most advertisers then subscribed to the mistaken view that tabloid papers were read only sketchily. In addition, its circulation was declining by about 70,000 a year and had dropped below 800,000 by 1933. In anticipation of its closing, the *Daily Mirror* was deserted by its principal owner, Rothermere.

Rothermere's disengagement enabled the paper to change direction. Bartholomew was created editorial director in 1933, and the paper was skilfully steered towards a gap in the market. Advertisers' traditional orientation towards middle- and lower-middle-class readers had encouraged the lower end of the market to be neglected. However, the shift in the outlook of many advertisers indicated that a paper which recruited new working-class readers would get advertising support. The inspiration behind the paper's relaunch was essentially a marketing one, and this was reflected in the close involvement of a leading advertising agency, J. Walter Thompson (JWT), in every stage of the paper's rebirth. JWT carried out market research into readers' preferences, advised on layout, relinquished members of its staff to become key members of the new *Mirror* team, and, above all, urged its clients to back the new venture with advertising.

A change in market direction for the *Daily Mirror* required a corresponding shift in the paper's politics. As Cecil King, the paper's advertising director put it,

> Our best hope was, therefore, to appeal to young, working-class men and women. ... If this was the aim, the politics had to be made to match. In the depression of the thirties, there was no future in preaching right-wing politics to young people in the lowest income bracket.

The political shift of the *Daily Mirror* was nevertheless cautious. It backed Baldwin as Prime Minister in the 1935 general election, gradually adopted an anti-appeasement policy, but drew back from anything as extreme as support for the Labour Party. It also developed an ambiguous social identity that mirrored its political uncertainty, combining traditional features about debutante balls with racy articles aimed at young working people.

Although commercial pressures encouraged an editorial adjustment, they actively discouraged the *Daily Mirror* from moving too far down-market or editorially too far to the left. The *Mirror*'s management became nervous about alienating its traditional, predominantly Conservative, and disproportionately middle-class readership. They also became even more apprehensive about the paper becoming stereotyped as a working-class tabloid at a time when working-class audiences generated much less advertising than middle-class audiences. Indeed the *Daily Mirror* even undertook a promotion campaign in the advertising trade press boasting of its upper-class, 'A' readership (the top 5 per cent of the country). 'Only one of the six popular national papers', the *Daily Mirror* declared in 1938, 'can claim more "A" class readers.'

The really important change in the *Daily Mirror*, however, was not its flirtation with reformist politics, but its exclusion of politics in favour of material with a wider appeal to women and young readers. Between 1927 and 1937 the *Daily Mirror* cut by half the proportion of its news devoted to political, social, economic, and industrial issues.[11] The shift meant that, in 1936, the *Daily Mirror*'s coverage of domestic public affairs was less than half that of its sports coverage, and little over one-third of its coverage of crime, sex, and other human interest content. Even more striking, its analysis of public affairs, whether in the form of editorials or feature articles, accounted for a mere 2 per cent of its editorial content.[12] The *Daily Mirror*'s relaunch constituted a key moment in the incorporation of the press by the entertainment industry.

The relaunch of the *Daily Mirror* was extremely successful. Its circulation rose to 1.5 million by 1939 and, after an initial period of difficulty, its advertising revenue also increased substantially. The *Mirror*'s success prompted a similar marketing operation on its sister paper, the *Sunday Pictorial*, in 1937, under the aegis of Cecil King and Hugh Cudlipp. The *Sunday Pictorial* also moved away from right-wing politics and a middle-class social identity without becoming left wing or working class. 'Our "A" class readership', the *Sunday Pictorial* reassured advertisers, 'is greater than that of any other Sunday paper.'

Advertising patronage still inhibited the development of radical journalism. Yet the rise of working-class living standards, and changes in the way in which advertisers selected media, had encouraged a move away from right-wing politics by part of the popular press. The foundation had been laid for the development of a powerful social democratic press that would press for reform in the different social and economic context of the Second World War.

Notes

1. Circulation figures for the inter-war period are not entirely reliable. The principal sources for circulations used in this chapter have been T. B. Browne's annual *Advertisers' ABC; Royal Commission on the Press 1947–9 Report* (London, HMSO, 1949); N. Kaldor and R. Silverman, *A Statistical Analysis of Advertising Expenditure and of the Revenue of the Press* (Cambridge, Cambridge University Press, 1948); W. Belson, *The British Press* (London, London Press Exchange Ltd, 1959); the Audit Bureau of Circulations; and individual publishers.

2. In fact most of Beaverbrook's senior editors kept their jobs for exceptionally long periods of time, though this was less true of his more junior employees.

3. Northcliffe's unpredictability increased to the point of insanity, possibly induced by syphilis.
4. *Report on the British Press* (London, Political & Economic Planning, 1938), p. 132.
5. The content analysis was based on a sample of twelve issues of each daily, and six issues of each Sunday paper in 1936. Public affairs is defined as political, social, economic, industrial, scientific, and medical affairs. For a summary of the results, see chapter 7.
6. *Royal Commission on the Press 1947–9 Report*, Appendix 7, p. 250.
7. *A Survey of Reader Interest* (*News Chronicle*, 1934).
8. 'A statistical survey of press advertising during 1936' (London Press Exchange Ltd records). The figures exclude certain forms of classified advertising.
9. 'The Sun-Maid plan 1929–30' (J. Walter Thompson Ltd records).
10. G. Harrison and F. C. Mitchell, *The Home Market: A Handbook of Statistics* (London, Allen & Unwin, 1936), p. 6.
11. *Royal Commission on the Press 1947–9 Report*, Appendix 7, pp. 257–8.
12. See note 5.

6

The press
under public regulation

Nostalgia has encouraged the belief that the British people closed ranks with bulldog determination under the unchallenged leadership of Churchill during the Second World War. This mythical view obscures the political and social crisis of the early war years, which led to a major confrontation between the government and the left press.

Many senior politicians and officials doubted the commitment of the British people to winning the war. A significantly named Home Morale Emergency Committee of the Ministry of Information reported in June 1940 on 'fear, confusion, suspicion, class feeling and defeatism'. Even the ministry's parliamentary secretary, Harold Nicolson, confided in his diary during this period, 'It will now be almost impossible to beat the Germans.'[1] For at least the first two and a half years of the war, the relationship between the authorities and the press was dominated by an excessive and probably misplaced concern about the state of public morale.

This anxiety was combined with growing concern amongst conservative politicians and civil servants about the growth of radicalism in Britain. In February 1942 the ministry's Home Intelligence Division reported a wave of admiration for Soviet Russia and a growing suspicion amongst sections of the working class that financial vested interests were hampering the war effort. A month later the ministry commented on what was to become a familiar theme – the flowering of 'home-made Socialism' of which important elements were 'a revulsion against "vested interests", "privilege", and what is referred to as "the old gang"' and 'a general agreement that things were going to be different after the war'.[2] In these circumstances, left-wing criticism in the press took on an added meaning. Not only did it seem, in the eyes of some, to be undermining military discipline and impeding efficient production, but also it was adding to political divisions at home when the nation desperately needed to be united against the common enemy. Indeed the maintenance of public morale came close to being equated by some ministers and officials with suppressing radical criticism of any kind.

Yet a succession of military defeats provoked mounting attacks on 'the old gang'. In 1940 Neville Chamberlain was forced to resign as Prime Minister. The new Coalition government under Churchill also came under growing attack as the military situation deteriorated. A cumulative political crisis developed which was only partially defused by changes in the Cabinet and leadership of the armed forces in 1940, 1941, and 1942. Press censorship thus became part of a beleaguered administration's battle for survival.

The circumstances of the Second World War also called for special measures. The strategic objective of the blitz was not only to impede war production but also to destroy the ability and will of the civilian population to service the war effort. This inevitably made regulation of the press a more sensitive issue than it had been during the First World War.

Censorship and resistance

Amid mounting fears of invasion in the summer of 1940, the government issued regulations which gave the Home Secretary sweeping powers to control the press. The most important of these was Regulation 2D which gave the Home Secretary the personal power to ban any publication which published material 'calculated to foment opposition to the prosecution to a successful issue of any war in which His Majesty is engaged'. The regulation also denied the offending publication any right of appeal or recourse to the law courts. As one angry MP declared, 'Its effect will be to put the Ministry of Home Security in a position by no means inferior, as regards the scope of its powers over newspapers, to that occupied by the distinguished Dr Goebbels in Germany.'[3]

A major campaign was organized against these new measures. Leading members of the old political establishment, including Lloyd George, were mobilized, and much of the press joined in the protest. Concerted opposition was mounted in the Commons with the result that the government secured ratification of the regulations by only thirty-eight votes – the smallest majority on any issue gained by the new government. This opposition was important because it secured two vital concessions that limited the way in which the regulations were subsequently implemented. First, Sir John Anderson, the Home Secretary, gave an undertaking that no amendments would be made to the regulations without parliamentary consultation. Cabinet memoranda show that three months later this pledge was effective in blocking moves to ban publications which were deemed to 'disrupt the unity of effort' in the country.[4] Secondly, Sir John Anderson indicated in the Commons that the regulations would apply only to papers opposed to the continuance of the war. When government ministers later wanted to close down a pro-war paper, they felt it necessary to reinterpret the scope and purpose of the regulations. This created a delay which enabled effective opposition to be mounted against them.

Silencing the Communist press

Following a unanimous Cabinet decision, the Communist *Daily Worker* and the *Week* were closed on 21 January 1941. The *Daily Worker* had modified its anti-fascist editorial policy, following the signing of the Nazi-Soviet pact in 1939, and attacked the war as a struggle between imperialist powers. The ostensible ground for banning the two papers was that they were impeding the war effort by setting people against the war. This was not borne out by research undertaken by the Ministry of Information, which indicated that both publications had little influence on public attitudes. The *Daily Worker* accounted for less than 1 per cent of total national daily circulation, while the passionately anti-fascist *Week* had an even smaller audience.

But if the two papers did not damage public morale, they clearly damaged the morale of the Cabinet. The *Daily Worker* campaigned on a number of sensitive issues – notably the inadequacy of deep shelters and civil defence preparations – which the Cabinet was not in a position to remedy in the short term. The *Daily Worker* also published vituperative personal attacks on ministers – including a cartoon portraying Bevin, the Minister of Production, as being in the pay of capitalist bosses – which caused deep personal offence.

The ban on the two papers was also part of a wider government campaign against Communism in Britain which was being organized by the interdepartmental Committee on Communist Activities, including representatives from the Foreign Office and MI5, strongly supported by leading right-wing ministers. That the ban was motivated, in part, by political prejudice – and not simply by a concern about the papers' impact on public morale – is underlined by the unwillingness of the authorities to allow the *Daily Worker* to start publication again when the British Communist Party came round to full-hearted support of the war.

The government chose to close down the two Communist papers by ministerial decree rather than by prosecuting them through the law courts. Summary execution was preferred, partly because the government feared that it might lose the case and partly because, as a private memorandum from the Home Secretary explained, a law suit would provide the *Worker* with 'a good opportunity for propaganda against what it would describe as the government's effort to "gag" the press'.[5] Although the government's actions clearly amounted to an attack on press freedom, the self-appointed watchdogs against the abuse of executive power were mostly silent or approving. When the Home Secretary informed the Newspaper Proprietors' Association of the ban, only one person objected. In parliament the more successful of the two motions opposing the government's actions attracted only eleven votes.

Harassment of the left press

The assault on the Communist press was part of a wider move to curb criticism from left papers. The *Daily Herald*, which had been outspokenly critical during the early stages of the war, moderated its tone when the Labour Party joined the coalition. Pressure was brought to bear upon the paper through its TUC-nominated directors. Appeals to loyalty also helped to subdue criticism of the government in *Reynolds News*, the paper of the Co-operative Movement. But the *Daily Mirror* and *Sunday Pictorial*, which moved sharply to the left during the war, were much more difficult to deal with. They were not controlled by the labour movement, nor were they answerable to a dominant shareholder (as the Cabinet discovered after a secret investigation into the shareholders of the two papers).

At first pressure was exerted informally through a series of meetings between senior members of the government and directors of the two papers. When this failed, Churchill urged a more direct approach. Both papers, he argued in a Cabinet meeting on 7 October 1940, published articles that were subversive. He went on to suggest that a conspiracy lay behind this criticism. 'There was far more behind these articles', Churchill warned, 'than disgruntlement or frayed nerves. They stood for something most dangerous and sinister, namely an attempt to bring about a situation in which the country would be ready for a surrender peace.'[6]

The new Home Secretary, Herbert Morrison, asked for time to consider the issue. The next day he circulated a sharply worded memorandum to his Cabinet colleagues in which he suggested that 'There is much in the papers (*Daily Mirror* and *Sunday Pictorial*) which is calculated to promote a war spirit. They seem to be clearly anxious for the defeat of Hitlerism.' After arguing that government action would be counterproductive, he declared, 'It is a tradition of the British people that they still remain obedient to the constituted authorities while retaining their liberty to ridicule and denounce the individuals who are actually in authority.'[7]

An unlikely struggle developed in which Morrison, the archetypal machine politician, vigorously defended press freedom against Churchill, a former journalist famous for his eloquent speeches in defence of liberty. In the next Cabinet meeting, Churchill accused the *Daily Mirror* and *Sunday Pictorial* of 'trying to rock the boat' and demanded 'firm action to deal with this menace'. He was strongly supported by, among others, Sir John Anderson who was in favour of issuing a warning to the two papers and then closing them down if they did not change their attitude. Morrison opposed this, arguing that such action would divide the Commons on party lines and amount to 'interference with the liberty of the press'.

In the end the Cabinet agreed, at Beaverbrook's suggestion, to exert pressure on the two papers through the Newspaper Proprietors' Association (NPA). A meeting was arranged between Beaverbrook and Attlee, representing the government, and the NPA. The proprietors were warned that compulsory censorship might be introduced if the *Daily Mirror* and *Sunday Pictorial* were not more restrained. The proprietors protested strongly against compulsory censorship at the meeting, but they subsequently urged the senior management of the *Daily Mirror* and *Sunday Pictorial* to exert a moderating influence on their staff. The effect of this intervention was limited. 'We shall pipe down for a few weeks,' Cecil King, a director of the two papers, commented in his diary.

Churchill's allegation that the two papers were motivated by a desire to secure 'a surrender peace' was unjustified. Both papers were totally committed to winning the war. Indeed they had opposed appeasement with Germany before this had become government policy: they had also backed Churchill for the leadership on the grounds that he would push for a more vigorous prosecution of the war. The tone of the *Mirror* was every bit as belligerent as that of Churchill himself: 'We appeal to every worker and every employer to play the man . . . stick to your job unless it is foolhardy to do so' (30 September 1940). The *Sunday Pictorial* was no different. Pillorying Lloyd George as 'the Marshal of the weak and the terrorized' when he proposed a negotiated settlement, it had even less time for pacifists. 'Put the lot behind barbed wire,' it urged.

The real reason for the attack on the two papers was that they had become increasingly critical of the government. The *Sunday Pictorial* (29 September) called the reverse at Dakar 'another blunder' while the *Daily Mirror* referred pointedly to 'futile dashes at remote strategic points'. Both papers began also to urge social reform at home. But they left no doubt in the mind of their readers that victory against Hitler was what mattered most. 'However bad the "pluto-democratic" world may be,' declared a *Daily Mirror* columnist, 'it is at least better than the depravity that would suppress all independent action and thought under the devilish way of life commended by Nazi fanatics.'

Clashes between the government and the *Mirror* and *Pictorial* recurred throughout 1941 and early 1942, largely because both sides had irreconcilable views about what constituted the national interest.[8] Leading Conservative ministers believed that criticism of officers in the *Daily Mirror* – including a reference to 'brass-buttoned boneheads, socially prejudiced, arrogant and fussy' – served to undermine the respect for rank that was the basis of good discipline in the army. They also felt that the *Daily Mirror*'s calls for post-war reconstruction were needlessly introducing political controversy and dividing the nation at a time of national emergency. The *Daily Mirror*, with an average circulation of 1,900,000, had become in their view a serious obstacle to winning the war.

Daily Mirror journalists, on the other hand, saw themselves as contributing to the war effort. They argued that Britain, in its hour of need, could not afford the incompetence that arose from snobbery and privilege: responsible jobs should go to those selected on the basis of ability rather than of birth. And plans for a new deal after the war were not divisive in a society already divided by class inequalities: on the contrary a programme for 'winning the peace' would help win the war by motivating people to contribute even more to the war effort.

These differences flared up into a full-scale confrontation in March 1942. The occasion, though not the cause, of the confrontation was a cartoon published in the *Daily Mirror* by Zec which showed a torpedoed sailor adrift on a raft in the open sea with the caption: 'The price of petrol has been increased by one penny – official.' This was interpreted by Churchill and many of his Cabinet colleagues to be an unprincipled attack upon the government for sanctioning oil company profiteering at the expense of people's lives. Its real intention was quite different: Zec meant it as an attack upon the needless waste of petrol by dramatizing the human sacrifice involved in shipping oil to Britain. This was how it was understood by most people, according to a Home Intelligence Report, as well as by most MPs who commented on it in a subsequent Commons debate.[9]

The misconceptions about the Zec cartoon were symptomatic of the demoralization within the Cabinet. In the three months preceding the confrontation with the *Daily Mirror*, the allies had suffered defeats at Guam, Wake, Hong Kong, Manila, the Dutch East Indies, Rangoon,

Benghazi, and Singapore. In the embattled atmosphere of Cabinet discussions, the press came to be blamed by ministers on the left as well as the right for some of the things that were going wrong. Bevin, the Labour Minister, demanded in a highly emotional state, 'how was he to "press" people almost into the Merchant Navy if they were then to see the suggestion (in the Zec cartoon) that they were being "pressed" in order to put the price of petrol up for the owners?' The *Daily Mirror*'s staff had become scapegoats for failure. 'We will flatten them,' Churchill told his Information Minister, Brendan Bracken.[10]

The assault on the *Daily Mirror* was, however, part of a more general struggle for political survival. A *Daily Mirror* editorial on 16 February 1942 came very close to demanding a new administration in a sweeping indictment:

> The assumption that whatever blunders are committed, and whatever faults are plainly visible in organization, we must still go on applauding men who muddle our lives away, is a travesty of history and a rhetorical defiance of all the bitter lessons of past wars.

Many politicians thought that the government would be forced to resign between the winter of 1941 and the summer of 1942. Churchill himself believed that he might be ousted. 'My diary for 1942', writes a member of Churchill's personal entourage, 'has the same backcloth to every scene: Winston's conviction that his life as Prime Minister could be saved only by victory in the field.' Even the general public, previously more loyal to the premier and his administration than the political élite, showed signs of turning against Churchill.[11]

The attack on the *Daily Mirror* was thus a pre-emptive strike against the government's principal critic. Its purpose, as discussion amongst Cabinet ministers made clear, was not only to silence the *Daily Mirror* but also to intimidate the rest of the press into adopting a less critical stance. Churchill demanded the immediate closure of the *Daily Mirror* in a full Cabinet meeting on 9 March 1942. The matter was referred to a Special Committee under the chairmanship of Sir John Anderson. The committee was advised by the law officers (rather surprisingly in view of the terms in which censorship regulations had been introduced) that it was legal to close down the *Daily Mirror* because, although it supported the war, it impeded its 'successful prosecution'. Indeed the Lord Chancellor urged immediate suspension of the paper since the experience of the last war suggested that quick, decisive action would be effective. 'When the then Home Secretary quite illegally suppressed the *Globe* newspaper,' he recalled, ' ... there was a row in the House in one debate in which the government received overwhelming support, and nothing was ever heard of the *Globe* newspaper again.'[12]

The committee did not, however, endorse the proposal to close the *Mirror*, although it suggested that 'it would be helpful if an example could be made' to curb press criticism. Those opposed to an immediate ban stressed that 'It was clear from the debates in parliament at the time when Regulation 2D had been enacted that it would be used to deal with Communist, Fascist or Pacifist Anti-War agitators' – but not, they pointed out, 'for the purposes now suggested'. There had to be a public redefinition of the government's censorship powers before anything could be done.[13]

At this stage a near consensus had been reached in favour of banning the *Daily Mirror*. The hawks, who wanted immediate suspension, had been strengthened by the recruitment of Bevin, the only trade union leader in the Cabinet. The opposition of the doves, on the other hand, had weakened. They stood out for giving the *Daily Mirror* one last chance in which to reform itself, while at the same time seemingly consenting to the paper's suppression if it did not 'improve'. Even Morrison, the principal dove and the minister who would be responsible for carrying out Cabinet policy, apparently agreed that if the *Daily Mirror* people 'did not amend I would suppress them'.[14]

Morrison announced that Defence Regulation 2D empowered the government to ban pro-war papers which undermined the war effort, even if the offence was not intentional but merely arose from 'a reckless and unpatriotic indifference'. He added that the *Daily Mirror* would be banned without further notice unless 'those concerned recognized their public responsibilities'. The same warning was given personally to the *Daily Mirror*'s senior management, and a report of the meeting released to the press.

Most members of the government clearly did not anticipate the storm of protest that followed. A large group of MPs demanded a special debate in the Commons. In a packed House a Liberal MP, Wilfred Roberts, aptly quoted an article published in the USA by the Minister of Information, Brendan Bracken. In this Bracken had argued that 'the savage censorship imposed on the French press played no small part in the fall of France. It encouraged defeatism, and bred complacency. A blindfolded democracy is more likely to fall than to fight.' A Labour MP, Frederick Bellenger, then cited an article written by Herbert Morrison during the First World War in which he had urged all soldiers not to fight 'your German brother' in an imperialist struggle. Morrison was pointedly asked why he was not now extending the same freedom of expression to others.

As the debate progressed, it became clear that it was the government rather than the *Daily Mirror* which was on trial. While loyal Conservative MPs rallied to Morrison's defence, the great majority of Labour and Liberal MPs were opposed. The Coalition administration was confronted, as Morrison had feared, with an issue that divided the Commons along party political lines.

Newspaper proprietors and editors were also not as compliant as they had been over the closure of the *Daily Worker*. While many Sunday and local papers supported the government, the majority of national daily papers sided with the *Mirror*. It thus became clear that closing down the *Daily Mirror* would lead to a major confrontation with a powerful section of the press.

The strength of opposition was such that the *Daily Mirror* was never really in any danger of being closed down after March 1942. Thereafter official displeasure took the form of harassment, such as Churchill's personal request that Cecil King be conscripted into the armed forces.[15] The victory was not, however, entirely one-sided. The *Daily Mirror's* outspoken radicalism became more subdued and the paper's most controversial columnist, Cassandra (Connor), decided it was time to join the army.

The defence of the *Daily Mirror* overlapped with a major campaign to lift the ban on the *Daily Worker*. Mass rallies were organized in Trafalgar Square and in London's Central Hall. The Labour Party Annual Conference voted down its national executive's recommendation by backing the ending of the ban. The Co-operative Congress and the Scottish TUC followed suit. In the face of this escalating pressure from the organized working class, the government relented. The ban on the *Daily Worker* was lifted on 26 August 1942 – more than a year after the USSR had become one of Britain's closest allies.

The defeat of censorship

The *Daily Mirror* and *Daily Worker* campaigns were part of a wider victory against the abuse of censorship powers. The notorious Regulation 2D was never again used after 1942. All proposals for compulsory censorship of the press were rejected. An ingenious scheme for bringing pressure to bear on newspapers by allocating rationed newsprint to publications solely according to their contribution to the war effort was also turned down.

Admittedly, the government drew back from taking full advantage of its censorship powers partly because the press proved, on the whole, to be co-operative. The Chairman of the Newspaper Emergency Council, for instance, wrote to the Ministry of Information in 1939 that 'Our respective tasks and duties are complementary.'[16] Some editors even took the Ministry of Information to task for being too permissive in its advisory guidelines about what should not be published. The press, including critical and independent-minded papers like the *Daily Mirror*, consciously sought to bolster public morale at the expense of objective reporting. Coercive censorship was made, to some extent, unnecessary by self-censorship.

The authorities were also restrained from exercising greater control over the press through purely pragmatic considerations. Military censorship of dispatches sent by war correspondents accompanying the armed forces provided a discreet means of regulating uncomfortable news. A number of senior Ministry of Information officials also became convinced that compulsory censorship was unnecessary, once they came round to the view that public morale was holding up. Some also felt that the credibility of a largely co-operative press would be undermined if it was seen to be directly controlled by the government. These arguments from the Ministry of Information helped to deflect more authoritarian attempts to censor newspapers. When the military situation improved after the summer of 1942, and the position of Churchill's administration became secure, ministers also became notably less sensitive to criticism.

But widespread commitment to the ideal of a free press also played an important part in stopping illiberal politicians like Churchill and Anderson from taking control of the press. Press freedom was one of the symbols of democracy that Britain was defending against Nazi Germany. This became a rallying slogan for anti-censorship campaigns which the government could not afford to ignore. When a senior official in the Ministry of Information wrote that 'It would be improper to propose in this country either a moral or a political censorship of opinion, for that would be contrary to the last 300 years of English history,' he added a significant postscript: 'It would also be perilous in view of the recent events surrounding the *Daily Mirror* and *Daily Worker* and the parliamentary and public attention that has been paid to them.'[17] In resisting the abuse of arbitrary censorship powers, relatively obscure politicians like Bellenger and Roberts, along with a large number of now-forgotten labour movement activists, kept alive the tradition of an independent press. The political processes of a democratic society saved government from itself.

Freedom from commercial controls

Ironically it was partly the government's economic intervention in the press industry that caused leading politicians to be subject to such unwelcome scrutiny by left-wing newspapers. Newsprint was rationed, on a statutory basis, from 1940 in order to husband a scarce resource and ensure its equitable distribution. An unintended effect of this control was to liberate the press from some of the economic pressures that had previously inhibited the development of radical journalism.

Newspaper managements voluntarily curtailed the amount of advertising they took because newsprint rationing reduced papers to less than one-third of their pre-war size. This self-imposed rationing was formalized in 1942 by new regulations which restricted the proportion of newspaper space which could be allocated to advertising. As a consequence, the money that people paid for their papers once again made a substantial contribution to the finances of the press. London dailies, for instance, derived 69 per cent of their revenue from sales in 1943, compared with only 30 per cent in 1938.

Newsprint rationing also redistributed advertising expenditure. Newspapers which had difficulty attracting advertising before the war found agencies begging them to take their orders due to the general shortage of advertising space. This meant that radical editorial policies and low-paid readerships no longer carried a financial penalty.

These changes did not in themselves account for the sharp move to the left made by some papers during the war. The experience of the war changed the outlook of journalists and expanded the demand for radical journalism. As A. C. H. Smith has shown, a radicalizing rapport developed between the *Daily Mirror* and its audience. Readers' letters and documentary-style reporting influenced the tone and orientation of the paper, helping it to acquire a distinctively working-class voice. But while economic controls did not cause the wartime transformation of the *Daily Mirror* and *Sunday Pictorial*, they provided the economic environment that made the shift possible.

Economic pressures had restrained both papers from moving further to the left in the late 1930s. But the wartime liberation from advertisers meant that they could aim solely at a working-class readership. They could also develop clear political identities in keeping with their more homogeneous audiences. Survey research shows that the *Sunday Pictorial* entered the war with a disproportionately middle-class readership and re-emerged after the war with a mainly working-class one. Similarly the *Daily Mirror* had the most cross-sectional readership of all national dailies in 1939, but its readers were solidly proletarian by 1947. The readership of both papers was also overwhelmingly Labour immediately after the war.

Newsprint rationing also reduced the polarization between quality and popular papers. Popular papers were no longer under intense pressure to seek ever larger audiences because circulation levels were 'pegged' during much of the war. By reducing costs and redistributing advertising, newsprint controls also increased the profitability of many newspapers. These changes coincided with a new interest not only in war news, but also in public affairs in general. As a consequence the proportion of space devoted to public affairs doubled in all wartime popular national dailies, save in the already politicized *Daily Herald*.

Wartime controls thus contributed to the development of a radical and less entertainment-oriented press. The aggregate circulation of the *Daily Mirror* and *Sunday Pictorial*, combined with that of the *Daily Herald*, *Reynolds News*, and *Daily Worker*, amounted to nearly 9 million copies in 1945. This formidable grouping of papers was supplemented by the progressive *Picture Post*, an illustrated weekly with a readership (as distinct from circulation) of well over 4 million people. Not since the mid-Victorian period had the left been so well represented within the press.

These publications provided a strong impetus behind social democratic change in wartime Britain. This can be illustrated by the reception given to the Beveridge Report, published in 1942, which provided the basis of many of the reforms later implemented by the Attlee government. The report was hailed by the left press with banner headlines, congratulatory editorials, and detailed summaries of its recommendations. It 'will so much break the old order', proclaimed the *Sunday Pictorial* (6 December 1942), 'that it will rank as little short of a Magna Carta for the toiling masses in Britain'. According to the *Daily Herald* (2 December 1942) the report was a 'massive achievement'. The *Daily Mirror* (2 December 1942) was scarcely less lyrical. Anticipating counter-arguments, it also published a sober article by Beveridge entitled, 'Britain Can Afford It'. The report also received sympathetic coverage from liberal papers such as the *News Chronicle* and *Manchester Guardian*, and even from the Conservative *Daily Mail*. As Cecil King noted at the time, 'The volume of press support is so great that it seems to be assumed in the House that it will be politically impossible to drop the Report.'

What might have been a relatively obscure official document, which the Tory Minister of Information had initially wanted to be published quietly, was transformed with the help of press publicity into a cornerstone of the new consensus. Indeed a British Institute of Public Opinion survey in 1943 found that no fewer than 86 per cent of people wanted the Beveridge Report to be adopted. Radical newspapers were thus helping to lay the foundation for Labour's 1945 landslide victory more than two years before Labour's election campaign even began.

In short, state regulation during the Second World War helped rather than hindered the growth of radical journalism. The introduction of economic controls freed the press from the regressive influence of advertisers, while attempts to gag the radical press were largely thwarted. Partly as a consequence, radical journalism gained ground in the national press, and this helped to reinforce the diffusion of Labourist views in wartime Britain.

Notes

1. Ministry of Information (INF) 1/250, Report to Policy Committee (June 1940); H. Nicolson, *Diaries and Letters 1930–45* (London, Collins, 1967), p. 96.
2. INF 1/292, Home Intelligence Weekly Report 73 (16–23 March 1942), Appendix.
3. *Parliamentary Debates*, 363 (1940), col. 1,307.
4. CAB 66/12, WP 402 (40) (8 October 1940).
5. CAB 66/14 (23 December 1940).
6. CAB 65/9, WM 267 (40) (7 October 1940).
7. CAB 66/12, WP 402 (40) (8 October 1940).
8. See, for instance, W. Armstrong (ed.), C. King, *With Malice Toward None* (London, Sidgwick & Jackson, 1970), pp. 94–9 and 103–7.
9. H. Cudlipp, *Walking on the Water* (London, Bodley Head, 1976), pp. 134–6; INF 1/282 Home Intelligence Weekly Report 78 (23–30 March 1942); *Parliamentary Debates* 378 (1942), cols 2,233–2,308.
10. Simon, CAB 66/23, WP 124 (42) (17 March 1942); Bevin and Churchill cited in A. J. P. Taylor (ed.), *Off the Record: W. P. Crozier, Political Interviews 1933–43* (London, Hutchinson, 1973), pp. 311 and 325.
11. Eden cited in J. Harvey (ed.), *The War Diaries of Oliver Harvey 1941–5* (London, Collins, 1978), p. 94; Churchill cited in Lord Moran, *Winston Churchill* (London, Sphere, 1968); INF 1/292 Home Intelligence Weekly Report 72 (February 1942).
12. In fact the *Globe* was suspended only briefly.
13. CAB 65/25, WM 35 (42) (18 March 1942).
14. A. J. P. Taylor (ed.), *Off the Record: W. P. Crozier, Political Interviews 1933–43* (London, Hutchinson, 1973), p. 325.
15. Cecil King was medically unfit for the armed forces. This was the reason why he had not joined up in the first place.
16. INF 1/187, Letter to Censorship Bureau (10 September 1939).
17. INF 1/238, Memorandum from R. H. Parker (15 April 1942).

7

The press in the
age of conglomerates

The leading historian of the British press, Stephen Koss, portrays the post-war period as the apogee of political journalism. 'By 1947', writes Koss, 'the party attachments of papers – as they had been understood to operate over the preceding hundred years – were effectively abandoned.' The press became fully independent of political parties and hence government: 'the halting transition from official to popular control' was allegedly complete.[1]

This supposedly resulted in a marked improvement in the quality of political reporting and analysis. According to Koss,

> newspapers grew steadily more catholic and less partisan in their ordinary news coverage. When confronted by a general election, they usually expressed a party preference, but always with at least a gesture of pragmatism and often for a different party from the one they had previously endorsed.

This more open-minded style of journalism is attributed by Koss to the emergence of a new type of proprietor who was 'a businessman first and foremost', oriented towards what sold rather than what furthered a party interest or ideological viewpoint. The man who 'personified' this pragmatic, undoctrinaire approach, in Koss's romantic view, is Rupert Murdoch, whose 'papers, both in Britain and elsewhere, lurched from one party persuasion to another for reasons that were seldom articulated and manifestly more commercial than ideological'.

This analysis is broadly echoed by many other accounts of the post-war press. Their common theme is that newspapers were emancipated not only from party tutelage but also from the personal dominion of press magnates. According to John Whale, for instance, 'the newspaper's staff is left to get on with the job' in the modern press because many of the new proprietors 'have global problems of trade and investment to occupy their minds'. Like Koss, he sees control of the contemporary press as residing increasingly in the market-place.

Like all persuasive mythologies, these portrayals connect with an element of truth. But their overall assessment is misleading because they inflate short-lived trends into permanent transformations, and ignore developments which run counter to their conclusions. Sadly the reality of the post-war press is very different from these accounts, celebrating the arrival of 'market democracy'.

The re-emergence of interventionist proprietors

During the immediate post-war period a substantial section of the press remained subject to the direct personal control of aggressively interventionist proprietors: the second Viscount Rothermere, Beaverbrook, Camrose, Kemsley, and, after 1948, David Astor. The Labour movement papers, the *Daily Herald* and *Reynolds News*, were also tethered to the editorial line laid down by their political masters.

However, this hierarchical pattern of control gave way to a greater delegation of editorial authority in the regional press and in a growing section of the national press. The person who typified this change was Lord Thomson, who acquired the Kemsley empire in 1959 and *The Times* in 1967. Within the framework of an agreed budget, his editors enjoyed a high degree of autonomy. Publicly he declared, 'I do not believe that a newspaper can be run properly unless its editorial columns are run freely and independently by a highly skilled and dedicated professional journalist.' His British editors have broadly corroborated this statement. Harold Evans, for instance, could recollect only one occasion in his fourteen years as editor of the *Sunday Times* when he received political guidance from Lord Thomson: the proprietor, he was told in 1974, would be unhappy if the *Sunday Times* supported the Labour Party in the forthcoming general election.

Similar changes occurred elsewhere in Fleet Street during the 1960s. The *Daily Herald* was freed from following the Labour Party line; Sir Max Aitken proved to be less dictatorial than his father, Lord Beaverbrook; the proprietor-editor regime at the *Observer* came to an end; and, perhaps, most important of all, Cecil King was ousted in 1968 after authorizing a front-page article in the *Daily Mirror* calling for the removal of the Prime Minister and the establishment of a national government without discussing the matter with the paper's editor. King's lordly action was in the seigneurial tradition of his uncle, Lord Northcliffe: his dismissal by his fellow directors in response to what they called his 'increasing preoccupation with politics' seemed, at the time, to signify the end of an era.

These changes in the control of the press coincided with the rise of specialist correspondents. Their number increased and they acquired an increasing degree of autonomy. As Jeremy Tunstall's research in the late 1960s showed, specialist correspondents tended to hunt in packs and to exchange information and ideas with each other regularly. This fostered the development of a group consensus and encouraged journalists to resist pressure from their editors.

The devolution of authority within newspaper organizations, at a time of broad political consensus, encouraged a more bipartisan approach to political reporting and commentary. This was reflected, for instance, in the growing number of newspapers which invited politicians to write articles opposing the editorial line of their leaders during general election campaigns. But although the interventionist tradition of proprietorship waned during the 1960s, it did not disappear. This was highlighted by a private management inquiry commissioned by publishers, which concluded in 1966:

> When all allowances have been made for variations within the industry, its most striking feature, and possibly its greatest problem, is its dominance by a small number of highly individualistic proprietors with their own personal interests and philosophy of management.

This was clearly a reference to the proprietorial regimes at the *Telegraph*, *Express*, and *Mail* groups.

The extent to which political partisanship declined during the post-war period has also been overstated. Thus Stephen Koss's sweeping claim that national newspapers 'often' supported 'a different party from one they had previously endorsed' proves, on close inspection, to be inaccurate. The *Daily Express*, *Daily Mail*, *Daily Mirror*, *Daily Telegraph*, *Daily Sketch*, *Daily Herald*, and *News Chronicle* each backed with unwavering loyalty the same political party in post-war general elections.[2] Only *The Times* (before 1983) and the *Guardian* approximate to Koss's mythical norm.

Moreover, national newspapers became markedly more partisan from 1974 onwards. This was partly in response to the growing polarization of British politics. But it also reflected the cumulative impact of a new generation of partisan, interventionist proprietors. The extent of their editorial involvement has perhaps been exaggerated by the recent spate of journalists' memoirs and reminiscences which have tended to focus on untypical periods of conflict between proprietors and editors caused by changes of ownership and editorial strategy. But they leave no doubt that Koss's portrayal of Murdoch and other contemporary proprietors as market-led pragmatists is deeply misleading.

Indeed Koss's claim that the political orientation of Murdoch's papers fluctuated in response to the shifting currents of public opinion could not be further from the truth. Murdoch's British papers moved to the right because he became increasingly right wing. Moreover these changes were imposed by Murdoch regardless of the views of his readers. The *Sun* switched from Labour to Conservative in the February 1974 general election despite the fact that over half of its readers were Labour supporters. After 1975 it developed into a partisan Thatcherite paper *in opposition* to the opinions of its readers (only 40 per cent of whom supported the Conservatives in the 1987 general election).[3] All his other papers have also become partisanly Thatcherite in an era characterized by the weakening of partisan loyalties and the rise of the Liberal-SDP Alliance.

These changes were brought about by Murdoch in a personalized style of management reminiscent of the earlier press barons. 'I did not come all this way', he declared at the *News of the World*, 'not to interfere'. Stafford Summerfield, its long-serving editor, found to his dismay that the new proprietor 'wanted to read proofs, write a leader if he felt like it, change the paper about and give instructions to his staff'. A series of clashes with Murdoch, partly over the issue of whether the editor should be accountable to the paper's board or to Murdoch personally, hastened Summerfield's departure.

A subsequent editor of the *News of the World*, Barry Askew, also records Murdoch's extensive editorial interventions when he was in London. 'He would come into the office', Askew recalls, 'and literally rewrite leaders which were not supporting the hard Thatcherite line.' Askew, who was not a Thatcherite enthusiast, lasted only nine months.

Murdoch reconstructed the *Sun* by working closely with two compliant editors, Sir Larry Lamb and Bernard Shrimsley. But he adopted a more circumspect approach towards *The Times* and *Sunday Times* when he acquired them in 1981. During his bid for Times Newspapers, he was asked whether he would change their character. 'Oh no, no, I would not dream of changing them at all,' he had replied. But to satisfy critics who openly doubted his word, Articles of Association and independent directors were introduced at Times Newspapers in order to prevent Murdoch from interfering in their editorial contents.

Although Murdoch never issued a direct editorial instruction to the editor of the *Sunday Times*, Frank Giles, he made his views forcibly known. 'Murdoch, the paper spread out before him,' Giles recollects, 'would jab his fingers at some article or contribution and snarl, "what do you want to print rubbish like that for?" or pointing to the bye-line of a correspondent, assert that "That man's a Commie".' Further pressure was funnelled through Gerald Long, the new managing director appointed by Murdoch, prompting the editor to establish a dossier called the 'Long Insult File'. Undermined by a sequence of calculated humiliations (Murdoch used to berate his editor in front of his staff and entertain visitors by firing an imaginary pistol at his back), Frank Giles retired early to make way for Andrew Neil, a Conservative journalist, who has piloted the paper from the centre-right, more towards the new right.

The editor of *The Times*, Harold Evans, received a similar treatment. Murdoch 'creates an aura', recollects Evans.

> The aura he created in 1981–2 was one of bleak hostility to Edward Heath and the Tory rebels, and contempt for the Social Democrats. He did this by persistent derision of them at our press meetings and on the telephone, by sending me articles marked worth reading which espoused right-wing views, by jabbing a finger at headlines which he thought could have been more supportive of Mrs. Thatcher – 'You're always getting at her' – and through the agency of his managing director, Long.

The latter bombarded him with memos containing reprimands such as 'the Chancellor of the Exchequer says the recession has ended. Why are you having the effrontery in *The Times* to say that it is not?'

Murdoch sought to exercise control indirectly at *The Times* by declining to fix an editorial budget. Evans was consequently compelled to seek permission for editorial decisions involving significant extra spending. As relationships soured due to the centrist political orientation of the paper, and its slow growth of circulation against a background of heavy losses, Murdoch actively fomented opposition among a group of journalists personally hostile to the editor. In an atmosphere thick with intrigue, in which Evans's personal aide was secretly reporting to the opposition group, Evans resigned in 1983 rather than 'be subjected to a thousand humiliations, challenged on every paperclip'. He was replaced by two Conservative editors, each more right-wing than the last.

Another active interventionist, Victor (later Lord) Matthews, became head of the Express group between 1977 and 1985. 'By and large editors will have complete freedom,' he promised, 'as long as they agree with the policy I have laid down.' During his first flush of enthusiasm as proprietor, he forced his editors to endure lengthy discourses of homespun political philosophy, which then had to be recreated as editorials. Only the most outrageous *ex cathedra* judgments seem to have been resisted. 'I had to plead against the *Evening Standard*', remembers a former editor, 'being expected to call for a nuclear first strike on Moscow, "to rid the world of communism, just like that".' His staff were also a little taken aback by his novel sense of news values. 'I would find myself in a dilemma', Matthews publicly declared, 'about whether to report a British Watergate affair because of the national harm. I believe in batting for Britain.'

But what perhaps most clearly reveals how little Matthews conformed to Koss's idealized view of the new generation of proprietors was Matthew's troubled relationship with his new paper, the *Daily Star*, launched in 1978. Ironically it owed its existence to commercial considerations since it was conceived primarily as a way of making better use of under-employed printing machines and staff. Matthews was also persuaded initially that it had to be relatively radical since it was aimed at a 'down-market', mostly Labour-voting audience. But when the *Daily Star*'s editor, Peter Grimsditch, argued on commercial grounds that the paper should support the Labour Party in the 1979 general election, Matthews vetoed this on explicitly political grounds. Even after the election, he responded to the paper more as a partisan reader than as a market-orientated publisher. For example on reading the proofs of a *Daily Star* leader critical of the Thatcher government's first budget, he angrily phoned the editor, 'There aren't any poor. You can take my word for it. There are no poor in this country.' This insight was dutifully incorporated by the editor into the editorial. In the end, Grimsditch was sacked and the paper became another Tory tabloid. It vigorously supported the Conservative Party in the 1983 election, even though only 21 per cent of its readers voted for Mrs Thatcher.

The third major figure to emerge in Fleet Street was Robert Maxwell, who acquired the Mirror Group in 1984. A former Labour MP, with a powerful, domineering personality, he brought to an end the relatively autonomous regime that had existed when the group was owned by Reed International during the 1970s and early 1980s. In the early days of his proprietorship, he was in the office almost every night phoning, according to Alastair Hetherington, as often as six times in the evening to staff who were working on political reports. 'I certainly have a major say', he declared recently, 'in the political line of the paper [*Daily Mirror*].'

But the reassertion of proprietorial control has not been uniform throughout the national press. Although the third Viscount Rothermere, a tax exile in France, claims to map out 'the overall strategy my papers will take', in practice his overseeing role allows considerable freedom of action to editors in the Mail group. Lord Matthews was ousted in 1985 by Lord Stevens, the controller of United Newspapers with a less personalized managerial style than his predecessor. Lord Hartwell, who combined the role of proprietor with that of editor-in-chief of the Telegraph group, was forced to sell out in 1985 to the right-wing Canadian businessman, Conrad Black, who has so far proved to be a relatively absentee landlord. Tiny Rowland, the new proprietor of the *Observer*, also plays a relatively non-determining role. But, as we shall see, this is not from choice.

Concentration of media ownership

During the post-war period concentration of national press ownership increased, although the trend towards concentration was not continuously sustained (see Table 1). In 1946 only one publishing group (Odhams) ranked among the top three publishers of both national daily and Sunday papers. In 1987 the three principal publishers were the same – Maxwell, Murdoch, and Stevens: they controlled between them 73 per cent of national daily and 82 per cent of national Sunday circulation.

Table 1   *Concentration of ownership of daily and Sunday newspapers, 1947–85*

	The three leading corporations' shares of:				
	Total daily and Sunday paper circulation	Total daily paper circulation	Total Sunday paper circulation	National daily circulation	National Sunday circulation
	%	%	%	%	%
1947	42	42	66	62	60
1961	65	67	84	89	84
1976	53	49	80	72	86
1985	58	55	79	75	83

Sources: derived from *Royal Commission on the Press 1947–9 Report* (1949), Appendices 3 and 5; *Royal Commission on the Press 1961–2 Report* (1962), Appendices 2, 3, and 4; *Royal Commission on the Press 1974–7 Final Report* (1977), Annex 3; *32nd Annual Report of the Press Council 1985* (1986), Table 4.
Note: The three leading publishing corporations have been defined in terms of their market share of *each* of the categories of publication listed in this table. Total daily and Sunday paper circulation has been calculated by multiplying daily paper circulation six times to obtain a total weekly circulation of daily and Sunday papers.

The leading publishers of regional newspapers also consolidated their position (see Table 2). Their biggest gains were registered in the local weekly press, where the leading five publishers increased their market share by 275 per cent between 1947 and 1985. In a growing number of sub-regions extensive monopolies were also created in which all or nearly all paid-for papers were owned by the same group.

Table 2   *Concentration of ownership in the provincial press, 1947–85*

	The five leading chains' share of:			
	Regional evening newspaper circulation	Regional morning newspaper circulation	Local weekly circulation	Local weekly freesheet circulation
	%	%	%	%
1947	44	65	8	—
1961	53	70	13	—
1976	58	69	25	NA
1985	53	73	30	33

Sources: derived from *Royal Commission on the Press 1947–9 Report* (1949), Appendices 4 and 5; *Royal Commission on the Press 1961–2 Report* (1962), Appendices 2, 3, and 4; *Royal Commission on the Press 1974–7 Final Report* (1977), Annex 3; and N. Hartley, P. Gudgeon, and R. Crafts, *Concentration of Ownership in the Provincial Press* (Royal Commission on the Press 1974–7, Research Series 5); *32nd Annual Report of the Press Council 1985* (1986), Tables 4 and 5 and D1 and D2.

Note: The five leading chains are not all the same in each category of publication.

Although local freesheets mushroomed in the 1970s and 1980s, they have also come to be organized into chains. The five principal, freesheet groups – all of them major publishers of paid-for newspapers – accounted for one-third of the weekly freesheet market by 1985.

But the most important change in the pattern of press ownership was the increase in the domination of the press as a whole by just three proprietors (see Table 1). This trend was temporarily reversed by the rise of Murdoch in the 1970s but was resumed with the consolidation of his empire. The top three publishers controlled in 1985 58 per cent of *total* daily and Sunday newspaper sales compared with 42 per cent in 1948.

The development of press concentration is part of a more general trend towards increasingly centralized control over the leisure industries. The top five companies in each media sector controlled in the mid-1980s an estimated 40 per cent of book sales, 45 per cent of ITV transmissions, between half and two-thirds of video rentals, record, cassette, and compact disc sales, and over three-quarters of daily and Sunday paper sales (see Table 3). Some of these companies overlap: Pearson, for example, has major interests in one of the top five ITV, book publishing, and regional newspaper groups. Murdoch, in turn, has the second largest holding in the Pearson Group.

The introduction of new television technology created opportunities for the major newspaper publishers to expand their media empires.

Table 3   *Concentration of media ownership*

Market share of top five companies in selected media sectors	
	%
ITV programmes (transmissions)	45.5
National dailies (circulation)	95
National Sundays (circulation)	92
National and regional dailies (circulation)	75
National and regional Sundays (circulation)	91
Books (sales)	40
Single records (sales)	58
LPs, cassettes, and compact discs	60
Video rentals	66

Sources: IBA Annual Report and Accounts (1985–6); *32nd Annual Report of the Press Council 1985* (1986); *Jordans' Review of Marketing and Publishing Data* (1984); *British Phonograph Yearbook* (1986); British Videogram Association (Gallup, 1986).

Leading proprietors have interests in the newly established Super Channel through their holdings in ITV companies. Maxwell has bought the largest cable television network in Britain; Murdoch owns the largest pan-European cable television channel, Sky Channel; and Pearson (controlled by the Cowdray family) is a co-founder of British Satellite Services, which won the franchise to develop the new British direct broadcast satellite television system.

But perhaps the most alarming feature of this trend towards media concentration is that it is beginning to develop on a global scale. Many leading publishers now have media interests outside Britain (see Table 4). Indeed the most spectacular example of this is Rupert Murdoch who currently controls not only the largest selling daily and Sunday paper in Britain but also a string of over 100 papers stretching from Hong Kong to New York, the fourth largest television network in the USA, key television stations in Australia as well as the international entertainment service, Sky Channel, a major interest in the publishing group, Collins, and a controlling interest in the American movie major, 20th Century Fox. He has now acquired a greater potential influence over the global flow of information than anyone in the history of the western media.

Conglomerates, profits, and politics

The other key related change in the post-war press was its integration into the core sectors of financial and industrial capital (see Table 4). Between 1969 and 1986 nine multinational conglomerates bought over

Table 4 *The conglomeration of the British press*[a]

	Main British press interests	Selected other media interests	Selected non-media interests
Pergamon Holding Foundation (Maxwell)	*Daily Mirror* *Sunday Mirror* *Sunday People* *Daily Record* *Sunday Mail* (Total newspaper circulation 10.5 million)	British Cable Services TF–1 TV (France) Orbis (USA) Pergamon Press Maxwell Communications Corporation	E. J. Arnold (furniture) Hollis Plastics Paulton Investments Jet Ferry International (Panama) Milthorp Machinery (Australia)
News Corporation (Murdoch)	*Sun* *News of the World* *The Times* *Sunday Times* *Today* (Total newspaper circulation 11 million)	Sky Channel Collins (Fontana) Channel Ten – 10 (Sydney) Herald and Weekly Times Group (Australia) Metromedia (USA) 20th Century Fox (USA)	Ansett Transport (Australia) Santos (Natural gas – Australia) News-Eagle (Offshore oil – Australia) Snodland Fibres Whitefriars Investment

	Main British press interests	Selected other media interests	Selected non-media interests
United Newspapers (Stevens)	Daily Express Sunday Express Daily Star United Provincial Newspapers United Magazines Morgan-Grampian Magazines (Total newspaper circulation: 6.8 million)	TV-am Asian Business Press (Singapore) Specialist Publications (Hong Kong) Capital Radio Inter Media Group (USA)	JBS Properties M G Insurance Moncroft Finance PRN Holdings (USA) David McKay Inc. (USA)
Reed Group[b]	IPC Magazines IPC Business Press Reed Regional Publishing (Total newspaper circulation: 0.5 million)	Butterworth IPC Business Press (USA) Trade News Asia (Singapore) Européenne de Publications SA (France)	Reed Finance (South Africa) Reed Canadian Holdings WPM Finance (Bermuda)
Associated Newspapers (Rothermere)	Daily Mail Mail on Sunday Weekend Northcliffe Newspapers (Total newspaper circulation: 5.1 million)	London Broadcasting Company Herald-Sun TV (Australia) Esquire Magazine Group (USA)	Blackfriars Oil Consolidated-Bathurst (Canada) Transport Group Holdings Jetlink Ferries

International Thomson Organization (Thomson)[c]	Thomson Regional Newspapers *Scotsman* Northwood Publications Whitehorn Press Standbrook Publications Illustrated Newspapers (Total newspaper circulation: 1.4 million)	Thomson Data Associated Book Publishers Thomson Publications (South Africa) Thomson Communications (Denmark) Radio Forth	Thomson North Sea Thomson Travel Rym SA (Tunisia) International Thomson Organisation – Canada (parent company)
Pearson (Cowdray)	Westminster Press Group *Financial Times* *The Economist* *Northern Echo* (Total circulation: 1.5 million)	Longman Penguin Yorkshire TV NAL (USA) British Satellite Broadasting	Midhurst Corporation (USA) Lazard Partners Royal Doulton Camco International (USA)

	Main British press interests	Selected other media interests	Selected non-media interests
Lonrho (Rowland)	Observer George Outram and Co. Scottish and Universal Newspapers (Total circulation: 1.3 million)	Radio Clyde Border TV Radio Ltd. (Zambia) Times Newspapers (Zambia) Melody Records (Zimbabwe)	Whyte and Mackay Firsteel Group Consolidated Holdings (Kenya) Constructions Associated (Zimbabwe) HCC Investments (South Africa)
Hollinger (Black)	*Daily Telegraph* *Sunday Telegraph* (Total newspaper circulation: 1.8 million)	Sterling Newspaper Group (Canada) TG & K Press Media (USA) Standard Broadcasting Corporation (Canada)	Hanna (USA) Ravelston Holdings (Canada) Argus (Canada) Norcen Energy Resources (Canada)

Sources: Who Owns Whom 1987; Company Reports; Press Council Annual Report 1985.
Notes: [a] All circulation figures exclude freesheets and magazines. [b] No dominant shareholder. [c] Not including North American chain of TV, radio, and press interests.

200 newspapers and magazines with a total circulation of 46 million at the time of purchase (excluding publications resold to each other). Some of these (Atlantic Richfield, Lonrho, Trafalgar House, Reed, Hollinger) were primarily engaged in activities outside publishing and their involvement in Fleet Street was sometimes shortlived. Others (the conglomerates controlled by Murdoch, Maxwell, the Cowdrays, and Stevens) were originally printing or publishing companies which expanded into activities like gas, engineering, transport, and banking. There are now only two national newspapers – the *Guardian* and *Independent* – which do not have, or are not controlled by, a major interest outside the media.[4] All the major regional press chains also diversified into activities outside publishing.

This integration of the press into finance and industry created conflicts of interest. As *The Times*, then owned by the Thomson Organization, candidly told the last Royal Commission on the Press, 'Coverage of Thomson Organization activities in Thomson newspapers tends, certainly, to be drily factual.' Occasions when it has been alleged that ownership interests influenced reporting include the cancellation at the *Daily Mail* in 1974 of an investigation into an oil rig owned by a sister company, Blackfriars Oil, and a series of articles in the *Observer* during 1985–7 which attacked the Al Fayed brothers' take-over of the House of Fraser after the paper's proprietor had failed to acquire it.

But these occasional abuses were less significant than the growing co-option of the press in support of the general interests and ideology of capital. The economic diversification of the press resulted in an intricate pattern of interlocking directorships in which controllers of the press increasingly came to work alongside other business leaders on the same boards. Graham Murdock has also shown that in 1976–7 two-thirds of the chairmen and vice-chairmen of the ten largest press groups were educated at public school and/or Oxbridge, the recruiting grounds of much of Britain's industrial and financial élite.[5] Many also belonged to exclusive London clubs (their favourites being White's and the Royal Yacht Club), also frequented by élite members. All these affinities and points of contact – similar social origins, shared educational experiences, overlapping social networks, and close working relationships – fostered common ideological positions between controllers of the press and other groups within the capitalist class.

The economic absorption of the press subtly changed its relationship to the party system. The archetypal proprietors of the inter-war period had been maverick politicians who viewed the world from the optic of Westminster and were heavily engaged in internal party battles. In contrast most of their post-war successors (with the notable exceptions of

Cecil King and Lord Hartwell, were increasingly involved in running large multinational corporations, and remained at several removes from the inner circle of senior politicians and their close advisers.

Indeed for some post-war proprietors, newspaper ownership was little more than an investment in corporate public relations. It extended their range of business and political connections, increased their corporation's prestige, and, through judicious editorial appointments, contributed to the maintenance of public opinion favourable to private enterprise. As the Chairman of Atlantic Richfield (which spent $20 million subsidizing the *Observer*) explained to his shareholders in 1978:

> Despite the social upheaval of the last few years, Atlantic Richfield's primary task remains what it has always been – to conduct its business within accepted rules to generate profits, thereby protecting and enhancing the investment of its owners. But ... senior management recognise that the Company cannot expect to operate freely or advantageously without public approval.

The ownership of newspapers thus became one strategy by which large business organizations sought to influence the environment in which they operated. This strategy was pursued mainly on the basis of an arms-length relationship between newspapers and conglomerate newspaper companies during the 1960s. But in the more recent period, newspapers campaigned more actively for the general interests of big business, under closer proprietorial supervision. This development signified an important, long term shift: newspapers had become the agencies not of 'freelance' politicians or of the political parties but of politically aligned, large business conglomerates.

Indeed a number of major press groups – Trafalgar House (which controlled for a time the Express group), United Newspapers, and Pearson – gave in the 1970s and 1980s substantial donations to the Conservative Party. Owning (and in some cases subsidizing) newspapers was merely another way of sustaining the party which they believed best served their economic interests.

However, part of the lure of the national press for some proprietors was its social prestige. The ownership of national newspapers led to the bestowal of honorific titles on an almost automatic basis and provided access to an élite social world. It also offered a way of mainlining into the romance of Fleet Street which, as Leonard Woolf once observed, is 'a magnetic field of highly charged importance, influence ... and vocational delusions'. These were clearly important attractions for Lord Thomson, who spent some £8 million subsidizing *The Times* (though part of this was funded by tax-payers in the form of tax remissions).

But what is clear is that the rewards of newspaper ownership were not defined solely in terms of profits. Indeed many national newspapers made substantial losses during much of the post-war period until the introduction of new cost-cutting technology in the mid-1980s. Thus in 1966 five out of eight national newspapers made losses totalling £4.3 million. By 1975 four national dailies and six out of seven national Sunday papers made an even larger loss. In 1982 the national press was reported to have made a net loss of £29 million. Thus when conglomerates bought up the rotten boroughs of the national press, they were seeking more than just an immediate return on their investment.

Compliance and resistance

The new generation of proprietors encountered some resistance from journalists, who continued to enjoy a relative but still significant degree of autonomy. Conflict increased particularly during the 1980s in response to proprietorial pressure on journalists to provide more favourable coverage of the Thatcher government. A substantial group of journalists at the *Daily Mail* even sent a formal note of protest to their editor in 1983 complaining about the paper's excessive partisanship during the general election campaign. Similarly, growing resentment at the *Sunday Times* about the paper's move to the right, following Murdoch's take-over, prompted a steady exodus of the best known writers from the Harold Evans era. Among them was sadly John Whale, whose celebration of non-interventionist proprietorship had been confounded by events.

But in only one instance has journalists' opposition to proprietorial changes proved successful. When Tiny Rowland acquired the *Observer* in 1981, he clearly wanted to introduce major changes. He told one group, for instance, that he wished to improve the paper's coverage of southern Africa because its liberalism was abetting the advance of Communism. In traditional proprietorial style, he appointed a new roving Africa correspondent without consulting the editor.

However he was forced, like Murdoch, to accept new Articles of Association and independent directors at the *Observer*, designed to prevent him from interfering editorially. But whereas Murdoch moved with consummate skill at Times Newspapers, first encircling unwanted editors with people he could trust, Rowland blundered in with an ill-judged ultimatum that alienated most of his supporters.

Donald Trelford, the *Observer*'s editor, wrote an article reporting that Zimbabwe's armed forces were torturing and killing their own citizens in the dissident Matabeleland province. This put Rowland in a difficult position since his corporation, Lonrho, derived £15 million of its profit from investments in Zimbabwe. Rowland also had an uneasy relationship with the Zimbabwe Prime Minister, Robert Mugabe, since he had backed his principal rival, Joshua Nkomo, in the recent elections there. Seemingly seeking to protect his commercial interests, Rowland instructed Trelford to withdraw his article.

Trelford refused to spike his article and was backed in his stand against his proprietor by all his editorial staff and independent directors. In the highly publicized row that followed (in which Lonrho cancelled advertising in its own paper) Rowland had little real choice but to back off. Lonrho's corporate image, already tarnished by Edward Heath's celebrated attack on it as 'the unacceptable face of capitalism', would have been seriously damaged if Rowland had agreed to Trelford's offer of resignation. In the event, Trelford survived as editor. However his paper has suffered from his proprietor's continued reluctance to make a major investment in its development.

But confrontations of this sort have been rare. Proprietors generally choose the editors they want. Editors have also normally been appointed on a short-term basis, and most of them have been happy to work within a framework of implicit understanding that has made unnecessary heavy-handed proprietorial intervention. Editors' freedom of action has usually been constrained by the budget allocated to them, formal policy guidelines, and the past tradition of their paper.

Although tension between journalists and national press managements has increased, a number of factors have operated to minimize conflict. Fleet Street journalists have long been well-paid and few of them have political convictions which are far to the left. A survey of specialist correspondents in 1968, for instance, found that only 2 per cent of those working for right-wing Labour or centrist papers said that they were 'well to the left' of their publications.[6]

Conforming to hierarchical requirements has brought rewards in terms of good assignments, promotion, and consequent peer group esteem. Failure to conform has also invited escalating sanctions – copy that regularly goes unused or heavily revised, being passed over or moved to less interesting work, or being squeezed out altogether. This is why journalists have tended to gravitate towards papers whose editorial outlook is congenial to them.

Newspapers have also developed routines for gathering news, organized around powerful groups and institutions adept at meeting the press's needs – most notably the various branches of the state. Most journalists have been socialized into news values which ascribe particular weight and authority to these news sources, and hence legitimize their heavy dependence on them. The structures of news-gathering and professional norms have thus evolved in a way which privileges dominant definitions of reality and so underwrites the centre-right orientation of the national press.

Restoration of market controls

Underlying many accounts of the post-war press is the assumption that market democracy superseded the personal dominion of press magnates. Newspapers are said to have become less the personal mouthpieces of right-wing proprietors and more products shaped by what people wanted.

This orthodox view is misleading not only because it overlooks the revival of proprietorial control in the last two decades, but also because it is based on a mistaken conception of the market-place as the means by which public demand is neutrally registered. As we shall see, the competitive processes of the newspaper market misrepresented – due to the distorting influences of press oligopoly, advertising, and mass-market pressure – the diverse nature of public demand in post-war Britain.

The key changes in the functioning of the market occurred in the 1950s when newsprint rationing was greatly relaxed and finally abolished in 1956. This had the effect of redistributing advertising away from radical papers in favour of their more Conservative rivals. This was not due to the revival of ideological bias among advertisers but to inequalities of income and wealth in post-war Britain. Admittedly political prejudice seems to have coloured some advertising decisions. A small number of advertising agencies frankly told the second Royal Commission on the Press (1962) that left publications were sometimes boycotted for political reasons. The ill-fated, radical *Scottish Daily News*, founded in 1975 as a co-operative, was also rejected by some advertisers because of its politics. As one advertiser put it, 'I'm not going to keep a newspaper which, the first time I get a strike, will back the strikers.' An initial feasibility study for the left-wing *News on Sunday* also suggested, on the basis of interviews with advertising agency executives, that some advertisers discriminated against socialist publications during the mid-1980s.

But the evidence suggests nevertheless that political bias in advertising selection declined in post-war Britain. Advertising agencies came to rely even more heavily on calculations of rival publications' cost effectiveness in terms of the readers that they delivered, based on increasingly detailed survey research into their characteristics and purchasing behaviour, and less on intuitive assessments of editorial influence coloured by subjective ideological judgments. This was reflected, for example, in the first two handbooks on advertising media planning published under the auspices of the Institute of Practitioners in Advertising. The first, issued in 1955, contained a whole chapter on the 'character and atmosphere' of advertising media, laden with speculative judgments about 'the intangible effects of accompanying editorial and advertising'. Its successor, published in 1971, was openly disparaging about this approach.[7]

In fact, the reallocation of advertising during the 1950s was a short-term response to newsprint rationing. Controls had artificially inflated advertising in Labour papers by creating a space shortage. The lifting of controls led to a 'normal' distribution of advertising which reflected the fact that Labour papers were read disproportionately by low income families.

The rapid growth of working-class consumption did not redress this shift because class differences of income and wealth (though significantly reduced during the Second World War) remained remarkably constant during most of the post-war period.[8] Indeed special factors led to a growing gap in advertising support for down- and up-market publications in the 1960s and 1970s. The rapid growth of financial and classified advertising helped quality papers much more than tabloids. These last were also more adversely affected by the rise of television as an advertising medium because their readers tended to be heavier viewers of ITV.

This changing pattern of advertising patronage helped to undermine the social democratic press. This was the result not of direct, blackmailing pressure on editorial copy – a relatively rare phenomenon to which radical critics have perhaps paid too much attention – but of the cumulative influence of advertisers on the economic viability and market orientation of radical papers.

The death of radical papers

The impact of the relative redistribution of advertising away from down-market papers in the 1950s was exacerbated by a cumulative deterioration in the cost and revenue structure of the national press during the period 1957 to 1965.[9] Increased competition led to rising levels of outlay at a time when circulations declined steadily. As a consequence vulnerable papers became more at risk.

One of these, the *Daily Herald*, found it particularly difficult to attract advertising because its readership was overwhelmingly working class and disproportionately male and ageing. In 1945 its advertising revenue per copy sold (an index that takes account of differences in circulation) was more than that of either the *Daily Express* or *Daily Mail*. By 1964 it had dropped to less than half of either paper.

The *Daily Herald* also lost readers as a consequence of its continuing commitment to the Labour Party during the Conservative ascendancy of the 1950s. But its loss of advertising far exceeded its loss of sales, and was a more important cause of its downfall. In 1955 the *Daily Herald* had an 11 per cent share of both national daily circulation and advertising revenue. By 1964 its share of circulation had declined modestly to 8 per cent but its share of advertising had slumped to 3.5 per cent.

Indeed despite its loss of sales, the *Daily Herald* still retained a substantial following. It was not true, as Sir Dennis Hamilton suggested, that the *Daily Herald* 'was beset by the problem which has dogged nearly every newspaper vowed to a political idea: not enough people wanted to read it.' When it closed in 1964, it had a circulation of 1,265,000. This was more than five times the circulation of *The Times* of which Sir Dennis Hamilton was then editor-in-chief.

The *News Chronicle*, a long-established Liberal daily, succumbed in 1960 with a substantial circulation of 1,162,000. This was roughly on a par with the highly profitable *Daily Telegraph* buoyed up by up-market advertising. Similarly the *Sunday Citizen* (formerly *Reynolds News*) folded in 1967. It was a quality paper in terms of the relatively extensive coverage it gave to public affairs. But by 1965 it obtained per copy sold one-tenth of the advertising revenue of the *Sunday Times* because it did not appeal to an élite audience.

The closure of these three social democratic papers was part of an epidemic that also killed off the *Empire News, Sunday Dispatch, Sunday Graphic*, and *Daily Sketch* between 1960 and 1972. All these papers succumbed to similar pressures to those that decimated the centre-left press. They all had a predominantly working-class readership and, in terms of mass marketing, relatively 'small' circulations. They thus fell between two stools: they had neither the quantity nor the social 'quality' of readership needed to attract sufficient advertising for them to survive.

Adjusting to the advertising system

One response of down-market papers to the economic realities of post-war publishing was to try to break out of their working-class ghetto. The editorial implications of this are graphically illustrated by the troubled post-war history of the *Daily Herald*.

The *Daily Herald*'s management responded initially to the paper's growing shortfall in advertising not by modifying its editorial policy but by seeking new and more imaginative ways of selling the paper to the advertising industry. In particular, it sought to combat the negative image of the paper's readers as poor by initiating research which showed that they were heavy spenders on certain products such as canned meat, desserts, cereals, and beer.

The diminishing success of this promotion encouraged the *Daily Herald*'s management to undertake in 1955 a fundamental review of the paper's editorial strategy and market position. Two clear options emerged from this review. One, partly inspired by market research into what people read in popular papers, was to devote less space to political and industrial coverage and more to human interest stories, photographs, and strip cartoons. This was identified as the most promising way to rebuild a mass circulation and, in particular, to 'bring in woman – vital to the advertising department'.[10]

The second option, and the one that was eventually adopted, was to attract more advertising by seeking to upgrade the paper's readership. This strategy led to the appointment of John Beavan as editor in 1960 with the remit to lure former *News Chronicle* readers and, above all, to attract 'the intelligent grammar school boy and girl'. The paper moved up-market, and included features about books, classical music, opera, and even ballet. It also loosened its ties with the Labour Party and the TUC, and moved politically to the right.

Yet despite these changes, the *Daily Herald*'s readership remained obstinately proletarian. Indeed even by 1963–4, only 13 per cent of its readers were middle class. Yet its owners were conscious that the traditional, loyalist union sub-culture from which the *Daily Herald* sprang was in decline. The paper's management, influenced by the Gaitskellite revisionism of the early 1960s, concluded that the cloth-cap, traditional Labour Party identity of the paper was putting off potential readers and that the only way to blast the paper successfully into the middle market was to relaunch it under a new name, the *Sun*. As a prelude to this, the TUC was persuaded to sell its share of the paper in 1964 to the International Publishing Corporation (IPC) which had acquired the Odhams shares in the paper three years earlier.

The intention behind the new launch was to construct a new coalition of readers composed of working-class, 'political radicals' (the old *Herald* readership) and young, upwardly mobile 'social radicals'. 'The new paper', according to an internal memorandum, 'is to have the more representative make-up essential to advertisers.'[11] But the difficulties inherent in this strategy were dauntingly revealed in pre-launch research which showed the enormous gulf that separated the two wings of the coalition. 'Social radicals', defined largely in terms of their attitudes towards race, hanging, and issues like increasing access to (but not abolishing) public schools, turned out to be only marginally more inclined to vote Labour than Conservative or Liberal, and to be not greatly more likely to read the *Daily Herald* than the *Daily Telegraph*. Ranking high amongst the favourite reading of 'social radicals' were the society gossip columns of the *Daily Express* and *Daily Mail* expressing social values fundamentally at odds with the class-conscious, often resentful attitudes of many *Herald* readers recorded by Odhams's previous surveys.[12]

These findings suggest that it would have been more sensible for the *Daily Herald* to have been relaunched as a more popular, working-class daily. But this strategy was rejected by IPC because it would have meant spending money attacking another paper in the same group, the *Daily Mirror*. Instead the launch proceeded along its preconceived lines, seemingly unaffected by the corporation's own research.

In the event, the editorial staff of the *Sun* never succeeded in finding an editorial formula which reconciled the two very dissimilar groups that they were seeking to attract. IPC's market research showed that the paper failed both to please old *Herald* readers and to attract young, affluent social radicals.[13] The paper struggled on as an underfinanced, deradicalized hybrid until it was sold at a low price to Murdoch in 1969.

The *Sun* was then reoriented towards a mass working-class market broadly along the lines identified by the Odhams research department as a major option in 1955. The recasting was done with consummate skill but in a right-wing mould that combined Conservative politics with soft porn, social iconoclasm, and an increased emphasis on entertainment, making it Britain's best selling national daily. Thus the only consistent advocate of the Labour Party in Fleet Street during the previous fifty years – revealed by survey research to have had the most devoted readership of any popular daily as late as 1958[14] – was first enfeebled and then converted into a paper which supported politically everything that the *Daily Herald* had opposed.

Consensual pull of the mass market

In some respects the post-war career of the *Daily Mirror* paralleled that of the *Daily Herald*. But the pressures that led to the deradicalization of the *Daily Mirror*, and major editorial changes in the popular press as a whole, were more complex than those underlying the *Daily Herald*'s desperate struggle for survival, and need to be set in a wider context.

National newspaper circulations reached a peak in 1951, and there-after went into almost uninterrupted decline until the 1980s when national dailies registered a small recovery. This decline was partly a belated adjustment to the end of newsprint rationing which had artificially inflated newspaper circulations by causing households to buy more than one daily. But it also reflected from the late 1960s onwards a modest decline in the number of households regularly buying a national newspaper. In addition popular nationals lost some circulation to quality papers. Throughout much of the post-war period, popular newspaper publishers thus felt themselves to be swimming against a strong tide.

Advertising expenditure on the national press steadily increased. But popular nationals' share of total media advertising gradually declined after 1953. More important, their advertising profit margins became seriously eroded during the 1960s and 1970s because most popular papers failed to increase their advertising rates in line with rising costs in an attempt to fend off competition from ITV. Popular papers responded to mounting economic problems by doubling their cover prices in real terms between 1962 and 1985. But this policy, born out of crisis, merely redoubled publishers' anxiety about losing readers.

But the main cause of mounting economic pressures on the press was its rapid escalation of costs. National newspapers more than quadrupled their paging after 1945. Editorial and production staffs got bigger and were paid steadily larger salaries in real terms. The annual expenditure of the average London and national daily rose from £1.5 million in 1946 to £28.1 million in 1974 – a fourteenfold increase.[15] Costs were further inflated by the circulation war that began in 1981, leading to the award of £1 million as top bingo prizes in 1985, and an unprecedented level of television promotion in 1986–7.

National newspapers thus emerged from their cocooned existence in the 1940s, when newsprint controls had curbed costs more than revenue, into an intensely competitive environment where the pursuit of readers became increasingly important. It was against this economically uncertain background that the *Daily Mirror*'s management began to worry in the 1950s that the paper was failing to respond to new popular trends. In particular it became anxious that the leftward current which had sustained the paper's rise was moving the other way. They deliberately distanced therefore the *Daily Mirror* from the Labour Party and propelled the paper nearer the centre of political gravity in the mass market – towards the right.

The paper's management also consciously courted young and upwardly mobile readers from a mixture of motives. They brought in additional advertising because they were particularly sought after by advertisers; they seemed to embody important, new social trends; and they were the most accessible part of the market because their newspaper reading habits were relatively unfixed. The effect of this redirection was to make the paper's readership more socially and politically heterogeneous. By 1964 a third of the paper's readership opposed the Labour Party. This was perceived by the *Mirror*'s management to impose a limitation on the paper's radicalism. As Cecil King, then Chairman of the Mirror Group, explained in 1967,

> Today newspaper circulations are vast assemblies of people of all social classes and all varieties of political view. A controller who tried to campaign for causes profoundly distasteful, even to large minorities of his readers, would ... put his business at risk.

But Cecil King's market fears, and those of his senior colleagues, perhaps masked their own personal inclinations. After all, Murdoch did not shrink from pushing his papers in a political direction that was contrary to the views of many of his readers. In reality, King's early radicalism had waned as he got older. This was reflected in his choice of political advisers to the Mirror Group during the 1950s and 1960s – Alfred Robens, George Brown, and Richard Marsh. They were all senior Labour politicians who subsequently left the Labour Party to support the Alliance or the Conservative Party. King's successor and former close colleague, Hugh Cudlipp, also left the Labour Party for the SDP. The new controller of the Mirror group, Robert Maxwell, belongs to the far right of the Labour Party.

As a consequence the political identity of the *Daily Mirror* changed. The class divisiveness of the paper's 'us and them' rhetoric of the 1940s softened in the 1950s and early 1960s into the more inclusive and acceptable rhetoric of 'the young at heart' against 'the old', the modern against the traditional, 'new ideas' instead of 'tired men'. The *Mirror*'s commitment to the Labour Party remained but it changed in character. Increasingly it took the form of opposition to the Conservative Party rather than positive advocacy of a socialist alternative. The hard-hitting investigative reports that had characterized the *Daily Mirror* at its best became less frequent. Eventually, under Maxwell, the paper's old radical motto, 'Forward with the People' was revived in a new, consensual form, 'Forward with Britain'. The change symbolized the post-war reorientation of the paper, brought about by both managerial and mass-market pressure.

But a no less important feature of the paper's change was the declining attention it gave to public affairs, and the greatly increased proportion of space which it devoted to sport, pictures, and entertainment features. This shift was part of a more general transformation of the popular press.

Table 5   *The editorial contents of selected national daily and Sunday newspapers,*
1936–76[a]

Percentage of editorial space	Daily Express			Daily Herald/ Sun			Daily Mail		
	1936	1946	1976	1936	1946	1976	1936	1946	1976
Advertising (proportion of total space)	43	18	44	42	17	40	46	18	36
Editorial (proportion of total space)	57	82	56	58	83	60	54	82	64
Photographs[b]	13	7	13	9	5	16	15	7	14
Illustrations[b]	4	4	5	2	4	6	5	4	5
Public affairs news[c]	14	29	12	23	34	8	15	27	12
Public affairs features[c]	4	10	6	10	11	6	4	12	8
Finance	10	4	7	6	1	1	9	3	10
Sport	22	18	27	19	20	30	20	19	23
Human interest news	20	20	16	14	14	14	14	19	17
Human interest features	10	6	12	8	4	20	15	3	10
Consumer and women's features	7	2	4	5	3	2	8	2	5
Horoscopes, cartoon strips, quizzes, and competitions	4	3	6	3	3	8	3	4	5
Arts and entertainments	6	4	7	6	4	7	5	5	9
Other features	5	5	4	6	4	7	7	6	3

	Daily Mirror			Daily Telegraph			Sunday Express			People/ Sunday People			Sunday Pictorial/ Sunday Mirror			Observer		
	1936	1946	1976	1936	1946	1976	1936	1946	1976	1936	1946	1976	1936	1946	1976	1936	1946	1976
	29	16	42	47	35	48	51	16	56	38	22	44	24	25	46	46	36	49
	71	84	58	53	64	52	49	84	44	62	78	56	76	75	54	54	64	51
	21	8	18	8	2	9	14	4	13	11	4	21	26	25	20	3	3	12
	7	15	8	1	1	1	4	6	9	2	2	2	6	6	6	1	–	3
	10	18	9	19	40	26	8	20	5	10	15	2	7	10	5	20	28	16
	2	7	4	3	9	4	10	19	12	4	11	6	10	16	6	6	19	14
	4	–	1	20	8	20	5	2	2	1	1	1	2	–	2	7	2	10
	15	9	28	14	11	18	21	20	25	25	28	30	18	20	27	17	12	16
	21	29	17	14	12	13	15	11	12	18	15	13	11	14	13	7	5	5
	27	5	16	10	10	2	23	9	17	23	17	22	15	26	28	6	7	8
	6	4	2	3	1	5	4	2	10	3	3	5	8	5	5	4	2	11
	6	16	10	1	1	1	4	6	6	8	8	6	14	3	5	3	5	1
	4	1	8	6	3	10	3	4	6	3	2	6	7	3	6	25	20	15
	7	10	5	9	7	3	8	7	4	7	2	10	9	3	4	5	4	5

Notes: [a] Sample 252 issues. [b] These are also tabulated in terms of their content. [c] Defined as political, social, economic, industrial, scientific, and medical affairs. All figures have been rounded off to the nearest whole number.

Depoliticization of the popular press

The effect of mounting pressure to maximize circulations was to force popular papers to respond to large aggregates of market demand at the expense of minority interests. The implications of this were spelt out in expensive market research commissioned by publishers. This revealed a remarkable consistency of reading preference throughout the period 1947 to 1987, notwithstanding the rise of television. The most read items in popular papers were found to be human interest stories and certain entertainment features such as cartoons and horoscopes. Public affairs coverage in newspapers obtained a smaller overall following, largely because it was of limited interest to women and young people. Within the broad category of politics, items about home politics and industrial news often had an above average readership among men. Even so, these more popular political stories were found to have less of a following among men than sport. Women's features, which brought in related advertising, were also shown to be heavily read by the majority of women.

The managements of popular newspapers responded by giving more space to content with a common denominator appeal. They expanded human interest content, entertainment features, sports, and women's articles (see Table 5).[16] This growth took place at the expense of public affairs coverage which declined, as a percentage of editorial space, by at least half in all our sample popular papers between 1946 and 1976. Indeed public affairs took up less space than sport in all these papers by 1976.

In effect the make-up of popular papers reverted back to its pre-war character in response to similar market pressures. However, the reduction of political coverage was carried to even more extreme lengths in the case of three papers – *The People/Sunday People*, the *Sunday Pictorial/Mirror*, and the *Daily Herald/Sun*. In the last case, editorial space devoted to public affairs was down by almost two-thirds in 1976 compared with thirty years earlier. A supplementary content analysis also reveals that public affairs stories were less often chosen as lead, front-page articles in popular newspapers in 1976 compared with 1936.

The increasingly frenetic pursuit of readers also led to a general lowering of journalistic standards, as reporters came under mounting pressure to come up with good human interest stories. This led to a growing number of well-publicized excesses such as the invention of an overnight love tryst between Prince Charles and Lady Diana Spencer on a lonely railway siding in the royal train (*Sunday Mirror*), the fabrication of a fictitious interview with Mrs Marica McKay, the widow of the Falklands VC hero (*Sun*), the touching up of a photograph of 'Lady Di' to give a hint of nipples in a low-cut dress (*Sun*), and the offering of 'blood money' to relatives and friends of the 'Yorkshire ripper', Peter Sutcliffe (*Daily Mail, Daily Express, Daily Star,* and *News of the World*). It also resulted in artificial flavouring and additive being injected into an increasing number of routine stories.

Growing gap between quality and popular newspapers

In contrast to the popular press, quality papers continued to maintain their commitment to serious political coverage. The *Daily Telegraph* and the *Observer,* for example, actually increased their coverage of public affairs as a percentage of editorial space between 1936 and 1976, while reducing or merely continuing at the same level their human interest content (see Table 5).

But the increasing polarization between popular and quality papers did not reflect a growing cultural gulf between élite and mass publics. Indeed one of the most striking findings of market research is the relative similarity it has regularly revealed in the preferences of popular and quality paper readers. Thus to take but one example, the most read stories in Sunday quality papers during the period 1969–71 were human interest stories about ordinary people, followed by human interest stories about celebrities – precisely the most read stories in the *Sunday People* and *Sunday Mirror* during the same period.

The growing divergence between quality and popular papers was a consequence of how they were financed. Quality newspapers were much more dependent on advertising. They also differed from popular papers in that they did not obtain significantly more advertising if they sold more copies to a non-élite audience. There were thus strong economic disincentives against quality papers adopting editorial strategies with a wide public appeal (even if paradoxically more human interest stories would have appealed to many quality paper readers).

The bizarre dynamics of the newspaper market were dramatically revealed when *The Times* increased its circulation by 69 per cent between 1965 and 1969 through a more popular diet of news and features and an aggressive advertising campaign. Many of its new readers were students or lower middle class. Advertisers objected to paying premium rates to reach people who were outside their target market or who could be reached more cheaply through other media. The paper's advertising failed to keep pace with its growth of sales with the result that additional copies were sold at a loss. *The Times* then changed editorial direction, revised its promotion strategy, and raised its price. It succeeded in jettisoning between 1969 and 1971 many of its new readers as a deliberate act of policy.

In short, structural inequalities in society have given rise to unequal advertising subsidies for newspapers: these have structured in turn the press, giving middle-class minorities the most commanding vehicles for articulating and representing their interests. Other minorities have been unable to sustain quality papers, written from a different class perspective, because they have lacked the necessary pulling power among advertisers.

Curtailment of choice

The range of choice of newspapers was further curtailed by the rising costs of publishing. No radical national paper was launched in the first forty years after the Second World War largely because the left was intimidated by the huge sums involved. The most likely source of finance was the TUC which decided in 1984, after much debate, that it could not afford to launch a new daily at a time when its membership was falling.

The only new national papers (excluding the *Sun*) to be established between 1931 and 1985 were the *Daily Star*, *Sunday Telegraph*, and *Mail on Sunday*. All these papers were Conservative, thus reinforcing the Conservative preponderance of the national press. They all originated from leading press groups, consolidating their oligopoly.

Beguiling promise of new technology

Many commentators argued in the mid-1980s that the introduction of new technology would provide a way of reforming the press. They pointed out that major savings could be achieved in four ways. Journalists and advertising staff could 'key' in copy to computers, linked to page make-up and plate-making, thereby dispensing with 'hot metal' type and making redundant most composing, lithographic, and paste-up staff. The purchase of powerful, new web-offset machines could make possible the employment of fewer printers. Facsimile transmission, enabling simultaneous production at satellite printing plants, could also reduce distribution costs and enable more intensive use of printing presses. Lastly, new technology could revolutionize the social organization of production. Powerful print unions could be broken; production workers could be employed on lower wages or be replaced by relatively unskilled workers; and a simplified, mass production system of printing could replace the old discontinuous process in which shop-floor control was effectively subcontracted to craft unions.

These savings, it was widely argued, would transform the press.

Groups with limited resources would be able to start new papers and thus greatly extend the diversity of the press. Minority papers would also be able to flourish as never before because they would be economically viable with small circulations. In this new environment of specialized publishing, mass circulation formula journalism – allegedly the product of Victorian technology – would wither and die.

It was not only right-wing press managements which advanced these arguments; they were also echoed by distinguished journalists and politicians on the centre and left of the political spectrum in what proved to be a general mobilization of public opinion against Fleet Street's production workers. Ian Aitken, political editor of the *Guardian*, pronounced that only the intransigence of some in the print unions prevented the emergence of 'entirely new newspapers representing all points of view'. His counterpart at the *Observer*, Robert Taylor, argued that, with new technology, 'the tyranny of the mass-circulation Press, with its mindless formula journalism appealing to the lowest common denominator, will be weakened'. Shortly after the Wapping dispute ended, Bill Rodgers, Vice-President of the Social Democratic Party, enthused, 'Murdoch may have done more for the freedom of the press than a dozen Royal Commissions'.

The man who initially embodied all these hopes for the future was Eddy Shah, a publisher of freesheets in the north-west and the victor of a famous confrontation with the National Graphical Association. He announced in 1985 to general acclaim that he was setting up a new national daily and Sunday paper in a green field site, miles from Fleet Street, using the latest in print technology. He seemed to many at the time to be the harbinger of a new era.

But it was in fact Rupert Murdoch who made the first, decisive move by building a new printing plant in Wapping, East London. Although he told the print unions that he intended merely to print a new local daily there, he secretly established a massive, new technology complex, costing over £66 million, capable of printing all his national newspapers. An alternative production work-force was recruited with the help of the maverick electricians' union and trained to operate the new technology. An alternative distribution system was also established through an Australian transport company, Thomas Nationwide Transport, to prevent effective sympathy action by organized labour. As a final precaution, Murdoch reconstituted his Wapping plant as a separate company so that picketing by his Fleet Street employees outside Wapping would be technically illegal.

Murdoch then issued an ultimatum to the print unions requiring them to accept a legally binding, no-strike agreement in which 'new technology may be adopted at any time with consequent reductions in manning levels' and in which anyone involved in industrial action during the term of the contract would be dismissed without appeal. The print unions, although agreeing belatedly to new technology and voluntary redundancy, refused to sign an agreement which they believed meant signing away their members' rights. A strike was called and Murdoch's Fleet Street production workers mounted a forlorn, nightly vigil outside the coils of razor wire surrounding the Wapping plant. Their frustration flared into occasional violence during ritualized mass pickets, which resulted in some print workers being jailed and their unions heavily fined. After more than a year, the strike was called off amid bitter recriminations. The whole episode had been an object lesson in tough multinational, business management in which Murdoch had used an Australian ally to help break a British strike in order to increase the cash flow for the expansion of his media interests in the USA.

His success was followed by a wave of redundancies in Fleet Street, as rival press groups introduced new technology. Some of them also completed arrangements to leave Fleet Street for a free enterprise zone in London's docklands, which offered major tax advantages. However, a number of new papers were also launched in 1986–7, initially seeming to confirm optimistic predictions about the impact of new technology.

These predictions were never fulfilled because they were based on the false assumption that production workers' wages constituted the major part of national newspaper costs. In reality, they accounted for only 21 per cent of national press costs, according to the last available figure (1975) for the period before new technology was introduced.

In the event, new processes resulted in only a modest lowering of run-in costs. *Today* and *Sunday Today* were launched with an initial outlay of £22.5 million; the *Independent* with an establishment fund of £18 million; *News on Sunday* with £6.5 million; and the *London Daily News* with an outlay of well over £30 million in its first year. Indeed the launch of the supposedly mould-breaking *Today* and *Sunday Today* served only to show how little things had changed. One of Shah's central problems – apart from his lack of editorial and managerial expertise – was, ironically, his lack of sufficient finance. A substantial part of his launch fund was swallowed up setting up a new technology plant (instead of contracting out to an independent printer). This led him to economize on pre-launch preparations which contributed to the production problems and indifferent editorial quality of the early issues of his papers. He then ran out of money after only ten weeks and found it impossible to secure further credit, largely because the equity proportion of his capital amounted to only £8.5 million. As a consequence the first national newspapers to be launched by an outsider in half a century were taken over by a leading press conglomerate, Lonrho. Along with other subsidiary backers, Lonrho injected a further £24 million into the Today group, effectively doubling its establishment cost. *Today* was then sold to Murdoch in 1987.

It also became clear that new technology was not inaugurating a new era of minority journalism. Among the new papers, the *London Daily News*, *Sunday Today* and *News on Sunday* folded, while the *Independent* ran up substantial losses. *News on Sunday* initially required just under 800,000 to break even, the *Independent* (with a 'yuppie' readership and high advertising rates) an estimated 400,000. Only the soft porn *Sunday Sport* prospered, because its skeletal staff enabled it to break even after it passed around 350,000.

While new technology increased competition, it did not greatly extend the diversity of the press. The continuing high costs of publishing still restricted the ownership of newspapers to those with large resources, and the unequal allocation of advertising still constrained what could be realistically attempted. This was reflected in the new papers which were launched. *Today* and *Sunday Today* were innovatory only in their use of colour; *Sunday Sport* was almost a parody of the excesses of tabloid journalism; the *Independent* emerged as yet another paper, however distinguished, catering for the top 25 per cent of the market; and the *London Daily News* challenged the *London Evening Standard* by going for the same affluent segment of the metropolitan market. Only the *News on Sunday* extended the political range of the press. But the odds were heavily stacked against this undercapitalized and editorially inadequate venture: its initial equity capital amounted to less than the amount spent by the *Daily Mirror* and *Today* just on television promotion alone in the first quarter of 1987. It closed in November 1987.

Ironically one effect of new technology and national papers' flotation of Reuters in 1984 was to increase their profitability. This financed a further escalation of the circulation war, with an unprecedented outlay of £25.3 million in television advertising by London dailies and national newspapers in the first three months of 1987. The effect of this rising promotional expenditure was to increase the run-in costs of new papers. Over the medium term, the savings secured by new technology may well be spent in ways designed to shield established papers from competition.

Retrospective

During the post-war period, the press became fully integrated into the core sectors of capital. Ownership ties between newspapers and business corporations were further cemented, at the top level, by institutional, social, and personal links, encouraging newspaper controllers and business leaders to adopt similar ideological positions.

The shift to a more delegated pattern of control in part of the national press during the 1960s was reversed during the 1970s and 1980s. A new generation of predominantly right-wing proprietors emerged who adopted a more interventionist and personalized style of management. Yet, even in those papers where proprietors were relatively inactive, control was still exercised through the selection of senior management and mediated through the structures of news-gathering and the consensual values of journalists.

The impact of new, right-wing proprietors was reinforced by the distorted operation of market forces. Rising costs and advertising reallocations helped to decimate the social democratic press, and contributed to the taming and depoliticization of the radical papers that survived.

The rightward shift of the press was also a response to the decline of the Labour Party. But the changing complexion of the national press overstated the decline of the left and overemphasized the greater resilience of the right. This was reflected in the yawning gap that developed between editorial and electoral opinion, particularly from the 1970s onwards. By 1983, for example, the Conservative Party had the support of 74 per cent of national daily circulation but only 42 per cent of the vote.

Partly as a consequence of increasing concentration of ownership, the press failed also to reflect the growing diversity of public opinion. Indeed the national press – although numbering between 17 and 21 titles during the period 1969–87 – had unanimous editorial opinions on a surprising number of issues. For example every national daily and Sunday paper supported the aborted union 'reforms' proposed by the government in 1969. During the 1975 referendum every national newspaper supported Britain's entry into the EEC. In 1980 every national paper opposed the TUC's 'day of action'. In 1981 every national paper, which expressed an editorial opinion, supported the more right-wing candidate, Denis Healey, in the Labour Party's deputy leadership contest. In 1985 all national papers applauded Neil Kinnock's attack on the 'hard left' of his party.

The rightward drift of the press had significant political consequences. In particular, the closure of large circulation centre-left papers weakened one central institutional prop sustaining a popular radical tradition in Britain. The *Daily Herald*, which had been read principally in the industrial heartlands of Britain, had helped to sustain a working-class,

Labourist sub-culture. The *Sunday Citizen/Reynolds News* had reinforced the values and commitments of the Co-operative movement. The *News Chronicle*, whose radicalism had periodically upset its post-war owners, belonged to an older, ethical Liberal tradition. Together these three papers reached, on their death-bed, an aggregate readership of 9.3 million people according to the official readership surveys of the advertising industry.

Press reporting of industrial relations helped to undermine support for trade unions. For example a content analysis, undertaken for the Royal Commission on the Press 1977, revealed that national dailies tended to focus on the disruptive consequences rather than causes of strikes. The three most frequent, dominant themes in reports were loss of output, loss of work by those not involved, and danger or inconvenience to the public. Strikers were thus tacitly portrayed as being primarily in conflict with the public rather than with management. Since the reasons why workers were on strike were often unexplained or given little prominence, they were also often made to appear as if they were causing disruption for no good reason.[17]

The press also mounted a sustained and effective attack on the Labour left. This culminated in the tabloid campaign against 'loony left' councils in 1976–7 the impact of which stemmed from a series of seemingly factual reports which featured left-wing councillors doing manifestly dotty things. Thus 'loony left' councils in London were alleged to have banned black bin liners as racist, proscribed the nursery rhyme 'Baa Baa Black Sheep', ordered its employees not to call each other 'sunshine', spent almost £0.5 million on '24 super-loos for gypsies', and insisted that gays should go to the top of the council house waiting list. Not one of these reports proved, on investigation, to be true.[18]

By contributing to the disorganization of oppositional forces in Britain, the press helped to stabilize the social order. Reaching a larger, average daily audience than television even during the mid-1980s,[19] newspapers generally endorsed the principal tenets of capitalism – private enterprise, profit, the 'free market', and the rights of property ownership. By regularly invoking the consensual framework of the 'national interest' and by projecting positive symbols of nationhood, in particular the monarchy and sporting heroes, the press promoted national identification at the expense of class solidarity. The press also reinforced political and social norms by mobilizing public indignation against a succession of public enemies projected in stereotypical ways – youth gangs, squatters, student radicals, muggers, football hooligans and union militants.

In a more indirect way the press reinforced support for the social order by the way in which it depicted reality. Its expanding consumer sections concerned with television, records, books, travel, motoring, fashion, health, homes, bingo, and personal finance tacitly encouraged the view that shared access to goods and services constituted a consumer democracy that transcended and was more important than the hierarchy of power. Newspapers' focus on political and state office as the seat of power decentred capital and masked the central influence of industrial and financial élites. By reporting political and economic news usually in the form of disconnected events, the press also encouraged acceptance of the social ordering of society as natural – the way things are. Above all, its greatly enlarged human interest content tended to portray the world in terms of a series of individual dramas shaped by the randomness of fate and elemental human emotions like love and greed. By thus blocking out alternative, structural explanations of how society operates, the human interest stories of the tabloid press contributed as much as political commentary to sustaining the social cohesion of post-war British society.[20]

Notes

1. S. Koss, *The Rise and Fall of the Political Press in Britain*, vol. 2 (London, Hamish Hamilton, 1984).
2. The only partial exception to this was the *Daily Mail* which advocated a Conservative-Liberal coalition in the October 1974 general election.
3. This percentage does not exclude those who did not intend to vote or who were undecided, as recorded by MORI.
4. The *Daily Worker/Morning Star* and *Newsline*, accounting for less than 0.2 per cent of national circulation in the early 1980s, have not been included as national papers since they did not have a proper nation-wide distribution. They have also been excluded in the assessment of national press content in the last part of this chapter.
5. G. Murdock, 'Class, power and the press: problems of conceptualisation and evidence' in H. Christian (ed.), *The Sociology of Journalism and the Press*, Sociological Review Monograph 29 (Keele, University of Keele, 1980).
6. J. Tunstall, *Journalists at Work* (London, Constable, 1971).
7. J. W. Hobson, *The Selection of Advertising Media* (London, Business Publications, 1955); J. R. Adams, *Media Planning* (London, Business Books, 1971). There was, however, a reaction against over-dependence on quantitative approaches in media planning during the late 1970s and 1980s.
8. For more detailed data about advertising allocations, see J. Curran, 'Advertising and the press' in J. Curran (ed.), *The British Press: A Manifesto* (London, Macmillan, 1978).

9. *Survey of the National Newspaper Industry* (London, Economist Intelligence Unit, 1965).

10. '*Daily Herald* reader interest surveys recommendations', p. 8 (London, Odhams Ltd records, 1955).

11. 'Attitudes to newspapers and newspaper reading' (London, International Publishing Corporation (IPC) records, 1964), p. 3.

12. 'National newspaper readership studies: feature readership in national dailies' (London, IPC records, 1964).

13. 'Report of an investigation into the transition from the *Daily Herald* to the *Sun*' (London, IPC records, 1968).

14. 'Report of a survey to study attitudes to daily newspapers' (London, Odhams Ltd records, 1958).

15. Estimated from *Royal Commission on the Press 1947–9 Report* (London, HMSO, 1949), Table 4, p. 82, and *Royal Commission on the Press Interim Report* (London, HMSO, 1976), Table E5, p. 96.

16. A representative sample (twelve issues of dailies and six of Sundays per year) was selected in a way that gave appropriate weight to each quarter of the year, each week in the month, and each day in the week. A code-recode comparison of a representative sample of 1,491 items yielded 83 per cent agreement in their classification.

17. D. McQuail, *Analysis of Newspaper Content*, Royal Commission on the Press Research Series 4 (London, HMSO, 1977). The impact of this press coverage was reinforced by that of television. See Glasgow University Media Group, *Bad News* (London, Routledge & Kegan Paul, 1976) and *More Bad News* (London, Routledge & Kegan Paul, 1980).

18. Goldsmiths' Media Research Group, *Media Coverage of London Councils: Interim Report* (London, Goldsmiths' College, University of London, 1987).

19. 70 per cent of people over the age of 4 watched television on an average day in 1984 (BBC Audience Research). By comparison 73 per cent of people aged 15 and over read an average issue of a daily paper not including evening papers (JICNARS, January–June 1984).

20. For further discussion of this, see J. Curran, G. Whannel, and A. Douglas, 'The political economy of the human interest story' in A. Smith (ed.), *Newspapers and Democracy* (Cambridge, Mass., MIT Press, 1980).

Part II

Broadcasting history

8

Reith and the denial of politics

There are two accounts of the origins of the BBC. The first is that the Corporation was the personal achievement of John Reith. The second is that its emergence was accidental. According to the first view the BBC's monopoly of broadcasting was an inevitable consequence of the Corporation's cultural mission, while for the second, as R. H. Coase has written, 'The problem, to which the monopoly was seen as a solution by the Post Office, was one of Civil Service administration. The view that a monopoly in broadcasting was better for the listener was only to come later.'

These theories appear to conflict. According to one view Reith made history fit his vision. According to the other, a great institution took a particular form because no one appreciated its future importance. Both, however, have a central flaw in common: they disregard political and social change in the world outside broadcasting.

Discovering an audience, a director, and the money

Broadcasting – the transmitting of programmes to be heard simultaneously by an indefinitely large number of people – is a social invention, not a technical one. The capacity to broadcast existed long before it was recognized. 'Wireless telegraphy' was developed during the First World War for military purposes. It was used as a substitute for the telephone, but one with the disadvantage that it was impossible to specify the audience which heard the message. An American engineer, David Sarnoff, first saw the possibilities of radio in 1916. 'I have in mind a plan of development which would make radio a "household utility" like the piano or electricity,' he wrote. 'The idea is to bring music into the house by wireless.'

Yet for some time after popular broadcasting had started in the 1920s, wireless was regarded as little more than an experimental toy. It took

Northcliffe, a pioneer in the commercialization of leisure, to demonstrate the potential audience for the new invention. He arranged a promotion stunt for the *Daily Mail*. Dame Nellie Melba was to be broadcast singing from Chelmsford. This event which began 'with a long silvery trill' and ended with *God Save the King* attracted a much larger audience than had been expected. It made the wireless manufacturers aware for the first time of a potentially huge market for them to supply.

In 1922 there were nearly a hundred applications to the Post Office from manufacturers who wanted to set up broadcasting stations. This demand created the need for control. As Peter Eckersley, one of the company's first employees, wrote later, 'The BBC was formed as an expedient solution to a technical problem. It owes its existence to the scarcity of air waves.' The Postmaster General solved the problems of radio interference by persuading rival manufacturers to invest jointly in one small and initially speculative broadcasting station: The British Broadcasting Company. John Reith was made its Managing Director.

How would the BBC have developed if its first director had been a career civil servant, a banker, or a Bloomsbury intellectual? Many of the features of broadcasting which are taken for granted today would certainly be absent. Reith's domination of the Corporation in its early days was massive, totalitarian, and idiosyncratic, and for many decades the traditions of the BBC seemed to flow directly from his personality. The British Broadcasting Company was set up as a business. Reith turned it into a crusade. 'Scotch engineer, Calvinist by upbringing, harsh and ruthless in character', as A. J. P. Taylor has described him, Reith used 'the brute force of monopoly to stamp Christian morality on the British people'. While waiting to find out whether his application for the directorship had been successful Reith wrote in his memoirs, 'I kept my faith alive night and morning and encouraged myself with the text "Commit thy way unto the Lord, trust also Him and He shall bring it to pass".' Later he was to exhort his staff to dedicate themselves to 'humility in the service of higher pursuits. The desire for notoriety and recognition', he warned, 'sterilizes the seeds from which greatness might spring.'

This ability to impose his will on staff was helped by his size. Churchill nicknamed him 'Wuthering Heights' and senior staff would stand on stairs to argue with him, 'so that I can see you eye to eye, Sir'. His administrative style, and indeed his private diary, were characterized by abuse. Memoranda sent to Reith would return peppered with 'rubbish', 'stupid', 'soft minded idiocy', 'he lies'. Frequently he saw his life in nautical terms: the Corporation was a ship and he was at the helm. He was pompous, humourless, arrogant, and, like most megalomaniacs, paranoid and self-pitying. Yet the near absurdity of his vision enabled him to foresee the power of the new service.

Broadcasting was to be financed partly by a tariff on wireless sets, and partly by a licence fee. These sources soon proved inadequate for the rapidly expanding station. Listeners evaded the tariff by building their own sets with cheap foreign components. They then evaded the full licence fee by applying for experimental licences. The BBC complained, and the manufacturers were angry that the monopoly of wireless production was not proving as profitable as they had hoped. Hence in 1923 the Sykes Committee was set up by the Post Office to inquire into the Company's finances. This rejected advertising as a source of revenue because 'The time devoted to it ... would be very small and therefore exceedingly valuable'. Radio advertising would interfere with market competition by favouring large firms. Instead the report recommended that a simple licence fee should be raised to finance the service.

The Crawford Committee, two and a half years later, unquestioningly accepted the necessity of a broadcasting monopoly, and recommended that the private company be replaced by a 'Public Commission operating in the National Interest'. The service was felt to have outgrown the petty limits of a business enterprise. 'Formed at a moment when broadcasting was still embryonic – regarded by many as a toy, a fantasy, even a joke,' the report argued, 'the company by strenuous application to its duties aided by the loyalty of its staff has raised the service to a degree which reflects high credit on British efficiency and enterprise.'

In 1926 the British Broadcasting Company closed, and the new British Broadcasting Corporation opened. Reith was delighted that the unique status of his organization was recognized. 'The Royal Academy and the Bank of England function under Royal Charter,' proclaimed the 1927 *Handbook*. 'So does the BBC. It is no Department of State.'

The BBC as a public corporation

The BBC came to be seen, in the words of William Robson, as a 'sociological invention of immense significance', and a 'breathtaking administrative innovation'. Hilda Matheson, the first head of the Talks Department, wrote in 1933 that the Corporation was 'wholly in keeping with the British constitution, and it is more and more common to find it quoted as a possible model for the management of other national services for which private control and direct state management are equally unsuitable'. What, then, was the novelty of the BBC's organization and to what extent was Reith responsible for it?

Reith did not invent the notion of a public corporation. Neither did the Corporation simply emerge accidentally. Reith exploited a theory because it was convenient to do so. The Post Office, which played a critical role in the BBC's development, was itself an early example of a nationally run business. William Beveridge had commented in 1905 that the GPO was the 'one socialist experiment ... that now works well'. Forestry, water, and electricity were all important public corporations set up in the years before the BBC was even thought of. Lincoln Gorden, the economist, wrote that by the 1920s, 'Public boards had become all the rage, politicians of every creed when confronted with an industry or a social service which was giving trouble or failing to operate efficiently – created a board.'

The First World War had been critical in establishing the conditions for the acceptance of a 'Public Service Utility'. Despite bitter opposition the centralized control of health, insurance, coal, and ultimately the rationing of food had been introduced. These were seen as exceptional wartime measures. By the 1920s, however, a generation of reformers who had been civil servants during the war were experienced in organizing the centralized distribution of resources. Indeed for a brief period after the war even the government accepted a more interventionist role. The BBC was formed in this period.

The development of the public corporation depended on the rejection of both market forces and politics in favour of efficiency and planned growth controlled by experts. Briggs has pointed out that the acceptance of the BBC and its monopoly was a consequence of the 'substantial and influential support' the Company received between 1924 and 1925. The monopoly remained in Reith's keeping because 'a large number of important people and a large section of the interested public felt that it was right that this should be so'. These influential people were those who were personally impressed by Reith: the Post Office officials; the director of the wireless manufacturers' association; even the Prime Minister, Baldwin.

However, the idea of the BBC also had more general support. There was a widespread dissatisfaction with the *ad hoc* nature of industrial competition. Even in the 1920s, during the first post-war slump, there was a sense that there must be alternative ways to manage the distribution of resources. Men like Beveridge, who had demonstrated the justice of centralized control in the arrangements for social security and in the rationing of food during the First World War, were opposed to the social consequences of industrial competition. In 1934 Beveridge was to argue:

> In a free market economy consumers can buy only that which is offered to them, and that which is offered is not necessarily that which is most advantageous. It is that which appears to give the best prospect of profit to the producer.

This kind of attitude, which Beveridge later developed and popularized in his broadcasts, was surprisingly widely held in the early 1920s. For example Sir Stephen Tallents, who was to play a prominent role in the BBC as well as in the British documentary movement, had worked on rationing with Beveridge, and held very similar opinions. Reith's view that capitalist competition was not wrong but could be inefficient was therefore hardly original.

The BBC was to be used repeatedly as a prototype of the public corporation, especially by Herbert Morrison. Perhaps the feature which particularly attracted socialist writers was the BBC's distance from the world of capitalist industry. The Corporation made no profits. But in addition the goods it made, programmes, were in theory accessible to an infinite number of consumers. It was also a completely new enterprise with no capitalist inheritance to weigh it down. As Robson wrote, 'The BBC is an engine of the mind ... it represents socialized control not encumbered with compensation.'

It was this aspect of broadcasting which Reith grasped. He argued that it was in the very nature of the medium that it should be available for all, for it 'ran as a reversal of the natural law that the more one takes, the less there is left for others'. In broadcasting, he wrote, 'There is no limit to the amount which may be drawn off. It does not matter how many thousands there may be listening; there is always enough for others.'[1] In order to exploit broadcasting fully, Reith had argued, it must be governed by social and not financial priorities.

Thus considerations of profit would have restricted the service to the populous urban areas. Reith was determined that the BBC must serve the whole nation. However, Reith also saw that a national service was vital for the defence of the Corporation's monopoly. 'About a week ago', he wrote in 1923, 'we got wind of a projected attack.' This was to be 'based on the grounds that under the present system we had already reached the limits of our expansion. The deduction to be drawn was that the British people would never be supplied with adequate services unless the principle of competitive commercialism were admitted.' Reith rejected commerce because it would have diminished his empire and lowered its status. But he also believed it to be inefficient in the management of national resources. Many shared this view.

Even the government had come to see some kinds of goods as exceptional. In 1926 the film industry, suffering from foreign competition, was protected by import controls, because films were of 'outstanding national importance'. The BBC had been established because the government was anxious not to exercise unfair patronage by granting a monopoly to any one commercial company. But it had also been considerably affected by the report of a Post Office official, F. J. Brown, on a visit to the USA where 'an epidemic of broadcasting was raging'. Thousands of American companies had started broadcasting and President Hoover had demanded central control over the new technology, claiming that it was as if '10,000 telephone subscribers were crying through the air for their mates'. As a result of interference, Hoover declared, 'the ether will be filled with frantic chaos'.[2] The British government realized on the basis of the American experience that broadcasting was a new kind of resource whose management demanded a new form of administration.

The BBC was founded on a rejection of politics. From the start of broadcasting there had been anxieties that the service would become an agency of government propaganda. Sir Charles Trevelyan, a Labour representative on the Sykes Committee, asked the Company's lawyer whether 'for public reasons a government could intervene to prevent anything it regarded as undesirable being broadcast'. He was told that there might be control of the news, but that a government was unlikely to bother with concerts, lectures, speeches, or the weather.

While Reith believed that the BBC should be above politics, politicians at first believed the BBC to be beneath them. Direct public ownership was rejected because it was felt 'A Member might well shrink from the prospect of having to defend in Parliament the various items in a government concert.'

Reith despised politicians and disliked party politics. Although at various times he had political ambitions, he hated the 'toadying, the cringing pursuit of popularity' which he believed characterized politics. 'It is pathetic', he wrote, 'how apprehensive Labour leaders are of their followers and how little control they seem to have over them.' Reith often misjudged the significance of political events (he felt that the split and collapse of the Labour government in 1931 was unimportant, 'Silly, over money'). 'The whole horrid technique of politics should be abolished,' he wrote in his diary. 'Government of a country is a matter of proper administration, in other words efficiency. It need not be different in nature from the government of a business – only in degree' (29 November 1936). Perhaps the most significant feature of Reith's distaste was the sense that politics led to vacillation and compromise when firm government was needed. Reith was not alone in this view. Indeed an interest developed during the late 1920s and early 1930s, from the extreme right to the fellow travelling left – and including the Keynesian centre – in the benefit of planning.

'The Next Five Years Group' and Political and Economic Planning (known then as PEP!) were groups involving members with different political allegiances but who were agreed on the need for more social planning. 'It may be', wrote one reformer in *The New Outlook*, 'that the Party structures will act for some time as an obstacle in the way of new developments.' Macmillan summed up this position:

> Most of us recognize that the old system of free unplanned Capitalism has passed away. Most of us agree that a leap forward to complete state planning is politically impossible. But ... our search is for some practical scheme of social organization ... which is neither.[3]

On the left, the XYZ club and the New Fabian Research Bureau soon became the natural home for planners and economists.

It has been argued by Scannell and Cardiff that the BBC legitimized its model of broadcasting, not by the huge audience the service soon attracted, but by reference to the élite of 'the great and the good who trooped into studios to educate and inform on every subject from unemployment to the Origin of the Species: Shaw, Wells, the Webbs, Beveridge, Keynes and Huxley – the roll call is endless'. Broadcasting, they argue, was dominated by a specific, reforming, fraction of the middle class. 'They saw themselves as superior to the aristocracy, for they were efficient and uncorrupt, and claiming to act for the general good, they presumed (naturally) to speak and act on behalf of the working classes.' Robert Skidelsky has argued that Keynes's economic theories provided the basis for a new liberal politics in the 1940s, which avoided class struggle and yet implied 'Keynes's most characteristic belief: that public affairs should and could be managed by an elite of clever and disinterested public servants' (*Encounter*, April 1979). The BBC provided a cultural institution which performed the same function. Indeed the economic and political structure of the BBC was also a product of the experience and beliefs of this reforming intelligentsia. Reith's view of what he intended the BBC to be, those pressures he perceived as threatening, and the alternatives he rejected, were typical of what has been seen as a 'middle opinion'. Indeed it might be claimed that the success of the BBC vindicated the view that a strong middle-class consensus lay beneath the dissent and turmoil of the 1930s.

However, this view should perhaps be modified. Marwick has admitted in an article called 'Middle opinion in the thirties' that 'They did not in their own day achieve much, these advocates of political agreement, the "soft centre" as they were not unjustly called.' Indeed, the 'great and the good' were, as Hugh Dalton wrote in 1936, 'more or less eminent persons who are disinclined to join any existing political party, but who are prepared to collaborate with others in writing joint letters to the Press, and in such organizations as the Next Five Years Group'. They were a band of leaders – but they had no followers. As Pimlott has argued in *Labour and the Left in the 1930s*, their policies might have developed 'into the basis of a powerful campaign for a British New Deal as a frontal assault on mass unemployment'.[4] But in fact the supporters of middle opinion were politically isolated. Keynes and Beveridge had to wait until the Second World War to see their ideas implemented. Yet the BBC was not merely a dream or a plan for reform. It was a rapidly growing institution. By the middle of the 1930s it had become an established and central component of British culture.

Perhaps pressures other than those of the liberal intelligentsia were at work in the making of the BBC? Certainly, unlike Beveridge's plans for insurance, the BBC cost the government no money. The personal connections of the BBC producers were with Bloomsbury literati rather than with liberal reformers. Reith was more an evangelist than a liberal. 'Anything in the nature of a dictatorship is the subject of much resentment these days,' he wrote in 1924. 'Well somebody has to give decisions.' While liberals planned, Reith bullied, wheedled, and built an empire. 'It is occasionally indicated to us that we are apparently setting out to give the public what we think they need and not what they want – but few know what they want, and very few what they need.'

Reith was authoritarian and successful. In the 1930s the new liberals were neither. Moreover, although they dominated broadcast talks, this category hardly dominated the BBC's output. Despite Reith's preoccupation with culture, contemporary critics most frequently accused the Corporation of philistinism. 'The company undoubtedly saw itself as a cultural force', wrote R. S. Lambert, 'by which it meant something constituted to avoid the postures of vulgarity.' Perhaps the BBC was less dominated by the concerns of the liberal intelligentsia and more successful in the 1930s because it was paternalist. Perhaps, also, it gave the public what it wanted rather more than Reith was prepared to admit. For, as the BBC *Handbook* shows, by 1934 the BBC was broadcasting more light music, comedy, and vaudeville than any other European station. It was hardly the stuff of social revolution.

The BBC and political independence

How was the BBC's independence from partisan political pressure to be achieved? The directors of the private company were replaced by publicly appointed Governors in 1926. These were to be the trustees of the public interest. At first the Governors and Reith disagreed about how the responsibility should be divided between them.

Thus Philip Snowden's wife Ethel – described in Beatrice Webb's diaries as having 'caricatured social climbing' (19 March 1932) – arrived at the BBC expecting an office, a secretariat, and a full-time job. Appointed a Governor as a 'convenient representative of both Labour and Women', she believed the Director General should play an administrative role, and that the Governors should make all policy decisions. Reith detested her, and commented that she thought that 'there ought to be a board meeting every day ... an abominable exhibition by her. A truly terrible creature, ignorant, stupid and horrid.' He saw her as a threat to his own position. Indeed he was quite correct to do so. Hugh Dalton, the Labour politician, recorded in his diary (3 August 1930) that Ethel Snowden had asked G. D. H. Cole – another Governor – to help her get rid of Reith. 'Who would she suggest as his successor?' Cole had asked. 'I would gladly take it on myself,' Ethel had replied.

Herbert Morrison wrote in his important work on nationalization, *Socialization and Transport*, 'It is a matter of argument whether the Director General of Broadcasting should, or should not, be a strong personality.' Reith's views were quite straightforward: he wanted to be in control, and he wanted the Governors to back up his decisions.

The Corporation was supposed to be independent and non-partisan: in practice it was not even indirectly accountable to Parliament. In a Report on the Machinery of Government written in 1918, the Webbs had opposed the increased use of public corporations because

> when a board is set up without explicit status provided for ministerial responsibility to parliament – the situation is obviously unsatisfactory. Only ministerial responsibility provides safeguard for the citizen ... and consumer.

However, these objections were not understood. The government had felt in 1925 that 'The progress of science and the harmony of art would be hampered by too rigid rules and too constant supervision by the state.' So, between Reith, anxious to avoid having the content of broadcasting politically manipulated, and therefore determined to evade political control, and the government, anxious to avoid responsibility for trivia, the BBC was left with no effective accountability. This omission came to be treated as though it were a principle. Herbert Morrison later claimed to have invented it. Robson wrote in 1935 that it was

> in strict conformity with the English tradition ... derived as a practical expedient to perform a particular function, without any concern for general principles – or indeed any awareness that questions of principle were involved.

It is perhaps better seen as the elevation of an uneasy compromise into an ideal type.

The BBC and the General Strike

The BBC's practical interpretation of impartiality was soon tested during the General Strike in 1926. Reith knew that the survival of the Corporation (whose constitution had not yet been formally accepted) depended on its conduct during the crisis.

One effect of the strike was to create a national audience for broadcasting. At the end of 1926 Hilda Matheson was able to write, 'The public and wireless listeners are now nearly synonymous terms.' Beatrice Webb noted in her diary that 'The sensation of the General Strike centres around the headphones of the wireless set.' Although there were only 2 million licence holders these represented a far greater number of listeners, and 'communal listening' was a feature of the crisis as people gathered in halls and outside shops to hear the news.

The BBC seemed more important because of the absence of all other sources of information. An old age pensioner in the 1950s told Julian Symons that he still had 'the little homemade crystal set which worked lovely with the iron bedstead for an aerial . . . and which told me what was *really happening*'. Despite the inadequacy of its news the Corporation emerged from the strike with a national audience and increased authority.

Another effect of the General Strike was that the BBC invented modern propaganda in its British form. During the First World War persuasive techniques had been crude. All Germans were characterized as vicious beasts intent on murdering children and raping nuns. Anthony Smith has argued that a rejection of the

> propagandists of the First World War, and the ensuing reaction against the black-out that they had perfected were among the profoundest influences on the men who came to lay the foundations of broadcasting in the early nineteen twenties.

The First World War view of propaganda was still accepted by many during the strike. Its main proponent was Churchill and its main instrument the *British Gazette*. This was a daily news-sheet that few took seriously, so evidently biased were its contents. Churchill wanted to commandeer the BBC, as the government had the right to do. Reith argued that if the BBC was taken over the strikers would merely close the service down. Apart from destroying 'the pioneer work of 3g years', by shattering public confidence in broadcasting, 'It was no time for dope, even if the people could have been doped.' He argued that to suppress information was likely to exacerbate the crisis. His most telling point was that by gaining the trust of both strikers and the government the BBC could positively facilitate a resolution of the crisis:

> In the end conciliations of some kind must supervene and ... the BBC could act as a link to draw together the contending parties by creating an atmosphere of good will towards its service on both sides.

Reith argued that the trust gained by 'authentic impartial news' could then be used. It was not necessarily an end in itself.

He stated, however, that 'Since the BBC was a national institution and since the Government in this crisis was acting for the people ... *the BBC was for the Government in the Crisis too.*'

Indeed it was Reith's own political judgment which controlled policy throughout the strike. Briggs has pointed out:

> He preferred mediation to showdown. If his views had coincided with those of the sponsors of the *British Gazette* he would have had fewer qualms about allowing the BBC to fall directly into the hands of the government. As it was, his personal conviction gave strength to his resistance on constitutional principles.

Reith, as another writer, Patrick Renshaw, has argued, 'would have supported the union against the owners. But he was certainly not prepared to support the TUC against the Government.' However, Reith's 'distinct' view seems very close to that of the most implacable opponent of the strike, Churchill. Martin Gilbert argues that Churchill was quite prepared to accept a conciliatory policy towards the resolution of the coal-miners' dispute with the owners; it was only the general and political strike he was opposed to.

Until 1926 the press had prohibited the BBC from collecting any news. The strike allowed the Company to develop a news service of its own. This reported statements by the strikers as well as the strike-breakers. One of the bulletins on 4 May started with the TUC statement, 'We have from Land's End to John O'Groats reports of support that have surpassed our expectations.'

During the strike no representative of organized labour was allowed to broadcast, and the Leader of the Opposition, Ramsay MacDonald, was also banned. These restrictions were imposed by the government. Reith thought them wrong, but said he could do nothing about them. Willie Graham, one of the strike leaders, wrote angrily to him:

> The Government emphatically deny that they interfere with the BBC in any way. On the other hand the company states that it was not a free

agent. I am sure that you will agree that it is impossible to make any sense of these two statements.

Called by some workers the 'British Falsehood Corporation', the BBC learnt how to censor itself during the strike in order to forestall government intervention. Nevertheless the General Strike marks the end of the propaganda based on lies and the start of a more subtle tradition of selection and presentation.

Throughout the strike the government had emphasized that the strikers were politically motivated and hence unconstitutional. The BBC emerged from the crisis with an ethic of political neutrality, which was expressed as much in the tone of its broadcasts as in any formal regulations. This was to have profound consequences for politics.

Governments and the BBC in the 1930s

The General Strike initiated a pattern that was to recur throughout the 1930s: the BBC was forced to pass off government intervention as its own decision. In 1935 it was proposed to include talks by a communist and a fascist – Harry Pollitt and Sir Oswald Mosley, respectively – in a series on the British constitution. The Foreign Office protested, arguing that Pollitt could not be allowed to broadcast as he had recently made a speech supporting armed revolution. The BBC responded by referring the matter to the Governors, who declared that, 'More harm than good could be done if a policy were adopted of muzzling speeches.' A BBC official told the Foreign Office, 'We can't chuck Pollitt unless, under our charter, we are given direct instruction from government that he is not to broadcast.'

The Foreign Office remained adamant that Pollitt should not broadcast. They suggested, however, that the question could resolve itself into the undesirability of *Mosley* speaking.[5] The matter was finally brought to an end when the Postmaster General wrote to Reith pointing out that as the Corporation licence was due for renewal, it would be wiser to comply with government demands. The BBC then asked for permission to say why the programmes had been banned.

The government reacted sharply. According to a Cabinet minute:

> It would be neither true nor desirable to state publicly that the talks would be an 'embarrassment to the Government' at the present time. But it would be true to say that 'they would not be in the national interest'.

Despite the feeling of Corporation officials like Tallents and Graves that the BBC's chances of survival were better if it were seen to be acting in strict accordance with the Charter, the series was dropped and no mention made of government pressure.

An even more remarkable example of the BBC's relationship with the government occurred in the period immediately before the outbreak of the Second World War. On 25 August 1939 the Labour leaders Hugh Dalton and Harold Laski, together with the General Secretary of the TUC, Walter Citrine, wanted to broadcast a direct personal message and warning to the German people. In an interview with them, the Director General of the BBC, Ogilvie (who had replaced Reith in 1938), refused to tell them whether their request would be granted. In the event, news that a 'statement' had been made was broadcast, but nothing whatsoever was mentioned about its contents.

Ogilvie, Dalton pointed out, clearly wanted to consult the Foreign Office but refused to admit this. The next day the Labour leaders complained to the Foreign Secretary, Halifax, of the way in which the BBC had treated them. By this time Ogilvie apparently claimed that he had told Dalton and Citrine that he was going to consult the Foreign Office.

Walter Citrine complained to Halifax that 'Our people are getting pretty fed up with being expected to shout with the government one day and being treated like a lot of children or nobodies the next.' He went on to say that Ogilvie (who had been a Conservative MP) 'might be good enough to help them [the Tories] collect material to rag Lloyd George with – but that doesn't satisfy me that he is fit to be Director General of the BBC'.[6] This incident demonstrates the continuous and insidious dependence of the Corporation on the government. It is not merely that the decision whether to broadcast the message was referred to the Foreign Office. In addition, Ogilvie was predicting Foreign Office policy, and indeed covering for it. Earlier, the BBC had been concerned to make government pressure on its decisions public. In 1939 it was protecting the Foreign Office, and passing off Foreign Office demands as its own policy.

Since 1927 the BBC had been strenuously courting government departments in an attempt to evade press restrictions on its reporting. 'We ought to be the arbiters of what Government news goes out,' wrote a Corporation official, 'not a commercial company like Reuters.'[7] A close relationship with civil servants grew up and government pressure was often exercised informally and personally. 'Vansittart would like the BBC to get pro-Franco in our news and stop using words like insurgent,' Reith wrote in his diary in 1937. The Corporation was most concerned that disputes with governments should not be resolved by the emergence of any official regulations.

This cautious self-protection was shrewd, and may have been the only strategy available. However, it made the BBC vulnerable to bullying. At various times it was implied that the licence fee might not be allowed to rise, or even that the Corporation's licence to broadcast might be terminated. As a result the most important constraint came to be the Corporation's anxiety to pre-empt the threats.

The BBC, society, and programmes

During a decade of depression and industrial decline, the BBC grew, quadrupled its staff, raised salaries, and acquired vast buildings. One writer, D. G. Bridson, recalled his shock at being asked to work for the BBC. 'In 1935 I mentally bracketed it with Parliament, the Monarch, the Church and the Holy Ghost,' he wrote.

However, the Corporation also intended to become part of the Establishment. Its development into an authoritative institution was a complex process. This was expressed in the choice of outside broadcasters, and what they were allowed to say. It was also expressed in how the Corporation treated them, and its own staff. It was expressed in the distance between what it claimed to do and what it did.

In a decade of hunger marches and 'red united fighting fronts', the BBC regarded a succession of royal broadcasts as the triumph of outside broadcasting and actuality reporting. Broadcasting in the 1930s was dominated by state openings, royal anniversaries, visits, deaths and births, and by the Coronation. 'The floral decorations for His Majesty's broadcast', ran one press release, 'will be one bowl of hiskura (mauve) and a small vase of grape hyacinths.'

In 1923 Reith had exercised a servile cunning in his attempt to persuade the Dean of Westminster to allow the Duke of York's wedding to be broadcast. It would, he suggested, even have advantages 'from the devotional point of view'. Many who 'by sheer force of circumstance, or negligence had little to do with the Church' would hear the 'measured cadence of the sacred words'.[8] The experience, Reith implied, might change their hearts.

Reith's greatest coup was the annual Christmas message delivered by the Monarch. These events were usually preceded by an 'Empire programme', making contact with far-flung colonial stations. 'Goodbye Wilmington', ran one, 'and a Happy Christmas to you all ... behind us the mountains which encircle Vancouver are still lost in darkness ... though a faint radiance announces that dawn is on its way.'[9] George V's funeral resulted in an eighty-page BBC policy document, 'Procedures on the death of a sovereign'.

Reith and the Corporation did not merely present traditional pageantry to a wider audience. They established a new manner for royalty which was more appropriate to the twentieth century. Reith made suggestions for what royalty should say, and how they should say it. He recognized what kinds of occasion a royal presence would grace – and benefit from. One of the bitterest complaints of Reith's old age was his omission from royal Garden Party invitation lists. He felt he had 'done much to serve the House'. Indeed the BBC was responsible, at least in part, for moulding a new domestic and populist image for the Monarchy.

The BBC was a little less sensitive to the needs of trade unionists. One of the clearest aspects of what came to be known as the 'William Ferrie incident', was the incomprehension of the Corporation's bourgeois but liberal-minded staff, when confronted with a worker.[10] Ferrie, a Communist trade unionist, was invited to reply to a talk given by Sir Herbert Austin, who had spoken on the immense improvement of working-class conditions during the twentieth century. This was in 1932. Ferrie committed the Corporation equivalent of original sin by departing from his written script when he reached the microphone. He began to tell the public how the BBC had censored him, and horrified Corporation officials rushed to fade out the programme. Ferrie later wrote:

> I was particularly incensed at their demand that I should put across that the slogan 'Workers of the World Unite' is not a revolutionary slogan. I also refused to drop my h's and talk as they imagine a worker does.

His talk had quite clearly been altered to make it more politically acceptable. But the way in which it was done is even more revealing. The BBC censored him in ways that the officials would hardly have recognized as such. 'Your language', commented Mary Adams, 'was too literary and impersonal.' Ferrie, to her surprise, came 'in an agitated state', to see her at her Chelsea home. He arrived at the studio with three colleagues 'for support'. All of this seemed odd to middle-class BBC producers, even though Mary Adams was sympathetic to the union case. It seems in retrospect a perfectly regular way for a working-class trade unionist to deal with an institution that seemed bent on intimidating him.

The BBC was more intentionally autocratic in its treatment of its own staff. Reith would banish rebels from the centre of the empire to the periphery. 'You're a very dangerous man Harding,' Bridson recalls Reith telling one, 'I think you'd better go up North where you can't do so much damage.' Indeed by 1937 the only doubts about the Corporation's monopoly were centred on the rights of its staff. There were several symptomatic scandals during the 1930s. The first was the forced resignation of P. P. Eckersley, an engineer and programme innovator of enormous talent who had worked for the Corporation since 1926. Eckersley wrote his own epitaph, 'He had ideas: We stopped them.' He was obliged to resign because he was cited in a divorce case.

The second was over the pressure brought to bear on the editor of the *Listener*, R. S. Lambert, to discourage him from continuing with a libel action. Lambert was warned that he had no future career in the Corporation if he pursued the case. Later he argued that 'This opinion crystallized the dangerous doctrine that the individual owes more loyalty to his employer, than to his fellow employees.'

Reith's view was succinct. 'It's a mug's game', he wrote in a book called *Personality and Career*, 'to pull contrary to your boss.' In 1937 the Ullswater Report recommended, under pressure from Attlee, that a Staff Association should be set up, and for the first time the BBC's workers had organized representation.

The BBC saw itself as a humane and enlightened employer, which had always pursued strictly egalitarian and meritocratic appointment procedures. In 1934 an internal report commented complacently that there was 'a good proportion of women to men on the staff'. This was true, but most of the women were secretaries.

Hilda Matheson and Mary Somerville had set up the key Talks Department and the Education Service when the Company started. It was a woman's initiative which had started the Sound Archive. Women, however, were never announcers, rarely presenters, and the proportion of women in administrative and creative posts declined. Between 1926 and 1936 the Corporation's staff had increased fourfold yet, as the BBC's annual reports show, the number of women in creative jobs had risen by little more than one-third, and in senior administrative positions by barely one-quarter.

Nevertheless, the atmosphere in the BBC, a new exciting glamorous place where it was better, as Peter Eckersley remarked, 'to have discreet affaires than to remarry', is summed up by Maurice Gorham:

> The BBC secretaries were beginning to bloom though they reached full flower later. By that time many of them were pin money girls. It was a great sight to see them going out at lunch, high heeled, sheer stockinged, beautifully made up, talking disdainfully in high clear voices.

By the 1930s the BBC had become an august institution. It was not a crude agent of the status quo, rather it advocated acceptable change, in some areas, in certain circumstances, sometimes.

The BBC and journalism

Indeed, by the end of the decade the sheer amount of news that broadcasting and the press were flooded with was so large that, had it wished to, a government could hardly have pre-censored it all. However, a new tradition in reporting imposed new criteria of selection on the news. Journalists stopped being passionate advocates, saw themselves rather as independent professionals, and their writing as a negotiated product of conflict between partisan views. This self-image and its practical consequences were most fully developed in the BBC. Reith was not opposed to conflict. On the contrary, he fought the press for the right to broadcast on contentious issues. But the BBC and the new 'professional journalist' retained a monopoly over deciding its limits.

The BBC and appeasement

The BBC's brokerage was subject to pressure. In the eyes of the BBC's programme-makers, politics was an activity which only happened between major political parties. Two kinds of political dispute never reached the air waves: divisions within parties and the expressive politics of the streets. Winston Churchill, repeatedly excluded from broadcasting because his views were seen as eccentric, wrote to Reith saying he wished he could buy broadcasting time. He preferred the American commercial system 'to the present British method of debarring public men from access to a public who wish to hear'. In 1933 Churchill and Austen Chamberlain complained that the BBC 'had introduced an entirely new principle of discrimination into British public life, namely the elimination from broadcasting of any Members of Parliament who were not nominated by the Party leaders or the Party Whip'. Such a crucial innovation, they protested, should be decided by parliament, not arbitrarily imposed by the BBC.[11]

The most important dispute the BBC ignored, and one which cut across party loyalties, was that of the government's policy of appeasing German territorial ambitions. Churchill claimed that the BBC conspired with the press to exclude all opponents of this policy from any access to the public. Gilbert and Gott have suggested that appeasers were effective for so long mainly because of their success in keeping the opponents of German rearmament out of public office. However, the control of public knowledge and opinion was also crucial. An early reference to Polish rearmament lost a producer his job in 1932. Speakers were banned because of their hostility to the fascist states. Later, the BBC was to apologize for its attitude during the 1930s by explaining that, while mistaken, it was merely following the trend of opinion of the times. Yet the BBC's silence is extraordinary as it was itself making extensive plans for the Corporation's conduct and survival during a possible war.

Reith's diary first mentions preparations for war in 1933: plans for the physical protection of transmitters and broadcasting stations were in hand by 1935; Reith was involved in discussions over the organization of a Ministry of Information in the event of war by 1936; details of trains in which to send personnel from London were established by 1937. Thus the BBC was secretly preparing for a war which it did not officially expect, while the public were kept in ignorance of these cautious foresights.

The BBC at the end of the decade

Reith resigned in 1937, restless and dissatisfied. The BBC no longer stretched him, and he hoped for something better which never came. Increasingly, as the prospect of high office receded, he regarded the Corporation which he had created with resentment. It had not, he came to feel, treated him well.

By the end of the 1930s the BBC seemed a natural and inevitable solution to the problem of administering a national broadcasting system. It had won the right to discuss controversial politics against the determined opposition of suspicious governments and a jealous press. But it developed unnecessary conventions, and had become too defensive. The real test of the Corporation's independence was to come during the Second World War.

Notes

1. J. W. C. Reith, *Broadcast Over Britain* (London, Hodder & Stoughton, 1924), p. 52.
2. F. J. Brown, 'Broadcasting in Britain', *London Quarterly Review*, 145, 3 (January 1926).
3. H. Macmillan, 'Looking forward' in the Next Five Years Group, *The New Outlook*, 1 (8 May 1937).
4. See B. Pimlott, *Labour and the Left in the 1930s* (Cambridge, Cambridge University Press, 1977).
5. 'The citizen and his government' (1935–6), *BBC Written Archives*.
6. The unpublished diary of Hugh Dalton (25–29 August 1939). For a further development of this affair, see J. Seaton and B. Pimlott, 'The struggle for balance: the BBC and the Labour Movement 1920–45' in J. Seaton and B. Pimlott (eds), *Politics and the Media in Britain* (Aldershot, Gower, 1987).

7. 'Relationship between the government and the BBC: the Foreign Office', *BBC Written Archives*.
8. Duke of York's wedding, *BBC Written Archives* (Royalty).
9. Christmas broadcasts, *BBC Written Archives* (Royalty).
10. The William Ferrie incident, *BBC Written Archives*.
11. The Churchill and Chamberlain complaint, *BBC Written Archives* (Churchill).

9

Broadcasting and the blitz

The 'Dunkirk spirit' and the comradeship of the air-raid shelter during the blitz have long been part of our national self-image. How much was this myth and how much reality? Officials concerned with civilian morale in the Ministry of Information and the Home Office who had seen ordinary people as unintelligent and weak during the phoney war in 1939 came to see them as dependable, shrewd, and courageous by 1940. What was the cause of this change?

It is clear that the BBC, almost certainly the most important instrument of domestic propaganda during the war, conducted a campaign intended to convince the public of its own endurance and solidarity. The BBC emerged from the war as both a symbol and an agent of the victory. More than at any other time, the BBC was part of, and seen to be part of, the history of the nation.

'The people will break'

When war was declared in 1939 most people expected a cataclysm. Pre-war pessimism about popular morale had largely been forgotten, yet it had been common to many groups who were otherwise opposed to each other.

During the 1930s another war was felt to be imminent. The main aim of many politicians was to avert the repetition of a disaster like that of the First World War. Even pacifists organizing peace pledges came to feel, like Vera Brittain, that they were trying 'Canute-like to reverse the inexorable'. Indeed memories of the First World War dominated the British as they entered the Second.

The success of the fascist dictatorships had led to a growing distrust and fatalism about the political will of the 'masses'. J. A. Hobson argued in the left-wing *Political Quarterly*:

No one could have predicted the possibility of the collapse of all codes of decent conduct, all standards of justice, truth, and honour, not only in international affairs but in the revealed nationalism of the brutalitarian state, the facile acquiescence of whole peoples in the absolute domination of self-appointed masters, and the amazing credulity of the educated classes under the spells of the crudest propaganda. (January 1938)

Many on the left believed that the organization of the resistance to fascism would lead to totalitarianism at home. 'If you go to war to save democracy', Kingsley Martin wrote in the *New Statesman* (1 September 1939), 'you will give up democracy in doing so, and find that you are fighting for the overseas investment of your own capitalist classes.' Even after the outbreak of war Sir Charles Trevelyan, a former Labour Minister of Education, wrote privately, 'I have a deep-seated feeling that none of the people want to fight, and that the war will collapse.' It was thus felt by some on the left either that the workers would refuse to fight a war against fascism abroad, because it would only lead to fascism at home, or that they would not fight anyway, because of the iniquitous lack of justice in Britain.

The marches and demonstrations of the 1930s had led the right to believe that British workers were too anarchistic and socialist to be trusted to fight. Those in authority were also anxious about the effects of class division on morale. As early as 1926 a pioneering social scientist, Lasswell, had written, 'Governments of Western Europe can never be perfectly certain that a class-conscious proletariat will rally to the clarion of war.'

Indeed the whole concept of 'public morale', which so preoccupied the government during the war, originated in the 1930s. It was a concept based on naïve psychological and sociological assumptions; in particular, that individuals' attitudes and behaviour were peculiarly susceptible to manipulation in the conditions of modern 'mass' society. 'Morale' was seen as single and malleable. The success of the fascist dictators had confirmed these views, and demonstrated that the urban masses acted in response to crowd psychology and not according to rational political calculation. One reason for this view of the masses, as Bruntz indicated, was the widespread belief that superior allied propaganda had helped to shorten the First World War. *The Times* in 1918 had argued that effective propaganda had hastened victory by a year, and consequently saved a million lives. Indeed, as Shils pointed out, the Nazis may have overestimated the effect of propaganda because they concluded that 'If Germans failed to be tricked by propaganda this time, success was assured.' In addition, the decades between the two wars had seen the dramatic success of commercial propaganda in advertising. The people, then, were thought to be persuadable.

Parallel to this anxiety was the belief that the new technology of destruction, the bombing attack on cities, would lead to a collapse of civilian society. These fears were based on exaggerated projections of the number of deaths which could be expected for each ton of explosives dropped, and on the biased intuitions of military 'experts' about how civilian populations would respond to bombing. 'In simple terms', Titmuss wrote, 'the experts foretold a mass outbreak of hysterical neurosis among the civilian population.' Psychoanalysts argued that under the strain of bombing, people would 'regress', and behave like frightened and unsatisfied children. A group of eminent psychologists reported to the government that 'The utter helplessness of the urban civilian today when confronted with the simplest task outside his ordinary work is likely to be a potent factor ... in the war effort.' Experts confidently predicted that for every survivor injured by bombs at least three others would be driven mad.

It was therefore widely believed that the British worker would be devastated by an attack from the air. Perhaps this fear explains the curious official ambivalence about the approaching war during the late 1930s. Detailed preparations were made for war, yet rearmers were still banned from the microphone. An atmosphere of dignity, gloom, and appeasement dominated broadcasting even after the declaration of war. Harmon Grisewood recalled that at the end of September 1939 the new Director General, Ogilvie, suggested that a lady cellist, playing a duet with a nightingale in a wood, should be broadcast to Germany. Ogilvie believed that the sound would induce peaceful and harmonious thoughts in the belligerent fascists.

The first months of war

When the war started normal programmes were replaced by news bulletins interspersed with serious and appropriate music. 'Almost everything is obscured at present,' the *New Statesman* commented on 9 September. 'For the first days of the war the BBC monotonously repeated news which was in the morning papers and which it had itself repeated an hour earlier. While each edition of the papers repeated what had already been heard on the wireless.' The news black-out was as complete as the black-out of the streets. During the phoney war the BBC paid for nominal independence by doing exactly what the government wanted. Jack Payne noted that the music department was 'deep in memos', one of which listed the eighty banned German and Italian composers, including Monteverdi, who had died in 1643. Another BBC employee claimed that the only explanation for the failure of the Germans to devastate Bush House was that 'no BBC administrator had remembered to send Hitler the memo reminding him to have it done'.[1]

When more varied programmes started from new provincial centres in unlikely country houses, they were rather less well-organized versions of what had gone on before. Basil Deane, who ran the Entertainment National Service Association (ENSA), the organization responsible for the entertainment of the troops, wrote, 'Public anxiety was not lessened by the forced gaiety of variety artists whose personal jokes and excessive use of each other's Christian names – syndicated familiarity – savoured of self-advancement and was out of key with the national mood.' Many early propaganda broadcasts had a peevish, hectoring tone. A month after the outbreak of war a British Institute of Public Opinion poll showed that 35 per cent of the public were dissatisfied with the BBC and 10 per cent did not listen to it. In the winter of 1939 to 1940 Mass Observation reported that rumours were rife; the people apparently did not believe the newspapers, the Ministry of Information, or the BBC. They trusted only their friends.

The 'phoney war' forced the BBC to regionalize and extemporize. The most important change was the Corporation's dramatic growth in size. In 1939 the BBC had 4,000 staff, by the beginning of 1940 6,000, and by November of that year nearly 11,000. Roger Eckersley, the staid brother of Peter Eckersley, wrote, 'I knew directly or indirectly most of the senior staff up to the outbreak of war. Now, I shared lifts with complete strangers.' It became increasingly difficult to control the hordes of new staff and this in itself led to a period of anarchy and change. The new employees were quite different from the regular Corporation men. George Orwell broadcast to the colonies and India, William Empson to China, Herbert Read organized poetry readings, Edward Blunden arranged talks, and Basil Wright and Humphrey Jennings made programmes on the principles of documentary. According to Orwell:

> The British Government started the present war with the more or less openly declared intention of keeping the literary intelligentsia out of it, yet after three years almost every writer, however undesirable his political history or opinions, had been sucked into the various ministries or the BBC. ... No one acquainted with Government pamphlets, the Army Bureau of Current Affairs lectures, documentary films and broadcasts to occupied countries ... can believe that our rulers would sponsor this kind of thing if they could help it.

The notion of a Corporation converted from philistine reaction to progressive culture became part of the fable of the BBC at war. It was a particularly public example of a common tension that characterized much war work. Conservative administrative authorities were forced to work with creative intellectuals. Scientific 'boffins' invented curious bombs for the military; literary and artistic 'boffins' did intelligence work. The Ministry of Information was notorious for the strange collection of dilettantes, anthropologists, and advertising copy writers which it employed. Duff Cooper, who directed the ministry, wrote that a monster had been created, 'so large, so voluminous, so amorphous, that no single man could cope with it'.[2] 'Frustrated' was the word he came to hate most: the plaintive cry of brilliant amateurs thwarted by bureaucracy. Yet the intellectuals were more prepared to take risks as they had no careers to jeopardize. The *Radio Times* became filled with pictures of distinguished chemists putting bicycle power to strange purposes, and professors of literature 'thinking' about future programmes; the image of 'boffins' at least provided an accommodation and role for experts. For a brief period it was respectable, and even useful, to be serious. Nevertheless the BBC, wrote Orwell, felt 'halfway between a girls' school and a lunatic asylum'.

Programme changes

The first radio personality of the war was not a patriotic politician or a staunch common man, but Lord Haw Haw. By 1940 William Joyce dominated German propaganda to England. His voice was rich, apparently upper class, 'Cholmondely-Plantagenet out of Christ Church',[3] and caused much speculation. It was difficult to avoid Joyce's wavelength when tuning into British stations, as Rebecca West recalled. 'There was an arresting quality about his voice which made it a sacrifice not to go on listening.'

Everyone in Gosport knew that Haw Haw knew that their town hall clock was two minutes slow. In Oxford everyone knew when the Germans were going to bomb the Morris works; Lord Haw Haw had told them. The myth of the English aristocrat with inside knowledge of the German High Command – a kind of diabolical Peter Wimsey – was powerful. What Lord Haw Haw said was less important than what the British came to believe he had said.

It has been argued that Haw Haw was ineptly used by the Germans, who failed to keep him adequately informed about military developments. However, both the government and the BBC were seriously worried about the broadcasts. Robert Silvey of the Audience Research Department was commissioned to conduct a survey of Joyce listeners for the

BBC. 'It produced highly reassuring results,' he wrote in the BBC *Handbook*. 'It showed that the British welcomed the new guest to the fireside as a diverting entertainment in the first bleak wartime winter.' But the survey included some less comfortable findings: by the end of 1939 over 30 per cent of the population was listening to Joyce regularly. The BBC's Home Broadcasting Board had sneered that only 'adolescents, and middle-aged women' listened to him. Silvey's work revealed that every kind of person heard the programmes. The reassuring feature of the audience, little understood at the time, was that Haw Haw's listeners were particularly discriminating ones. Most read one or more newspapers; 34 per cent of the listeners were *Times* readers. Those most exposed to enemy propaganda were those least likely to be taken in by it. Yet Joyce's ability to hold an audience demonstrated either that the BBC was failing to entertain or that its news was distrusted.

The fall of France in 1940 demonstrated the potential power of enemy propaganda. It was widely believed that German broadcasts were responsible for the failure of the French civilians to resist the German invasion, and for the strength of the French 'fifth column' of collaborators. British officials felt that radio was crucial, yet the BBC was too solemn, aloof, and boring. The problem was urgent.

1940 and cheerful patriotism

Dunkirk has been seen by most historians as a key turning point in the war. A massive defeat was turned into a triumph, and the British, curiously relieved to be without allies, found a new determination to win the war. Calder sees Dunkirk as the point at which the 'old gang' of pre-war reactionaries was finally exposed. Found to be guilty they were thrown aside. After Dunkirk, he argues, people were concerned with winning the war, and ensuring a 'New Deal' for the peace. Mass Observation noted a steady growth of left-wing opinion from this period.

What is remarkable is the absence of any evidence of popular pressure for a negotiated peace. Rationally invasion seemed certain, and defeat, accompanied by appalling devastation, seemed likely. Yet where, during the 'phoney war' period, there had been a degree of indifference, now there was a closing of ranks. It was not that morale was high, nor that anybody believed Britain was likely to win the war: rather the war was accepted. The public decided to try and survive it as best it could.

Broadcasting contributed to this shift in mood. It ceased to be merely exhortative. It became more sensitive to popular feeling and, in consequence, more successful in moulding or at least channelling public opinion.

Dunkirk meant that the war changed from being an affair of soldiers abroad to one of civilians at home. It was quickly followed by the Battle of Britain and then the blitz. The kind of war that people had expected had arrived. Yet, though devastating, the catastrophic effects widely predicted in the 1930s did not occur. Survivors went on with what Churchill called 'their job of living through the blitz'. Even Mass Observation, which documented the panic and virtual disintegration of civilian life in the worst hit towns at some times during the winter, noted the remarkable capacity of the public to adapt to new conditions. In London, Tom Harrisson wrote, 'the unfailing regularity' of German attacks 'greatly raised the ability to adjust, and created the best organized centre in the country'.

The First World War was traumatic partly because the horror of a large-scale modern conflict had been far greater than anybody had ever imagined. The Second World War – especially on the civilian front – was bearable precisely because literature, memory, and rhetoric had led everybody to expect a repetition. Yet civilians in cities, like men in trenches, were prisoners. In the First World War the troops called trenches on the Western front by familiar names, Piccadilly, Liverpool Street, Elephant and Castle, Penny Lane. In 1940 it was the real places in Britain which suffered. They could not escape. There were civilian front and relief lines. In the First World War men would be regularly moved back from the front to security behind the lines. In the Second World War (as Titmuss argued) the underprivileged survived the stress of attack partly because there was a variety of 'safety valves' they could use. The government never stopped the nightly 'trekking' out of the city centres, nor did it resist the take-over of tube stations as deep shelters. On any one night of the blitz seven out of ten Londoners slept in their beds. But in any single week during the blitz nearly everyone spent at least a night in the shelters or the equivalent. Civilians thus survived the stress partly because – like the soldiers in the First World War – they took some relief from the front.

The prevailing atmosphere in 1940 amongst the civilian ranks was, as in the 1914 army, one of 'us' against 'them'. The opposition was as much to the unbelievable bureaucracy of British administration, as to the Nazis themselves. Strachey expressed this mood when he wrote:

There is no public record of the labour of the interdepartmental committee, of the co-ordinating committee, the Board of Enquiry, or of the Treasury minute, or indeed of the final Cabinet minute which settled upon the word 'incident' as the designation of what takes place when a bomb falls on a street.

One way of dealing with the Second World War was to refer firmly to the First. Like many of his listeners the broadcaster J. B. Priestley's own image of fighting was based on memories of 1914–18, and he particularly liked to draw parallels between trench life in the First World War and civilian mores in this one.

In his memoirs, Priestley referred to a folksong of the Great War:

> 'It's hanging on the old barbed wire
> I've seen 'em, I've seen 'em.'
> ... [E]ven the devilish enemy, that death-trap the wire, has somehow been accepted, recognized, acknowledged, almost with affection.

A similar point about public attitudes in the Second World War was made by John Strachey:

> No the people didn't call Germans Huns ... or dirty bastards. No one knows in what region of the unconscious the English people decided that their formidable enemy were best called Jerry.... There is in it an acceptance of destiny; of a destiny to resist. There is a refusal to take the panoply of the German might at its own evaluation.

Both writers are pointing to an attitude of familiarity, though not of contempt, for the enemy. This had first developed amongst soldiers in the proximity of the trenches. In the First World War it had separated them both from those who lived in the security of high commands, and from everyone in the safety of home. In the Second, such irony was an appropriate attitude for civilians' nightly encounters with bombers.

To what extent did the BBC lead, follow, or play a part in the creation of a new rhetoric to handle the experience of being bombed nightly?

The war brought the blue joke and an anarchistic, almost surreal, assault on authority to the radio. Shows like ITMA (It's That Man Again) never challenged the basis of authority, rather they consolidated it by making a joke of its misuse. In the 1930s radio comics had been warned that there were to be 'no gags on Scotsmen, Welshmen, clergymen, drink or medical matters'. ITMA thrived on innuendo, and on a skilful nudging at the previously taboo.

The programme was based on a formula. It had a repertoire of characters with stock phrases. Funf, 'the enemy agent with the feet of sauerkraut', made a joke of the spy panic of 1940. 'This is Funf speaking,' he would intone muffled by a glass. 'After you Claude – No, after you Cyril,' RAF pilots would quip as they queued to begin the attack, using another ITMA catchphrase. Each programme had eighteen-and-a-half minutes of talk into which an attempt was made to pack 'at least one hundred laughs'.[4]

A great strength of the show was its topicality. The writers visited factories and army camps to pick up current slang. The programme would be rewritten up to the hour before it was broadcast in order to include jokes on the latest news. ITMA summed up public frustration and gave it vent. In an early show transmitted from Bush House, itself next door to the Ministry of Works, Tommy Handley issued a memo. 'To all concerned in the Office of Twerps. Take notice that from today, September the twenty-fourth, I the Minister of Aggravation, have power to confiscate, complicate and commandeer.' In 1940 there was a period of remorseless exhortation of the public by the government. Frank Owen noted in the literary magazine, *Horizon*, that he was obliged to pass thirty-seven government posters on the way from his house to the Post Office. The Ministry of Food was particularly active in impressing on the public the virtues of the carrot. An ITMA sketch took note:

> *Door opens.* Voice: Do you know what you can do with a carrot?
> Tommy Handley: Yer.
> *Door closes.*

Frank Worsley, the producer, thought that the humour of ITMA was 'the closest radio had come to the everyday jokes that ordinary people have always made. ... The characters were not trying to be funny in themselves, they were only funny in relation to the situation.'

One of the show's most popular characters was 'Mrs Mopp, the vamping vassal with the tousled tassle', a charlady who worked for a pompous civic dignitary. 'Can I do you now sir?' she would ask. Mrs Mopp was perhaps the most famous version of a familiar figure of the period. She glares at German bombers during an attack in an *Express* cartoon by Giles (20 November 1940). 'Never mind about it not being arf wot we're giving them – lets git 'ome,' demands her husband. The same figure – phlegmatic and grumpily imperturbable – was dug out of ruins. She was a mythical figure, and real people were frequently credited with her well-known characteristics. 'Mrs Wells is an obstinate woman,' John Strachey wrote about one lady who survived an air raid. 'You may drop big bombs on her, you may kill her dearly loved husband before her eyes, you may bury herself and her daughter under her home: but you do not alter her.' People who signed themselves 'Mrs Mopp' sent letters to the *Listener* and the *Radio Times*; she was discussed in the *New Statesman* and she asked the Brains Trust questions.

Mrs Mopp was an image of the working-class woman at war. Her characteristics were an indefatigable appetite for work, and stubbornness. She did not mean to be heroic, but simply to get on with things. Titmuss saw her in 'a certain Mrs B., a beetroot-seller by trade', who brings order and comfort to a shelter in Islington but who returns daily to her stall.

When 'charladies' had first been mentioned in a broadcast in 1938 by John Hilton, the programme received hundreds of letters correcting his language. He should have called them 'char-women' for, wrote the aggrieved listeners, they were hardly ladies.[5] By 1942 charladies were featuring regularly in BBC programmes – recognition of a kind of the importance and power of working-class women. 'Kitchen front' programmes were broadcast 'for the busy working woman – the charlady'. 'Mrs Mopp', said Priestley on the radio, 'could easily believe there weren't any women in Germany ... just tramping, bragging, swaggering males, silly little boys.' 'When I think of the country now,' said another speaker on the Home Service at the height of the blitz (*Listener*, 9 September 1941), 'I see representing the country an embattled Mrs Mopp shaking her fist at the sky. "I'll do yer," she says, "I'll do yer".'

The other woman the BBC gave the nation was 'the girl next door', Vera Lynn. She sang sweet but not sexy songs. The typical 'crooning' style implied an intimate relationship between the singer and her listener. This was hardly appropriate, and possibly embarrassing, to the communal listeners of the Forces Programme. Vera Lynn was the solution. A Vera Lynn song was a cross between a hymn and a pub song.

Yet nostalgia and sentiment were not thought by the BBC to be proper fare for fighting men. 'Why should we hear so much from Vera Lynn?' Deputy Director Graves wrote angrily. 'How can men fit themselves for battle with these debilitating tunes in their ears?' The BBC Board of Governors remarked testily, 'Sincerely Yours deplored – but popularity noted'.[6] Military authorities demanded something more martial, yet the show survived, simply because it had such a vast and enthusiastic audience. 'The girl next door' was loyal, sincere, faithful, ordinary, and unsophisticated. She was 'the mainstay of most war fiction', Tom Harrisson noted in a review of war literature written in *Horizon* (December 1941) and was the heroine of a number of films.

'The people are changing'

According to contemporary commentators, the war made the public more serious-minded. This view has been accepted by later historians. Perhaps it should be qualified. Robert Silvey certainly felt in 1946 that there was no evidence that public taste had 'deepened'. Val Gielgud, Director of Drama during the war, recalls that when a 1940 production of *Hamlet* was interrupted at the grave scene, the BBC was inundated with letters from people who wanted to know what happened next. Yet there was undoubtedly a shift in interests. The public appetite for news broadcasts became insatiable. Less predictably, the audiences for serious music increased sharply, and drama ratings doubled between 1939 and 1941. At the start of hostilities the BBC had assumed that the people would be 'too tired for much heavy stuff', and in too sombre a mood to appreciate variety. Both assumptions were revealing – and both proved wrong.

It was generally believed that the masses were becoming more informed, and the success of programmes like the Brains Trust was seen as evidence of this. 'One of the surprises of wartime radio', wrote Howard Thomas, the programme's producer, 'is that five men discussing philosophy, art and science, should have a regular audience of ten million listeners.' As many people listened to the Brains Trust as to the most popular variety shows. Such was the influence of current affairs and discussion broadcasting that the Brains Trust formula replaced orthodox debating in innumerable social clubs and societies. It was particularly popular with local Conservative Associations.

The Brains Trust panel consisted of three regular members and two visiting guests. The original trio were Julian Huxley, the scientist, the philosopher Joad, and Commander Campbell, a retired soldier. In retrospect Campbell seems like a character from Evelyn Waugh, or perhaps Captain W. E. Johns – an enjoyable overdrawn caricature with a background of exotic experience: he claimed to be able to sleep with his eyes open, to have solved the mystery of the *Marie Celeste*, to have seen and smelt sea serpents, and to have 'married' a South Sea Island girl by eating some fish with her.

Brains Trust questions were wide-ranging. 'Why should we learn algebra?' asked a class of Manchester schoolgirls. 'Why can you tickle other people but not yourself?' asked a bus conductor. 'What is hate?' enquired a schoolmistress. A group of RAF pilots who asked why flies could land on ceilings started a dispute which lasted months. To be mentioned on the Brains Trust was fame indeed. A week after *War and Peace* had been recommended by the panel it had gone out of print. This kind of impact was hard to ignore. In 1941 the Ministry of Food was exhorting women to make the new, economical, soya 'Joad in the Hole'.

The importance of the show was recognized by Whitehall in other ways. There was concern about the programme straying into delicate political areas, highlighted by the fact that Joad and Huxley were socialists. In 1942 questions on religion were banned because the churches complained that the programme had an agnostic bias. In 1943 the government banned the discussion of politics, and MPs were excluded from the panel. When Huxley attacked patent medicines and called for a National Health Service the Tories complained. After a period of increasing restriction the original panel were forbidden to appear together. From 1943 each was allowed to broadcast only one programme in three.

The Brains Trust was somewhere between a culture and an institution. Like other programmes it provided a new currency of conversation. Women in shelters discussed Campbell's views on hypnosis. (He claimed it could be beneficial: 'I knew a man who put his wife to sleep with it at weekends.') In 1940 the *Listener* reported that Gilbert Murray's jokes were swapped in bus queues. 'Veni, Vidi, Vichy,' he had said. 'I came, I saw, I concurred.'

The success of the Brains Trust was the basis for many theories about public opinion during the war: left-wingers felt that a population interested in the panel's views on social justice would also be susceptible to socialism. Whether or not this was right, the programme presented to the listener an image of himself as engaged, participant, and capable of confounding experts. Perhaps the real significance of the Brains Trust was that it represented a shift not just in public attitudes, but in the Corporation's willingness to cater for them. Despite restrictions and political interference the Trust provided for and encouraged an immense public curiosity about the natural world, the world of affairs, and about questions of ethics, philosophy, and psychology, and in so doing it began to foster a less aloof and distant image of the Corporation.

Yet the most dramatic image of the radio at war is of families clustered around their sets listening with reverence to speeches by Churchill, the news, or J. B. Priestley's Sunday night talks. These commanded some of the largest audiences ever known. 'By 1941 over 50 per cent of the adult population listened to them,' reported Silvey. It is therefore worth considering them closely.

Before the war the BBC had rarely allowed Churchill to broadcast. The Corporation even censored him after the war had begun. He was considered too anti-German. Churchill had come to hate the BBC. Yet his speeches as Prime Minister, always delivered first to parliament, were perhaps the most dramatic events of wartime broadcasting. He claimed that he merely gave words to what people felt: 'The people's will was resolute and remorseless, I only expressed it, I had the luck to be called upon to give the roar.' Churchill believed that military success, rather than propaganda, was the only way to win a war. 'If words could kill,' he broadcast in 1939, 'we would all be dead already.' Despite his claim to the contrary, Churchill was of course an expert propagandist, and the government, whatever it said in public, remained desperately concerned with the public mood throughout the war.

If Churchill expressed confidence in the people, J. B. Priestley claimed to represent them. His first series of 'Postscripts' started after Dunkirk at the peak listening time after the Sunday evening news. The series turned him into a household name. 'I found myself', he wrote, 'tied like a man to a gigantic balloon – to one of those bogus reputations that only the media know how to inflate.'

Churchill combined an appreciation of practical problems with a deep, almost metaphysical romanticism, based on an appeal to honour, national pride, and a sense of history. Priestley was just as practical but looked to the future. He helped to give the war an aim beyond military victory by focussing attention on the world to be built in the aftermath. Priestley talked about a level of society with which Churchill had had little contact and of which he understood less. While Churchill talked of Henry V and quoted Macaulay, Priestley's examples were Falstaff and Sam Weller.

Priestley's success, however, had essentially the same foundation as that of Churchill. It was based on an appeal to traditional values; indeed, on an appeal to a traditional social order. Priestley's Postscripts made a virtue of getting on with the job in hand, even when there were no alternatives. Like Churchill, Priestley linked current events with the past. He reminded listeners after Dunkirk of Hardy's descriptions of the Napoleonic wars, and described it as another English epic. 'So typical of us, so absurd, yet so grand and gallant that you hardly know whether to laugh or cry.' Official propaganda, Priestley claimed, encouraged people to see the war as an interruption. It was, he said, rather 'a chapter in a tremendous history'.

Postscripts continually emphasized the rural nature of Britain. In the First World War officers read *The Field* and *Country Life* in the trenches, and war poets contrasted the seasons and images of nature with the war. Priestley, broadcasting to the most urbanized population in the world, referred in ten out of his seventeen talks to the country and nature. 'I don't think that there has ever been a lovelier English spring than this last one', he said at the start of the Battle of Britain, 'now melting into full summer.' Later, after the news that the British had been obliged to sink the French fleet, he started the broadcast by saying that he had seen two heartening things that week. 'The first was a duck and the second was a dig in the ribs.' The duck swimming with her ducklings, 'triumphant little parcels of light', was in a country pond; the dig in the ribs was given by Churchill to Bevin in parliament before the grim announcement. Priestley talked about factories and the blitz, British restaurants and London humour, but the village or the Welsh hills were more frequently the setting for his talks. Priestley provided his listeners with a way of handling their experiences. 'I don't like danger,' he said in November 1940, when Londoners were facing their twenty-eighth consecutive night of bombing, 'but the fact that we are all at least within reach of danger seems to me a better, not a worse, feature of the war.' In the First World War men in the trenches, and the writers who recorded their lives, had survived its horrors by rejecting romantic heroism. In the Second, Priestley made the everyday and commonplace heroic.

Priestley demanded 'more flags and less red tape, hard work and high jinks'. He challenged the old order and called for more social justice. Like Ed Murrow later, he praised the courage of individuals and criticized their leaders for ineptitude. In his second series of Postscripts he proposed to talk about money, class, and equality. 'I received', he wrote, 'two letters.' One was from the Ministry of Information, telling him 'that the BBC was responsible for the decision to take me off the air'. The other was from the BBC saying 'that a directive had come from the Ministry of Information to end my broadcasting'. They were both anxious to make it clear that 'the order to shut me up had come from elsewhere'. The Minister of Information, Brendan Bracken, had seen Priestley earlier and warned him to say more about Dickens and less about the government. As with the Brains Trust there had been complaints in parliament about Priestley's socialism. Churchill felt it intolerable that the BBC should broadcast criticism of the government, and ordered Priestley to be gagged. Already, within the Corporation, the Controller of Talks had written to Ryan, the Controller of News:

> Priestley has definite social and political views which he puts over in his broadcasts. ... The question which I want to raise is one of principle, whether any single person should be given the opportunity of acquiring such influence ... merely on the grounds of his merits as a broadcaster, which are, of course, very great.[7]

Priestley's removal was widely greeted as a sign of government censorship. The *New Statesman* printed a selection of the letters of protest, 'representative of the many others we have received'. Even the *Radio Times* printed letters of complaint for several weeks.

The removal of Priestley showed how limited was the official concern for reform. Priestley's programmes proposed different priorities from the war aims laid down by Churchill. To talk of new orders and redistribution was, in the view of the government, merely to distract the public from the urgent business of winning the war. Yet it was at precisely this point in the war that even the officials in the Ministry of Information were beginning to urge the government to plan post-war reconstruction. The public, they argued, needed the prospect of a better future to enable them to cope with the rigorous present. Priestley had merely started the shift in propaganda a little early. Later it was to be taken up with growing enthusiasm by the government itself.

Harold Nicolson dismissed the talks as 'sentimental banalities'. Priestley himself was puzzled by their success. Subsequently they have been seen as a major contribution to a change in public mood. Yet the most notable feature of Priestley's talks was that a concern for ordinary people and their future emerged and was expressed by very traditional images of rural England, village communities, and nature. This was hardly the rhetoric of a revolutionary.

The news

The most important wartime programme was the news. Information about the conduct of the war was the main determinant of morale on the Home Front. Indeed the BBC's claim to accuracy and objectivity was, in itself, a propaganda weapon – a demonstration of the superiority of democracy over totalitarianism. This was particularly true because the BBC – much more than the press – was the 'voice of Britain'. Unlike newspapers, its messages reached a wide foreign audience in neutral and occupied countries. Broadcast news also seemed to be an authoritative reflection of official policy and opinion. There were allegations on the left that the real facts of the situation were kept from the people; these were particularly relevant during the period of the 'phoney war' when many on the left expected imminent defeat. The Service Ministries, on the other hand, viewed radio news with suspicion for a different reason: they saw it as a threat to morale.

News, like everything else for the duration, was determined by the necessity of winning the war. The Corporation's sense of priorities was often very close to that of the government. There was narrow-minded and bigoted censorship. But some of the omissions which the BBC was later blamed for were more a result of the contemporary understanding of what could be done in the war, than of deliberate suppression. Thus, for example, the BBC did not so much fail to inform the public about the holocaust – indeed what it knew it told – rather this news was not given a prominent position, and there was little consideration of what might be done to save the remaining Jews. This was largely because the BBC accepted the government's views that the allied victory was the only 'realistic' condition for effective action.[8]

However, such was the demand for news that when little of the real thing was available because of military inactivity, the public created its own. Rumours acquired a special influence. The Ministry of Information waged a relentless and unsuccessful campaign against them. Mass Observation divided them into three categories: impressive, informative, and inhibited.[9] The first were a compensation for non-involvement in the war; the second were based on an attempt to improve the teller's prestige, and the third kind, the inquiry claimed, were based on fear. Mass Observation argued that rumours arose from a general distrust of published and broadcast sources, and so were a product of official censorship. But they may also have been a simple reflection of anxiety, a context in which to talk about the war. The BBC always argued that rumours could be stopped only by more comprehensive news.

Several departments contended for the right to control the BBC. Even more believed that they deserved it. The Ministry of Information was concerned to encourage morale at home; the Political Intelligence Department to scavenge information from abroad; the Foreign Office to maintain friendly relations with allies and neutral countries; while the Ministry of Economic Warfare was interested in the immediate effects on the enemy's industry and morale, even if this involved ignoring the interests of the neutrals.

At the start of the war an official wrote that the Ministry of Information 'recognized that for the purpose of war activities the BBC is to be regarded as a Government Department'. (He added: 'I wouldn't put it quite like this in any public statement.'[10]) This implies a rather different relationship between broadcasting and the government than that which the BBC claimed. Yet the control by the ministries was often irregular and contradictory. For a time even the BBC's Director Generalship was divided: one Director to say yes to the ministry (broadcasters joked) and the other to say no to the staff.[11]

The Ministry of Information, which had most direct control over broadcasts, had been the butt of much humour when it was formed: the inefficiency of its organization seemed to be surpassed only by the scale of its notional operation. It was believed to be staffed by brilliant but dotty amateurs. Nigel Riley (who resigned from the ministry) pointed out that in 1940 of 999 ministry employees only 47 were journalists. The ministry was supposed to build morale, yet until 1941 it based its judgments on little except hunches and intuition. Stories about the department's gentlemanly eccentricities were legion. One incident involved a ministry official dispatched to lecture in the provinces on the wickedness of gossip. Complaints came back that his speech had been almost entirely composed of long quotations in Latin. 'Oh,' replied the department, 'Latin? It's usually Greek with him.'

Reith, who was appointed Minister of the Department in 1940, was deeply depressed by its pointlessness and disorganization. Nevertheless, before Churchill dismissed him later in the same year, he had begun to define the work of the ministry and to discipline its staff. Reith believed that it was essential to have news and propaganda controlled by the same authority. By the end of the war, Ian Maclaine has argued, the ministry was actively defending the press and broadcasting from the Service Ministries.

Broadcasting and the press

Which did people believe more, the newspapers or broadcasting? Intellectuals certainly did not trust the Corporation. They recalled its role during the General Strike. 'What could possibly take the place of newspapers?' wrote the editor of the *Picture Post* (18 December 1940). 'There surely cannot be any sane man or woman who would argue that the Ministry of Information, or its near relation the BBC, have so far offered a serious alternative to the newspapers in conveying information?' Yet there were also grounds for distrusting the press. Newspapers had deceived the public in the interest of the Establishment over the abdication crisis.

The war heightened a long-standing rivalry between press and radio. The *Listener* was voicing a widely held BBC view in 1941 when it claimed that while radio was concerned to report events as they occurred, news in the press was regarded as entertainment. A Home Service talk in March 1941 maintained that newspaper stories might have come 'from a report from a Mexican correspondent of a Portuguese journal quoted in a Roman paper'. The public had little idea of the tricks employed by the press in presenting events.

Mass Observation reported that radio was the most important medium of information in 1941, and that by the end of the war it had replaced the newspapers for some kinds of news, particularly immediate accounts of battles.[12] When more systematic surveys asked people to rank the media on which they based their opinions, radio came far below personal experience and several points below newspapers. Yet between January 1940 and the end of the war in Europe the authority of the press fell steadily, from third to sixth place in people's ranking. In contrast the position of broadcasting remained constant throughout this period between fifth and sixth place.[13] By the end of the war people had come to trust broadcasting more – at least in comparison with other sources of information.

Topicality and the BBC

The Second World War made topicality the dominant news value. German scoops had shocked the public and done much to discredit the Corporation at the start of the war. Topicality then became the key weapon in the BBC's defence against the expansionist censorship of the Service Ministries. The Ministry of Information recognized the importance of getting news on the air as quickly as possible. A memorandum ordered 'Action to strengthen confidence in BBC news. Confirmed items to be included in earliest available bulletins, even at the expense of friction with the Press.'[14]

From 1939 the BBC's news section grew rapidly, gathering material from an increasingly wide range of sources, including monitoring foreign broadcast sections. The BBC also developed the ultimately 'topical' news, the 'on the spot' or 'outside' broadcast. By late 1944 teams of broadcasters were regularly accompanying British units both in France and the Far East. Commentators developed a way of reporting conditions at the front which related the soldiers' experience more closely to their families at home. 'If you've got a brother or a husband or a sweetheart in Normandy today,' started one famous report from the war zone in 1944, 'there's a fair chance you might see your name riding along the dusty roads, your name on a truck, on a lorry, on a bulldozer, on a tank, somewhere in France.' The style of war reporting was also closely modelled on an earlier form of outside broadcasting: sports programmes. A reporter describing a bombing raid on Hamburg was angrily compared by a *Radio Times* correspondent (30 September 1944) to 'someone at a Welsh Rugby International – not a person watching death and destruction'.

The war led to a victory for those who believed in the superiority of the scientific assessment of public opinion. At the start of the war the government believed that this could be tested by consulting pressure groups and opinion leaders. By the end of the war the public was being polled, probed, and tested by a multitude of official surveys. These new sources of information made it clear that in everyday matters of which the public had experience, it was essential that news should be given quickly and accurately. If people had been bombed out of their homes and their towns devastated, it was imperative that the BBC should be able to say so. Knowledge of the extent of destruction was an important factor in coming to terms with it. At the start of the blitz Maurice Gorham had written, 'The news sounded all the more alarming for being so vague.' But by November 1940, although scrupulously censored for information which might be useful to the Germans, it had become more precise. In

Britain, at least, 'topicality' became the dominant news value as a consequence of the war.

The 'manner' of the news

Before the war the BBC's announcers had been anonymous: this was felt to be more dignified. However, from the start of the war they were named, and this innovation excited considerable comment at the time. The change was introduced in order that, in the case of invasion, the public would not be taken in by orders issued by the enemy. After the war it was discovered that the Germans had carefully trained substitute announcers to sound like Alvar Lidell and Stuart Hibberd to be used during the proposed invasion of England. However, the BBC maintained some pre-war standards. The announcers, despite sleeping in a lavatory adjoining the studio, and living for days underground, continued to present the news in dress suits. When the BBC received a direct hit which made an audible thump in the middle of a bulletin, the announcer paused, a whispered 'Are you all right?' was heard, and then he continued, with Corporation-bred aplomb, to read the news without comment.

Before 1939 style had often seemed more important than comprehensibility in BBC news broadcasting; during the war ease of understanding became paramount. There was a new anxiety about syntax and vocabulary, and scripts were scrutinized for difficult words and constructions. The Corporation also became more sensitive about the voices of its news readers. Clement Attlee, Deputy Prime Minister as well as leader of the Labour Party, complained that the monopoly of upper-class voices was likely to offend workers. Indeed this anxiety was shared, and a Home Morale Emergency Committee in the Ministry of Information suggested that 'something might be done to diminish the present predominance of the cultured voice upon the wireless. Every effort should be made to bring working-class people to the microphone.'

The Corporation responded by employing Wilfred Pickles, whose voice combined the properties of being both working-class and northern. Broadcasting had developed a unique pitch of speech in the 1930s and 1940s, a high and hard voice. One news-reader, Joseph Macleod, wrote that he had two voices. One was low, gruff, and Scottish. The other, which he always used when broadcasting, was 'young, suave, rather pedantic and intolerant, a voice in a higher register'. The war also made the tone of voice a more sensitive matter than before. Macleod lost his job, ostensibly because his style of announcing was too 'tendentious'. He was accused of putting too much emphasis on certain words, and apparently sneering at the government. He was dismissed, according to Harold Nicolson, soon after Bracken had 'spoken openly about the left-wing fanaticism of certain members of the BBC, especially in the news room'. Clearly the tone of an announcement could establish the public attitude towards the news. One news-reader wrote of the problems posed, for example, by announcing the suicide of the Commander of the *Graf Spee* after the ship had been lost. If the announcer sounded pleased the item 'would sound gloating. While if he sounded sympathetic it would sound fifth column.' The BBC's solution to this problem was that announcers should sound as 'official, neutral, and unaffected as possible'. The BBC announcer, it had been decided, should sound like a civil servant.

Another, more urgent, reason why announcers became so careful of their words and their timing was the problem of the sarcastic comments which German broadcasters had at first managed to slip in during pauses in bulletins. The only way to stop this was to read the news smoothly and unhesitatingly. By the last months of 1940 the only words a German commentator managed to intrude was an exasperated, 'Oh that's not fair!'

The news, enemies, allies, and neutrals

Another, more romantic image of the Corporation at war was of the BBC as provocateur, spy, and supporter of resistance movements. The Corporation recruited many refugees to staff the foreign broadcasts, and these formed a new and exotic element within the Corporation's staid departments. 'The Hungarian Unit,' read a dry memo of the period, 'a duel averted by Duckworth.' A recurring tension in all of these sections was between the demands of the centrally controlled news service, and the interests of individual nations. The Danish section complained that they were not allowed to deal with events in Denmark itself in sufficient detail. According to Bennett, the correspondents who supplied the service with its information from neutral Sweden even organized a news strike in an attempt to change the BBC's policy.

Other countries complained that the broadcasts implicitly criticized the occupied countries. Listeners who took risks to hear the BBC felt that they should be complimented on their resilience, rather than condemned for their failure to do more. Indeed, like home broadcasting, the Foreign Service suffered from a tendency to exhort rather than inform or support in the first year of the war. Richard Crossman argued that too many of those employed in directing propaganda had come from the advertising world. 'Do you suffer from National Socialism?' was their line. 'Then buy British Democracy!'

Another tension was the extent to which the broadcasts should encourage (as one BBC administrator put it) 'listeners to *do* something rather than *feel* something'. It seemed presumptuous to instruct foreigners in sabotage when the British had little experience of it, and were themselves safe. More significantly, the dramatic success of the 'V' campaign, when in 1941 Dutch, French, Belgians, and Scandinavians in occupied Europe were asked to use the letter 'V' as a rallying sign, revealed the dangers of such a strategy. In one Vichy town, Moulins, graffiti Vs for 'Victoire' were so numerous that the Germans imposed fines and penalties on the whole town. In Prague 'multitudes of little Vs had appeared on all sides'. From Belgium it was reported that 'never has so much chalk been sold so quickly'. The campaign, initiated almost accidentally, was evidently a success. Its effects, however, were disastrous. It merely exposed those who were prepared to be active resisters to the Germans at a time when there was no possibility of any allied invasion. Men lost their lives in a campaign with no practical goal. In addition, the BBC was in effect making foreign policy. The campaign was stopped. Crossman later argued that it was a great mistake for those involved in psychological warfare to suggest that they have 'a mystical substitute for military action'. Broadcasting had to be as concerned with preventing resisters from acting unwisely as with prompting them to action when the right moment came.

It is not easy to assess the effect of the BBC's foreign broadcasts. Indeed it is difficult enough to decide what the overall impact of resistance was on the German war effort. Every clandestine listener, however, had already committed an act of resistance, and the BBC's service provided information – even if of a selective kind – to populations who were starved of news. The BBC's bulletins provided most of the material for the underground press in occupied Europe. M. R. D. Foot has concluded that the role of broadcasting was to 'keep the mechanism of the canal gates of freedom oiled and in decent order, till the water levels of fluctuating public opinion could move up and down again'.

This image of the heroic BBC was not, however, shared in the USA. 'To Americans, not very enthusiastic about British cooking, the warmed up remnants of the original meal were not very palatable. News bulletins – one half an hour long – often contained items from yesterday's American press,' wrote an academic, Emmanuel Katz, in 1944. The constant stress on the collapse of social barriers in Britain only emphasized how tenacious they had been, and to what extent they still survived. However, American public opinion was never wholly pro-

British, and the attitudes towards broadcasting were part of a wider feeling about the war.

In matters concerning the allies the BBC's policy was dictated by government. When the Russians started to fight the Nazis, the cover of the *Listener* was devoted to a pageant in honour of Russia, while the *Radio Times* was packed with tributes to Russian workers. This was a period of extraordinary enthusiasm for Russia and all things Russian. As Elizabeth Bowen wrote of a character in her wartime novel, *The Heat of the Day*, 'The effect of her was, at first glance, that of a predominating number of London girls this summer when the idealization of Russia was at its height – that of a flying try at the Soviet comrade type.' However, the BBC was told not to include the *Internationale* in the popular Sunday evening concert of allied national anthems. The Corporation abandoned the series rather than be embarrassed by the sound of the communist song.

Conclusion: 'my country true or false?'

In 1939 the Home News Service editor had said that in the event of war the BBC would 'tell the truth and nothing but the truth, even if the news was horrid'. By the end of the war the Corporation was arguing that the pursuit of truth had been victorious. 'Today', the 1946 *Handbook* proclaimed, 'we can point to the history of broadcasting in Europe and say that certain good principles in broadcasting have defeated the worst possible principles.' During the war the BBC seldom lied if it could avoid doing so. Indeed as the war began with a series of devastating defeats for the allies it might have been difficult to disguise the situation. However, that the BBC could claim independence was at least partly because it suited the government that it should do so. For the government continually intervened in the conduct of the Corporation, and merely chose not to control it directly.

Veracity, however, was perhaps the only acceptable aim for a democratic news policy. More practically, telling the truth was probably the most effective propaganda with which to face a sustained war. 'You must hate propaganda to do it well,' Richard Crossman wrote, 'and we British did hate it and therefore took more trouble to conceal what we were doing.'

The contemporary judgment of the BBC's performance was enthusiastic. 'In a world of poison the BBC became the great antiseptic,' said Léon Blum, the French socialist leader. Recently the claims of broadcasters that they have independence have been challenged. 'Bias' and opinion are fundamental conditions of the production of news, not accidental pathologies. Hence the work of the BBC during the war has been viewed with greater scepticism. A belief in its independence is little more than a self-adulatory part of the British myth.

The BBC cannot simply be distinguished from its totalitarian opponents in terms of its intentions. In both Britain and Germany broadcasting was seen as a crucial instrument in the war effort. Indeed both countries even shared practical concerns: hopes should never be raised unless they could be met; controversy between enemy allies was, as Goebbels claimed, 'a small plant which thrives best when it is left to its natural growth'. He continued that 'News policy is a weapon of war. Its purpose is to wage war and not to give out information.' The BBC also viewed news as part of propaganda. However, the use of the 'news' weapon was determined by quite different constraints and pressures in a democratic society.

British home propaganda depended on an informed public. The BBC remained a civilian institution, whose employees saw themselves primarily as broadcasters. Once committed to a policy of informing the public, the war acted as an incentive within the Corporation for an improvement in the news services. Although the BBC broadcast optimistic official figures for enemy fighters shot down in the Battle of Britain, tended to treat raids on Germany as victories, cut, edited, and censored news, its main purpose remained that of telling people what was happening.

If the Service Ministries and the government were concerned to limit the amount and kind of information broadcast, the main pressure within the Corporation was to tell the people as much as possible. This did not mean telling them everything, but the heritage of obligations imposed by the Corporation's public service monopoly meant that the public knew more than might have been expected.

In Britain, Asa Briggs has observed, the mystique of radio meant little. In Germany, the new medium had been credited with almost magical powers of suggestion. These views affected the way in which broadcasting was used in both countries. The dominating image of the BBC during the war (indeed the dominating image of the war in Britain) was one of relentless domesticity. 'Every time I listen to these programmes I cry,' a factory worker told Mass Observation about a radio link-up between soldiers and their families. 'You hear the women giving the men their messages ... they can hardly get through sometimes.' Another describes her day. She gets back from work 'about nine o'clock, and they've got the wireless on. Dad's asleep in the chair – the kiddies are in bed.' Families were united around the radio; 52 per cent of respondents to one survey always listened to the news with their families, 76 per cent preferred to do so if possible. In Titmuss's classic account of the development of welfare policy during the war, he saw the security of the family as the crucial guarantor of good morale. By 1945 the radio had become an essential element of the image of the family in its home.

Before the war the BBC had regarded the regular expectation of particular kinds of programmes as 'lazy listening'. In contrast, during the war the BBC made considerable efforts to develop such habits. Regular programmes produced predictable audiences. The knowledge of these could be used in propaganda appeals and information campaigns. Indeed the predictability of the daily broadcasts was a kind of security in itself. 'At the moment, all similes for safety are slipping,' wrote C. A. Hodson in 1941. 'How can one say as safe as houses?' But the BBC at least seemed dependable. Modern programme planning, a matter of inducing habit, was at least in part a consequence of the war.

By 1945 the Corporation had apparently become less aloof. Programmes like ITMA, Hi Gang, and Worker's Playtime introduced a more vigorous tradition of speech and humour to broadcasting, one that was closer to the music hall tradition than the well-mannered 'variety' of pre-war programmes. They were part of a feeling that the British war, unlike that of the prudish Germans, was taken seriously, but never solemnly. Even government propaganda came to appreciate the 'common man's sense of humour':

Those who have the will to win
Eat potatoes in their skin,
Knowing that the sight of peelings
Deeply hurts Lord Woolton's feelings

exhorted the Ministry of Food. Humour was part of the protective self-image with which the British faced air attacks and the possibility of invasion. It was an image that the BBC helped to create, and was determined to encourage. Harold Nicolson even broadcast talks on the subtle superiority of British humour to that of the status-conscious Germans (*Listener*, December 1942).

There was, of course, another war which did not get much broadcasting time. This was one of apathy, and dingy making-do rather than cheerful resilience. Life in shelters was not always a protracted East End party; it was squalid, with inadequate sanitary arrangements, little food, and chaotic overcrowding. Novels of the period document the dreariness and austerity of life in Britain after several years of war, and newspapers campaigned against the petty-mindedness of official regulations and bureaucracy. The BBC did not campaign for the public on any of these issues.

However, the Corporation succeeded in producing a dignified but humorous image of what kind of people the British were. It was not that the BBC 'came closer to the people'. Rather it represented them as a liberal, compassionate, reforming administrator might have seen them. The BBC innovated within a repertoire of very traditional ideas. Subsequently it has been argued that there was a significant change in public mood during the war. The people became determined that there would be greater social justice after it. Certainly the war changed the BBC, and it changed public taste.

Yet the day after the war in Europe ended, the public changed again. The audience for the news dropped by half, and never returned to wartime levels.

Notes

1. D. G. Bridson, *Prospero and Ariel: The Rise and Fall of Radio* (London, Gollancz, 1971), p. 269.
2. D. Cooper, *Old Men Forget* (London, Hart-Davis, 1953), p. 79.
3. Harold Hobson, *Daily Express* (14 January 1940).
4. T. Kavanagh, *Tommy Handley* (London, Hodder & Stoughton, 1949), p. 73.
5. *Listener* correspondence, *BBC Written Archives* (John Hilton).
6. Board of Governors' Minutes (5 July 1941), *BBC Written Archives*.
7. Maconachie to Ryan (6 September 1940), *BBC Written Archives*.
8. See for further development of this example, J. Seaton, 'The BBC and the Holocaust', *European Journal of Communication*, vol. 2, 1, 1987.
9. Mass Observation (October 1940), File 473, 'What the people are talking about today'.
10. A. P. Waterfield to W. Palmer, *Ministry of Information Files*, INF 1/238.
11. A. S. Hibberd, *This is London* (London, Macdonald & Evans, 1950), p. 307.
12. Mass Observation, *The Press and Its Readers* (London, Art & Technics, 1949), p. 41.
13. 'The British Institute of Public Opinion Survey, the attitudes towards the press and broadcasting and other sources of information (1940–5)' in H. Cantril (ed.), *Public Opinion 1935–46* (New Jersey, Princeton University Press, 1951).
14. *Ministry of Information*, INF 1/250, Home Morale Emergency Committee, Item 13 (22 May 1940).

10

Social revolution?

It is a commonplace of twentieth-century social history that world war has been the agent, or at least the catalyst, of major change. What has been less noticed is the extent to which wartime forms of organization – born of the unusual conditions and needs of the moment – have created structural fossils in important areas of policy, surviving immutably in peacetime, but with no particular relevance to the post-war world.

Broadcasting and education provide interesting examples of this process. Both were drastically reorganized at the end of the Second World War. In each case the most striking feature of the reforms was the imposition of a 'tripartite' division, based on a supposed hierarchy of talent. The changes represented a sharp move away from a view of society as an aggregate of individuals towards an official concept of particular groups with separate needs.

Broadcasting

Reith's programme policy depended on an assumption of cultural homogeneity: not that everybody was the same, but that culture was single and undifferentiated. He had been determined to avoid the mediocrity which he believed would accompany freedom of choice. 'It is occasionally indicated to us that we are apparently setting out to give the public what we think they need – not what they want,' he wrote in 1924. 'But few know what they want and very few what they need.' Advisory panels of 'experts' were established to lay down canons of taste in music, and to adjudicate correct pronunciation. Their purpose was to give authority to cultural values, not to represent listeners' interests.

Reith believed that the function of broadcasting was primarily educative: its purpose was to train 'character'. According to this view, your class of origin and what you learnt mattered less than how you lived and how you learnt. This principle was the basis for his programming policy. Men might be unequal, but they could all try equally. Hence the Corporation defended a policy of mixed programming, in which talks, light music, chamber music, quizzes, vaudeville and plays succeeded each other. The service was not planned to provide appropriate listening for different interests, or to allow people to avoid what was serious in favour of the trivial. Reith was determined that the audience should encounter everything that broadcasting could offer.

Mixed programming determined many aspects of the Corporation's policy between the wars. In 1934 a BBC administrator wrote that 'the most advantageous single extension or change in programme policy'[1] would be to stop broadcasting programmes at regular times and so break the audience's conservative listening habits. This was part of the Corporation's campaign against what was contemptuously known as the 'tap' listener 'who wants to have one or more very light programmes available at all hours between breakfast and bedtime'.[2] 'The BBC', the 1932 *Yearbook* claimed, 'definitely aims at having an interval of four or five minutes between programmes ... it is obviously irritating for a listener who, switching on his set to hear, say, the news, finds himself listening to the last minute of an opera or vaudeville turn.' Listening was a serious business.

The BBC's belief in cultural homogeneity was a useful weapon in the defence of its broadcasting monopoly, particularly against the commercial wireless exchanges. These retransmitted a selection of BBC and continental programmes to simple home 'speakers', improving reception and making it cheaper. The number of such stations had risen from 34 in 1929 to 343 by 1935. The BBC argued, in the 1931 *Handbook*, that the relay system

> contains within it forces which uncontrolled might be disruptive of the spirit and intention of the BBC charter. The persons in charge of wireless exchanges have power, by replacing selected items of the Corporation's programmes with transmission from abroad, to alter entirely the general drift of the BBC's programme policy.

The BBC was defending its own position, and what it assumed was a generally recognizable set of cultural values. Reith's objection to audience research was also based on the principle of cultural homogeneity. He did not want to know popular preference, because of the danger that programme organizers would pander to it.

The BBC had a distinctive model of the listener. 'Broadcasting is not mass projection, though it seems to be so, it is an individual intimate business,' wrote Hilda Matheson, the first head of the Talks Department in the *Sociological Review* (no. 3, 1935). The personal relationship between listener and programme was elevated into a principle. The class and tastes of groups of listeners were irrelevant. Any variety in programmes was justified by the changing moods of the average listener and not by reference to the interests of different groups. In this way, 'entertainment' had its appropriate place: it was meant to provide periods of relaxation in the broadcasting diet of the Reithian 'average' listener.

The Reithian approach was paralleled during the 1920s and 1930s by similarly 'unitary' assumptions in state education. The content of state education between the wars was common to all schools: children merely received more or less of it. At the top of the ladder children had access to 'the whole world of learning', while at the bottom they had 'the hems of learning only'.[3] The curriculum was governed by notions of a 'general liberal education', a direct legacy of Matthew Arnold's philosophy of education.

Educational policy reflected the traditional psychology of the nine-teenth century, argued the Spens Report on secondary education in 1938:

> with its emphasis on faculties and its belief in the doctrine of formal education and mental transfer which played an important part in perpetuating a curriculum common to all pupils.

It was assumed that most boys and girls were equipped with the same mental endowments, that most of them developed the same way, and at almost the same rate of progress. Although some scholarships were available to the academic secondary grammar schools, these were very scarce, and most pupils paid fees. University scholarships were even more rare. Yet all the children in grammar schools followed a pattern of education which was designed to secure university places which only 3 per cent of them actually attained. Even in non-academic secondary schools, the curriculum was merely a weaker version of the university-dominated teaching of the grammar schools.

State education, like state broadcasting, was (in theory) designed to enable the hard-working and able to develop those faculties which were regarded as common to all. In education there was also emphasis on the development of 'character', a nebulous and undefined moral concept, taken undiluted from the 'muscular Christian' ethos of leadership training which governed public schools. Until Cyril Burt's ideas on scientific intelligence testing were accepted during the 1940s and 1950s, the ideology of 'character' pervaded educational policy as well as broadcasting.

In many ways, of course, education and broadcasting are not

comparable: for one thing, state education hardly grew at all during the 1930s while broadcasting developed very quickly. For another, broadcasting was centrally controlled with a national monopoly, while education was administered locally, and alongside (rather than in competition with) a prestigious private sector. Nevertheless, broadcasting and schooling as communicators of accepted values have enough in common for the similarity to be striking. The similarities in the organizational changes, which occurred as a result of the impulse for reform created by the Second World War, are more remarkable still.

Reform, the war, and education

The needs of war radically altered education and broadcasting. The Education Act, 1944, which introduced compulsory secondary education for all, has been seen by many as the finest achievement of a great reforming minister, R. A. Butler, who based it on what he described to his biographer, Ralph Harris, as a 'sensationally ingenious report'. More recent assessments have been less enthusiastic. According to Brian Simon,

> Through the late 1940s and 1950s when so much might have been accomplished, the development of secondary education for all was restricted and distorted by the dead hand of a doctrine brought to a point during the depressed 1930s – the doctrine that in effect secondary education is not for all.

The Education Act recommended that schools be reorganized 'firstly to provide opportunities for a special cast of mind to manifest itself ... indeed to develop specialized interests and aptitudes'.[4] The Act was not the result of radical political pressure, but of official initiatives within the Board of Education itself. In 1938 the Spens Report had suggested that 'It is becoming more and more evident that a simple liberal education for all is impractical.' It drew a distinction between those children 'who work with hands, work with tongue, or work with pen' and suggested that 'one child differs from another far more than is generally supposed'. The Norwood Report and the 1944 Act went further and argued that these differences were held in common by groups of children. They distinguished between three kinds, the child 'who is interested in learning for its own sake, who is interested in causes and who can grasp an argument. ... [He] is sensitive ... he is interested in the relatedness of related things ... he will have some capacity to enjoy from an aesthetic point of view.' A child of this kind was to go to a grammar school, the distinct feature of which 'lies in the intellectual ideal which it upholds'. This category of school was to retain the values which had been intended for all schools before the war, and was to produce the new professional and managerial élite.

The second kind of child 'often has an uncanny insight into the intricacies of mechanisms, whereas the subtleties of language construction are too delicate for him. To justify itself to his mind, knowledge must be capable of immediate application.' These children would 'go into industry' and were to attend the new technical schools.

The third kind of child 'may have much ability but it will be in the realm of facts. He is interested in things as they are ... he must have immediate return for his effort.' These residual children were to attend the new secondary modern schools. These schools were to be separate but equal and were, according to the report (incredibly) to have 'parity of prestige'. The purpose of the modern schools was distinct because these children would need education for their leisure: 'This homely aspect of education is often the basis of future happiness, and is as vitally necessary as it can be interesting.' It was implicit in the Norwood Report and the Act that there were children who could think, children who could do, and the rest.

This division of schools and children was not consciously based on any scientific evidence, but was justified on the grounds that 'these rough groupings have in fact established themselves in general educational experience'. Immediately the Act was published Cyril Burt attacked its underlying psychological assumptions. He argued that his own work had long since demolished the myth of separate 'mental types', and that the proposed reforms had overlooked the fundamental discovery of his work on intelligence: that anyone who was above average in any one aspect of intellectual performance was likely to be above average in all of them. 'It is difficult to see', he wrote, 'how even administrative necessity can lead us to discern the indistinguishable and to find three types of mind when they do not exist.' However, Burt's attitude was surprising, for the process of selection and division was to be carried out with his own 'scientific' intelligence testing. More strikingly, the proportions of children which it was projected would attend each kind of school closely approximated to Burt's 'normal curve' of the distribution of intelligence within the population. Indeed, in an article devoted to 'The psychology of listeners', Burt wrote: 'Politically no doubt all men are born equal. Mentally however, as the results of surveys incontestably show, the range of individual differences is far wider than had ever been suspected.'[5]

The classification of children proposed by the Act depended on the war experience of Burt's followers in training and assigning members of the armed services to appropriate jobs. Psychologists used increasingly detailed tests developed from Burt's work, not only to guarantee that the various services had equal shares of intelligent personnel, but also to distinguish between 'skill' and 'character', and to identify a whole range of special mechanical, logical, and clerical abilities. 'The value of vocational or educational classification', wrote Vernon and Barry about their work as psychologists during the war, 'lies not merely in the closer co-ordination of human capacity with job ... but also with their effects on morale.' Workers, they argued, were happier if they were not disturbed by association with those with abilities far beyond, or behind, their own. Thus during the war 'streaming' was developed and rationalized.

The effect of the war is also revealed in the provision of the new 'technical' schools. During the war there had been a shift in the subjects in which children were examined towards the sciences, in response to the increased need for technical skills. Lord Hankey wrote in 1941 that 'Technical colleges, although ill housed, ill equipped and understaffed had responded without hesitation to the needs of the services and industry and had magnificently reorganized themselves to train men and women for the war effort.' It was these experiences, a dramatic increase in the need for technical and scientific workers, and the reorganization of schools and training to produce them, which had led to the creation of the new 'technical schools' and the perception of the 'practically able' child.

In the Act it was expected that these new schools would take some of the children who would previously have gone to grammar schools, and direct them into more technical and industrial work. These schools simply failed to appear. This was partly because money was not available. Also during the war the government had been able to direct the allocation of the entire work-force; in a post-war world this was far more difficult. Moreover, hopes that private industry would seek technically educated school-leavers for training did not materialize; employers continued to prefer young people with a 'general' academic education where they could get them.

R. A. Butler had written in 1942 that

> Education cannot by itself create the social structure of a country. I have to take the world as I find it and the world I find is one in which there is a very diversified range of types. Educational progress must be along the grain of human nature.[6]

Yet arguably the Act and its implementation was precisely an attempt at massive social engineering. It was not, as Simon has argued, merely a rationalization of the status quo, but marked a major change in the official perception of the child. It also represented a new recognition of class, and the fragmentation of culture. The old, liberal culture survived, but was confined to the curricula of the 'professionals' in their grammar schools; while in modern schools children for whom exams were inappropriate were to be taught how to entertain themselves.

Reform, the war, and the BBC

The war also revolutionized the BBC. During the war Reith's 'cultural unity' was abandoned. After a visit to the troops in France, Ogilvie, Reith's successor as Director General, had come back convinced that the morale of the forces would be improved by knowing that their families at home were listening to the same programmes with them, but also that the Corporation's whole programming would have to change. Ian Hay, a BBC comptroller, had written in 1939, 'We shall need a lot of entertainment before this business is over.' It was recognized that the new forces service would have to be quite different from a 'watered-down version of our peacetime programmes', for 'if we give them serious music, long plays, or peacetime programme talks they will not listen'.[7] The lure of the continental stations could not be ignored during the war and programme changes would inevitably have more long-term consequences. An official wrote ominously, 'We shall not be able to return to our Sunday policy when the war ends.'

More light music, comedy, crooning, and jazz were justified not only by the immediacy of wartime demands, but also, crucially, by a new model of the psychology of the listener. The first step argued that the service had to be changed because troops were listening to it communally in the mess or in camps. Then it was suggested that different programmes were appropriate to different occupations. Very quickly the audience research department was trying to establish which kinds of music had the best effect on factory production.

Modern wars change the status of entertainment: leisure is seen as an aspect of 'public morale'. This was particularly true in Britain after 1940. Nevertheless, the Corporation was anxious not to be accused of producing 'programmes fit for morons', and the *Listener* printed many letters on this subject. 'I think you will find this army more highbrow than you suppose,' wrote one officer (15 February 1941).

What had first been seen as a temporary expedient became a permanent feature when the General Forces Programme was changed to the Light Programme in 1946. Grace Wyndham Goldie commented on the consequences of this innovation for the internal structure of the Corporation: 'It is not only that this is lighter, more gay, fresher in its approach; but for good or evil it is more closely related to the box office than any broadcasting in England has ever been before' (*Listener*, 26

December 1940). Competition was introduced between various parts of the Corporation. It meant the recognition of distinct groups whose tastes the BBC was obliged to identify rather than to change. This internal reform was of more fundamental importance than that of the competition later offered by commercial television. An editorial in the *Listener* claimed that 'the position is that the Forces Programme is carefully planned and not a casual proliferation of high jinks for low brows' (13 March 1941). Yet providing the public with what it wanted had become central to the Corporation's plans.

The introduction of a 'Light' Programme inevitably had implications for the Home Service. As early as 1940 the Home Service Board had decided that the 'barometer of listeners' preferences' should be a regular item on its agenda. However, the Home Service also broadcast the main news bulletins, and came to be seen as the part of the BBC which was most concerned with 'citizenship, family and home'.

The final and most revealing innovation was the introduction of the Third Programme. An internal memorandum in 1944 had suggested that the BBC should provide three competing services. Programme A 'should be of the highest possible cultural level, devoted to artistic endeavour, serious documentary, educational broadcasting, and the deeper investigation of the news, corresponding in outlook to a *Times* of the air'. Programme B, 'the real home programme of the people of the United Kingdom', would 'give talks which would inform the whole democracy rather than an already informed section, and be generally so designed that it will steadily, but imperceptibly, raise the standard of taste, entertainment, outlook and citizenship'.[8] Programme C was to divert, and needed little detailing.

The Third Programme was a survival of the Reithian ethic of 'mixed' programming. It emphasized that it should be judged by the whole programming of the service rather than individual items.

> The daily broadcasting schedules rush by the listener like the scenery past the windows of an express train. . . . The Third Programme from the beginning has arrived at a standard which has brought it into conflict with this ephemeral characteristic of broadcasting.[9]

Elsewhere, Harold Nicolson wrote, 'Every cultural pill is coated with sugar; and an item which it is felt might be unpalatable is tendered with a tone of apology, or with the horrid cheeriness of the scoutmaster, the padre, or the matron.' The Third regarded broadcasting as an art.

The 1950 White Paper on the future of broadcasting argued that 'listeners will now normally have a wider choice of contrasting programmes', while Nicolson, who had been involved in the creation of the Third, was at pains to point out that 'at no time, I am glad to say, did we entertain the doctrine that the listening public should be segregated between sheep or goats'. Sir William Haley, the Director General who had originally thought of the Third, put the classification clearly in a lecture given in 1948:

> Before the war the system was to confront [the listener] with pendulum-like leaps. The devotees of [Irving] Berlin were suddenly confronted with Bach.... Since the war we have been feeling our way along a more indirect approach. It rests on the conception of the community as a broadly based cultural pyramid, slowly aspiring upwards.

This concept resembled the hierarchy of ability.

Progress or rationalization?

By the end of the war British broadcasting and education had been radically reformed. Is it a coincidence that the two most important vehicles of national culture were reorganized almost simultaneously and in each case along very similar lines?

The reforms may have been made possible by the new weight given to public opinion by the war. However, in both areas of policy the form which the changes took depended on a new official way of looking at children on the one hand, and at listeners on the other. In this, distinctions were in effect being made between the tastes, abilities, and interests of different social groupings.

Listeners and children are not obviously analogous. Yet what is striking is the similarity in proportions of people assigned, quite independently, by education and broadcasting authorities to three categories. It is as though in the natural order of things there were three types of children and three types of listeners reflecting a three-way divide in society as a whole. It was expected that the population would divide as follows:[10]

Grammar schools 5%	Third Programme 6%
Technical schools 15%	Home Service 20%
Modern schools 80%	Light Programme 74%

In both cases the figures were based more on a hunch than statistics, and in both cases they proved wholly unrealistic. In education the technical schools barely got off the ground and completely failed to produce the technical administrators that had been expected; instead the grammar school section expanded. The estimate of the Third Programme audience of serious listeners was wildly optimistic; it never attracted more than 1–2 per cent of listeners. Neither projection was officially justified in terms of social class; yet in both cases what seems to have occurred is the imposition on social policy of official assumptions based on military and administrative experience.

There has been much discussion about the social effects of the war. Calder and Marwick have pointed to a major upheaval; Addison has suggested the culmination of a long, slow revolution in attitudes; Pelling argued that there was not much fundamental change at all. What is clear is that there was a dramatic and permanent increase in the power and scope of government. Whitehall's view of society and human nature, essentially meritocratic and hierarchical, pervaded policies which in normal times would have been fought out in the political arena. The reforms in both broadcasting and education reflected an approach to organization which had more to do with a civil service conception of the world as itself writ large, than with the reality of the world as it existed. Thus in Whitehall there were administrative, executive, and clerical grades (and in the services there were officers, NCO's, and privates). Officials found their own tripartite system natural and efficient. In creating new structures for the public they assumed a similar pattern of talent and need. In broadcasting, as in education, reforms contained a contradiction. On the one hand they were progressive in that they sought to cater for the whole society; but on the other they reinforced class divisions by giving new life to old hierarchical assumptions.

Notes

1. Filson Young to Dawney, BBC Internal Memorandum, 'Programme policy', *BBC Written Archives* (3 March 1934).
2. 'Programme revision committee', *BBC Written Archives* (June 1934).
3. Board of Education, *Inspectors' Report* (1932), p. 12, para 7 [Cmd 4068].
4. *The Nation's Schools: Their Plans and Purposes*, Ministry of Education Pamphlet 1 (London, HMSO, 1945).
5. Sir Cyril Burt, 'The psychology of listeners', *BBC Quarterly*, IV, 1 (April 1949), p. 7.
6. Lord Butler, *The Education Act of 1944 and After*, The First Noel Buxton Lecture, University of Essex (Harlow, Longman, 1965), p. 21.
7. Ryan to Nicolson, BBC Internal Memorandum, *BBC Written Archives* (17 January 1940).
8. 'Programme development', BBC Internal Memorandum, *BBC Written Archives* (14 February 1944).

9. BBC, *The Third Programme: Plans for October–December 1944*.

10. Sources for education figures, Ministry of Education circular 731 (1944), quoted in P. H. J. H. Gosdon, *Education in the Second World War* (London, Methuen, 1976); and for broadcasting, *Listener* (February 1946), and BBC Internal Memorandum, 'Projection for the Third Programme', *BBC Written Archives* (14 May 1946).

11

The fall of the BBC

In 1946, when television broadcasting was resumed, the BBC's popularity at home and prestige abroad were even greater than before, largely because of the wartime experience. Yet barely a decade later, the BBC's monopoly of the air waves was destroyed. Television and subsequently radio were placed on a new competitive footing. More than anything else, this has shaped the aims, structure, and output of all television programming over the last quarter of a century.

The change was not brought about by public pressure, but by a small group within the ruling Conservative Party. It was opposed by bishops, vice-chancellors, peers, trade unions, the Labour Party, and most national newspapers. Reith compared the introduction of commercial broadcasting into Britain with that of dog racing, smallpox, and bubonic plague.[1] The objections to commercial broadcasting were diverse, but most were anti -American, and opposed the encouragement of crude materialist desires. Criticisms of this kind were particularly vehement on the left. More recently, however, some socialist writers have taken a different view, arguing that commercial television was, in fact, a cultural liberator, taking the control of broadcasting out of the hands of a patronizing and paternalist establishment, and increasing the scope of genuinely popular influences.

Austerity, monopoly, and the Beveridge Report

The BBC's prestige contributed to its undoing. The Corporation had assumed that it was invulnerable and so had the 1945 Labour government which consequently did not hurry to renew its licence. In 1947 Beveridge was asked to conduct an inquiry into the BBC's affairs. He might have been expected to sympathize with Reith's legacy of benevolent, high-minded despotism at the BBC, for Beveridge had once claimed that his ideal society would be run by neither parliament nor dictators, but by professional administrators – 'social doctors' – who would organize society 'to adapt the social and economic relations of clients so as to produce the maximum economic health'.[2] However, as a liberal, Beveridge was highly critical of the Corporation.

He distrusted the tone and character of the BBC, which 'beginning with Londonization, going on to secretiveness and self-satisfaction, and ending up with a dangerous sense of mission became a sense of divine right'. He was constantly on the watch for 'the four scandals of monopoly: bureaucracy, complacency, favouritism and inefficiency'. Written in Beveridge's inimitable style, the report nevertheless finally recommended that the Corporation's licence be renewed, because the alternative, American-style commercial television, seemed far worse.

The recommendations of the Beveridge Report were ignored by the Conservatives after they beat the Labour Party in the 1951 general election. Instead, Selwyn Lloyd's dissenting minority report, which was in favour of commercial broadcasting, became the basis for the commercial lobby. Nevertheless, Beveridge's findings influenced the form of British commercial broadcasting. First, the report preferred spot adverts to sponsored programmes because they gave advertisers less control over programme content. 'A public broadcasting service', the report commented, 'might have its controlled and limited advertisement hour, as every newspaper had in its advertising columns, without sacrificing the independence of standards of broadcasting.' Second, the report advocated the regionalization of broadcasting and the decentralization of the BBC. These arguments affected the organization of the commercial system when it was introduced.

The commercial television lobby has been seen by some writers as a tiny group of back-bench MPs, 'who worked night and day on the project'. However, they were supported by the immense power of the great entertainment industries. Pye Radio, the largest West End theatre management, and J. Walter Thompson, the advertising agency, were all involved in the campaign. Although a member of the group declared in the House of Commons that 'Any suggestion that the Bill was fostered by commercial interests is a complete figment of the imagination of the Party opposite', the speaker at the time was a director of various electronics firms who expected to profit out of an increase in the market for televisions.[3] 'At what point', H. H. Wilson asked, 'were the members speaking as MPs representing their constituencies, and when were they speaking as directors, managers or employees of advertising agencies, market research organizations or radio and television manufacturers?'

However, the most important organizer of the lobby was a broadcaster, Norman Collins. He had been director of the Light Programme, and controller of BBC Television. When he was not appointed Chief Executive of Television, Collins resigned from the BBC. He told *The Times* that he had left

> because of a clash of principle... whether the new medium of TV shall be allowed to develop at this, the most crucial stage of its existence, along its own lines and by its own methods, or whether it shall be merged into the colossus of sound broadcasting.

The commercial lobby fought a hard and frequently unscrupulous battle. It was successful because important members of the government, including the Prime Minister, Churchill, were not prepared to defend the BBC. Significantly the campaign also had the active support of Lord Woolton. He had modernized the Conservative Party organization before the 1951 election and brought a new kind of candidate into parliament. This group represented industry and advertising rather than law or hereditary wealth.

Woolton wanted free enterprise to dominate the 'new age of post-war prosperity'. 'Our individual lives today', he complained in a broadcast, 'are hemmed in by no less than 25,000 controls.' He wanted to associate the party with the long-term material aspirations of the people, and believed that commercial television would help to do this.

The opposition to commercial television was organized by the National Television Council with Christopher Mayhew as its secretary. Support came from surprising quarters. 'The Establishment', wrote Henry Fairlie, 'came as near as it has ever done to organizing a conspiracy against the government of the day – a Conservative Government.'[4] This group objected to the cultural consequences of commercial television: it would 'vulgarize, bowdlerize, and coarsen', wrote one critic.

The argument became more fierce when it was learnt that in the USA the Coronation had been shown interspersed with NBC's television chimp, J. Fred Muggs, selling tea. A deodorant had been advertised just before the ritual anointment. Horrified MPs suggested that if a commercial system were started here, royal tours would be interrupted by commercial breaks extolling the makers of the Queen's chairs and carpets.

Nevertheless the Act introducing commercial television was passed in 1954 because most Tories believed that in some way it would promote industry, commerce, and the free market. The new service was named, by some genius of euphemism, 'Independent Television'.

Commercial television and the new world

'A whole new world has come,' proclaimed the first commercial television *Yearbook* in 1955. 'We've won, and now we can really get going,' said

Norman Collins. 'The importance of the introduction of commercial TV goes far beyond any question of the merits of commercial versus public service broadcasting,' wrote Wilson, 'for it may also seem to symbolize a change within the Conservative Party, and give expression to an accumulation of influences which are securing the future of British society.' ITV brought about a revolution, it has been claimed, because it challenged the complacent pre-war conservatism of the BBC. The Corporation was staffed by narrow-minded, middle-class professional bureaucrats who had little sympathy for working-class interests. Norman Collins complained of the 'apathy, disinterest and often open hostility towards the new medium' that existed within the BBC. Lord Simon of Wythenshawe, chairman of the BBC Governors, claimed that during the early 1950s only about one-fifth of the business the Director General presented to the board was concerned with television. Indeed in 1946 when Haley was shown a television demonstration he had remarked that he would not have one in his house.

The BBC, one producer wrote, regarded radio as 'the father figure, established and responsible', while television was seen as a 'spendthrift tiresome adolescent'.[5] The BBC bureaucrats, secure in the imperial comforts of Broadcasting House, deluged television producers in the unheated wastes of north London with memos. These detailed the proper procedures for the purchase of books and why it was outrageous to suggest that book covers should be cut up, even to be shown on the screen. The tensions were exacerbated by the influx into television of cameramen, technicians, and directors who were used to the high living which characterized the precarious film world. 'Disorder has been repeatedly reported from the television studios ... new employees do not seem to have become one with the Corporation,' read one ominous memo of the period. 'Perhaps', another memo replied, 'a brief course on the history of the Corporation might be of assistance?'[6]

Indeed during the 1950s the Corporation appointments policy was apparently designed to keep the new service in order, rather than accelerate its development. Gerald Beadle was an amicable BBC administrator, quietly approaching retirement in the Western Region, when the call came. 'About 1953', he remarked, 'every BBC directorship in London was filled by younger men than me ... but then in 1956 something quite unexpected happened ... at the age of fifty-seven I was appointed Director of TV.' Beadle was to hold this post during the critical early years of commercial television.

Beadle was a typical example of the BBC administrator of this period. The Corporation man, as Burns has argued, did not work for the BBC, he worked *in* it – as a secular church of professional excellence. One writer noted that a Corporation producer 'breathes the BBC ritual welcome to eminent persons as they arrive' (to have their personalities 'brought out', rather than be put on the spot), 'How good of you to come!' (*Encounter*, October 1960). The Corporation saw itself as a particularly dedicated branch of the civil service, and this image affected its approach to television.

However, the BBC's performance during the 1950s needs scrutiny. Despite the overwhelming bureaucracy, a remarkable generation of television producers and directors started work during this period. They were to dominate the entire output of British television, on both channels, for the next twenty years. Even the Corporation's lack of interest in television had benefits. Because it was seen as relatively unimportant it was left alone. Goldie claims this allowed programme-makers far greater initiative.

The most serious charge against the BBC was that it starved the new service of funds. In 1950 the BBC's television budget was only one-half of that allocated to the Home Service. However, in the period of experimental broadcasts during the 1930s, television had been able to develop only because the BBC had been willing to subsidize it out of wireless revenues. (In the USA, where it depended on advertising funds, the service was forced to close because the pictures and reception were inadequate to attract a commercially useful audience.) The BBC also pursued a policy of national coverage and by 1956 98 per cent of the country was able to receive television. This was achieved only by a massive redistribution of resources away from the rich south-east, where there were many television owners, to the more remote regions. A national service was an investment which could not at first have been made by the commercial companies.

Competition new and old

It has been argued that commercial competition changed the BBC. Competition forced the Corporation to consider public wants more seriously. 'The BBC will have to abandon the ivory towers for the beaches! People prefer fun,' wrote one critic (*Daily Mail*, 15 February 1957). Peter Black comments that a kind of myth developed, based on an image of 'the energetic thrusting showbiz visionaries elbowing aside the complacent bureaucrats of the BBC, by presenting a series of audacious novelties that blew the stale air of monopoly out of television and sent the invigorating breezes of free enterprise whistling through it'.[7] Others have argued that subsequently broadcasting has been dominated by the need to maximize the audience.

Yet competition came to the BBC long before Independent Television was thought of. The decisive break with Reithian paternalism occurred during the war, when the General Forces Network was established. Similarly the BBC had always been obliged to prove that the size of its audience legitimized its receipt of the licence fee. Indeed the BBC had been subject to competition from foreign commercial stations since the 1930s. It was the challenge of Luxembourg which had broken the dismal Reithian Sunday on the radio. However unctuously it was defended, the BBC had abandoned the concept of planned programming considerably before the introduction of Independent Television, while programme-makers have always been most sensitive to the competition offered by colleagues. Anthony Smith has argued in *British Broadcasting* that 'Producers within the BBC were more often conscious of an internal competition within the different sections of the BBC.' This, he claimed, led in the 1960s to 'an enormous flowering of talent and inventiveness'. Such internal pressure had the greatest effect on standards and innovation within both authorities.

In addition the threat posed by commercial competition was more limited than its advocates have suggested. At first the two authorities fought a bitter ratings war. They soon discovered that the public would watch anything in preference to a party political programme. (The parties reacted swiftly and ensured that these broadcasts were shown simultaneously on both channels.) When ITV offered the audience the Hallé Orchestra, the BBC's share of the audience rose. When the BBC offered the people *La Bohème*, the numbers watching fell to 2 per cent. However, both soon discovered the comforts of competition and the security provided by the dependability of the enemy's programming. It was found that documentaries and current events programmes achieved their maximum audience only if they were shown at the same time. As Burns commented, 'Competition now seems to be accepted as a fact of life for both the BBC and ITV, and is defended by both. There is one obvious reason for this; it makes life easier for them.' A rigidly conventional use of time and categories of programmes was reinforced by competition.

Commerce and the audience

It is often assumed that ITV changed television because it won the battle for the audience. This is not the case. Indeed commercial television had little effect on the growth of the television audience, nor did it decimate the numbers watching BBC.

Between 1955 and 1956 the commercial companies struggled to

acquire an audience. Howard Thomas wrote that by January 1956, 'The situation was very grim. The costs of running commercial television were enormous for the audience was simply not large enough to attract advertising revenue.'

However, the situation improved. In a well-publicized campaign in 1957 Sir Kenneth Clark was claiming a 79:21 preference for the commercial channel. In December of the same year, out of 539 programmes listed by TAM in the top ten ratings, 536 were from ITV and only 3 produced by the BBC. 'Once they had a choice', Black wrote, 'the working-class audience left the BBC at a pace that suggested ill will was more deeply entrenched than good.' The first *ATV Showbook* put the point more jubilantly: 'We've got the audience,' it proclaimed. Norman Collins said that the BBC would soon 'grind to a halt'.

Certainly the BBC panicked. *Ariel*, the staff magazine, became full of warlike metaphors about 'beating back the enemy' and getting into 'fighting formation'. As large numbers of staff left the Corporation for the higher salaries and more makeshift offices of the commercial companies, Sir Ian Jacob wrote, 'I doubt whether any organization in peacetime has been subject to comparable strain' (*Ariel*, 3, 1956).

Corporation officials became obsessed with maintaining a 30 per cent share of the audience. Television was typically being interpreted in terms of the audience distribution of radio. Furthermore its audience was being seen in terms of an obsolete distribution of the population between classes. According to this view, the commercial companies would concentrate on entertainment (like the Light Programme, which drew 68 per cent of the audience), leaving more serious programming to the BBC (like the combined Home and Third services which drew 32 per cent of the audience).

The apparent collapse of the audience posed a dilemma. The BBC might be destroyed because its share of the audience would no longer justify the collection of a licence fee from all viewers. Or the BBC might be destroyed because it would be forced to emulate the commercial programmes.

However, the argument about which service had won the largest audience was confused, in the first place because the two authorities counted their audience in different ways. 'For us,' wrote Robert Silvey, the head of the BBC's audience research, 'it meant people, and for ITV it meant TV sets. Our method was based on questioning samples of the population about their previous day's viewing; ITV's on metered records of when TV sets in a sample of homes had been switched on.' Although both methods showed trends in viewing behaviour, they could not be directly compared.

Indeed the commercial companies had not 'won' a 70 per cent share of the total viewing audience as Clark had implied. Rather this was the proportion of those viewers who had purchased a new television set which could receive both channels. At first this was a tiny fraction of the total audience. Even as late as 1960 the ITA estimated in its annual report that fewer than 60 per cent of licence holders had two channel sets. Given their considerable financial investment, it was hardly surprising that viewers with new sets at first preferred the novelty of commercial television. Nevertheless, throughout the period the BBC's total audience was over twice that of ITV.

Indeed the introduction of commercial television had no independent effect on the overall growth of the television audience.

As Table 6 shows this was fast but steady. The pattern of gradual growth was interrupted only once, when two years before the start of ITV the Coronation produced a dramatic rise in viewers. The BBC did not 'lose' an audience, nor did commercial choice increase the speed of audience growth.

Public service: private enterprise

Commercial television in Britain was hardly revolutionary. Indeed it was carefully modelled on the BBC. The traditions of public service were inherited by the new authority.

The ITA was responsible for regulating the commercial stations and made no programmes. Like the BBC, ITV was licensed only for a limited

Table 6 *Growth of television audience*

Year	No. of new TV licence holders
1946–7	14,560
1947–8	57,000
1948–9	112,000
1949–50	344,000
1950–1	420,000
1951–2	685,319
1952–3	693,192
1953–4	1,110,439
1954–5	1,254,879
1955–6	1,235,827
1956–7	1,226,663
1957–8	1,123,747
1958–9	1,165,419

Source: BBC Handbooks (1946–59).

period, a system which ensured that the whole of British broadcasting came under periodic review. Like the BBC it had a publicly appointed controlling board. 'The BBC triumphed', Peter Black wrote, 'because all of those chosen as members of the IBA might equally well have been BBC Governors.'

The new service was more limited than the BBC. It was banned from broadcasting its own opinions, and the injunction that it should observe 'impartiality in the treatment of all controversial issues' has been interpreted narrowly to imply a balance of views within each programme. As Smith points out, the prohibitions 'listed in the 1954 Act are broadly consistent with the general editorial policy of the BBC, but they have been used over the years to oblige independent TV not to do certain types of programme'. Hence ITV has been given less political independence than the BBC.

Thus Independent Television was made in the image of the BBC. Introduced after a controversy which *The Economist* called 'a soufflé of high principles and politics' (15 June 1954), which disguised a simple profit motive, commercial television was nevertheless formed as a public service.

Commerce, finance, and television

Indeed television was so expensive it had always seemed likely that it would have to be financed commercially. 'Had there been no war in 1939', Briggs remarks, 'it is conceivable that commercial TV would have come to Britain fifteen years before it did.' Even in the limited experimental stage, television was an exorbitantly expensive medium. In 1937 a BBC *Handbook* had estimated that an hour of television cost twelve times as much to produce as the most expensive programme on the radio. Even Reith, in his evidence to the Selsdon Committee in 1934, claimed that he had 'no objection in principle to the sponsor system and we do in fact do something which is near to that and might do it in the future'. Sir William Haley wrote in 1945, 'Television will cost more than the Corporation's usual sources of funds can easily provide.' Beveridge had rejected sponsorship, but was not hostile in principle to some commercial involvement in television.

The BBC itself had been pressing for some kind of commercial financing of television since the 1930s, partly because it was felt that business interests could have little serious effect on what was seen as a trivial means of entertainment. Within the BBC, television was regarded as an extension of the Light Programme. As such it might be expensive, but it could hardly be important. 'In terms of the ethos which had been cultivated within the BBC during the fifties', wrote Burns, 'Light Entertainment remained an unfortunate necessity, its marginal character inescapably perpetuated in the adjective tagged to it.' Commerce, television, and programme policy had been closely linked since the 1930s.

New programmes and the new style

Perhaps the most important innovation which ITV introduced was the change of mood which it brought to broadcasting. The atmosphere of the new companies, owned and run by showmen like Val Parnell and the Grade brothers, was quite different from the stifling solemnity of the BBC bureaucracy. 'It was more like Klondyke than Maida Vale,' wrote Howard Thomas. When Thomas went to see Lew Grade at ATV about new programme ideas he would be met by a cloud of cigar smoke, and Grade would throw open a drawer bulging with receipts and bills. The haggling would then begin. Describing Parnell and Grade negotiating a new contract for ATV Thomas wrote, 'They sat like boxers pausing between the rounds of a heavyweight championship.'

Once ITV had begun broadcasting, it no longer had to fight the moral scruples of the establishment and its first priority was to capture an audience. 'Variety,' claimed the first *ATV Showbook*, 'although accumulating the largest number of viewers, has been taken to task by critics of commercial television who have asked for "more cultural programmes and less airy frolics".' The article continued, 'Many will agree with ATV chief executive Val Parnell when he says there is a lot of culture to be gained from watching a great clown performing.' However, it was not the big top or the *Commedia Dell'Arte* which drew the ATV audience, but rather the giveaway shows, Double your Money, Take your Pick, and Beat the Clock. The Labour MP, Tom Driberg, compared the audience's howl of laughter at one of these shows to that of the circus crowd in ancient Rome (*New Statesman*, 25 December 1959).

Independent Television did not, however, 'soundly beat the BBC at its own game', as a *Daily Mail* critic claimed in 1956. BBC drama, serials, and documentaries were consistently preferred to those of ITV. Consequently in 1956 news, documentaries, classical music, current events, and drama on ITV were cut by one-third. 'A craven definition of "serious"', Black claims, 'killed off promising programmes whose only offence was that though entertainment, they were a novelty.'

ITV's most important contribution to television was to develop a format for the news. The BBC bulletin had been read by an unseen newscaster accompanied by still photographs. Cardiff and Scannell argue that this failure left a gaping hole in the very centre of television programme output. The function of a daily news service is not simply the continuous up to the minute monitoring, processing and defining of immediate national and international news events. It also serves to define the currency and topicality of events and issues for current affairs programmes.[8]

Independent Television News attracted an immense audience. It used journalists as news-readers, allowed them to write their own scripts, and showed them on the screen.

Robin Day, one of ITN's first newscasters, commented in his memoirs that 'The man on the screen had a further task, to win the professional confidence of his colleagues.' ITN developed television journalism in new directions, despite the limitations imposed upon it by the Television Act. The obligation to exercise balance proved particularly difficult. 'Any problems?' Day once asked the news director. 'Yes,' Cox replied bitterly, 'a call from a chap called Pontius Pilate who says his case has not been properly put.' The success of the ITN approach in turn provoked the BBC into improving its own news services.

However, ITV also inherited many traditions from the BBC. One disgruntled critic claimed, 'The BBC has precedents for everything, for handling a monarch's abdication, a State Opening of Parliament or a boy scouts' jamboree.'[9] The opening years of television seem little more than an extension of the wireless, where history was relentlessly marked by a succession of royal events (with outside coverage).

More significantly the BBC solved many of the political and social dilemmas that confronted television. The BBC showed the first televised election, and established the rules governing politicians' access to television, while the practical consequences of 'neutrality' and 'balance' in a visual medium were developed by a new generation of BBC producers and presenters. Goldie employed several young Labour ex-MPs defeated in the 1951 general election to make current events programmes. Later she claimed her choice was vindicated because Mayhew, Taverne, and Wyatt moved from the left to the middle and right of the political spectrum. These shifts in attitude might also demonstrate the power of the ethic of consensus which came to dominate television journalism. The commercial companies simply took over the conventions developed within the BBC. Both, wrote Stuart Hood, 'interpreted impartiality as the acceptance of that segment of opinion which constitutes parliamentary consensus. Opinion that falls outside that consensus has difficulty in finding expression.' Hood suggests that the median of acceptable opinion may shift, but the consensus, once arrived at, is always shared by both companies.

The BBC had also set precedents for the solution of technical dilemmas in television journalism before ITV started. New rhetorics of documentary and current affairs coverage were established. At first most cameramen had been trained in the cinema, and had little experience of journalism. 'In those early days', one producer wrote, 'I often discarded glamorous pictures of cherry orchards, or flocks of bleating lambs, or children dancing in playgrounds because, though improbably useful in a travelogue, they did nothing to a study of, say, the relationship of Yugoslavia to the USSR.'[10] She concluded that as pictures would always override words a style had to be found which ensured that they would reinforce rather than distract from the meaning of a piece. It was also recognized that the use of film raised problems of authenticity. Viewers could easily be led to believe that a film taken in the past actually portrayed events happening in the present. One solution was to use someone who had helped to make the film as the programme presenter. Reviewing the BBC magazine series Foreign Correspondent in the *Listener* (May 1959), Goldie had written that they

> were using film but we were not trying to make films. We wanted the programmes to be dominated by the personality of the commentator. ... We were all feeling our way but when the series finished we felt that we had hit on a new form that had come to stay in television. The key to the new form is the use of film to illustrate a personal experience.

This form was quite opposed to the style of the British documentary movement, in which the film purported to represent an authoritative reality, rather than any personal view.

These innovations and cautious explorations of the specific properties and opportunities of televised politics and current affairs were made well before ITV started. They solved dilemmas that were common to any television service. ITV did not challenge or alter the rules established by the BBC; it merely helped to develop them further.

End of a monopoly: vulgar new world

The introduction of Independent Television did not mark such a decisive break with the BBC. Rather the brash new companies owed more to the Corporation than has usually been recognized. The BBC had already begun to change in fundamental ways before ITV was started. The commercial station provided a stimulus for the maturing of a national television service. Sir Hugh Greene claimed that dramatic changes were to come later in the 1960s, and these were as much to do with a shift in the political climate as with any administrative innovations.

This is not to deny that the BBC had a radically different manner and organization from Independent Television. Like the British Raj, the BBC combined privilege and moral purpose. It was a world in which 'unsoundness' was a major crime. Independent Television provided an alternative source of employment for dissidents and had no deadweight of custom or dignity. Personnel moved continually and freely between the two authorities by the 1960s.

However, commercial television was also modelled on and limited by the BBC. Originally intended as a political counterweight to what was seen as the BBC's 'red' bias, ITV was as vulnerable to political pressure. The BBC depended on public support for the legitimacy of its licence fee, as ITV depended on it for advertising revenue.

It has often been claimed that ITV was a vulgar debaucher of cultural standards. In the pursuit of profit it merely pandered to the lowest common denominator of public taste. More recently a far more subtle case has been advanced which is not so crudely anti-commercial. This claims that ITV was rather an energizing, populist force which gave expression to working-class culture.

Notes

1. J. C. W. Reith, *House of Lords* (22 May 1952), H. L. 176: 1,293–1,451.
2. Quoted in J. Harris, *William Beveridge* (Oxford, Clarendon, 1977), p. 311.
3. Captain L. P. S. Orr MP, *House of Commons Debates* (22 June 1954), 529:327.
4. H. Fairlie, 'The BBC' in H. Swynnerton Thomas (ed.), *The Establishment: A Symposium* (London, New English Library, 1962).
5. G. Wyndham Goldie, *Facing the Nation: Television and Politics 1936–1976* (London, Bodley Head, 1977), p. 45.
6. 'Television staff policy', *BBC Written Archives* (1955).
7. P. Black, *The Mirror in the Corner* (London, Hutchinson, 1972), p. 115.
8. P. Scannell, 'The social eye of television', *Media, Culture and Society*, 1, 1 (1979).
9. H. Fairlie, 'TV: idiot box', *Encounter* (August 1959).
10. G. Wyndham Goldie, 'TV report', *Listener* (23 October 1968).

12

Class, taste, and profit

Post-war affluence was measured in consumer durables. Cars, refrigerators, and washing machines made it easier to do what had always been done. Television changed people's social life and habits. Commercial television was believed to alter their aspirations and values as well.

In the late 1950s and early 1960s television was central to a debate about supposed changes in the British class structure. The growth of a mass television audience and the setting-up of a commercial service were seen as agents of a revolution that was eroding class distinction and increasing social mobility. Television has more often been seen as a destructive than as a creative force. In the 1950s many regarded it as a threat to traditional ways of life, and hence to the basis of traditional political loyalties.

In 1962 the Pilkington Report summed up this debate. The Director General, Sir Hugh Greene, later called the report 'the most important piece of work on the purposes of broadcasting which has appeared in this or any other country'.[1] Pilkington attempted to establish the criteria for producing – and judging – good broadcasting. In fact the report was very much a product of its time, and was constrained by current sociological fashions.

The myth of the disappearing working class

During the 1950s it was argued that affluence was destroying the working class. The general elections of 1955 and 1959 seemed to support the view that there were no longer two nations: fewer and fewer people were prepared even to support the Labour Party. Two complementary explanations were put forward. According to the first, as the working class had become richer it was actually disappearing through assimilation into the middle class. According to the second, a working class had continued to exist but prosperity had undermined an awareness of its own interests: capitalism was successfully eradicating the consciousness (though not the reality) of class.

The first view was particularly popular among right-wing Labour politicians (who used it to justify an attempt to remove socialism from the party's constitution). 'The steady upgrading of the working class,' wrote Anthony Crosland in his book *The Future of Socialism*, 'both occupationally and still more in terms of political and social aspirations, renders Labour's one-class image increasingly inappropriate.' It was also widely held by social scientists who invented the inelegant term 'embourgeoise-ment' to describe the alleged process. As Butler and Rose wrote after the 1959 general election, 'It is more than ever possible to speak of the Conservatives as the country's usual majority party ... the Labour Party has to face the fact that its support is being eroded by the impact of age and social change.'

Between 1951 and 1958 real wages rose by 20 per cent. The proportion of manual workers who owned their own homes rose from 32 per cent to 39 per cent in the four years before 1962.[2] Between 1951 and 1964 the number of television sets rose from 1 million to 13 million. Indeed as televisions were clearly not useful, the widespread ownership of sets merely appeared to confirm what Crosland called the 'pubs, pools and prostitutes' view of the working class which was seen to 'waste all its higher income on alcohol, tobacco, gambling and fun ... if not actually women'.[3]

During the same period working-class habits also changed. People went on more holidays, went to the cinema less frequently, began drinking more at home and less at pubs. As these goods and habits had previously been the prerogative of higher social classes, it was assumed that their use also entailed middle- and upper-class views and beliefs.

The second explanation of the decay of the working-class depended on the centrality of culture. The rituals which were a source of strength to working-class life were disappearing, partly (so it was argued) because of the homogenizing influence of television. Paradoxically working-class culture was celebrated just as it seemed to be about to vanish. Indeed its condition was detailed by a generation of academics whose origins were working class, but all of whom had been upwardly mobile.

'To live in the working class', wrote Richard Hoggart, 'is to belong to an all-pervading culture, one in some ways as formalized and stylized as any that is attributed to the upper classes.'[4] Jackson and Marsden in their book on working-class life argued that two and a half centuries of urban life 'have established distinct working-class styles of living with very real values of their own. Values which are perhaps essential to society and which do not flourish that strongly in other reaches of society.'[5] In a chapter headed 'An acceptance of the working-class life', they remarked that obliterating these values and way of life, 'can be so quick in a technological society ... the mass media, the central planning office, the bulldozers are all characteristic instruments of change'. In a related series of studies Wilmott and Young compared the warm closeness of a Bethnal Green working-class community with the more isolated life of a new suburb. In the East End the emphasis was on the informal collective life and the extended family, the pubs and the open air market. 'There is a sort of bantering warmth in public,' they claimed, which in the new suburb, Woodford, was reserved for the family home. There seemed to be more uniformity in gardens, attitudes, and behaviour in Woodford than in the East End. 'Maybe uniformity is one of the prices we have to pay for sociability in a more mobile society,' they concluded.[6]

Television was important because it was seen as replacing old communal forms of leisure with isolated and standardized entertainment. 'In many parts of life', Hoggart argued, 'mass production has brought good: culturally the mass produced makes it harder for the good to be recognized.' Indeed for writers like Hoggart culture was the most important aspect of a society's achievement.

Hoggart applied F. R. Leavis's concern with the moral quality of élite literary culture to a broader problem of working-class life. For Leavis, Annan wrote, 'The analysis of the text is only important in so far as it reveals the profundity or morality of the writer's moral consciousness.'[7] Leavis was concerned to evaluate the purpose of literature. 'Where there is not in the literary critical sense a significant contemporary culture', he wrote, '*the mind* is not fully alive.'[8] Hoggart was concerned to judge modern working-class culture. He concluded that 'Most mass entertainments are in the end what D. H. Lawrence described as "anti-life". They are full of corrupt brightness and improper appeals and moral evasions.' Progress had been reduced to material improvement: 'It only offered an infinite perspective of increasingly good times. Technicolour TV, all smelling, all touching, all tasting TV.'

Thus the Pilkington Report was the product of two contemporary concerns: that the working class was being absorbed into the middle class, and that working-class culture was decaying because of the industrialization of leisure. Raymond Williams wrote that 'From 1956 to 1962 there was an intense development of ideas in the field of culture and communication, and by the time of the Pilkington Report this had reached the level of open and conventional politics.'[9] The committee had been asked to review the development of television. In fact they did much more, producing a report which judged the nation's culture. Television, the report argued, was 'one of the major long-term factors that would shape the moral and mental attitudes, and the values of our society'.

Yet the working class did not disappear, and neither did working-class culture. There is little evidence that people lose a sense of their social identity simply because they become comparatively better off. Indeed the really remarkable feature of the period was not affluence – the rise in living standards looks far less impressive when it is compared with the growth in other European countries – but full employment. For the first time there was work for everyone, and it gave working-class culture, taste, and life a confidence which it had rarely had before.

The Pilkington Report depended on a sentimentalization of an earlier 'golden age', just as Hoggart and Wilmott and Young had before it. Indeed it demonstrates a puritanical distaste for the effects of improved material conditions. Although its concern with the influence of television on social and cultural behaviour is important, the standards by which it judged the mass media were based on false premises about the nature of working-class life.

The power of the media

The Pilkington Report also depended on a crude view of the power of the media to influence individual behaviour. Advertising, and in particular its newest and most dramatic form, the television commercial, was regarded as immensely persuasive. The effect of advertising was dramatized by the contrast with the war, when advertising had not only been limited, but also pursued rather novel goals. A cartoon by Fougasse in 1942 wryly made the point: it compared the huge pre-war billboard extolling the public to 'Eat more and more Meatio' with the tiny wartime poster which read, 'Save Meatio, don't use more than you need!'[10] In this context the post-austerity explosion of advertising amazed the public, and academics and politicians became very sensitive to its effects.

Television advertising in particular was regarded as sinister. It was often equated with 'brain-washing' techniques which had been exposed during the Korean war. 'It may well be', wrote Daniel Bell in the *Listener* (December 1956), 'that our fears are excessive, that the pliability of the consumer, like that of the "indoctrinated" communist youth, is an exaggerated fact.' The fashion for 'motivation research' seemed to suggest that advertisements relied on an appeal to people's irrational and subconscious feelings in order to sell goods. The model of the consumer as a rational hedonist was replaced by another in which many goods were purchased not for their intrinsic worth or usefulness, but in an attempt to assuage anxieties. Marketing, dependent on the 'eight hidden needs' (most of which could be reduced to one – sex), was claimed to have dramatic effects. 'The ability of advertisers to contact millions of us simultaneously through television has given them the power to do good or evil on a scale never before possible,' one persuader put it.[11] Leavis wrote that 'a new brand of applied psychology ... and a highly specialized profession' had been developed. 'Years of carefully recorded and tabulated experiment [led advertisers] to develop their appeal in the confidence that the average member of the public will respond like an automaton.'[12] Television advertising, which reached people in the defenceless privacy of their own homes, seemed to assume that consumers were unable to introspect sufficiently to understand their own motives.

The working class were felt to be the group most vulnerable to the ambitions of advertisers. 'There is one kind of person who seems particularly responsive to advertising: the man or woman who is moving up from one class to another,' Mark Abrams argued in a broadcast in 1956. 'These people – and there are an incredible number in Britain – have to shed their old buying habits and acquire new ones. The class-destroying function of modern advertising is cumulative,' he suggested:

> The initial effect is to encourage people to want to buy consumer goods formerly enjoyed by their social betters. As they achieve this and become more socially mobile, advertising and television provide them with knowledge that enables them to fill their new role.[13]

Indeed the first television commercials seemed to confirm this view of the direct impact of the media on behaviour. Shops almost immediately sold out of the advertised goods, and jubilant market researchers discovered that the public recalled the commercials long after they had first been shown. But this was only a temporary effect.

Indeed later research has shown how complex the relationship between media message and audience behaviour is. The public is not a passive empty box merely waiting to be filled with the injunctions of advertisers. How people react to what they see is determined by their class, age, and the beliefs they already hold. Nor is the public subconscious so easily manipulated as many assumed. As one contemporary market researcher pointed out, surveys which concluded that housewives did not like macaroni which cooked to a wet sticky mass because wet sticky masses aroused sexual guilt in them were not treated with the scepticism they deserved.[14] Some critics reacted cautiously to the power of advertisements: 'I cannot think so poorly of British Fathers', wrote Driberg in the *New Statesman* (20 December 1958), 'as to accept the diagnosis proclaimed by one ITV advertiser last week, "Every daddy *deserves* a Brylcreem home dispenser for Christmas".' However, most critics believed it to be overwhelming. Advertising executives were credited with a power they would have been delighted to exercise, but which was far in excess of their rather unpredictable performance.

This overestimation of the manipulative power of the media influenced the Pilkington Report. It led to a crude view of the public – and particularly the working-class audience – as passive, gullible, and misled.

Real and false wants

The Pilkington Report dismissed expressed public preferences as unreal and the product of commercial manipulation. A Labour Party report on advertising written in 1962 developed some of these arguments. Advertising, it claimed, could not be defended by the assertion that it merely reflected the times. For, in order to make advertisements, individuals were obliged to make decisions. In so far as advertisers determined what was shown they were responsible for their choices. Some people, the report argued, had claimed that advertising 'reinforces attitudes of materialism, only too prevalent in society'. In the committee's opinion,

> This charge is probably the opposite of the truth: for it seems more likely that what advertising does is to interfere with the appreciation of material goods to the extent that it substitutes for a genuine assessment or perception of their qualities, vague sentiments and fantasies.

The choices that were expressed under these conditions were consequently not 'real'.

The Pilkington Report's assessment of commercial television depended on a similar view of the exploitation of working-class false consciousness for profit. The argument was based on two premises. First, that the public's expressed choice was not a real one because it had not been offered the entire range of possible options from which to choose. It made its choice of television programmes from a culture already limited by the imperatives of profit. Second, the public was in itself limited: the choices it made were deformed by the inadequacies of its education, wealth, and leisure. The working class has, of course, been particularly damaged in these ways.

The report's attitude towards cultural choice was particularly clear in its discussion of entertainment. ITV defended itself by arguing that its programmes were popular. Pilkington replied that

> to give the public what it wants is a misleading phrase ... it has the appearance of an appeal to democratic principle, but the appearance is deceptive. It is in fact patronizing and arrogant, in that it claims to know what the public is but defines it as no more than the mass

audience, and it claims to know what it wants, but limits its choice to the average of experience.

The commercial companies suggested that there was no need to consider entertainment as it was so unimportant. However, for Pilkington, the individual programme was analogous to the text for the literary critic. As such it was as essential to judge 'trivial entertainment' as more serious programmes. Pilkington found most entertainment programmes unsatisfactory.

However, as Crosland pointed out, it was patronizing and perhaps unwise to dismiss expressed public wants as irrelevant. He argued that the range of newspapers and television programmes was 'still considerable, certainly wide enough to offer genuine comparison'. Indeed most people, for most of the time, chose the escapist, the diverting, or the trivial. Policy should not ignore these needs, but should also seek to encourage minority interests.

The Pilkington Committee's fears that the public was passive led it to consider audience preferences as little more than the expression of commercial manipulation. Consequently the report became insensitive to public taste. Indeed it endorsed the BBC's popular music policy when this was clearly out of touch with what people wanted to hear, as the success of the pirate stations soon demonstrated.

Entertainment, politics, and advertising

The Pilkington Committee was romantically committed to a concept of folk culture. Its emphasis on the importance of the 'authenticity' of cultural products meant that many other considerations were ignored. For instance television entertainment programmes often implicitly supported particular political values. Yet the report's emphasis on considering the purpose of programmes has meant that long-term political consequences have rarely been discussed. In addition the report depended on a series of misleading images about the nature of working-class life and culture which affected its tone and distorted its recommendations. Often Pilkington seemed perilously close to despising what was popular and entertaining, and approving only that which was rigorous and demanding.

This was unfortunate, because the report's identification of programmes as the central focus for any assessment of broadcasting is crucial. Moreover, its recognition of the structural effects of advertising on the quality of programmes is original and shrewd, and still pertinent a generation later. In addition, attempts by Pilkington to mitigate the impact of advertising by giving the third channel to the BBC, and by strengthening the power of the ITA over the companies were important factors in improving the commercial service. In particular, the report, which had been wonderfully orchestrated by Sir Hugh Greene, also gave the BBC the *élan* and confidence which were the basis for its most exciting expansion in the 1960s.[15] For the first time, the Corporation attempted to make broadcasting something like a quality popular newspaper. This is perhaps the most challenging model for a national broadcasting service.

Notes

1. Sir Hugh Greene, 'The future of broadcasting in Britain', Granada Guildhall Lecture (1972), p. 24.
2. M. Pinto Duschinsky, 'Bread and circuses; the Conservatives in office 1951–64' in V. Bogdanor and R. Skidelsky (eds), *The Age of Affluence* (Harmondsworth, Penguin, 1970), p. 55.
3. C. A. R. Crosland, 'The mass media', *Encounter* (November 1962).
4. R. Hoggart, *The Uses of Literacy* (London, Chatto & Windus, 1957), p. 16.
5. B. Jackson and D. Marsden, *Education and the Working Class* (London, Routledge & Kegan Paul, 1962), p. 223.
6. P. Wilmott and M. D. Young, *Family and Class in a London Suburb* (London, Routledge & Kegan Paul, 1960), p. 129.
7. N. Annan, 'Love among the moralists', *Encounter* (February 1960), p. 37.
8. F. R. Leavis, *The Common Pursuit* (London, Chatto & Windus, 1952), p. 192.
9. R. Williams, *Communications*, revised edn (London, Chatto & Windus, 1966), p. 10.
10. Fougasse (pseud. C. K. Bird), *The Changing Face of Britain* (London, Methuen, 1950), p. 15.
11. V. Packard, *The Hidden Persuaders* (Harlow, Longman, 1957), p. 259.
12. F. R. Leavis and D. Thompson, *Culture and Environment* (London, Chatto & Windus, 1933), p. 48.
13. M. Abrams, 'Advertising', *Listener* (15 December 1956), p. 1,089.
14. M. Abrams, 'Motivation research', *Advertising Quarterly* (November 1959), p. 311.
15. See M. Tracey, *A Variety of Lives: The Biography of Sir Hugh Greene* (London, Bodley Head, 1983).

13

How the audience is made

Commercial television produces audiences not programmes. Advertisers, in purchasing a few seconds of television time, are actually buying viewers by the thousand. The price they pay is determined by the number of people who can be expected to be watching when their advert is shown. Hence advertisers regard programmes merely as the means by which audiences are delivered to them. The sequence of programmes in any evening, week, or season reflects the quest of commercial customers to get the largest or most appropriate public they can. 'The spot is the packaging,' wrote a market researcher in *Advertising Quarterly* (June 1979); 'the product inside the package is an audience.' These are the realities which help to determine what kinds of programmes are made, when they are shown, and who sees them.

Commercial television was introduced because it was claimed that it would bring competition into broadcasting, and make the service more responsive to popular demands. The Independent Television channel was supposed to break the narrow élitism of the BBC's cultural policy. Indeed once it had been given a regional structure, it was also supposed to promote provincial culture and oppose the BBC's metropolitan bias. Finally, commercial television, its advocates claimed, would be less vulnerable to political pressure. Unlike the BBC, its finances would be independent of official control.

Few of these hopes were fully realized. The allocation of the franchise areas in which commercial companies were given the right to broadcast was designed to produce a system in which four (later five) of the largest and wealthiest regions made most of the programmes for the national network. The smaller companies made most of their programmes for local consumption; only a few of their products were to be shown nationally.

The first commitment of the commercial companies was to make a profit. Hence they were concerned to minimize the financial risks involved in making programmes. The smaller regions, whose audiences were not so attractive to advertisers, could not afford to invest in expensive programmes unless they were guaranteed a national showing. Similarly the large networking companies needed to be able to show their programmes in every region in order to cover their costs. Consequently decisions about which programmes were to be networked became centralized.

This centralization was formally established when the Independent Television Companies Association (ITCA) was set up in 1971. This decides which programmes are shown on the national network, and how much the smaller companies have to pay towards the costs of the major programme producers. The smaller companies, however, have complained that the ITCA is dominated by the five major programme networking companies.

The Independent Broadcasting Authority

Yet British 'commercial' television is not merely a product of market forces. If financial pressures were the only influence, the programme-makers' aim would always be simply to reach the largest possible audience for the smallest amount of money.

In practice this would mean a diet of American soap opera, variety shows, filmed series, quizzes, and chat shows, based on proven formulae, endlessly repeated. 'Minority' programming would cater only for groups defined primarily in terms of their consumption patterns. Current affairs would be confined to news bulletins, and advertising spots would be longer, more frequent, and more intrusive. In addition, even more programmes would be bought from abroad – particularly the USA – and fewer programmes would be made in Britain or directed at a British audience. Commercial broadcasting has not developed all of these features in Britain, because of the framework of public regulations within which it is obliged to operate.

The Independent Television Authority (ITA), and its successor the Independent Broadcasting Authority (IBA), which was given additional responsibility for commercial radio, have exerted a major influence on commercial television. The powers of the authority were widened following the report of the Pilkington Committee (1962), but the most public job of the IBA has been to license television franchises, and to reallocate these franchises periodically. The authority is also required to ensure 'balanced programming', 'due impartiality' in the treatment of controversial issues, and a high quality in programme production as a whole. To enforce its recommendations the IBA may determine the broadcasting schedule, prohibit the transmission of particular programmes, or even revoke the franchises of offending companies. In addition, the IBA continually monitors and controls the amount, timing, quality, and content of advertisements shown on commercial television.

When commercial television started in Britain in 1956, there was little idea of what form it would take. 'All we had in the beginning', recalled Sir Robert Fraser, the first Director General of the ITA, 'was an Act of Parliament, an untested authority, a little prefab in a mews by Marble Arch, and a bit of money we had to pay back.'[1] Nevertheless, the new controlling authority quickly developed a commitment to public service. Thus in the first months of broadcasting, as Sir Kenneth Clark has recalled, the ITA threatened to make current affairs programmes itself to counter a proposal to abandon such programmes by the commercial companies. The determination of the authority to maintain minority programming in peak viewing time was similarly demonstrated when it came to reallocate franchises. In 1967 some of the original commercial franchises were not renewed. As a result, programme scheduling on ITV has an important though secondary goal, that of securing the reallocation of franchises. 'Advertisers understand that current affairs and news programming is a condition of the survival of the commercial television companies,' wrote one advertising executive recently. 'It is no good complaining about them.'[2]

The IBA also intervenes in the construction of the programme schedules, requiring that one-third of all material broadcast by commercial TV companies should be 'serious non-fiction, sensibly distributed over the week as a whole in appropriate times'.[3] Without this intervention, a service which many people rely on as their primary source of news would carry very little current affairs coverage.

The IBA's intervention has also helped to maintain a wider range of cultural output than would otherwise have been the case. In 1956 'serious programming' accounted for 19 per cent of the companies' schedules. This rose to 26 per cent in 1959, and 36 per cent in 1965, a proportion which has been maintained. However, official figures have been inflated by the growing number of programmes which are classed as serious documentaries, but which are on entertainment topics (such as the Alan Whicker series). In addition, there are an increasing number of consumer-oriented programmes (on cars, holidays, and gardening, for example), some of which scarcely qualify for their official classification as 'serious and informative'. Nevertheless, programming on commercial television undoubtedly includes more serious material because of the IBA's influence, and many of these programmes have gained large audiences. The most striking example is ITV's News at Ten, which regularly features in the IBA's yearly 'Top Twenty' popularity ratings.

The Authority has also been important in maintaining the standards of entertainment on commercial television. It has limited the number of cheap American imports and the frequency with which programmes are repeated. The IBA has also assisted the smaller regional companies by charging the more profitable regions a higher rent for the use of the television transmitter which it owns, and thus making them subsidize the rental of the poorer companies. In addition, through its position on the committee which decides which programmes are shown on the central network, it has ensured that some of the regional programmes do get shown nationally.

Regions and audiences

The Television Act, 1954, had not specified how commercial television was to be organized. It had laid down no principles to guide the allocation of contracts. When commercial companies began to submit proposals to the ITA they suggested many different ways of dividing commercial broadcasting between competitors. Thus some contractors offered to provide particular kinds of programmes, all the light entertainment, or all the music; others proposed to make the programmes for particular times of day, 6–9 pm or 3–7 pm. However, Sir Robert Fraser decided that the system should be based on regional companies. In this way, he intended to prohibit the growth of a centralized monopoly based on London, and to 'give real creative power to the regions'.

Yet the principle of the federal structure seemed threatened from the very start. During the first two years commercial television was so expensive to run, reached such a small audience, and was so unprofitable that there was little interest in the smaller regions. It was during this disastrous period that Roy Thomson acquired Scottish Television at a very low cost. It was only when this company overcame its initial difficulties that the other regional services began to develop. Thomson, famous for having said that owning a commercial station was like having a licence to print money, soon made Scottish Television profitable. 'I like monopolies', he said, 'when I operate them.'[4]

Regional commercial broadcasting has survived, but in a form that makes sense in economic rather than cultural terms. Thus Tyneside and Teesside have little in common apart from geographical proximity. Yet they were given a combined television station because only the joint purchasing power of their audience was sufficient to make up a marketing unit. A more serious case is that of Harlech Television, supposedly a Welsh station, but actually required, for commercial reasons, to cater for a large English audience as well. It has been argued that some regional television stations, for example Border Television, may have strengthened, or even created, a sense of local identity. However, most of the regions have no real justification except in marketing terms. Apart from London, television regions have not even approximately coincided with local authority areas. This has at least inhibited the discussions of local political issues.

The regionalism of commercial television appears less firmly rooted in popular needs than in the convenience of the market.

Indeed the most important response by the commercial companies to regional differences within Britain has been to identify and sell distinctive characteristics in marketing terms. 'Granada has the skilled workers: surveys prove it!' read an advertisement in a 1959 trade magazine. 'Westward where women cook,' read another in *Campaign* in 1962. In 1979 Southern Television was pointing out that its A, B, and C1 housewives cook, and have time to be *femmes fatales* afterwards (*Campaign*, 5 July 1979). The differences between the habits and tastes of the various regional audiences became an essential feature of sales campaigns. In 1962 one writer claimed that 'The television regions made scientific selling more possible than ever before.'[5] New products could be launched in regions where they were most likely to be successful, and advertising campaigns could be tested by pilot surveys in a particular region. In the same way regional television meant that additional advertising pressure could be applied in any area where sales were slumping. The most important effect of the regional structure of commercial television was to change the marketing map of Britain.

Franchises and owners

The cost of developing commercial television was at first so great that franchises had to be given to syndicates which had the resources to undertake the necessary capital investment. This brought an important change in the kind of people who controlled broadcasting. Hitherto in the BBC responsibility had been vested in professional administrators whose social origins, training, and attitudes reflected the 'public service' philosophy of the Corporation. Independent television introduced a new type of executive, business-oriented and entrepreneurial, geared to the commercial criteria of the sponsors. Thus while the BBC was directed by Sir William Haley, who had started his career as a journalist on the *Manchester Guardian*, and who became editor of *The Times*, Associated Television's first director was Lew Grade, a show business and theatre impresario.

By the time that the franchises were reallocated in 1967, commercial television had become highly profitable, and consequently the justification for allowing it to be controlled by speculative capital no longer held good. Indeed such vast profits had been made from a publicly owned asset, the air waves, that the prospect of their reallocation created a flood of applications. There was an atmosphere reminiscent of Klondyke gold fever. Many of Britain's major corporations financed 'prospecting' companies composed of theatre managers and entertainment moguls spiced with a few peers or eminent members of the BBC. Although changes were made in the new franchises, the control of large corporations over commercial television was not significantly diminished.

In this way EMI, with extensive interests in the film industry, commercial radio, sports and leisure industries, and electronics, gained the major share of Thames TV, one of the five networking companies. The Associated Television Corporation gained control of another of the big five television companies, and added television to its investment in record companies, London theatres, and film production companies. Similarly the Granada group, with major interests in TV rental, cinema exhibition, bingo, social clubs, the music industry, and popular book publishing, acquired the major shareholding in what became Granada TV. Thus the redistribution of commercial franchises, instead of widening control, in practice merely consolidated the power of the great media empires.

Ownership and control of television

However, the control of commercial television companies cannot simply be equated with ownership. Those who actually produce commercial television programmes enjoy a significant degree of autonomy. But, most important of all, the pressure of market forces imposes powerful constraints on what can and cannot be broadcast. These operate irrespective of the formal ownership of commercial television. In a study of the way in which programming is determined in the USA, Wolf has argued that ownership does not explain the differences in programming between stations. 'It may be', he suggested,

> that those who saw such influences labored under a false analogy between the small town newspaper editor who may have shaped every word in his paper, and the television corporate executive, who according to the analogy controlled what was shown on the air.[6]

Indeed he concluded that in the USA the more diversely owned companies were less likely to take the networked programmes, particularly the news, current affairs, and documentaries, and more likely to replace them with old movies, old quiz shows, or old operas. They did this simply because of the pressure to attract the largest possible audience.

The economic and social organization of broadcasting is very different in Britain from that which Wolf describes in the USA. There, the more diversely owned companies were the smaller and less successful ones, which were more vulnerable to market pressures. Nevertheless, the inevitable pursuit of profit within a commercial system must have some similar consequences for the programming decisions which can be made in any country. Market forces operate as a continual limiting pressure on any commercial broadcasting system. Yet it is also clear that more socially diverse patterns of ownership could be an important factor in creating the conditions for more adventurous and varied programming.

The audience that advertisers want

The most important pressure on television scheduling is that of advertising expenditure. If television companies sell audiences, what kinds of audiences do advertisers want, and how are they packaged to attract sales? Indeed how does the real purpose of producing audiences for advertisers affect the apparent purpose of producing programmes for audience consumption?

The American system of programme sponsorship, in which advertisers pay for individual programmes, was rejected when commercial television started in Britain on the grounds that it gave advertisers direct power over programme content. Instead only 'spot advertising' was permitted. Advertisers could buy time slots only between or within programmes. At first, advertisements were limited to an average of six minutes per hour. Later, when it was seen that this led to an accumulation of advertisements in peak viewing times, which had above average amounts of advertising, it was decided to limit advertisements to no more than seven minutes in any one hour.

The decision to adopt restricted spot advertising had been hailed as a victory for public service broadcasting. 'The prohibition of sponsorship was an inspiration of the Television Act', declared Fraser, 'since it established the supremacy of the editorial principle.'[7] Spot advertisements were compared with newspaper advertising. They were seen as guaranteeing the independence of programme-making from the influence of advertisers: no rational person, it was argued, supposes that what newspapers publish in their editorial columns is determined by advertisers. Spot advertising would protect the editorial integrity of commercial television. 'Advertising will be an asset worn as a bright feather in the cap of free TV,' Sir Robert Fraser wrote, 'not as a soiled choker around the throat.'

However, spot advertising does not preclude advertisers from cal-culating how the editorial content of programmes affects the impact of their advertising message. 'After all', as an advertiser wrote as early as the 1950s, 'an advert is seen as part of a programme' (*Campaign*, 14 March 1956). Advertisers have prior knowledge of programme schedules which are published each quarter in advance of their transmission. They thus know the general character, if not the precise content, of the programmes with which their advertisements will be shown. There have been cases in which advertisers have avoided certain programmes on the grounds that their content is unlikely to dispose viewers to respond favourably to their advertisements. This is most common when the content of the programme clashes directly with the appeal of the advertisement (for example airlines have withdrawn advertisements from appearing in documentaries about air disasters). However, it has also occurred when a programme is thought to have associations that detract from the broad image of the product.

In contrast, some programmes may be preferred because they pro-vide an editorial environment conducive to a favourable response to particular advertisements, or because their prestige is thought likely to enhance that of the product or service advertised within them. Thus advertisements for newspapers appear near the news, and those for beer are often placed close to programmes on sport. The very fact that such intuitive judgments associated with programme content can influence how advertising time is bought must affect the decisions made by the companies about scheduling.

This pressure is, however, marginal. The main consideration of advertisers is not the programme environment of their advertisements, but the size and composition of the audience that the programmes will attract. Advertisers buy television time in two ways. Sometimes they buy a 'guaranteed audience', that is a fixed number of viewers. This may be made up of many small sections of the audience and spread over a whole range of programmes with low ratings. Alternatively it may be composed of a few large audiences during peak viewing times. In either case, what is bought is viewers. However, advertisers may also purchase particular advertising slots. The television companies may oblige advertisers to buy a 'package' of slots, composed of some of the peak viewing times the advertisers want, but combining other less attractive slots. Nevertheless, advertisers are more in control of the kinds of audiences their campaign will reach if they buy specific slots.

Commercial television rapidly became the leading advertising medium for mass consumer products and so was under pressure to put on programmes with an appeal to a mass audience. However, many patrons of commercial television have sought to reach particular constituents within the mass market, in particular women (who are the key decision-makers in many consumer purchases) and young people. Since commercial television derives its revenue from advertisers and not from viewers, the commercial system is thus led towards catering for these groups. Thus the success of commercial breakfast time television depends almost entirely on its capacity to attract an audience rich in consuming housewives.

Market research can provide a detailed breakdown of the audience profile for particular programmes. A massive investment is made in monitoring how many and what categories of people watch each programme. This research assists the television companies to produce programmes that will deliver the required audiences, and to provide them with an accurate measurement of the audiences which they have sold.

Research also helps advertisers predict from advance programme schedules what audiences they can expect to buy. This research takes the form of continuous monitoring of a representative sample of viewers, providing detailed figures for programme viewing analysed in terms of the size and class of audience. It is supplemented by additional surveys that analyse other more specialized characteristics of viewers. This research has established that certain types of programmes – soap operas, situation comedies, the main news bulletin, and variety programmes – have a generalized appeal that transcends differences in social class, age, and sex. It also reveals that other types of programmes – most notably political documentary programmes and serious drama – are not watched as much by women and young people. The results have shown a remarkable stability of viewing preferences since the introduction of commercial television. There has been little change in the pattern of mass viewing, apart from a small shift away from variety and sport.

The way in which commercial television time is sold generates pressure for quantity of audience, rather than quality of audience appreciation. It has even been suggested that some advertisers prefer television programmes not to be too involving, for fear of detracting from the impact of their advertisements. This has been called the 'Let's-give-the-public-the-shows-they-*least*-like-so-they'll-watch-the-ads' theory.[8] The widespread use of video-recording machines has made research into the effects of advertising even more complex. Little is yet known about the extent to which the public uses this technology to avoid adverts. But it is assumed that 'spooling on' is a common habit.

The IBA has attempted to offset the pressure for quantity of audience by circulating the companies with a weekly Audience Appreciation

Index, which monitors the quality of audience response to individual programmes. This index has consistently shown that information programmes are more highly appreciated than those concerned with entertainment. There seems to be an inverse relationship between audience size and audience enjoyment.

However, it is doubtful whether this intervention has yet had much influence on the time-buying decisions of advertisers, as no connection has yet been established between the audience's enjoyment or involvement in programmes, and their responsiveness to advertisements shown at the same time. The implications of audience appreciation research have only lately begun to be developed. It has been argued that within the two categories of information and entertainment programmes, those with large audiences tend to have higher appreciation scores than those with small audiences. Indeed some market researchers have come up with the less than remarkable finding that the more demanding a programme is, the better it has to be before people will watch it.[9]

The pressure on commercial television to maximize audiences naturally leads to a preference for 'entertainment' as opposed to 'serious' programmes. Within the broad category of entertainment there is a preference for programmes which have previously demonstrated their appeal to women and young people. Hence there is a bias against showing sport at some times of the day, as it mainly appeals to men. Commercial pressures have also led programme-makers to emphasize the personal and human interest aspects of documentary stories. Thus structural social problems are treated in the form of individual case studies. This kind of programme reaches a wider audience, particularly amongst women, than other documentary styles. The prominence given to certain types of programmes on commercial television is a direct consequence of the pressures generated by advertising for the production of certain types of audiences.

Advertising also generates a strong pressure for the television companies to produce predictable and regular audiences, as well as to maximize them. While the ratings for any particular programme may be hard to predict, because they depend so much on factors outside the control of any commercial company (in particular what the BBC is showing), viewing patterns over a year, as well as the categories and sequences of programmes, are very easy to predict.

Advertisers rely on programme schedules to produce the audiences which they pay for. This has encouraged attempts to use the sequence of programmes in order to manipulate the size of an audience over an evening. Consequently programmes with a broad audience appeal are shown early in the evening, in an attempt to capture viewing families for a particular channel for the rest of that night's programmes. Scheduling attempts to expand and consolidate the mass audience throughout the evening. It is this pressure which leads to the screening of 'minority' information programmes outside peak viewing times, and to the 'twinning' of BBC and ITV schedules for current affairs programmes. By doing this the companies may minimize choice, but they also minimize the loss of audience from programmes that get low ratings. In addition, current events programmes are thus seen by a far larger general audience than would otherwise be the case.

There is evidence that these attempts to manipulate the audience are only partly successful. Goodhardt has argued that most families watch television sporadically. The 'inheritance factor' (or the likelihood of watching the programme that comes next) seems effective for only one programme, not the whole evening's viewing. Nor would it seem that people become loyal to a channel because they are addicts of particular series. Out of forty serials screened between April and May in 1971 only 54 per cent of people who saw one episode of any serial also saw the next. Most of the people watching the second half of the story were different from those who had seen its beginning.[10]

Nevertheless, the commercial companies necessarily continue to try and maximize their audiences. The pursuit of the largest possible audience is not in itself harmful. But if it is narrowly interpreted, it may lead to schedules that are cautious, conservative, and very rarely break established patterns.

The needs of all advertisers using commercial television are not the same. Some have sought more specialized groups within the mass audience, and the financial significance of this kind of advertising is growing. This is indicated by the growth of corporate advertising, in which giant companies are merely concerned to project an image of their activities rather than any specific product. In addition, there has been an increase in consumer durables and motor advertising. These categories have risen as a proportion of total television advertising expenditure from 7 per cent in 1968 to 22 per cent in 1983.[11] This has been accompanied by a fall in food, drink, and household advertising directed at the mass market. Furthermore, there has been a growing tendency even amongst mass-market-oriented advertisers towards directing their campaigns at particular segments of the market.

The impact of this shift, however, has been muted by the difficulties involved in translating the aims of marketing strategies into buying television time. There have been fashions in market research which determine how the audience is offered to the advertiser. In the 1950s and 1960s motivational research was dominant. 'Beecham's buyers are a little more likely to strive, and are a little more neurotic,' stressed an Associated Rediffusion survey in 1962. 'Compared, that is with Aspro, Anadin and Disprin buyers, however, they are noticeably more extrovert.' Increasingly, though, there was a trend towards pilot studies of particular products and towards attempts to segment target markets with a fine precision.

However, despite attempts (by Leo Burnett and the British Bureau of Market Research in particular) to develop 'psychographic' profiles of television viewers, such methods remain impressionistic. No satisfactory method has been developed that enables advertising men to select time slots in a way that allows them to reach the types of personalities believed to be particularly susceptible to their advertising campaigns. Consequently commercial television companies have not been obliged to cater for particular groups (at least those defined by psychological categories) to any great extent.

Advertisers have been most interested in reaching 'light viewers', who are like the 'floating' voters in election studies. The success of a campaign may depend on the proportion of light viewers, who might not otherwise know about the product, that it can reach. For a time, light viewers were regarded as being particularly selective in their television watching habits. This was partly because a large proportion of light viewers were middle class, and were believed to be discriminating.

However, this view has now been challenged. Goodhardt has suggested that light viewers do not tend to watch particular types of programmes, nor do they prefer low-rating minority programmes. They tend to be as unselective as heavy viewers, but merely watch less television. Hence support of minority programmes does not seem to be a means of reaching the light viewer. On the contrary, it appears that advertising on high-rating programmes represents the most efficient way of reaching light viewers. Another study suggests, furthermore, that the pursuit of light viewers is in itself misguided. What matters is not how many advertisements of a particular product are seen, but how many in relation to the number of advertisements of a competing product.[12] The light viewer sees less than the heavy viewer of *all* the competing products on television. It may, therefore, be better to reach him or her through other advertising media.

A further problem for the advertiser is that neither minority programmes nor particular *genres* of programmes can be relied on to deliver specialized audiences. Goodhardt's analysis of the housewife audience for twenty different categories of programme showed that only Westerns are positively sought out by any viewers. Westerns were the only kind of programme with a slightly higher level of 'duplication viewing' – that is the likelihood of a viewer seeing more than one programme within this category – than could be explained by channel loyalty or overall rating figures. Most people, Goodhardt's work suggests, see further programmes of any particular *genre* only because they prefer one channel, or because the programme has a high rating, not because they are specifically interested in its content. 'People who watched one arts programme', according to Goodhardt, 'had no more tendency to see another arts programme than to see, say, a Western or a religious programme, or a sports programme with a comparable weighting.'

This characterization of television audiences as indiscriminate and promiscuous in their viewing habits has been challenged. Sue Stoessel has argued that the results of Goodhardt's research are misleading because they aggregate behaviour over several weeks. This obscures major changes in viewing behaviour from week to week. It is only by examining these detailed changes in viewing behaviour, she suggests, that preferences for individual programmes could be revealed. An analysis of changes in viewing figures over successive weeks reveals the effects of positive choice and preference, as does an analysis that distinguishes between audience behaviour in the different regions. In London, she argues, light viewers are more heavily concentrated amongst the audiences of some specific programme types. There are significant groups of viewers, at least in the London area, who do choose to watch programmes because of their content.[13]

This debate is likely to continue. The apparent failure of different categories of programmes to divide audiences into conveniently specialized groups has important implications. It may reduce the potential for commercial television to create new patterns of programmes. A low-rating current affairs programme has little to offer advertisers if it delivers, not a discriminating élite (like a 'quality' national newspaper), but large numbers of heavy viewers so hypnotized that they cannot even summon the energy to switch off the ballet or Third World poverty programme offered at the margins of peak viewing times.

Indeed the audiences for specialized programmes do not necessarily share other characteristics which would make them marketable packages for sale to advertisers. A shared interest in Westerns does not imply, for instance, a propensity to trade in a new car each year or a tendency to be a young couple setting up home for the first time. On the other hand, if Stoessel is correct, there is a market for élite and quality advertising in television, but it may not be most efficiently reached through this medium.

Indeed in so far as advertising has promoted minority programming hitherto, it has tended to be in a form that produces groups of viewers which are marketable. Travel programmes, and those about cars and cooking, have all developed partly because they cater for audiences with a shared interest in buying certain sorts of products. The advertising plans for cable and satellite television depend on the development of this commodity-based 'narrow-casting'. The greater choice of channels will, it is suggested, offer advertisers more refined groups of audience interest. However, those with less material interests in common have been, and will continue to be, less favoured.[14]

Public regulation and the public interest

In the past the IBA has played an important role in mitigating the adverse effects of advertising on broadcasting. Nevertheless, at times the Authority has been passive. For example it has been reluctant to ensure that companies have adhered to the programme policies on which they won franchises. It has been difficult for the Authority to be more active in its surveillance, partly because its statutory obligations are imprecise in many areas. However, political realities limit its power more fundamentally. The commercial television lobby is highly organized and politically effective. It employs public relations officers and cultivates an able group of MPs. In addition, many newspapers are sympathetic to the commercial television lobby. Its interests are also protected by an extensive network of contacts based on the interlocking directorships linking commercial television companies to other banking and industrial organizations. In contrast, the IBA is less effectively organized as a political lobby, and its powers of supervision – which are inevitably the product of political negotiation – are consequently constrained. Finally, the IBA may be 'punished' for its interventions into schedules or programme decisions. Thus, having been required to present more balanced programming over Christmas, the companies may retaliate by showing programmes which get only very low ratings.

However, the aims of the IBA have been furthered by the presence of the BBC as a 'public service' institution, committed to broad social and political objectives rather than to the maximization of profit. There has been a convergence between public and commercial broadcasting in which the two systems influence each other.

In addition, for much of its history commercial television has been in a strong bargaining position in relation to advertisers. ITV has been able in the past to resist some advertising pressure precisely because it has been in a seller's market. Companies have sold advertising time in ways which reduced the pressures to maximize audiences. The high profits and monopolistic position of commercial television have created an environment in which the IBA has been more effective.

Swinging sixties and sober seventies

In the 1960s and 1970s television came of age. The last two decades have seen a remarkable revolution not in the technology but in the content of broadcasting. In this period, television rapidly developed its own conventions – in the treatment of politics, interviews, documentaries, and plays – which were quite different from the earlier styles of radio or film. During the 1960s television humour began to take the form of satirizing itself – an indication of how widely the conventions of the new medium had been publicly absorbed.

This was partly a product of a more generally liberal mood, which made a wider range of possibilities available for broadcasters. After Pilkington, the BBC became a more adventurous organization. At the same time, the independent television companies became more secure, because more profitable. By the 1960s, moreover, television had taken over from the cinema a mass working-class audience.

In many ways the vast size of the television audience has posed problems for the medium. There is a continual pressure to screen programmes that will attract the highest audiences and cause offence to the fewest numbers of viewers. Yet the attempt to reach a big audience while meeting 'public service' criteria has been a creative tension.

Some commentators, like Stuart Hood, Michael Tracey, Anthony Smith, and even Sir Hugh Greene, have seen the period since the early 1970s as one of increasing caution in television. Not only has the reporting of the troubles in Northern Ireland provided many problems for the broadcasting institutions, but also the BBC and ITV have become more vulnerable to government threats over a broad range of issues.

Channel 4, minorities, and money

Yet it was a reinterpretation of the public service principle which produced Channel 4. The ideas behind the creation of this new channel were a product of the tensions identified during television's most creative and expansionist years. But it was also influenced by the political problems of the 1970s. However, by the time the station opened there had been a change not only in the general economic climate but also more damagingly, in the conditions of competition for television audiences.

Channel 4 'publishes' programmes made by independent production companies. It does not make any programmes of its own, although it does commission them. It is financed by the existing commercial companies who supply much of its material. The channel is not, however, directly controlled by the ITV companies. It is obliged to screen programmes for the various 'minority' interests that are not well served elsewhere in the television system.

The minority-based rationale of Channel 4 had a number of origins. Perhaps the most important was the experience of even the most distinguished and 'marketable' producers and directors that it was impossible to work, in Britain, outside the BBC or ITV companies.[15] Those who wanted to make programmes that did not conveniently fit into the patterns of viewing developed by the duopoly, or those who simply wanted a greater control over their own material, found it difficult to raise the necessary finance or find buyers for what they made. It was argued that there evidently were audiences within the mass of viewers with more distinctive tastes and needs, but the existing channels allowed these consumers little opportunity to demonstrate their preferences. A new pattern of differently organized production companies, liberated from the limitations of the ITV or BBC systems, would be able to find and develop these more specialized audiences. Therefore any innovation in the television service ought to make it possible for 'independent' producers to explore the interests of these minorities.

It was also strongly argued that television had failed to reflect Britain's contemporary cultural diversity. Reformers emphasized the needs of the various Black and Asian communities, as well as those of minorities like the young and the old, for programmes which dealt with their concerns and ways of life. Any new service, it was suggested, should produce material for these social and ethnic minorities.

Finally, some market researchers believed that the blunt instrument of television advertising could, by the 1980s, be refined. A new channel could offer programme incentives that attracted discriminating 'minorities' of selective television viewers and could sell them the things they had particular interests in. For the first time television would be able to deliver higher concentrations of the more affluent consumers that advertisers wanted.

The logic of Channel 4 looked appealingly neat. It would offer greater freedom of choice, and serve minorities neglected elsewhere. Unfortunately the minorities that producers, social reformers, and advertisers were interested in were somewhat different.

Channel 4 represents an important (and perhaps the last) reinterpretation of the public service role of broadcasting. In this version, the freedom of creative individuals to risk making the programmes they want to make is seen as the guarantor of public good. It was a Labour government which decided to back the new channel (although a Conservative one presided over its birth). Labour support was based on a feeling that the political consensus developed by the existing broadcasting services was too restrictive. Consequently the channel has been given the opportunity to create new conventions for dealing with controversial and political issues. It is not obliged to balance views within a programme, but only over the whole schedule and over time. It can, therefore, broadcast more clearly partisan material.

However, the channel's capacity to innovate depends on the politics of money. The only ultimate defence Channel 4 has for its new style and new programmes is their ability to attract advertising revenue. By the 1980s the Conservative government was using the success of Channel 4 to attack public service broadcasting, by demanding that greater numbers of programmes should be produced by 'independent' companies. Yet Channel 4's innovations had been completely dependent on the development of public service ideals.

The limitations of commercial broadcasting are largely the result of the economic pressures to which it is exposed. That British commercial television has been in some ways superior to others is due to the public service traditions and institutions that have so far determined its development. Nevertheless, the implications of a comment by Sidney Bernstein, the television industrialist, should always be borne in mind. 'Commercial television is a very unusual business,' he said,'... you don't necessarily make more money if you provide a better product.'

Yet the market and the audience for television programmes is altering dramatically under the impact of a whole series of technological changes. Whether the advantage of increased variety will be enough to offset the dilution of resources remains to be seen. Indeed the 1960s and 1970s may yet be regarded, in television terms, as a lost golden age.

Notes

1. Sir Robert Fraser, *ITA Notes* (October 1970).
2. P. Todd, 'Scarcity of TV time!', *Campaign* (26 January 1979).
3. *IBA Annual Report* (1978).
4. R. Thomson, *Contrast: Television Quarterly* (winter 1961), p. 107.
5. Associated Rediffusion, 'Cold and flu remedies', *Market Profiles*, 6 (1962).
6. F. Wolf, *Television Programming for News and Current Affairs* (New York, Praeger, 1972).
7. Sir Robert Fraser, *ITA Notes* (January 1970).
8. C. E. Setlow, 'TV Rating, there just might be a better way', *New York Times* (31 December 1978).
9. T. P. Barwise, A. S. C. Ehrenberg, and G. J. Goodhardt, 'Audience appreciation and audience size', *Journal of the Market Research Society*, 21, 4 (October 1979), p. 269.

10. G. J. Goodhardt, A. S. C. Ehrenberg, and M. A. Collins, *The Television Audience: Patterns of Viewing* (Farnborough, Saxon House, 1975).
11. N. Rogers, tables of advertising expenditure in 'It's all right for some', *Admap* (1983).
12. A. Roberts and S. Prentice, 'Reaching light TV viewers', *Admap* (March 1979).
13. S. Stoessel, reply to Roberts and Price, 'The real weight of light viewers', *Admap* (June 1979), p. 277.
14. M. Johnson 'Narrow-casting – problems and opportunities', *Admap* (June 1983).
15. See S. Lambert, *Channel 4* (London, British Film Institute, 1982).

14

The information society: video, cable, and satellite

Video, cable, and satellite technologies have been discussed in such extravagant terms, and introduced with such covert haste, that their wider social and economic implications have been ignored. We are in danger of seeing the emerging pattern as inevitable, and accepting its consequences fatalistically.

Sixty-year-old audience habits are about to change. But the impact will go far beyond what people do with their leisure. The information revolution affects what goods the country produces and Britain's survival as an industrial nation. It will affect how the national image is developed and our political priorities both at home and abroad. It is closely related to problems about the increased capacity of modern communications to monitor, collect, store, and sell information about individual citizens. Finally there is the possibility, even the likelihood, of direct impact on political behaviour.

Experts are divided between the neophiliacs and the cultural pessimists. Neophiliacs write of the disappearance of class (by which they mean that traditional types of work will be replaced), the disappearance of work-places (as the work-bench is supplanted by the home computer terminal), and the eventual relocation of the production process to the developing world as the management of information (about production and consumption) becomes the key commodity in the technologically advanced economies.

Such predictions seem premature. Neophiliac arguments bring to mind an earlier debate about the arrival of the 'post-industrial' society. Recent comments by Anthony Smith and John Howkins belong to the same tradition as Daniel Bell and Alain Touraine,[1] who argued in the 1970s that the expansion of the service sector, increasing expenditure on the production of knowledge, and ever larger investment in research, together with changes in the technologies of production and leisure, were creating a new social order. *Plus ça change*: as Krishan Kumar has argued, similar developments became apparent early in the history of industrialization, and do not represent any qualitative change.[2] Many of the neophiliac predictions of future patterns are based on naïve extrapolation from current trends, and ignore the idiosyncracies of historical development.

The pessimists, on the other hand, see changes in mass commercial culture as a subversion of 'standards'. In the discussion of broadcasting technologies the new 'cultural' pessimists, such as Nick Garnham and Richard Collins, join hands with the 'industrial' pessimists like Mike Cooley and Henry Braverman,[3] who share a concern with the impact of computer and information technology on employment. Thus broadcasting becomes the fulcrum of a wider social and economic upheaval. The pessimists see little evidence for the emergence of new cultural patterns and much evidence for the irreparable damage to old ones.

In practice this 'revolution' represents the continued industrialization of the service sector. New technology performs old tasks more efficiently: in particular the sorting, correlating, and ordering of information in bureaucracies. Many of the current problems in broadcasting policy concern the next stage: the domestication of the computer.

The problems posed by this development are common to all countries. Few countries, however, have such strong broadcasting traditions as Britain, or such determined neophiliacs at the helm. When the Conservative government came to power in 1979 an official ideology of non-interference in the market was buttressed by a vigorously neophiliac view of information technology. A key Cabinet Information Technology Advisory Panel (ITAP), including experts in electronics and industrialists but nobody with any broadcasting experience, concluded that industrial revival was to be stimulated by 'cabling up' the nation. The necessary conditions for this economic miracle (a high proportion of homes linked to high quality cable networks), it was argued, would best be created by providing an alluring range of television channels for the eager public. That these would inevitably offer a consistent diet of old films, sport, American soap opera, and light entertainment was regarded as incidental.

The committee urged in its 1982 report the adoption, not of North American models, but of a more sophisticated cabling system that would permit households to receive and use up to a hundred different channels. Thus the nation would be lured into the new infrastructure by stealth: having paid for cabling in order to receive more entertainment, television users would find themselves linked conveniently to a variety of multipurpose networks with opportunities for computerized shopping, working, and learning. 'It is as if', one commentator has suggested, 'the Roman Senate had sanctioned, without debate, the proposition that improvements to the supply system of the Roman legions should first be introduced by speeding up the chariots in the hippodrome.'[4]

So solid is the expectation of a virtually insatiable appetite for television that official calculations have been based on the assumption that the technological leap forward can be accomplished without support from public funds. Britain is the only country in Europe which expects the entire capital cost of laying a cable system to be paid for by the sellers and consumers of the recycled programmes and films, while in West Germany – and also in Japan – state investment in a comprehensive cable system has become a major, and expanding, element in the annual budgets.

British optimism, in contrast to the prudence of its competitors, may of course be vindicated. Yet the cost of cabling up Britain's larger urban areas alone, including less than half the nation's population, is estimated at between £4 billion and £5 billion: a large sum to be found from private sources, even those of television addicts.

Apart from the problem of initial finance, there are other grounds for wondering whether neophiliac hopes are not premature. Thus in the USA – where the success of cable had been seen as providing a model for Britain – the cable revolution seems to be failing, or at least stabilizing. In 1983 more cable stations closed in the USA than opened.

Indeed 'popular' programmes aimed at mass audiences, supposedly the basis of cable expansion, have failed to find adequate markets. Where cable has succeeded commercially there has been a cultural price. In 1981 the most profitable American cable network offered its viewers *Rocky II* forty-five times, *The Muppet Movie* thirty-seven times, and *Superman* fifty-three times – all within the space of six months.[5] The pressure of real or supposed mass taste has been inexorable: even in Manhattan, with its sophisticated viewers, CBS has been forced to end the brief experiment of providing one quality station.

In Britain there is an additional factor, more powerful than in the USA: video. The proportion of video-owning homes is already twice as great in Britain as in the USA and, despite the recession, video ownership continues to grow faster in Britain than in any other European country. By early 1985 approximately one family in four possessed a video: a development not taken into account by official calculations at the beginning of the decade. Thus in the battle for public viewing hours, cable will face a more formidable task than elsewhere. Indeed, by the late 1980s the cable revolution had failed to appear, let alone speed a new post-industrial society.

Sabotaging public service broadcasting

One reason for believing that cable – with or without government intervention – will not reveal an as yet untapped demand for a wider range of television programmes is that since 1979, and following an American trend, the number of 'live' television viewing hours per British inhabitant has actually declined. Between 1980 and 1983 average viewing in Britain dropped by as much as one and a half hours per week, with particularly large reductions during bank holidays when ratings are normally highest. Christmas 1982 saw a staggering 22 per cent average drop since the previous December, with barely any recovery a year later.

As we have seen, part of the reason is the parallel growth of video: time previously spent on current programmes is now devoted to video-cassettes. (Significantly 75 per cent of video usage is for BBC and ITV programmes at non-networked times, a statistic that throws doubt on the thesis that there exists a pent-up demand for material not at present available on existing channels.) Since, however, the downward trend preceded the take-off of video, other factors – boredom with the medium, for example – were presumably also involved. If so, pressure on the networks may not cease when video ownership reaches saturation point.

Certainly satellite, cable, and video in combination will accelerate the decline in audiences for existing networks: more viewing opportunities will mean fewer viewing hours. As ratings fall, something will have to be sacrificed. In the bitter struggle for survival an early victim is almost bound to be public service broadcasting. This ideal depends for its realization on funding. In the new hyper-competitive climate, funds will be in short supply. As the 1982 White Paper (*The Development of Cable Systems and Services*) pointed out, one hour of home-grown documentary can cost £20,000, and one hour of high quality drama as much as £200,000. By contrast, an hour of American soap opera can be bought for as little as £2,000. We may expect, therefore, a trend similar to that in the cinema in the 1940s and 1950s: fewer programmes made in Britain, and an ever-expanding proportion of imports.

Here Thatcherite market liberalism will have particularly disastrous effects. With the proposed abolition of quotas for foreign programmes, there will be little to restrain cable stations from importing much and commissioning little. With no rules to enforce a balanced diet of programming, the new stations will naturally turn, like their American counterparts, to the lowest common denominator of pop, chat, soap, and sport. Perhaps the wider range of viewing which satellite, cable, and video will provide will lead to an imaginative exercise by viewers of 'freedom of choice'. Existing evidence, however, suggests the opposite: freedom will be used to consume an even greater concentration of pop, chat, soap, and sport than now.

If this analysis is correct, a shift of power within the networks is likely to follow. Where broadcasting is protected through subsidy or monopoly, producers can be given their head; where commercial pressures necessitate a heavy reliance on imported package deals and low budget formula programming, producers will be reduced, in effect, to corporation men: executives carrying out company policy. With less money available, making fewer 'original' programmes, initiative will be at a low premium. In particular, there will be little incentive to make programmes about British subjects, political, social, or cultural, purely for domestic consumption.

There is a further danger or, at least, an area of uncertainty. Until recently the economics of television were determined by an invariable: people bought television sets to watch programmes put out by the networks. The relationship between programme-maker and viewer, through the medium of a single-purpose instrument, and the role of public policy in regulating programme content, were based on this simple truth. The old relationship is rapidly weakening and soon will hold no more. Watching 'live' programmes ('live' in the sense of received from the ether) is already only one of the purposes of a television set. When it becomes possible to use television not only for video, but also to make hotel reservations, monitor electricity consumption, and place bets, 'live' viewing may become a comparatively minor factor in the calculations of those who buy, sell, and produce television sets, with inevitable consequences for those who make programmes as well. At the same time, the obligations of public policy become more difficult to define when the 'content' of television is no longer so evidently a single 'cultural' product.

Politics and new technology

There will also be consequences for politicians and political parties. Broadcasting, and especially television, has been a vehicle of political integration, establishing what Denis McQuail has called the 'common coin of values, ideas, information and cultural expression'. Arguably television has set the political agenda: ordering public priorities and arousing public concern for good or ill.

Key to this process has been the national audience. The power of television has been based, to a considerable degree, on lack of choice: almost any nationally networked programme is certain to count its viewers in millions. Cable will increase the range of 'choice'. Without necessarily increasing variety or quality of subject matter (perhaps, as has been argued, reducing it), a larger number of highly competitive commercial stations will fragment and atomize: the national audience will vanish. Here we should avoid premature judgment. Such a change might have beneficial results or bad ones. Given the centrality of broadcasting to modern politics, however, it is virtually certain to alter the nature of the political game.

Will national political coverage be reduced in importance relative to local issues? Such a development might be positive. It might provide citizens with greater awareness of what affects them directly, and give more scope to local campaigns and pressure groups. On the other hand, the example of the existing local press gives little ground for optimism. Lack of initiative, cost, and the fear of writs have discouraged the vast majority of newspapers, including the big-circulation regional dailies, from acting as anything more than publishing houses for politicians' handouts.

If, therefore, a diversity of local television stations produces an increase in local political reporting, the benefits remain uncertain. What does seem likely is that the present 'privileged' status of news and documentary, which has been a prominent feature of public service television, will be eroded. Political coverage at least held its own as inter-channel competition increased: between 1956 and 1976 the time devoted to politics quadrupled on average. But this tendency may have already begun to be reversed. It has been pointed out that, during the 1983 general election, campaign coverage on the two major channels (BBC 1 and ITV) was restricted to little more than a series of interviews with leading personalities: examination of campaign issues was relegated to BBC 2 and Channel 4.[6] Cable stations with small budgets and instant commercial targets are scarcely likely to widen the range or deepen the level of discussion. Indeed for all its failings, television coverage of politics in Britain has been serious and sustained. Indeed it may be argued that political programmes with the depth of reporting of the quality press (though with its definition of the limits of political discussion) are served out, for largely historical reasons, to a *Sun-* and *Star*-buying public. It seems likely that the commercial pressures of cable and video may ensure that, instead of deriving political information from television, large numbers of people will, in effect, be deprived of any reliable political information at all.

Even if there is no reduction in the time allotted to current affairs and documentary programmes, cuts in budgeting are bound to have a deleterious effect on quality and, in particular, originality. National reporting all too easily becomes a collaborative exposure of the point of view of the spokesman for a particular interest, provided that the interest in question has Establishment approval. The reason is cost as much as bias: investigative journalism, digging beneath the surface, and asking uncomfortable questions, involves more time, resources, and financial risk. Here competitive pressures are likely to be the enemy of imagination, professionalism, and that which is controversial.

Censorship

Some political effects of the new technology are speculative. Others are already frighteningly apparent. One development in the second category is the closing of doors which many had regarded as permanently unlocked: the reimposition of censorship in a new form, made the more dangerous because it is occurring in response to a public mood that owes much to fear of the new technology itself.

While dismantling 'public service' standards in broadcasting the Thatcher government has given its support to legislation on video-recording which promises to introduce a system of bureaucratic pre-censorship of a kind unprecedented since Oliver Cromwell's 'licenses of the press'. Ostensibly the new censorship is concerned with pornographic and violent home videos, dubbed by the press 'video nasties'. In practice the implications will be far wider. The new legislation sets aside the earlier 'interpretative' view of screen images, as held by the British Board of Film Censors (BBFC). This view was concerned with evaluating the meaning and intention of scenes, and emphasized that it was in context that any given act had to be judged. This view is replaced, in effect, with an index of prohibited acts. All videos must be submitted to the board, and may be liable for censorship if they contain any material which deals with 'human sexual activity', 'images of human sexual organs' (even if the films are made as part of training programmes for medical staff), or 'mutilation, torture or other acts of gross violence' (like scenes of war and sporting events). Defence on the grounds of artistic or literary merit is therefore likely to be set aside.

Film censorship has a long and in some respects hilarious history. More recently, however, the BBFC has seen its role as one of 'leading' public taste as much as curbing it.[7] In the future it seems likely that a board of nominees, for the first time directly appointed by the Home Office, will apply specific standards of permissible and non-permissible sexual or violent acts.

Will the new regulations affect television and films in general? It seems likely. An increasing proportion of both are made with the video market in mind: the natural tendency will be to tailor such material to make it acceptable both for direct transmission and for censored sale to the public.

Perhaps the availability of unpleasant material to the public, especially young people, will be reduced by the new legislation. The demand for it, however, seems so widespread that, as with prohibition in the USA, a flourishing black market is to be expected. The history of censorship in general reveals little evidence of a beneficial effect on public morality or mental health. But whatever the possible benefits, the dangers of illiberalism are manifest: thus, for example, coverage of wars, deliberately and rightly intended to shock, may well be restricted.

Conclusion

Should we, therefore, side firmly with the cultural pessimists against the neophiliacs? The answer is that much depends on the behaviour of broadcasters and programme-makers and, more particularly, governments, in the face of technological advance. Both neophiliacs and cultural pessimists emphasize the *power* of new technologies. Machines and inventions are not inherently powerful, nor is the use to which they are put inevitable. While the new technology brings with it many dangers, and some opportunities, its impact will depend crucially, and especially in the early years, on how it is managed.

Notes

1. See, for example, A. Smith, 'The fading of the industrial age', *Political Quarterly* (June 1983), or *Goodbye Gutenberg: The Newspaper Revolution of the 1980s* (London, Oxford University Press, 1980); J. Howkins, *New Media, New Policies* (London, British Film Institute, 1982); D. Bell, *The Coming of Post-industrial Society: A Venture in Social Forecasting* (London, Heinemann, 1976).
2. K. Kumar, *Prophecy and Progress* (Harmondsworth, Penguin, 1978).
3. See, for example, N. Garnham, 'Public service versus the market', *Screen*, 24, 1 (1983); R. Collins, 'Broadband Black Deaths cuts queues: the information society and the UK', *Media, Culture and Society*, 5 (1983); M. Cooley, 'New technology and jobs' in P. Sieghart (ed.), *Microchips with Everything* (London, Comedia, 1983).
4. S. Hearst, 'The development of cable systems and services', *Political Quarterly* (autumn 1983), p. 388.
5. B. Winston, 'Unusual rubbish', *Sight and Sound* (summer 1982), p. 17.
6. P. Kellner, 'The last television election?', *New Statesman* (July 1983).
7. B. Brown, 'An interview with the film censor', *Screen*, 23, 5 (1982).

Part III

Theories of the media

15

The sociology
of the mass media

Do newspapers, broadcasting, and mass entertainment matter? Do they change society or merely reflect the changes created by others? This chapter will argue that the media do have an independent influence, but not in the sense that has often been assumed. The power of the press and broadcasting is not necessarily greatest when the political involvement in the media is most apparent.

One (determinist) tradition has stressed the relationship of the media with the governing class. It has argued that the media play an important part in modern society. Another (empirical or pluralist) school has looked at the response of audiences to the media, and has concluded that other social pressures overrule any independent effect. These two approaches have been regarded as opposed to one another. In fact, as we will show, they are not incompatible.

The Frankfurt School and the power of
the press and broadcasting

'Propaganda, propaganda, propaganda,' Hitler said after the unsuccessful Munich *putsch* in 1923. 'All that matters is propaganda.' Although the Nazis emphasized the importance of oratory and public meetings, they were also fascinated by the emergence of the new technologies of mass communication in the USA and Britain. In particular they saw radio and film as a means of extending the influence of demagogy.

When Hitler came to power in 1933, a group of German intellectuals opposed to the new regime – and seeking to explain the fascist success – turned their attention to the role of the media. The so-called 'Frankfurt School' of writers argued that the roots of the fascist or 'authoritarian' personality were to be found in the nature of the family. However, in explaining what made a population potentially fascist, or why there was no revolt before the Nazi regime began to use widespread force, they also

saw the press, radio, films, and even comics and popular music as
reinforcing these early influences. The new mass media strengthened
the habits and attitudes which made people susceptible to fascist
arguments.

The USA, mass culture, and Europeans

Many members of the Frankfurt School became refugees and settled in
the USA, for which they developed a profound distaste. Disorientated
and homesick they reacted against every aspect of the American way of
life. They concluded that American mass culture was an irreversible
force which was destroying superior European cultural traditions. What
was worse, mass culture produced precisely the kinds of personality traits
that made the population vulnerable to fascist domination. The Frankfurt writers believed, incorrectly, that the USA was also about to become
fascist, as Germany had done before.

However, their reaction to mass culture is better understood as part of
a more general European response to the USA. The Frankfurt analysis
of the role of the press, films, and later television is very similar to that of
the literary critic F. R. Leavis. Broadcasting, Leavis argued in 1932, was
'little more than a means of passive diversion but one that made active
recreation, especially active use of the mind, more difficult'. And, in an
essay called 'Mass civilization and minority culture', he concluded that
'The prospects of culture, then, are very dark. There is less room for
hope, in that a standardized civilization is rapidly enveloping the world.'
Many of Leavis's views on the USA during this period had been formed
by reading a book by Robert and Helen Lynd called *Middletown*. This
described the increasing isolation of individuals, social fragmentation,
and the pervasiveness of the profit motive in a typical American town.

Thus the Frankfurt School writers shared with many other European
social and literary critics a revulsion against American culture. Much of
the work of writers like Marcuse and Adorno on the media was based on
a rejection of that which was modern, mass, and American.

Liberalism and the individual and the
emergence of fascism

The Frankfurt critics, both in Germany and later in the USA, were
concerned to explain the failure of liberalism, and of the liberal emphasis
on freedom of speech, expression, and creativity. Writers like Adorno,
Marcuse, and Arendt (although she can only loosely be described as a
member of this group) pointed to what they saw as the weakness of these

concepts in practice. These ideals, the Frankfurt writers believed, had degenerated into a corrupt and selfish individualism. The mass media had played a major part in this process: manipulating society by vulgarizing its culture. In an essay called 'The end of Utopia', Marcuse wrote, 'Today we have the capacity to turn the world into hell and we are well on the way to doing so.'

According to the Frankfurt School the unique individual personality was being destroyed by society. Adorno wrote in *Prisms* of the illusory importance and autonomy of private life which conceals the fact that it 'drags on only as an appendage of the social process'. The celebration of the home, family, and the individual which characterized liberal thought and bourgeois life in the nineteenth and twentieth centuries was already decayed. 'Nothing proved easier to destroy than the privacy and private morality of people who thought of nothing but safeguarding their private lives,' argued Arendt.[1] Totalitarianism was seen as both a cause of this process, and an effect of it.

The Frankfurt School saw the loss of individuality as the cause of dependence on great mass organizations. This analysis implied that society had returned to a more primitive form of association. The interdependence of highly specialized individuals, or what Durkheim called 'organic solidarity', had been succeeded by a new and barbarous homogeneity. Only a 'mechanical' cohesion was possible, dependent on similarity and standardization. Horkheimer argued that, paradoxically, individuality was impaired by the decline in the impulse for collective action. 'As the ordinary man withdraws from participating in political affairs, society tends to revert to the law of the jungle, which crushes all vestiges of individuality,' he wrote.[2] In this analysis the Frankfurt theorists were claiming that totalitarianism emerged as a result of corrupt social institutions and the decline of liberal principles.

There was also another explanation of the success of fascism, which might be characterized as a paranoid theory of change. In this a stealthy process of substitution occurs. This constitutes a Gresham's law of culture and personality, in which bad inexorably drives out good.

The mass media are the key agents of this process. They replace real cultural values with their 'look alikes'. This view that the media provide an ersatz and inferior culture is an important element in the Frankfurt explanation of totalitarianism, which assumed that many of the changes brought about through the media would be fought if they were recognized. Horkheimer wrote in *The Eclipse of Reason* that

Just as the slogans of rugged individualism are politically useful to large trusts in society seeking exemption from social control, so in mass culture the rhetoric of individuality, by imposing patterns for collective imitation, subverts the very principle to which it gives lip service.

Adorno, in a book called *The Jargon of Authenticity*, explains how the 'mass media can create an aura which makes the spectator seem to experience a non-existent actuality'. This subversion of values is a process which Hayek (a writer who came to rather different conclusions) also observed. 'To make a totalitarian system function effectively,' he wrote, 'it is not enough that everybody should be forced to work for the same ends. It is essential that people should come to regard them as their own ends.' The easiest way to do this, he argued, was to substitute new meanings for familiar and respected values, like liberty and freedom.

There is a third explanation of the success of totalitarianism in the work of the Frankfurt writers. In this totalitarianism emerges as the inevitable product of capitalism: the final subjugation of every aspect of life to commercial values. 'The individual now reproduces on the deepest level, in his instinctual structure, the values and behaviour patterns that serve to maintain domination,' wrote Marcuse.

Thus the School suggests three competing explanations of the emergence of fascism. The first sees totalitarian success as a consequence of the attrition of institutions. As Lasswell wrote, 'The Nazis came to power because of weak democracy.'[3] The second suggests that formerly vital values were hollowed out, and replaced with deluding substitutes. The third that fascism did not emerge by default but by evolution.[4] But whatever the explanation, the Frankfurt writers were agreed on one point: the new mass media were not merely a tool of totalitarianism, they were a major reason for its existence.

Entertainment

Above all else (according to the Frankfurt School) radio, film, popular music, and television share an overriding concern to entertain. This was the ultimate form of corruption. Indeed for these writers, 'entertainment' occupies much the same kind of role as self-abuse in pre-Freudian medical literature.

Entertainment promised relief and relaxation but, Rosenberg argued, 'Far from dispelling unrest, all the evidence on hand now suggests that mass culture exacerbates it.' Indeed the atomized individuals of mass society lose their souls to the phantom delights of the film, the soap opera, and the variety show. They fall into a stupor. This apathetic hypnosis Lazarsfeld was to call the 'narcotyzing dysfunction' of exposure to the mass media.

Entertainment thus led to blindness and lunacy. 'It is becoming increasingly plain', wrote Adorno in *The Authoritarian Personality*, 'that people do not behave in such a way as to further their interests, even when it is clear to them what these interests are.' People, it was argued, became insensitive to their own needs.

'The unreal delights and the frenzied fascination' of the mass media prevented them from acting collectively. They became the irrational victims of false wants. Marcuse argued that addiction to the media resulted in an absolute docility: the public had 'been enchanted and transformed into a clientèle by the suppliers of popular culture'. Reisman developed the analogy in *The Lonely Crowd*: 'Glamour in politics, the packaging of the leader, the treatment of the events by the mass media, substitutes for the self-interest of the inner directed man the abandonment to society of the outer directed man.'

Industrialization and leisure

The Frankfurt School argued that leisure – empty time filled with entertainment – had been industrialized. The production of culture had become standardized and dominated by the profit motive as in other industries. In a mass society leisure was constantly used to induce the appropriate values and motives in the public. The modern media trained the young for consumption. '"The sphere of pleasure" has itself become a sphere of cares,' Reisman argued. Leisure had ceased to be the opposite of work, and had become a preparation for it.

The repetition of the forms of the mass media resembled the monotony of the assemby line: what Adorno called 'The ever-changing production of what is always the same'. In this process, it was argued, culture is consumed by the process of industrialization. Marcuse pointed at the practice of listening to serious music while doing other things (the phenomenon of 'Bach in the kitchen'). Music presented as 'classic', he suggested, 'comes to life as other than itself'. The fact that modern methods of reproduction have increased the quantity of music, art, and literature available to the public does not mean that culture spreads to the masses; rather that culture is destroyed in order to make entertainment.

'At its worst mass culture threatens not merely to cretinize our taste,' argues Rosenberg, 'but to brutalize our senses while paving the way to totalitarianism.' Lazarsfeld and Merton put the case succinctly: 'Economic power seems to have reduced direct exploitation and to have turned to a subtler type of psychological exploitation,' they wrote of the USA in the 1950s. Overt totalitarian force was increasingly obsolescent. Radio, film, and television seemed even more effective than terror in producing compliance.

Complexity and mass culture

The Frankfurt School argued that although the messages of the media might be simple, explaining them was not. The overt content of any programme, film, or newspaper was merely the basis for interpretation. The mass media appeared to confirm the traditional values of British puritanical middle-class society. The real message they communicated, however, was one of 'adjustment and unreflecting obedience'. It was necessary to analyse not only the content, but also the form of the media and the way in which they were used. 'The trouble with the educated philistine', wrote Arendt, 'was not that he read the classics, but that he did so prompted by the ulterior motive of self-perfection.' Nothing, for the Frankfurt School, was what it seemed. It was always worse.

Their view of the illusion of apparent social relations was part of a developing analysis during the 1940s. Lasswell's *Psychopathology and Politics* had claimed 'that the significance of political opinions is not to be grasped apart from the private motives which they symbolized'. Political motives 'derive their vitality from the displacement of private effects upon public objects'. Later, in a bleak article written in 1941 on 'The garrison state', Lasswell also suggested that although 'instrumental democracy may be in abeyance the media will doubtless continue to purvey the symbols of mystic democracy'.

Indeed capitalist culture was so powerful that it could even use opposition to further its own interests. As Benjamin wrote in *Illuminations*,

> We are confronted with the fact ... that the bourgeois apparatus of production and publication is capable of assimilating, indeed of propagating an astonishing amount of revolutionary themes without ever seriously putting into question its own continued existence – or that of the class which owns it.

It follows from this that only that culture which was not assimilable and difficult to understand could be the source of genuine opposition.

Mass society theorists and the power of the media

The concern of Adorno, Arendt, and their colleagues with the direct psychological impact of the new media was in part a product of their experience in Germany. The rise of Hitler encouraged the Frankfurt School to view all mass audiences with suspicion, as though they were indistinguishable in behaviour and malleability from the crowds at a Nazi rally.

These writers also, however, developed another more long-term concept of the power of the media. Marcuse commented in *One Dimensional Man*:

> Objections are made that we greatly overrate the indoctrinating power of the media and that by themselves people would feel and satisfy the needs that are now superimposed upon them. This objection misses the point. The preconditioning does not start with the mass production of radio or TV. The people enter this stage as preconditioned receptacles of long standing. In this more complex view the public do not abdicate rational consideration of their interest blindly. More subtly, the whole basis of rational calculation is undermined.

Nevertheless, even this more complex explanation has a simple goal. 'Ideology for the Frankfurt School works one way,' Swingewood has commented, 'that is from above, seeping into working-class consciousness as an alien and conservative force.' Even leisure had been reduced to an adjunct of capitalism, its sole purpose 'the restoration of the human labour force for labour',[5] while all human needs had been redirected into 'consumption' – the destructive exhaustion of resources rather than their creative use. As a consequence the Frankfurt School saw the function of the media, whether in the long run or more directly, as controlling the public in the interests of capital.

It is here that the Frankfurt analysis is most vulnerable. What appears to be a particular account of the media is actually a view of capitalist institutions in general. Indeed the very strength of the Frankfurt analysis is dissipated in its generality.

Pluralism: the role of personal influence on the reaction of the audience to the media

The power of the media, and the pessimistic Frankfurt model of industrial society, were tested, challenged, and apparently refuted by American empirical researchers. A series of major surveys seemed to show that the media had very little influence on popular opinion.

In an odd way, the small town American gossip came to the rescue of democracy. Survey findings seemed to prove that people were not the isolated atomized automatons suggested by mass society theory. Thus the inhabitants of places which sounded like the locations for John Ford movies – Eerie County, Decatur, Elmira, and Rovere – appeared oblivious to, rather than hypnotized by, the blandishments of media propaganda. Far more important influences were provided by friends, neighbours, and drinking companions – whether people were deciding which presidential candidate to vote for or what brand of cornflakes to have for breakfast. It was personal contact, not media persuasiveness, that counted.

Market research methods were used to investigate whether the press and broadcasting had an effect on public attitudes. However, the concept of an 'effect' which was used in this research was very limited. Media messages were compared to 'bullets' and the only effects evaluated were immediate changes in audience attitudes.

Conceptualizing the power of the media

Nevertheless, empirical research as a whole has at least begun to question the way in which we understand the effects of the media. Thus writers on the press and broadcasting have credited the media with the power to 'influence' or 'persuade' their audience, to 'change attitudes', or even to 'affect behaviour'.

Yet these terms are imprecise and obscure. What is it to persuade or influence? All of the terms which are used to describe what the media do have a behaviourist basis, in which a single and external force – the media – has an impact on a single subject – the person. The empirical studies, in a very limited way, have re-examined these concepts. In a narrow attempt to measure effects they have at least dislodged terms which otherwise have been unquestioned.

The empirical work is inadequate. The theories which underlie our understanding of the media might be revealed more usefully than in an attempt to measure problematic phenomena. Indeed the early survey tradition of the 1940s and 1950s eventually abandoned interest in the media. However, it is possible to discuss the problem of how the power of the media might be conceptualized in examining the empirical work. For, as yet, there is no adequate vocabulary to describe the relationships between the media, individuals, and society.

Reinforcement

Early surveys seemed to show that the media did not change people's minds. 'Paradoxically campaign propaganda exerted one major effect – by producing no overt effect on voting behaviour at all – if by the latter "effect" we naïvely mean a change in vote,' wrote Lazarsfeld in 1944. In fact the media confirmed people in the opinions which they already held. Propaganda marshalled the faithful. It did not 'win over' the wavering or the opposed.

As election campaigns progressed, however, people became more interested in politics, but only because more of them had made up their minds. 'Thus they became both more likely to pay attention', wrote Schramm, 'and less likely to be converted as the campaign goes on.' Previously it had been assumed that 'floating' voters, in their attempt to arrive at a rational decision, would be the most avid consumers of information. But, because they were undecided, they appeared to be uninterested. 'As a group', wrote Trenaman and McQuail later in 1961, 'the "don't knows" were less well informed than consistent voters by as much as 25 per cent ... showing a general lack of information, and not just an ignorance of particular policies or the policies of one particular party.' However, even 'reinforcement' was insufficient on its own.

Personal influence

The research showed that the audience was not homogeneous, and society was not a simple, centrally controlled hierarchy. There were strong defences against people being persuaded in spite of themselves. Further, some members of the audience had a role in the persuasion of others. Ideas, it was argued, 'flow from radio and print *to* the opinion leaders, and *from* them to the less active sections of the population'.[6]

The power which personal contact exercised over people's views was examined by Katz and Lazarsfeld in a study of women 'opinion leaders'. The study, done in the late 1940s, seemed to show that some individuals of high social status had little effect on other people's views, while some of low status were important opinion leaders. Personal influence 'intervened' between the message of the media and its reception by the public. Consequently it impeded any attempt at mass indoctrination by the media. What could be more satisfactory than to find that in a democracy wealth and power do not buy opinion?

It was also argued that opinion leaders were not a narrow élite. The same study showed that a high proportion of women were exercising influence over others in matters of marketing, fashion, movies, and politics. Moreover, the diffusion patterns of influence and the characteristics of opinion leadership were different for each area.

Thus it was concluded that the media had little or no independent effect on public opinion. Indeed rather than changing attitudes, behaviour, or the world it seemed that they merely confirmed the status quo.

Findings the researchers ignored

In fact it is possible to look at the findings of these surveys in another way and draw quite different conclusions. What appears insignificant when buried in a range of figures dealing with breakfast cereals and film stars becomes more interesting if taken on its own. Status and opinion leadership, for example, were not correlated in most areas, except public affairs. Here high-status women appeared to exercise considerably more influence than low-status women. The assumption that consumer behaviour and political behaviour obey the same rules is not supported in these findings. Hence it would be dangerous to take for granted that the media – as opposed to opinion leaders – shape opinions about consuming and opinions about voting in identical ways.

Election surveys of the 1940s and early 1950s are also open to reinterpretation. 'Not every public opinion change involved a personal contact,' Lazarsfeld, Berelson, and Gaudet admit in their study *The People's Choice*. 'Fifty-eight per cent [of the changes not the changers] were made without any remembered personal contact and were very often dependent upon the mass media' (these changes were widely distributed amongst those who changed their views at all). This effect was ignored.[7] It was concluded that the media had little influence. Becker and McCombs have also shown other contradictions in these studies. In the Eerie County survey a high proportion of electors who intended to vote Republican at the start of the campaign but who were exposed to Democrat propaganda switched to Democrat by polling day. Yet this finding was also ignored.

These studies did not show that the media had no effect, although this is what was concluded from them. They showed only that people did not necessarily change their minds because of direct media exposure. The media – as the studies empirically confirmed – raised interest, fixed opinions, and, crucially, informed the electorate. Most of what people knew about campaigns they had learnt from the media.

Understanding and information

Indeed during this same period, another approach to studying the effect of the media, that of experimental psychology, began to develop a rather different model of media influence from that of the surveys. 'The power of the media to persuade, at least where there is a democratic controversy,' wrote Poole, 'is very much less than is usually assessed, but their power to inform is enormous.' A series of psychological experiments carried out by Hovland during the 1940s examined the effects of films designed to inform American soldiers about the war in Europe. The films had little effect on 'morale' or 'motivation to serve'. Yet after they had seen the films the men talked significantly more about what was happening in Europe, and this knowledge persisted for weeks. 'The hammerlike blows of frenzied oratory', Hovland concluded, 'may produce acquiescence and later recrimination: autonomous decisions made under the cumulative pressure of facts do not exact this price.' The theory which lay behind this 'propaganda of facts', he points out, 'is not far removed from the logic of progressive education'.

These experiments also showed that people were particularly vulnerable to persuasion about subjects of which they had no direct experience. Moreover, the willingness of the public to believe what it is told is precisely related to the degree of trust it has in the source of the message. Since few people have first-hand experience of politics, and broadcasting is regarded as an especially authoritative source, these findings would suggest that the effects of the media on political opinion may be particularly strong.

Hovland later argued that the distinction drawn between his experimental results and those of survey research was misleading. His work showed that between one-third and one-half of the people he tested 'actually changed their views'. Yet the surveys had concluded that communications had little effect on attitudes. Hovland argued that some of these differences could be explained because laboratory studies examined immediate responses to media messages, while the surveys were typically conducted long after exposure. But also, he argued, the laboratory studies 'deliberately try to find some types of issue susceptive to change', while surveys attempted to assess the impact of the media on 'socially significant attitudes which are deeply rooted in prior experience and involving much personal commitment'.[8] That is to say, the surveys had investigated those attitudes least likely to be altered in the short term.

The active audience

Studies of the purposes for which members of the audience use the media, and the gratification they get from this use, have also emphasized that public response is varied and not homogeneous. Thus McQuail *et al.* have argued that people use the media for diversion (including escape from routine and unpleasant problems); for developing personal relationships (including substitute companionship); for confirming their personal identity; and for keeping themselves informed. It is implied that if people use the media to satisfy different needs they will also interpret and use the same media message in many different ways. Nevertheless, in the case of political communications, the most frequently expressed use of the media is that of surveillance, or using the media to acquire information.

Indeed the findings of the 'uses and gratifications' research are not incompatible with a stronger interpretation of the role of the media. Given the differences in education, work, and leisure opportunities it would be surprising if the audience response to the media was unitary. The problem is rather to integrate evidence about the differences in the quantity of people's media exposure; about variations in popular interpretations of the media; and about differences in the extent of recall, with other evidence about social divisions. Thus Katz asks, 'What needs, if any, are created by routine work on an assembly line and which forms of exposure will satisfy them?' It is also possible to ask whether the use of the media reinforces or ameliorates social differences. In either case, an explanation of variety in media use is an important part of any more adequate explanation of the power of broadcasting and the press.

Pluralism: the effects of what the audience knows

Since the 1960s attempts have been made to understand the effects of the media on knowledge as well as on opinion. Survey research had apparently shown that the media had little effect on attitudes; new evidence seems to show, by contrast, a dramatic impact on the range and depth of perceptions.

Changes in politics

Underlying these new approaches – and perhaps not unrelated to them – were changes in political behaviour. 'Party allegiance', wrote Blumler in his report for the Annan Committee in 1977, 'which was once the rock of Gibraltar of the reinforcement doctrine of political communications effects has increasingly become its shifting sands.' The class basis of party support was apparently eroding in all the western democracies.

Consequently as the consistent voter became more rare, the nature of the 'floating' volatile voter changed. Previous research had shown floating voters to be an ignorant and apathetic section of the electorate. Recent research provides a different profile: undecided voters are seen, typically, as increasingly likely to be better informed than the majority.

Indeed if class continues to become a less accurate predictor of voting decisions, the media will play a more important role in political choice. Television, which as Blumler shows in an essay written in 1979 has become the main source of election information for over 70 per cent of voters, might be expected to have the greatest effect on long-term political allegiances. For, as class and social networks become less important as the determining source of political reinforcement, it is suggested that voters will rely more heavily on information to make up their minds.

As Blumler and Gurevitch have pointed out, the media have an authoritative relationship with their audience. This is one of dependence and trust and it 'provides the media with a potentially independent power base in society'.

Agenda setting

In addition attempts have been made to discover the effect of the media in determining priorities: how far press, radio, and television coverage could change a sense of which events were more important. On the basis of a study of the emergence of issues during an American presidential campaign, Becker and McCombs argued that such an influence was major, but gradual. There was a distinction, however, between the effects of the press and television. With newspaper influence there was a delayed reaction. 'The newspaper agenda of political issues in June is a predictor of voters' agendas in October,' they claim. With television the impact was last minute, but immediate. By the end of the campaign, television had become the most important determinant of voters' ideas.

The media's ordering of priorities particularly influenced voters without strong views. Yet television's coverage of politics has now penetrated sections of the electorate who previously were little affected by political communication because they were uninterested. Consequently the agenda setting by the media seems to be becoming more significant to a larger proportion of the electorate.

The media's agenda of issues may be quite different from that of the political parties. As Seymour-Ure has shown, media coverage made a speech on immigration delivered by Enoch Powell to a small audience in a church hall familiar to 86 per cent of the population two days later. Before the speech only 6 per cent of a Gallup Poll sample thought immigration an issue of national importance; afterwards 27 per cent thought it was important, and nearly 70 per cent of the public believed that the government would have to take 'a harder line'. In effect, Seymour-Ure writes, Powell had 'won himself a national constituency, a platform in the media from which to state his views on most subjects with the certainty of having an audience'.

Neither Powell, nor the media, created the race issue in Britain. Nevertheless, argues Seymour-Ure, the publicity surrounding his speech at a crucial moment (during the debate on the controversial Race Relations Bill) pushed immigration to the front of the political stage, a position it has kept ever since.

The political effects of the media on public opinion are complex, and need to be examined in their historical context. The media may exert great influence over one group, but have little impact on the other members of a society. Thus in Portugal, the press – despite close censorship – was crucial in establishing a culture of opposition to the authoritarian regime amongst the educated classes. This was an essential condition of the success of the liberal revolution in 1974. Yet, after the revolution, a dramatic change in the political direction of the media (from right to left), between the first and second democratic elections, had no effect on voting behaviour at all.[9]

The first studies of the effects of the press and broadcasting had undermined earlier assumptions about the power of the media, suggesting that audiences were, after all, free. Anybody, it seemed, could make almost anything out of any message. Yet a re-examination of the evidence has thrown doubts on this view. It has been suggested that the media may not persuade the public directly; nevertheless they affect what people know, and what they think is important.

Media organizations

Of course, research into public responses to news and information is not the only way of considering the political role of the mass media. Another approach is to look at how news is produced: the processes of news-gathering, sifting, and editing, and the administration of news and entertainment organizations. The virtue of this method is that it helps us to understand what pressures shape the commodity presented to the public. Its limitation is that in considering how rival interests balance one another, there has been a tendency to ignore the broader problem of those important but powerless interests which have no influence at all.

Making news

News rooms are always under pressure: the unexpected is always about to happen, the scoop is only a telephone call away. This is the professional self-image. However, for journalists (as for politicians, doctors, and firemen) crises that are frequent enough develop a pattern: the unexpected becomes the predictable.

Journalists solve these pressures by developing a set of rules. Tuchman argues that 'the routinely non-routine is constituted in practical tasks: in work'. Tuchman, however, also suggests that objectivity is little more than a protective 'strategic ritual', a set of conventions about the origins and presentation of facts that allows journalists to defend their selection of newsworthy events and interpretations. In an extreme form, Tuchman's definition of news precludes any distinction between relatively good or bad journalistic practices. Nevertheless, this interpretation highlights the way in which accuracy is by no means the same thing as objectivity.

The events that are honoured by being made news are those that are easy to obtain. They are by no means necessarily the most significant events which have occurred. In order to get made into news, events have to happen in places convenient for the news-gathering agencies, to be of a recognized and acceptable kind, come from a reliable and predictable source, and fit into journalists' framework of news values. These rules and habits have become worldwide and, as Golding and Elliot argue, 'News changes very little when the individuals that produce it are changed.' Even the international flow of news is determined not by the importance of events but by the organization of the news-processing industries.

The popular image of journalists (elaborated in many movies) as intrepid hunters after hidden truths is hardly realistic. Specialist reporters in particular are closely involved with, and indeed dependent upon, their sources. Thus crime reporters identify with the police, defence correspondents with the services, and industrial relations experts with the trade unions.[10] But, in addition, journalists, who are better seen as bureaucrats than as buccaneers, begin their work from a stock of plausible, well-defined, and largely unconscious assumptions. Part of their job is to translate untidy reality into neat stories with beginnings, middles, and denouements.

The values which inform the selection of news items usually serve to reinforce conventional opinions and established authority. At the same time, a process of simplification filters out the disturbing or the unexpected. The need of the media to secure instant attention creates a strong prejudice in favour of familiar stories and themes, and a slowness of response when reality breaks the conventions.

Pseudo-events

Many items of news are not 'events' at all, that is in the sense of occurrences in the real world which take place independently of the media. An important development alongside the mass media has been the growth of organizations, professions, and skills aimed at manipulating the media.

In a pioneering study (*Public Relations and American Democracy*, 1951) J. A. R. Pimlott reviewed attempts to control news and public opinion in the USA. Prompted by his own experience as a civil servant closely involved with the implementation of Labour's post-war programme in Britain, he was concerned with the use of public relations to win support for central planning and social reform – in particular the New Deal. He also considered the dangers which public relations presented. The book takes issue with the '*laissez-faire* school' argument that free competition ensures a fair hearing for both sides of every major issue. In many cases, the author pointed out, it is 'nobody's business to put the other side'. In the early 1930s American unions had complained that because of inadequate resources, they were unable to compete with the publicity of employers. Pimlott felt that there was some justice in the trade union case during the Depression, that 'more than ever before strikes are being won or lost in the newspapers'. His conclusions were pessimistic. It was impossible to control the growth of public relations by government intervention. Nevertheless, newspapers could help 'by transferring some of the energy which they devote to attacks upon government propaganda to attacking the misuse of public relations by private industry'.

Indeed the notion that 'events' compete for attention in the press and broadcasting is misleading. Often the media are desperately anxious to secure enough content (of the kind they want) to fill their space or time.

In this way, much of what is perceived as 'news' is little more than free advertising. 'Not for nothing does the trainee journalist have to sit as part of his qualifying exams a test in how to write a press handout,' writes McBarnett. The local press is particularly vulnerable to pre-digested news. Much of what appears as 'political news' is in fact written by councillors, candidates, and MPs. The same process also determines much of what appears nationally, leading to what Boorstin has called 'pseudo-events' – activities whose only real purpose is to secure and control media coverage.

Entertainment

What is entertainment? All media industries compete to create it. Even with news and documentaries, the pressure to be 'entertaining' – to hold audiences by being immediately accessible and stimulating – overrides other considerations. A high proportion of media content has no other aim but to amuse, flatter, excite, mystify, or titillate the public and so keep its attention.

Thus Michael Tracey has argued that the most prominent anxiety of producers of political television was not the sensitivity of their relationships with the political élite, but rather the development of an entertainment formula. Discussion programmes were composed as much for dramatic excitement as for political balance. 'Did you see her on women's lib?' he quotes a producer enquiring. 'Marvellous woman. Never stops talking. Liable to throw something.'

Yet just as little 'serious' material is presented without a sugar coating, so too there is nothing – or almost nothing – that can be deemed 'pure' entertainment. Soap opera, comedy, variety, and pop may not be intended to have any effect on the views of their audiences. But, it can be argued, there is scarcely a joke or a lyric that does not reflect a social attitude, and one with political consequences.

Some writers have suggested that entertainment encourages political passivity. Gitlin has argued that it often 'provides a legitimation of depoliticized forms of deviance, usually ethnic or sexual, and a delegitimation of the dangerous, the out of bounds, the violent'.[11] The resolution of social problems typically presented in fictional programmes may influence how they come to be seen in the real world.

It is not only the content of the media which may have implications for attitudes but also the form of programmes. Dyer has argued, in his discussion of light entertainment, that the way in which stars are presented, pictures shot, and the studio audience used, may all affect the meaning communicated by programmes. In so far as 'leisure' is seen by programme-makers as being opposed to work, then entertainment 'has to do something about the reality of work, it has to have an attitude towards it'.

Audiences

It is often argued that the mass media 'reflect' society because they are obliged to please their audiences. Yet many researchers have commented on the apparent remoteness of producers from their potential viewers. 'It is not so much that people don't know what the audience wants,' Alvarado and Buscombe write, 'as that in the actual process of production people were working more to please themselves.'

However, while writers on political broadcasting have seen this ignorance of the audience as a problem – 'the vital missing link', as Tracey calls it – writers on creative and fictional broadcasting have seen it as a safeguard. 'A model of popular television', write Alvarado and Buscombe, 'which sees it either as a cynical manipulation, or a straightforward identity of tastes between producers and audience, would be an over-simplification.'

The demands of the audience do not, then, exert any direct pressure on producers. Producers have only a vague image of those who watch their programmes. Yet they have a clear, if unconscious, notion of who they are actually addressing: well-informed, critical, professional people like themselves.

Institutional pluralists

A recent argument is that television in particular is not so much a player in the political game as the referee: setting the rules and arbitrating between contending forces.

This view of the political role of the media has been expressed most clearly by Anthony Smith. 'Television', he argues,

> has become the Theatre of Politics in both senses of the term. Like the theatre of classical times its structures combine into a memory system. Its disciplines incorporate the moral norms of politics as these apply at a given moment of history.

Thus the nature of the rules and their application reflect the politics of the time. The decision about whether to interview a terrorist on television, or the choice of 'controversial' topics for discussion, precisely indicates the political mood as it is perceived by producers and editors. Changes in the relationship between 'current affairs', 'comment', and 'news', or what is seen as 'hard fact' determine the manner in which information is presented to the public. In this way the limits of the permissible, the acceptable, and the appropriate constitute a series of snapshots of prevailing attitudes.

These pressures, however, are always seen by these writers as emerging from a free market of influence. Reviewing research into media organization, Blumler has argued that 'Researchers may be near the heart of competition through communication that is waged in a democratic pluralist society.' Burns has suggested that the politics of broadcasting are the politics of accommodation, while Smith, in his book *The Shadow in the Cave*, argued that 'If broadcasting is to be used as a tool for the intelligent exchange of cultural products, political information and controversial disquisition, it needs to be left flexible and left alone.'

Yet 'negotiation' and 'amplification' are inadequate metaphors for a process in which so much power has come to be invested in the message carrier itself. Hirsch and Gordon have argued that commercial pressure has limited the range of opinion expressed in the quality press. 'The picture we suggest of the quality press is of a band of opinion occupying the broad centre of British politics from about half way into the moderate left through to the edges of the extreme right.' But broadcasting has usurped the role of the popular press as a supplier of political information to the mass audience, while preserving the same 'consensus band' of opinion as the quality newspapers. Thus the audience of BBC or ITV news includes most readers of the *Mirror* and the *People*: but these programmes' political values (not just their concern with information) are closer to those of *The Times* and the *Observer*.

That the media order events, and discriminate between them, is not in itself evidence of their systematic effect on public understanding. But while some groups can bring powerful pressures to bear on the work that the media do, others can bring none. The market for information is no more free than any other.

The new determinists: class and market

Another view of the press and broadcasting is that they reinforce and legitimize the present power structure. The media, it is argued, distract public attention from real problems by manufacturing events and inflating trivial issues. However, the press and broadcasting, the new British cultural critics have suggested, do not merely express the interests of the dominant class. This is not only because this class does not always have one simple unitary interest, but also because the media at times reflect other interpretations of society.

However, it should be noted that these writers – many of whom have been associated with the Centre for Contemporary Cultural Studies at Birmingham – rarely question the concepts of 'lived experience', culture, struggle, resistance, or social control in their work. These ideas are accepted as self-evident and unproblematic, and used as the basis for explaining other phenomena. This inadequacy limits the work of these writers.[12]

Ideology

Ideology, writes Stuart Hall, 'entails the proposition that ideas are not self-sufficient, that their roots lie elsewhere'. Indeed while the audience for the media contains most members of society, only a few groups have any control over what the media produce. Hall concludes that they 'reproduce the definition of the powerful, without being in a simple sense in their pay'.

Hall argues that the media do not simply trick their audience: to some extent they must meet its needs. The independence of the media is at times quite genuine. For instance Hall suggests that broadcasting organizations have 'a wide measure of autonomy in their programming'.[13] However, this independence, though not a device, is actually serving a highly sophisticated function within a complex system. Precisely because the media produce material which is good, impartial, and serious, they are accorded a high degree of respect and authority. Since, in practice, the ethic of the press and television is closely associated with a homogeneous establishment this provides a vital support for the existing order. In this way, the apparent autonomy of organizations like the BBC 'veils and mystifies the structure of constraints'. Independence, Hall argues, is not 'a mere cover, it is central to the way power and ideology are mediated in societies like ours'. Thus we seem to have a more sophisticated instance of 'false consciousness'. The public are bribed with good radio, television, and newspapers into an acceptance of the biased, the misleading, and the status quo.

Hall emphasizes that the media change the world. They do not passively reflect class interests that have already been well developed. The media often articulate interests not previously expressed. That they do so is not because of the intentions of those who produce them. Rather it is a consequence of the situation and function of the press and broadcasting. The media, Hall suggests in a 1977 essay, help us 'not simply to *know more* about "the world", but to make sense of it'.

The mass media are not, according to this approach, crude agents of propaganda. They organize public understanding. However, the overall interpretations they provide in the long run are those which are most preferred by, and least challenging to, those with economic power.

Class, culture, and experience

Part of this approach to the power of the media has been a concern with the way in which different classes experience their position. The work of E. P. Thompson and that of Raymond Williams has been an important influence here. Both of these writers have been concerned with the nineteenth-century reaction to industrialization (although this has often been mistaken for a reaction to capitalism). Thus Thompson has written about working-class movements which opposed industrial developments, and Williams has examined the social criticism implied in the aesthetic reaction to industrialization of the Romantic movement. Barnett has argued that Williams puts too much faith in the political force of cultural opposition. 'Where economistic strategies rely upon the spontaneous momentum of industrial struggles to accomplish the overthrow of capitalism,' he suggests, 'Williams's book contains a culturist argument that is logically similar.'[14] In this way the independence of working-class culture has come to be seen not only as a source of opposition to capitalism, but also as leading to a socialist rejection of it.

This tradition has led the cultural critics to focus on working-class response to, and use of, the media. Thus Finn and Grant argue that people are 'not merely on "the receiving end" of their objective class position'. Classes take over, interpret, and use ideologies which are presented to them: they make them their own. This is particularly true of the ideas transmitted by the media.

According to this view, the working class is imprisoned by an ideology it often rejects. Many workers are not taken in by the view of society handed down to them. This can be seen from 'oppositional' behaviour which is generally not overtly political. Thus Willis has considered the division in a boys' comprehensive between those who are subservient to the imposed system and take exams, and those who regard the examination system as a confidence trick that will not help them. Willis argues that the second group of disrespectful layabouts actually have a better understanding of the world and their place in it. He suggests that 'Oppressed, subordinate and minority groups can have a hand in constructing their own vibrant cultures and are not merely dupes.'

Yet the relationship between working-class culture and political action is hardly inevitable. The relationship between lifestyle and class is also more difficult to explain than these writers have implied. In addition, those who have written about the sociology of art, literature, or film have found no simple correlation between the social origin of artists, writers, and film-makers and the political implications of their work. Indeed, as Garnham has pointed out, just because cultural goods are made within the capitalist system it 'does not follow that these commodities will necessarily support the dominant ideology'. This is not to argue that there is no relationship between class, cultural products, and experience; only that a direct relationship cannot be taken for granted. At the same time, even if it is true that experience of the media has become an intrinsic part of working-class culture, it cannot therefore be automatically assumed to be good.

The market

The pluralists largely ignore market pressures. The new determinist writers, in contrast, give them a crucial role. However, the determinist analysis of working-class culture leads to a contradiction. Goods – including the products of the media industries – are produced, it is argued, not to meet needs but to earn profits. Hence the goods are often worthless or inappropriate in themselves. However, workers are not necessarily enslaved by the distortions of the market. By appropriating what the system throws up, the working class preserves its cultural autonomy. Thus claims Willis, 'from the rubbish available within a pre-constituted market', working-class groups 'generate viable cultures, and through their work on received commodities actually formulate a living and lived out concretized critique'.

The work of Willis, Hebdige, and others provides an analysis of particular groups within the working class. Yet on the one hand, any attempt to generalize these conclusions to 'working-class culture' has to be treated with caution because of the narrow base of the research; on the other, the new critics seem to want to have their cake and eat it. Is television a subtle form of exploitation, the more sinister for being good? Is it 'rubbish available within a pre-constituted market', to use Willis's phrase for consumer goods in general? If the former, then it is hard to see how – or why – the working class should adopt oppositional 'concretized critiques' of it in their lifestyles. If the latter, and working-class culture manages to incorporate or appropriate the media product and remain 'viable' and 'lived out', then how thorough is the exploitation?

Pop music produces an interesting example. Is rock 'n' roll an expression of youth culture? Or is it a prime instance of capital discovering a new market and exploiting it? Few people would want to say that rock is intrinsically bad, or that it is not an important element in working-class life. No industry is more brazenly oriented towards quick, easy profits; in few are market pressures more immediate. Yet it is hard to sustain the argument that rock is handed down 'rubbish'.

Pop or rock fans are hardly an oppositional body taken *en masse*. As Frith points out, they are well aware that the product they buy is made and sold primarily to make profits. The reality is that rock is not simply a market-oriented concoction of the recording studios of Decca or EMI. Nor is it authentic folk music living an independent life in the community. Nor, for that matter, is it a distortion of a musical tradition plucked out of its native environment. Rather it is the product of a complex set of relationships in which music, fans, the media, profit takers, and distribution systems all play a part.

News values and power

The new cultural critics are most interesting when they deal with the content of the media and its relationship to power. *Policing the Crisis: Mugging, the State, and Law and Order* by Hall *et al.*, for example, both describes the career of a category of news story, cases of 'mugging', and also analyses its influence on the judiciary, the police, and the public.

The authors show how the media created anxiety by giving a new name to an old offence. This in turn precipitated an aggressive sentencing policy which was seen as a necessary response to an earlier mistakenly 'soft' attitude towards offenders. Yet as Hall and others show, not only had the rate of increase in crimes of violence actually declined in the period before the emergence of the mugging story, but also far from becoming more lenient, sentences had steadily become longer. The curious inversion of facts, the authors argue, can be explained only in terms of the media's most general function of reworking ideology and maintaining the status quo.

The new cultural critics emphasize that their explanation of this process does not imply any deliberate conspiracy. 'Within its limits', Hall has written, broadcasting, for example, 'shows little evidence of intentional bias, but the trouble is the matter of unwitting bias'. Rather the coincidence of interests between the media and those with economic power is secured by professional and organizational values, and a shared perspective of the way in which society is organized. Thus Murdoch, writing about the reporting of an anti-Vietnam rally in 1968, argued that 'despite this element of autonomy, the basic definition of the situation which underlies the news reporting of political events very largely coincides with the definitions provided by the legitimate power holders.'

Social control

Thus the media are seen by the determinists as one powerful agency of social control – as a means of inhibiting opposition to the social order. In a similar argument, Bourdieu has described the function of the education system, which he sees as justifying the established order, by

> using the overt connection between qualifications and jobs as a smoke-screen for the connection – which it records surreptitiously under the cover of a formal equality – between the qualifications people obtain and the cultural capital they have inherited – in other words through the legitimation it confers on the framework of this form of heritage.

Differences in the use of the media, the distribution of tastes and preferences, are thus more than a mere expression of class. They are a vital means of making people accept different class opportunities, and those interpretations of events which are the least challenging to existing social arrangements.

Indeed in the analysis of the cultural critics, the media perform a special role in addition: they maintain and repair consensus as the nature of the status quo changes. Thus the crime of 'mugging', launched and amplified by the press, did not emerge accidentally. Rather it arose 'in the middle of a general moral panic about the rising rate of crime. Far from triggering into existence what did not previously exist, it clearly focuses what is widespread and free floating.'

The concept of social control seems to imply an imminent crisis, one that will eventually erupt but which is at present controlled. The emergence of the 'mugging' story is therefore interpreted merely as a symptom of a more fundamental crisis, one in which there has been a collapse in the willingness of the public to accept the authority of the state. The individual discrete 'moral panics' of the 1960s are seen as having been superseded by a more general breakdown. The only rationale, it is argued, for

> entrusting the management of the corporate capitalist state to a social democracy is either (1) that in a tight squeeze it can better win the collaboration of the working-class organization for the state, or (2) that if there is going to be a crisis Labour might as well have it!

In this way there is a danger that social structure is anthropomorphized: it becomes an active agent in pursuit of its own persistence.

However, despite the limitations of the concepts of social control, the determinist explanation of the role of the media is revealing. The media do not merely express the interests of the ruling class, rather they have an independent function in ordering the world. The media do not merely 'reflect' social reality: they increasingly help to make it.

Conclusion

As we have seen, the pluralist analysis of the effects of the media contains an apparent contradiction. On the one hand, it seems to show that the media do have an influence, both on what people know and on the political system. On the other hand it seems to suggest that, so far from having an independent power, the media merely reflect the balance of forces within society. Thus the pluralists are left saying that the press and broadcasting function as an ideological market-place, a focus for competing pressures without an impact of their own. At the same time in taking a favourable view of 'pluralist' balance, this position tends to ignore the extent to which the weaker and unorganized groups are excluded from the process altogether.

Is the determinist approach any better? The cultural critics share the pluralists' view that the media have a key political role, stressing the way in which press and broadcasting shape public understanding. They differ from the pluralists in their preoccupation with the real or supposed role of the media as an instrument of class domination.

Thus the determinists have pointed to a major weakness in the pluralist case: the model of a freely competitive market-place of ideas breaks down because some groups are unable to compete. At the same time the empirical evidence of the pluralists gives powerful backing to the determinists' conviction that the media exert an important and uncontrolled influence. Yet the determinist explanation in terms of class manipulation and exploitation is too mechanistic, obscuring a series of complex relationships which have yet to be explained.

Notes

1. H. Arendt, *The Burden of Our Time* (London, Secker & Warburg, 1950), p. 331.
2. M. Horkheimer, *The Eclipse of Reason* (London, Oxford University Press, 1947), p. 135.
3. H. D. Lasswell, 'The garrison state', *American Journal of Sociology*, 46 (1941), p. 462.
4. This 'strong' interpretation they share with F. Hayek, *The Road to Serfdom* (London, Routledge & Kegan Paul, 1944). He indicts socialism, they blame fascism.
5. H. Arendt, *The Life of the Mind*, vol. 2, *Thinking* (London, Secker & Warburg, 1978), p. 93.
6. E. Katz and P. Lazarsfeld, *Personal Influence: The Part Played by People in the Flow of Mass Communication* (New York, Free Press, 1955).
7. P. Becker and M. McCombs point this out in 'The development of political cognition' in S. H. Chaffee (ed.), *Political Communication: Issues and Strategies* (Beverly Hills, Calif., Sage, 1975).
8. C. I. Hovland, 'Reconciling conflicting results derived from experimental and survey studies of attitude change', *American Psychologist*, 14 (1959), p. 11.
9. For a further development of this case, and a consideration of its more general implications, see J. Seaton and B. Pimlott, 'The role of the media in the Portuguese revolution' in A. Smith (ed.), *Newspapers and Democracy: International Essays in a Changing Medium* (Cambridge, Mass., MIT Press, 1980); J. Seaton and B. Pimlott, 'Political power and the Portuguese media' in L. Graham and D. Wheeler (eds), *In Search of Modern Portugal: The Revolution and its Consequences* (Wisconsin, University of Wisconsin Press, 1983); B. Pimlott and J. Seaton, 'The Portuguese media in transition' in K. Maxwell (ed.), *The Press and the Rebirth of Iberian Democracy* (Westwood, Conn., Greenwood, 1983).
10. See J. Seaton, 'Trade unions and the media' in B. Pimlott and C. Cook (eds), *Trade Unions in British Politics* (Harlow, Longman, 1983).
11. T. Gitlin, 'Prime time ideology: the hegemonic process in television entertainment', *Social Problems*, 26, 3 (1979), p. 111.
12. James Curran does not share many of Jean Seaton's reservations about the writers discussed in this part of the chapter.
13. S. Hall, 'The external/internal dialectic on broadcasting', *4th Symposium on British Broadcasting Policy* (February 1972).
14. A. Barnett in R. Williams (ed.), *Politics and Letters: Interviews with the New Left Review* (London, New Left Books, 1979), p. 98.

16

The liberal theory of press freedom

According to classical liberal theory, the freedom of the press is rooted in the freedom of everyone to publish a newspaper, magazine, or pamphlet without being subject to pre-publication censorship by the state. This ensures that the press reflects a wide range of opinions and interests in society. If a viewpoint is not expressed in the press, this is only because it lacks a sufficient following to sustain it in the market-place. As the heroine puts it in Tom Stoppard's play, *Night and Day*, 'The *Flat Earth News* is free to sell a million copies. What it lacks is the ability to find a million people with four pence and a conviction that the earth is flat. Freedom is neutral.'

This neutrality of the market makes the press a representative voice of the people. 'The broad shape and nature of the press', argues John Whale for instance, 'is ultimately determined by no one but its readers.' This is because newspapers and magazines must respond to their readers if they are to stay in business in a competitive market.

Some liberal theorists have compared the processes of market accountability to the formal processes of the constitution. Newspapers, they contend, must submit to the equivalent of an election every day they go on sale whereas politicians seek election only at infrequent intervals. The press should thus be seen, according to this theory, as the fourth estate of the realm: a representative institution which reflects public opinion, critically scrutinizes government, and acts as a public watch-dog.

Embedded at the heart of this theory – although often obscured by layers of well-rehearsed argument – is the assumption that press freedom is a property right. It is generally assumed that proprietors have a legitimate right to manage directly their publications, or to delegate authority to others, as they see fit. However, the hidden hand of the free market ensures that proprietors' pursuit of their private interests corresponds to the public good. For, as we have seen, liberal theorists argue that the freedom to publish and compete in an unrestricted market produces a press which is diverse, accountable, and representative.

This theory of press freedom has been attacked by radical critics on the grounds that it masks the way in which capital is privileged in the seemingly open contest of the free market, and obscures the fact that the press tends to report and interpret the world in ways which are consonant with the interests of the dominant class.[1]

But perhaps more significantly, some liberal commentators have also criticized the traditional theory of press freedom. One line of attack has been to challenge the legitimacy of proprietorial control on the grounds that the creation of vast press empires has led to the concentration of too much power in a few hands. Editors, according to this argument, should determine what is published without interference from proprietors. Others have mounted a more far-reaching assault on classical theory, arguing that it is now out of date and no longer fits the facts of an industrialized, monopolistic press. In some versions this comes close to – indeed merges with – radical critiques of liberal theory.

The nature of these criticisms and misgivings will be illustrated by comparing the reports of three successive Royal Commissions on the Press, published in 1949, 1962, and 1977. The last two reports represent, as we shall see, staging posts in a progressive process of disenchantment with conventional views of the free market that underpin the liberal theory of press freedom.

Freedom to publish

'Free enterprise', declared the first Royal Commission on the Press, 'is a prerequisite of a free press.' Underlying this belief was a relatively untroubled conviction that the unrestricted freedom to publish produces a diverse and representative press. The Commission expected to find that 'The press as a whole gives an opportunity for all important points of view to be effectively presented in terms of the varying standards of taste, political opinion, and education among the principal groups of the population.' Wartime economic controls were blamed for preventing new publications from springing up to meet changes in public demand. Anticipating the time when these controls would be removed, the Commission rejected dividend control because it might inhibit the creativity of the market. It also dismissed proposals for assisting the launch of new papers on the grounds that they were unnecessary.

The 1977 Commission was forced to make a different assessment of the market. As the Commission put it bluntly, 'Anyone is free to start a daily national newspaper, but few can afford even to contemplate the prospect.' It also noted that the national press was overwhelmingly right wing. Indeed 'in February 1974 ... the share of newspaper (national daily) circulation held by papers supporting the Conservative Party was 71% greater than Conservative votes as a percentage of the votes cast.'

High entry costs were found to curtail the freedom to publish in other sectors of the press. Even establishing a new local evening paper in a town with no direct competition would cost in 1977, according to the Commission, between £2 million and £3 million. The cost of launching a new magazine in the main consumer sectors was also found to be high. As for new paid-for weeklies, there are 'not many places left with the right conditions to provide a permanent market'.

The assumption that 'anyone' is free to start a new paper has been an illusion ever since the industrialization of the press. That it is an illusion was exposed in unsparing detail by the last Commission. This part of its report thus dislodged a key foundation stone sustaining the traditional theory of press freedom.

Proprietors and chain ownership

The 1949 Commission argued that proprietors should be free to conduct their publications as they wished. This was justified principally on the grounds that proprietors had the right to safeguard their financial investments in a high-risk industry. It was also assumed that their freedom underpinned the wider freedom of the press as a whole.

Underlying the Commission's approach was the assumption that chain ownership would not develop into a major problem. 'There is no reason to expect', declared the Commission,

> that the aggressive expansion of chain undertakings [in the daily and Sunday press] which characterised the early period will be resumed. Neither in the local nor in the periodical press nor in the news agencies do we expect a significant trend towards further concentration of ownership.

The 1962 Commission was obliged to revise this assessment. It found that the share of circulation controlled by the major chains had 'substantially increased' in all parts of the press. The leading three proprietors' share of the national daily press had soared to 89 per cent. There were, it added, 'spectacular movements towards concentration of ownership' in the periodical press. Only amongst local weeklies was concentration 'negligible'.

In 1977 the third Commission was forced to revise even this conclusion. The greatest acceleration of chain ownership had occurred, it reported unhappily, in the local weekly press. Furthermore, new acquisitions had resulted in the same three proprietors dominating both the national daily and Sunday markets unlike before.[2] The Commission also highlighted a phenomenon which had previously received little attention – the emergence of sub-regional monopolies in which all 'competing' local morning, evening, and weekly papers were owned by the same group.

These changes in the press prompted a reassessment. Whereas the first two Commissions had taken for granted the right of proprietors to determine editorial policy, the third Commission talked of the need to 'protect editors and journalists from owners'. The exercise of proprietorial power no longer appeared legitimate on the grounds accepted by its predecessors – that of guaranteeing the diversity of the press. Indeed at a time when just three men controlled two-thirds of national and regional daily and Sunday newspaper sales in Britain, proprietorial authority was tacitly recognized to threaten editorial diversity.

Proprietorship of the fourth estate

This shift of attitude towards proprietorial authority was also influenced by changes in the character of press ownership. The first Commission had advanced as a subsidiary justification for proprietors the argument that they safeguarded the autonomy of the press. 'It is undoubtedly a great merit of the British press', declared the Commission, 'that it is completely independent of outside financial interests and that its policy is the policy of those who own and control it.' The Commission thus invoked the classical liberal view of the press as an independent fourth estate, uncompromised by vested interests.

But during the take-over boom of the late 1960s and 1970s most of the British press was bought up by or diversified into interests outside publishing. All but one of the leading publishing groups in both Fleet Street and the regional press became part of larger conglomerates with holdings in fields as diverse as North Sea oil, transport, mining, construction, engineering, finance, and the leisure industries. 'Rather than saying that the press has other business interests,' the last Commission concluded unhappily, 'it would be truer to argue that the press has become a subsidiary of other industries.'

This clearly undermined the case for proprietorial control as a guarantee of the press's autonomy to which the 1949 Commission had made such a fulsome and, in retrospect, embarrassing tribute. It also cast in a new light the 1949 Commission's contention that proprietors had the right to safeguard their financial interests, whatever the circumstances. If a newspaper's investigative journalism jeopardizes its parent conglomerate's interests, should the controller of that conglomerate have the right to suppress it? Should the freedom of the press be located in the property power of large business organizations whose activities, according to liberal theory, should be subject to independent press scrutiny?[3] These were questions which clearly troubled the 1977 Commission, and partly explains why it was much less enthusiastic about 'the rights' of proprietors than its predecessors.

Competition, consumer choice, and new technology

The first Commission attached great importance to the role of competition in making the press accountable. Due to competitive pressures, argued the Commission, 'whatever a paper's purpose and however it is owned, it cannot escape the necessity of offering the public what some at least of the public will buy'.

Although the Commission was troubled by the large number of newspaper closures during the inter-war period, it took comfort in the belief that this had been only a temporary phenomenon caused mainly by extravagance and lack of adaptability. 'In the provincial press as a whole,' it concluded, 'there is nothing approaching monopoly and we can see no strong tendency towards monopoly.'

The Commission's optimism was confounded by events. The total number of newspaper titles continued to decline (see Table 7). The cities in the UK with a choice of directly competing local morning or evening papers was reduced by 1974 to only London, Edinburgh, and Belfast (see Table 8). In 1975 only 18 per cent of towns with a local paper had a choice of weeklies under separate ownership, a proportion that was little over half of what it had been in 1961. In short, competition – the *deus ex machina* of liberal theory which makes the consumer 'sovereign' and proprietors accountable – had been seriously eroded in much of the regional press.

The last Commission found some solace in the emergence of freesheets, a development which has become even more pronounced since it reported. However, the rise of freesheets has caused a further reduction in the number of paid-for weeklies (see Table 7). Due to their dependent relationship to advertisers, freesheets do not constitute an important independent voice. Ironically many of them are now also published by the major chains. In 1985 the five largest publishers of freesheets were responsible between them for 220 free publications: the same publishers also controlled a further 266 paid-for papers. However, it has been forcibly argued that the trend towards fewer newspapers and chain

Table 7 *The number of newspaper titles, 1921–85*

	1921	1937	1948	1961	1976	1985	Percentage reduction 1921–85
							%
National press							
National daily	14	11	11	10	9	10	29
National Sunday	14	10	10	8	7	8	43
Regional/local press							
Morning	41	27	27	22	20	19	54
Evening	93	83	80	77	79	75	19
Sunday	7	7	6	5	6	4	43
Weekly and bi-weekly	1,485	1,303	1,307	1,219	1,072	839	44
Freesheets	—	—	—	—	185[a]	724[b]	—
Total[c]	1,654	1,441	1,441	1,341	1,193	955	42

Sources: Royal Commission on the Press 1947–9 Report, Appendix 2, Tables 2–3; *Royal Commission on the Press 1961–2 Report,* Appendix 3, Tables 3 and 5; *Royal Commission on the Press 1974–7 Final Report,* Annex 3, Table 4; *Press Council Annual Report 1985,* chapter 11, Table 1 and Table A.
Notes: a. This relates to 1975. b. In addition there were one local daily and four Sunday freesheets. c. Excluding freesheets.

Table 8 *The number of urban centres with competing local dailies, 1921–85*

	Urban centres with a choice of:	
	Local morning paper[a]	Local evening paper
1921[b]	15	27
1937[b]	6	10
1948	4	11
1961	2	9
1974	2	1
1985	2	—

Sources: Royal Commission on the Press 1947–9 Report, Appendix 2, Table 1; *Royal Commission on the Press 1961–2 Report,* Appendix 3, Table 4; and N. Hartley, P. Gudgeon, and R. Crafts, *Concentration of Ownership in the Provincial Press,* Royal Commission on the Press 1974–7, Research Series 5 (London, HMSO, 1977), Table 6.1.
Notes: a. Excluding London. b. Excluding Ulster.

ownership which so concerned the last two Commissions will be reversed. By reducing labour costs, new technology will allegedly result in fewer papers closing, facilitate the launch of new ones, and expose the chains to new competition.

As we have seen, these arguments need to be treated with caution.[4] Although new technology will undoubtedly refuel competition in the short term, it will not transform the economic structure of the national press. The savings involved amount to less than 20 per cent of national newspaper costs. Consequently new national newspaper launches will continue to require large financial resources, and the range of new voices will still be curtailed by high costs.

The cost reductions secured through new technology are also likely to be dissipated in the long term. To judge from past experience, increased competition will result in rising levels of editorial and promotional outlay and perhaps heavy discounting on advertising rates. This will increase the run-in costs of new papers and undermine the financial position of some marginal ones (unless there is a countervailing growth of demand).

But even if this does not happen, new technology will not nullify the main underlying cause of newspaper closures – the unequal competitive relationship between strong and weak papers. Successful publications have a built-in advantage over their rivals because they have more revenue and generally lower unit costs, due to greater economies of scale. They are thus in a good position to consolidate their market lead by spending more on editorial and promotional outlay. This strategy has the added advantage of weakening financially their rivals by encouraging them to spend more in an attempt to stay competitive. The dynamic imbalance of this relationship is not modified by new technology. As the 1977 Commission pointed out, 'even if all newspapers accomplish the change [in technology], competition may still result in some papers closing since the new technology does little to alter the relative position of competing titles'.[5]

Nor will the introduction of new technology undermine the incentive for chains to expand. Economies of consolidation make it advantageous for chains to buy up rivals often at prices above the going market rate. Their large financial resources and accumulated expertise also equip them to be successful innovators. The 1977 Commission was disconcerted to find that only two out of a sample of twenty-four local weeklies launched between 1961 and 1976 originated from independent publishers; and that over half the consumer magazines with a circulation of over 30,000 started between 1966 and 1974 came from just four publishing groups. 'The larger companies,' the Commission's research team concluded soberly, 'are better placed to incur the considerable costs that are required to enter some markets.'[6]

In short, the evidence carefully marshalled by the 1977 Commission suggests that there is no free market solution to the central problem which it diagnosed: namely that the process of competition reduces competition. New developments since its report do not justify overturning this verdict, certainly in the long term, despite the Panglossian hopes that have been generated by the introduction of new technology. Nor does the experience of other countries like France and the USA, where new technology was introduced a decade earlier than in Britain give any support to the claim that new technical processes will greatly extend the cultural and political diversity of the press.

Reform or reinterpretation

The last two Commissions' reports thus reveal the gradual weakening of beliefs that have legitimized the press for over a century. The incorporation of the press by big business and the growth of chain ownership has cast doubt on the legitimacy of proprietorial control by undermining the traditional arguments advanced to justify it. Continuing high entry costs and the erosion of competition in the local press have also subverted the idealized view of the free market which underlies the traditional theory of press freedom.

In these circumstances the last two Commissions had perhaps two options available to them, given their liberal-conservative make-up. They could endorse the status quo and seek to legitimize it by updating traditional liberal theory. This would have meant following the pattern of the USA where liberal theory has been skilfully reworked in a way that takes account of the monopolistic structure of the American press.

Alternatively they could propose a major programme of reform which would make liberal representations of the press correspond more closely to reality. This is the strategy which has been adopted in most European countries where a variety of schemes have been introduced in an attempt to 'repair' the free market. These have ranged from subsidies to assist the launch of new publications to grants and tax concessions designed to prevent newspapers from closing.[7]

The Commissions' programme of reform

Perhaps the closest the Press Commissions came to adopting an interventionist strategy was to advocate an anti-monopoly policy. This was tentatively initiated by the 1949 Commission which proposed that the Monopolies Commission should monitor changes in press ownership with increased vigilance. This had no discernible effect.

Its successor recommended in 1961 the setting up of a Press Amalgamations Court. A variant of this proposal became law in 1965. It required all large press groups to obtain the permission of the Secretary of State before they were allowed to purchase any newspaper. The effectiveness of this legislation may be gauged by the fact that not one of the fifty acquisitions of newspaper companies by major press groups during the period 1965–77 was disallowed.

The 1977 Commission argued that press anti-monopoly legislation should be greatly strengthened. Its advice was ignored by both Labour and Conservative governments. Consequently anti-monopoly law again proved to be ineffectual when it was put crucially to the test in 1981. Permission was given to Rupert Murdoch to buy *The Times* and *Sunday Times*, thereby giving him control of 30 per cent of national daily circulation and 36 per cent of national Sunday circulation, without the take-overs even being referred to the Monopolies Commission.[8]

The impact of successive Press Commissions in this area has thus been limited. They have manifestly failed to restrain the rapid growth of press concentration that has taken place. Yet, while promoting ineffectual mergers legislation, the last two Commissions opposed proposals for divesting the major press groups – originating from the centre as well as from the left of British politics.[9]

Restriction on joint media ownership

The first Press Commission urged that the ownership of the press and broadcasting should be kept separate. No attention was paid to its views when commercial television was introduced in 1954. The second Press Commission criticized the press's heavy involvement in commercial television but was prevented from making any explicit recommendation by its terms of reference. Contrary to the spirit of its report, press groups continued to retain large shareholdings in commercial television. Indeed they were even given a prescriptive right to participate in setting up local commercial radio stations in their circulation areas when independent radio was introduced in 1972.

This prescriptive right was ended by the Broadcasting Act, 1981, at the recommendation of the 1977 Press Commission. The IBA also adopted a policy of reducing press interests in broadcasting (although these are still very extensive) in response to the urging of both the 1977 Press Commission and the Annan Committee on Broadcasting. But the Press Commission's main recommendations in this area have been ignored. Press groups have not been debarred from having interests in local radio stations in their main areas of circulation and they have not been excluded from ITV franchises in those areas where they are dominant.

Press Council

The Press Council is perhaps the most concrete reform to come out of the Press Commissions. But the Council, as presently constituted, bears little relationship to what was originally conceived. The initial blueprint, proposed by the 1949 Commission, was for a powerful 'General Council of the Press', which was to be a well-funded and widely respected public body concerned not only with investigating complaints but also with such matters as the recruitment and education of journalists and the promotion of substantial research into the press.

An ineffectual body was finally set up in 1953, which functioned during its first ten years as little more than a public relations agency for the press industry. The reforms that followed the 1962 Commission's indictment were limited. The Council was excoriated by the 1977 Commission for its lack of independence, its failure to enforce clear standards, and its general ineffectiveness. The Commission made twelve recommendations for a complete shake-up of the Press Council's organization and procedures. Their implementation was essential, the Commission warned, if the Council was to 'fulfil the hopes that were held for it in 1949'.

The Council responded by rejecting nine out of the twelve recommendations. In 1980 the National Union of Journalists withdrew from the Council as a mark of its lack of confidence in the Council's proceedings, and has so far resisted TUC pressure to rejoin.

The Council is now in a difficult position. It can silence the growing volume of criticism directed against it only by being more assertive and independent. Yet this could undermine the financial backing and goodwill of proprietors essential for its continued functioning. Whatever may be said for this vulnerable institution (perhaps more than its critics allow), [10] it is now clear that the 1949 Commission's fond hope that the Council would effectively promote 'a sense of public responsibility and public service among all engaged in the profession of journalism' has turned out to be illusory.

Miscellany

The 1949 Commission advocated that broadly based educational courses for journalists should be started, which would promote higher standards of professionalism. What emerged were courses that were narrowly vocational and encouraged uncritical acceptance of traditional values in the industry. The last Commission advocated a widening of journalism education to little effect. Most of its detailed proposals were ignored; its chosen instrument of change, the Printing and Publishing Industry Training Board, was later abolished by the Thatcher government.

Press Commissions have also advocated other reforms – that newspapers should prominently display the name of their owner, that they should declare an interest when reporting on economic activities in which their parent or associated companies are financially involved, that Fleet Street papers should receive cheap loans to assist the introduction of new technology, and that the press should abide by a Charter of good practice drawn up by the last Commission, which would be policed by a reformed Press Council on a voluntary basis for a trial period. No attention has been paid to any of these proposals.

In short, successive Royal Commissions have had very little influence on the press. Most of their proposals have been ignored. The few reforms that have been introduced have proved relatively ineffectual. In so far as the Commissions have exerted any real influence, it has been largely negative in discouraging the adoption of any of the reformist measures implemented elsewhere in Europe.[11] They have thus contributed little towards relieving the problems identified in their reports through a programme of reform.

Reworking liberal theory

However, the significance of Royal Commissions on the Press is not confined solely to their influence on public policy. They also draw together different sources of evidence and different views in new processes of synthesis. They provide therefore unique opportunities for modifying and updating theoretical justifications of the press in a form that takes account of changes in its structure and ownership.

There is one passage in the last Commission's report which is of particular interest in this context, since it seems to indicate a new approach:

> We define the freedom of the press as that freedom from restraint which is essential to enable proprietors, editors and journalists to advance the public interest by publishing the facts and opinions without which a democratic electorate cannot make responsible judgements.

By defining press freedom in these collective terms, the Commission seemed to be modifying the traditional concept of press freedom as the property right of proprietors. The novelty of this approach was seemingly confirmed by the clauses in the Commission's proposed

Charter which upheld the freedom of conscience of individual journalists and the right of editors to accept any contribution 'notwithstanding the views of his proprietor'.

But this new approach was not sustained. The overriding concern of the Charter, reflected in numerous, detailed prohibitions, was to protect proprietors and their editors from journalists and their principal collective organization, the National Union of Journalists. The traditionalism that really informed the Commission's attitude towards the press was further revealed by its discussion of how proprietors might be prevented from abusing their power. It accepted the Newspaper Publishers' Association's argument that 'in reality editorial and managerial decisions were inseparable' and that writing certain freedoms into editors' contracts – such as the right to criticize the activities of other parts of the organization to which their papers belonged – was 'too constricting'. On the wider issue of internal democracy, urged by some as an essential safeguard against the abuse of proprietorial power, the Commission made the extraordinary admission that it had 'not examined the issues raised in such a way as to enable us to express a view on this complex and disputed subject'.

The Commission's reworking of liberal theory was inconsistent as well as faltering. For instance it portrayed the issue of the union closed shop in the press as a simple conflict between 'two valid but competing demands': on the one hand, the desire of employees to improve their earnings and conditions of work and

> for those on the other side, what matters most is the freedom of the press because they cannot 'conceive a civilized society that does not regard as its first priority the right of a man to express what he believes in whatever form he thinks appropriate, subject to the control of the law'.

In accepting this simplistic representation advanced by the Newspaper Publishers Association, the Commission was falling back on the classical liberal premise that the unrestricted freedom to publish guarantees 'the right of a man to express what he believes'. It was thus endorsing a view which its own analysis had previously disputed.

The Commission thus failed to construct a new set of persuasive arguments which would replace traditional liberal apologetics. But its euphemistic re-presentation of the concept of press freedom as a collective freedom from restraint, and its tentative acknowledgement of the need to curtail proprietors, was nevertheless significant. It reflected the last Commission's uneasy awareness that the rhetoric of liberal press theory no longer corresponded to the reality of the contemporary press.

The same uneasiness is reflected in the Commission's tentative espousal of a philosophy of public service. Newspapers, the Commission argued, should behave 'with proper restraint'; the press should be like broadcasting and recruit more graduates: young journalists should go on improving courses and 'learn about society'.

Indeed the Commission seemed intent, at times, on transplanting the public service rationale of broadcasting to the press. But its moves in this direction were inconsistent and contradictory. It wanted a public service orientation but was opposed to the framework of public regulation that underpins it. It favoured a more balanced, responsible approach to journalism but was also committed to the tradition of partisanship and outspoken comment upheld by the free market tradition of the press. Unable to define precisely what it meant by professionalism, the Commission was not very successful at promoting it. But its flirtation with the idea of public service was nevertheless revealing: it was an attempt to co-opt a different theoretical tradition in a bid to bolster the increasingly threadbare classical theory of press freedom.

Commissions' escapism

Unable either to rationalize away or to reform the problems they identified, the Press Commissions took comfort in the belief that the importance of the press has been greatly exaggerated. This argument was explicitly stated by the first two Commissions, and implicitly stated by the last one when it stressed the growing importance of the broadcasting media. By implication, the failure either to prescribe practical remedies or to declare the patient fit did not greatly matter.

Admittedly critics of the press have sometimes overstated its influence. But the Commission's downgrading of press influence runs counter to the new consensus of informed opinion. The minimal effects model of the press is rooted in American research conducted in the 1940s and 1950s: it is now rejected by most contemporary researchers into the press.[12]

All three Commissions also sought to diminish the problems they encountered by adopting a narrow, functionalist perspective of the press. By discussing newspapers exclusively in terms of the functions they perform for society as a whole, such as informing, entertaining, and acting as a public watch-dog, they classified out uncomfortable questions about how newspapers relate to power groups in society. All three Commissions thus took refuge in the largely forgotten, functionalist sociology of the immediate post-war period.

Indeed the ways in which the Press Commissions became reconciled to failure have a curiously old-fashioned look about them. They are rooted in the discredited, intellectual fashions of the yester-year, scarcely a firm foundation for continued evasion in the future.

Weak opposition

The lack of a coherent and convincing set of ideas legitimizing the present pattern of press ownership leaves proprietors potentially vulnerable to attack. The emergence of an assertive new generation of proprietors also makes the launching of a major new campaign against them increasingly likely.

The most probable source of such a campaign is the labour movement. It became increasingly alienated from the press when its mass circulation papers closed down during the 1960s. This alienation turned into growing hostility when the national press supported a series of aggressive campaigns against the trade unions from the late 1960s onwards.

The first sign of a shift in attitude was the publication in 1974 of a Labour Party Study Group report, *People and the Media*, most of whose proposals later became official policy. But it was not until 1983 that the Labour Party first included a programme for reforming the press in a general election manifesto. Even then it did little to build public support for its proposals.

The main campaigners for change have been the print unions. They played a leading role in setting up in 1979 the Campaign for Press and Broadcasting Freedom (as it became known). Although this is a public pressure group and publishes a campaigning periodical, *Free Press*, its impact has been confined mainly to the labour movement and people working in the media. Its main success to date has been the right of reply campaign in which it demanded with the backing of the print unions the right of victims of press distortions to put their case. But while this generated considerable parliamentary support for a statutory right of reply, it failed to spark off a public debate about the nature of press freedom.

The Labour Party's leadership has drawn back from launching a frontal attack on press proprietors. Although Neil Kinnock has floated the outline of a radical new policy for curbing the controllers of global media empires, he has not sought so far to mobilize public opinion behind it.[13] Indeed the most telling and effective criticism of the proprietors has come not from the labour movement, but from journalists like Harold Evans and Donald Trelford, whose political views are centrist rather than radical. In the absence of an effective, popular campaign from the left, press freedom will continue to be equated with the property rights of proprietors, perhaps more from the force of habitual assumption than considered conviction.

Notes

1. This is the underlying theme of part I of this book.
2. The Commission was less troubled than it might have been partly because its analysis of the evidence concealed the full extent of the trend towards concentration of ownership. Its main report did not examine chain ownership in terms of total daily and Sunday circulation as its predecessors had done, and did not take properly into account the long-term development of press concentration in the period before 1961.
3. In this context it is worth noting Colin Seymour-Ure's argument that the transfer of control of the press from political parties to unaccountable capitalist conglomerates with an interest in the outcome of government policy has undermined the legitimacy of the press. (See his 'National daily papers and the party system' in *Studies on the Press*, Royal Commission on the Press Working Paper 3, London, HMSO, 1977).
4. See chapter 7, pp. 78–113.
5. The Commission suggested, however, that new technology would be of disproportionate help to quality papers in reducing costs.
6. N. Hartley, P. Gudgeon, and R. Crafts, *Concentration of Ownership in the Provincial Press*, Royal Commission on the Press 1974–7, Research Series 5 (London, HMSO, 1977); *Periodicals and the Alternative Press*, Royal Commission on the Press Research Series 6 (London, HMSO, 1977).
7. For a summary of alternative European press subsidy schemes, see A. Smith, 'State intervention and the management of the press' in J. Curran (ed.), *The British Press: A Manifesto* (London, Macmillan, 1978).
8. The government's failure to refer News International's acquisition of Times Newspapers to the Monopolies Commission was none-theless probably a breach of the law, even in its unreformed state. See H. Evans, *Good Times, Bad Times* (London, Weidenfeld & Nicolson, 1983).
9. Proposals for divestiture came from, among others, Sir Geoffrey Crowther (Royal Commission on the Press, Oral Evidence, vol. 1, p. 5, London, HMSO, 1962), and Professor Jeremy Tunstall (Royal Commission on the Press 1974–7, unpublished evidence), both from the broad centre of the political spectrum.
10. After the last Press Commission's criticisms, the Press Council did become notably more efficient and its lay membership (even if selected by a carefully controlled Appointments Commission) was increased to half of the Council. But for a recent indictment, see

G. Robertson, *People Against the Press: An Enquiry into the Press Council* (London, Quartet, 1983).

11. However, the 1977 Commission contained a minority report, signed by two members, proposing a National Printing Corporation and a Launch Fund to assist the establishment of new publications. These recommendations were ignored.

12. P. Dunleavy and C. Husbands, *British Democracy at the Crossroads* (London, Allen & Unwin, 1984) and J. P. Robinson and M. R. Levy, *The Main Source* (Beverly Hills, Calif., Sage, 1986) are examples of recent assessments of press influence. This said, psychological and peer group influences do significantly limit the impact of the press. For a more cautious assessment, see J. Curran, 'The boomerang effect: the press and the battle for London, 1981–6' in J. Curran, A. Smith, and P. Wingate (eds), *Impacts and Influences* (London, Methuen, 1977).

13. See chapter 19, pp. 292–322.

17

Broadcasting and the theory of public service

British broadcasting was started as a public service, unified in structure and aim. Broadcasting – monopoly or duopoly – was always justified in these terms, and an assumption of commitment to an undivided public good lay beneath all official thinking on radio and television until the 1970s. In 1977 the Annan Report abandoned this assumption, and replaced it with a new principle of liberal pluralism. The ideal ceased to be the broad consensus – the middle ground upon which all men of good sense could agree. Rather it became, for Annan and those who supported or inspired him, a free market-place in which balance could be achieved through the competition of a multiplicity of independent voices. The result has been confusion and crisis, from which no new received doctrine has yet emerged.

So, by 1982, the Hunt Report on the introduction of cable television could begin to modify the principles of balance and quality even further. These were relegated to a part of the national service in the BBC and ITV. Although both the Hunt Report and the subsequent White Paper advocated some safeguards to protect the British system from the damaging effects of foreign satellite transmissions, and to guarantee the rights of the networks to televise events of national interest, the basis of public service broadcasting was abandoned. Thus cable television, free from constraining ideals, was left to produce programmes that 'were sufficiently attractive for the public to buy'.[1]

However, the most obvious long-term symptom of this change has been a shift in terminology. The concept of public service is elaborated in all broadcasting reports before that of the Annan Committee. As early as 1923 the Sykes Report argued that broadcasting was 'of great national importance as a medium for the performance of a valuable public service'.[2] The next report – that of the Crawford Committee in 1926 – suggested that in view of the scale, significance, and potentialities of broadcasting, the duties and status of the Corporation which it had just created 'should correspond with those of a public service, and the directorate should be appointed with the sole object of promoting the utmost utility and development of the enterprise'.[3]

Later reports developed the consequences of this view. 'The influence of broadcasting upon the mind and speech of the nation', commented the Ullswater Report, made it an 'urgent necessity in the national interest that the broadcasting service should at all times be conducted in the best possible manner and to the best possible advantage of the people'.[4] In 1950 the Beveridge Report on broadcasting characterized the ideal of public service more actively. 'Like the work of the universities,' Beveridge suggested, 'the work of broadcasting should be regarded as a public service for a social purpose.'[5] The Pilkington Report, which considered both the BBC and the commercial service in 1962, added to this definition: 'The concept of broadcasting has always been of a service, comprehensive in character, with the duty of a public corporation of bringing to public awareness the whole range of ... activity and expression developed in society.'[6] Indeed the organization of commercial television was as much a product of the ideal of public service broadcasting as the BBC's had been originally. Thus successive reports developed the idea of broadcasting as a public service – catering for all sections of the community, reaching all parts of the country regardless of cost, seeking to educate, inform, and improve, and prepared to lead public opinion rather than follow it.

The Annan Report, however, broke with this tradition for the first time. This change was noticeable, both in the evidence which was presented to the committee, as well as in the conclusion of the report. Even the reformers, whether of the left or right, disregarded the public service principle entirely. The BBC referred to it in only the most apologetic tone. The Annan Committee itself took a pluralist view: broadcasting should cater for the full range of groups and interests in society, rather than seek to offer moral leadership. 'For the individual life is a gamble, he is entitled to stake everything, if he desires, on one interpretation of life,' it argued. 'But broadcasting organizations have to back the field, and put their money on all the leading horses which line up at the starting gate.'[7] In one elegant metaphor, the whole basis of public service broadcasting had been dismissed.

Indeed the Annan Report's reinterpretation of public service unintentionally left British broadcasters defenceless against the threats posed by recent technological developments. By so transforming public service it left no grounds on which to manage or control the impact of the inevitable introduction of cable, video, or satellite broadcasting. After 1977, reports and White Papers on the future of these very technologies have not even attempted to assess the impact of unregulated competition for audiences, revenues, and programmes on the television system as a whole. Thus it was possible for the Hunt Report to suggest that viewers' willingness to pay for cable television simply constituted a new source of revenue. It was claimed that this would not divert resources from existing channels. (However, it was not apparently thought necessary to support this assertion by either evidence or argument.)

By contrast there was a radical development in the 1986 Peacock Report, which reinterpreted the role of the market in broadcasting.[8] While advocating what Samual Brittan, a leading monetarist journalist and theorist and member of the Peacock Committee, called 'the goal that British Broadcasting should move towards a sophisticated market system based on consumer sovereignty', the report perceived public service commitments as actually protecting consumer sovereignty. Brittan commented that 'The existence of a tax-financed BBC and the IBA regulation of commercial television were justified by Peacock as a second best, but very successful, attempt to replicate artificially the programme structure of a true broadcasting market'. More than that, the committee took up the elaboration of the public service ideal developed in Channel 4 provision, and suggested that a mature broadcasting service would operate like the publishing industry. 'Pre-publication censorship, whether of printed material, plays, films, broadcasting or other creative activities or expressions of opinion, has no place in a free society', the report argued, and recommended that the government 'embark forthwith on a phased programme for ending it'. Brittan went on to point out not only that the report widened the scope of its enquiries far beyond its original brief of considering the introduction of advertising on to the BBC (which it rejected), by assessing the future of broadcasting and how that could be best managed in the context of technological developments, but also that the report demonstrated the fundamental social significance of broadcasting. As Brittan commented

> Peacock exposed many of the contradictions in the Thatcherite espousal of market forces. In principle, Mrs Thatcher and her supporters are in favour of de-regulation, competition, and choice. But they are distrustful ... of plans to allow people to listen to and watch what they like, subject only to the law of the land. They espouse the market system but dislike the libertarian value judgements involved in its operation: value judgements which underlie the Peacock Report.[9]

The Peacock Report put public service back on the agenda at just the point when the broadcasting organizations seemed to have abandoned it.

Indeed this abandonment by the broadcasting organizations is a problem, for the authority of British broadcasting has always depended on the pursuit of public service. Indeed by relinquishing any claim to this, the broadcasting institutions have put into jeopardy a whole set of complex relationships between themselves, the state, their audiences, and their programme policy. What caused this crisis? What are its consequences?

The state and broadcasting

One cause of the collapse of the principle of public service broadcasting has been the deterioration in the relationship between the state and broadcasting institutions. In the Sykes Report Charles Trevelyan argued that 'We consider such a potential power over public opinion and the life of the nation ought to remain with the state.' Because broadcasting was so important it was seen as 'essential that permission to transmit, and the matter to be transmitted should be subject to public authority'.

Air waves were a scarce resource which did not obey national boundaries. Consequently the state was obliged to control the right to broadcast in all societies. In the early British broadcasting reports, however, there is a consensus that state regulation is the best guarantee of broadcasting independence and accountability. As the Crawford Report put it, only the state could license the BBC to be 'a public corporation acting as trustee for the national interest'.

In the 1920s the problem of the relationship of government with broadcasting was dealt with by making new rules and creating new machinery. It was taken for granted that the control over the administration of an organization could be kept quite separate from whatever the organization did. Hence it was possible for broadcasting to be politically accountable, and yet remain independent of any political influence. The Sykes Report noted that any detailed control of the work of the Corporation would make a government 'constantly open to suspicion that it was using an opportunity to its own advantage'. It was therefore decided that the minister responsible for the service would be able to answer questions in the House on matters of principle and finance, but he should not be held responsible for the programmes themselves. Later the problem seemed to disappear. Complaints about government intervention were rare, and the issue of excessive interference no longer seemed to exist.

In 1936 the Ullswater Report commented, 'We have no reason to suppose that, in practice, divergent views of public interest have been held by the Corporation and government departments.' Pilkington argued in 1962 that 'The practical resolution of the problem was made easier because the first priority of the department concerned with exercising the government's responsibility (the GPO) is with technical matters.' No conflict had arisen between broadcasters and governments over the definition of public interest.

However, by the 1970s this pragmatic argument was felt to be inadequate. Imperceptibly the problem had become one of defending broadcasters against the state. The relationship was increasingly characterized as one of vigilant and stealthy hostility. A cold war had been declared between them.

This was partly a consequence of the changing nature of politics in Britain. In a world of increasingly sophisticated news reporting this posed problems for both the BBC and the IBA. 'Politics' and political balance could be treated simply in two- or three-party terms in the 1950s. By the 1970s this was no longer the case. The emergence of the SDP made the work of 'striking a balance' far more difficult for broadcasters. In addition many fields which had previously been regarded as non-controversial and administrative had moved into the political arena. But also because of a proliferation of parties, interests, and pressure groups, because of a widening gap between the major parties and, most of all, because of the rise of issues – of which Northern Ireland was the most critical – for which the gentlemanly and constitutionalist assumptions of the early rule-makers could not cater. The problem of providing 'balance' in dealing with treasonable activities in Ulster – when, whether, and under what conditions to interview terrorists or members of illegal organizations, how to discuss the issue at all – forced the broadcasting directorates to make new rules and, in effect, to add to the corpus of Britain's unwritten constitution.

The questions which the public asked about broadcasting, the Annan Report claimed, were becoming 'more critical, more hostile and more political'. At the same time, there was a new public mood, 'at once inflationary in the expectation of what political power could achieve, and deflationary towards those in power who failed to give effect to these expectations'.

By 1977 the interests of governments were seen as inimical to those of broadcasting. The distinction between the broadcasting bureaucracies and what they produced had been challenged. Previously the quality and balance of a company's programmes were believed to be guaranteed by the good order of the administration. This view was now replaced by one of increasingly detailed suspicion. More than that, broadcasters' institutionalized caution about the power of governments had developed into a rejection of all kinds of intervention by the state.

This has had profound consequences for the legitimacy of the public service broadcasting organizations. The Annan Report argued that the authorities have a dual role: on the one hand they exist to ensure that broadcasters operate in the public interest and are responsive to public opinion, particularly as expressed in parliament. On the other hand, they exist 'also to defend broadcasters from undue pressure from whatever quarter'. But these are not complementary obligations; rather they are contradictory. The authorities are supposed both to reflect political pressure and to resist it. It used to be possible for the authorities to perform these two functions when the interests of the state and the broadcasting organization were seen as similar, if not identical. However, once their interests are opposed, the two aspects of the authorities' role are increasingly difficult to reconcile.

Accountability and broadcasting

This situation would matter less if other mechanisms designed to relate broadcasting institutions to society seemed less perfunctory. Since 1926 they have all suffered from attrition.

Reith rapidly turned the Governors, supposedly 'the trustees of the national interest', into creatures of the Director General. In both commercial television and the BBC, the Boards of Governors depend for their information upon the organizations they were designed to supervise, and they have no independent secretariat or research function. The Governors have remained relatively powerless, and do not see their job as one of representing external interests or views. Similarly the role of the advisory committees was ingeniously reinterpreted. Reith ensured that these acted as specialists (whether in music, speech, or religion) who merely offered their advice over particular policy issues to the Corporation, rather than experts in broadcasting as such.

Indeed the only independent source of power left within these supposedly governing bodies is that of the Chairman of the Board. This power derives from the Chairman's close personal association with the Director General – or the administrative head of the independent service. Yet this intimacy leads to what Heller has called 'the tendency of broadcasting authorities to identify their interests, and by implication the national interest very closely with the survival of the organization they supervise'.[10]

However, in the 1980s a series of political crises in which the role of broadcasting was crucial – the Falklands War, further trouble in dealing with Ireland, disputes about the interpretation of foreign events – all exposed the potential vulnerability of the governing body and the

Chairman to political influence. In this period the problem was not so much the identification of the Chairman with the institution, but rather the identification of the Chairman with the government in power.

Yet the broadcasting organizations had given up so much of the ground themselves. By 1977 the IBA claimed that accountability was only a minority interest. The Annan Report endorsed a system which was little more than a pious rhetoric. 'On balance', the report concluded, '... while some improvements could be made, the relations between government and parliament and the broadcasting authorities do not require much adjustment: the chain of accountability is adequate.' Annan apparently believed that accountability was a purely abstract idea – one which includes no reference to the public. But the paragraph nevertheless ends, 'We do not consider, however, that the relations between the broadcasters and the public are satisfactory.' If, as Annan suggested, broadcasting is to abandon the independence of public service, and be based, rather, on a principle of representative pluralism, then the inadequacy of the Governors, and advisory committees, becomes even more serious.

Independent professionals or men with an interest

The independence of broadcasting from the state has recently been seen as the most important condition of the service's accountability. This independence has in turn been reduced to the freedom of programme-makers. Yet as Beveridge once commented, 'To whom is a broadcaster responsible? If it is only to his own conscience the decision might better be described as irresponsible.'

This emphasis on broadcasters' rights is a consequence of focusing the assessment of broadcasting on individual programmes. Pilkington was the last report to elaborate the tradition of public service, and it also argued that 'A service of broadcasting should be judged, not by the stated aims of the broadcasters, but by its achievements.' The Annan Report endorsed this approach.

Nevertheless, broadcasting and broadcasting institutions cannot be understood merely as a collection of separate programme 'texts'. As an ACCT Report commented in 1972, judging broadcasting organizations by their product 'was like being asked to evaluate the Milk Marketing Board by drinking milk – relevant, but inadequate'.[11]

Broadcasting is a process which cannot be entirely understood from its products. Few would claim that the whole nature of the capitalist enterprise can be understood from the shop floor of one factory. Neither can all the pressures which condition broadcasting institutions be revealed by an examination of what Tracey has called 'the world of determination of a television programme'[12] – however important that study might be. The emphasis on programmes as the most important criterion for judging broadcasting reinforces the arbitrary role of professionals at the expense of more general considerations of public service.

The Annan Report claimed that 'Good broadcasting would reflect the competing demands of a society which was increasingly multi-racial and pluralist.' In turn, this variety could be secured only by giving the 'talented broadcasters' greater freedom of expression.

However, broadcasters are not necessarily influenced by a wide variety of interests. Much recent research has shown how little producers and directors consider their audience. The only information about viewers which seriously affects producers is knowledge of the size of the audience. This is not because audience research is incapable of providing more complex detail, but because to know more would put producers under even greater stress. 'For a sociologist', comments Burns, 'it was rather like watching the whole practice of medicine being reduced to the use of a thermometer.'[13] Producers value the opinion of their colleagues most, but they see very little even of them.

The public interest cannot simply rely on the quality of broadcasters, because to do so is to ignore the pressures which determine broadcasting choices. 'When one stresses the role of individuals manning the system,' Garnham argues, 'one is tempted to await a Messiah who will come over – and help transform the system.'[14]

However, the relationship of broadcasters to their organization has also altered. Burns argued that there had been a considerable change in attitude since the 1960s. Then staff expressed a devotion to public service 'and a belief in the BBC's normative role in the cultural, moral and political life of the country'. By the 1970s this had been replaced by a commitment to professional values. Indeed as Kumar points out, the emergence of professionalism as the dominating ideology is the product of a particular moment in the evolution of broadcasting organizations. Even the notion of 'lively broadcasting' which determines the professionals' judgements 'expresses a particular stance towards the audience, a judgement of what the audience can and cannot take, which reflects a particular conception of the purposes of broadcasting'.[15]

Indeed the new 'scientific management' of broadcasting organizations has greater power than earlier administrations, whose main concern had been to protect and assist programme-makers who had far higher status within the organization. 'Because of the need to allocate time and resources economically,' Burns argues, 'working relations became impersonally functional.' The steady march of rational managerialism had led to a withering of institutional ardour.

Consequently not only were the talented programme-makers upon whom Annan rested the future of broadcasting less committed to public service than before, but also they had become less important within broadcasting organizations.

Independence and the theory of broadcasting

The significance of broadcasting independence is also disputed. One side suggests that the independence is functional and must be extended to guarantee accountable broadcasting. The other argues that this same independence poses a serious threat to political institutions, whose control over broadcasting should be strengthened. Working from the same assumptions about the role of the media, Anthony Smith and Colin Seymour-Ure have arrived at diametrically opposed diagnoses and solutions.

According to classic liberal theory the independence of a journalist depended on his ability to follow the uninhibited dictates of his conscience. According to Smith, however, this is an illusory ideal. In discussing the 1968 crisis in French broadcasting he argues that, 'The ORTF strikers had stumbled across the central dilemmas of broadcasting and were demanding in the name of freedom ... a right which no broadcaster has ever really achieved – the right to be an individual member of a Fourth Estate.'[16] In its place Smith puts forward a far more sophisticated and powerful version of the theory, in which the independence of broadcasters is not an individual right – but rather a functional necessity.

Broadcasters are not free, but are 'brokers and megaphones, impresarios and mediators', he suggests. The 'independence' of broadcasting institutions from political control was one solution to a dilemma all broadcasting systems had to solve: namely the necessity not only of regulating the right to broadcast but also of ensuring that broadcasting served the interests of all sections of society. For, Smith suggests, 'The institutions of broadcasting inaugurated a special problem of unlegitimized and unselective power.' Broadcasters are obliged to negotiate political conflict – and not take sides in it – precisely because of the immense and dangerous nature of their power. In stable systems countervailing interests would always be able to enforce damaging sanctions if broadcasters became partisan.

This model implies that all political interests in society can, in practice, be reconciled. It is a logical extension of broadcasting institutions' own view of their role as arbiters that they come to see conflict and opposition as the products of failures in communication. Nevertheless, if there are real differences in interest, incompatible policies, and irreconcilable principles, then the role of the broker becomes untenable.

However, the functional independence of broadcasting institutions has many of the same policy consequences as the older liberal individualism. For, Smith argues, the way to meet recent criticisms is to give broadcasters more independence. The more perfectly broadcasters can do anything they want, the more adequate the service will be. As he is reported as commenting to the Annan Committee:

> If I am free to say anything I want to say except the one thing I want to say then I am not free. ... In broadcasting ... a single prohibition imposed on a national broadcasting authority or within it tends to corrode the whole output.

Colin Seymour-Ure views the 'independence' of broadcasters rather differently. The independence of the press – no longer the client of political parties – and 'now part of vast corporations who may have very direct interests in the outcomes of policy decisions' is vulnerable because it is compromised by ownership. Broadcasters, moreover, having abandoned the protection of 'public service' ideology are also susceptible to accusations of bias. Seymour-Ure argues that:

> Some Labour politicians used to take comfort in the fact that although the press might be disproportionately conservative, at least broadcasting was balanced. This is no longer true. No doubt broadcasters are not wilfully biased. But the simple fact of deciding their own programme content may in the extreme case lead to a projection of party politicians and leaders that might run entirely counter to the parties' own views.[17]

He suggests that the current interpretation of broadcasting independence has seriously damaged the political system.

The ideal of broadcasting independence – unlimited by any obligation to public service – has become increasingly inadequate. It has contributed to a growing anti-government ethos. It is hostile to many forms of political partisanship. It may inhibit political change and development. It may be that, as Seymour-Ure comments, the period of mass-based party organization is ending, for one effect of television in many countries seems to be 'the erosion of intervening structures between representatives and electors'. Nevertheless, any increase in the autonomy of broadcasting institutions may have more serious political consequences than had been expected. Rather it is the democratic processes which need support: not because broadcasters are malign but because of the inexorable pressure of broadcasting independence on the handling of politics.

Conclusion

Broadcasters have come to see the state as their enemy. Yet broadcasting institutions ultimately depend on the state for their legitimation. This authority cannot be replaced by a pluralist ideal of reflecting social and cultural variety. Indeed the adoption of this principle has left broadcasters peculiarly vulnerable to the more general attack on public service broadcasting.

Moreover, arguments with quite different aims from those of the broadcasters, but apparently related, are being used to undermine broadcasting responsibility and independence. Thus neither the emphasis on the authority of the viewers' right to choose from a greater variety of programmes, nor the elaboration of some aspects of the local and regional role of the media, let alone the distinction between a 'service' the public will pay for and a public service, are intended to strengthen the creative autonomy of broadcasters. On the contrary they are arguments which will enhance the power of commercial interests in determining the patterns of broadcasting provision.

Thus, without a commitment to public service, broadcasters are increasingly vulnerable to detailed political interference in the content of programmes. Broadcasting in Britain has in the past had a considerable degree of real autonomy from other institutions: it has not been in any simple sense biased. This autonomy is now threatened, partly because the consensus about what constitutes the 'middle ground' of agreed opinion has broken down, partly because the reliance on the skill of professional broadcasters which has replaced it is unjustified, and partly because of the erosion of public service broadcasting. Broadcasting needs to find a new relationship to the state – and a new form of commitment to public service.

Notes

1. *Report of the Enquiry into Cable Expansion and Broadcasting Policy* (Hunt Report, 1982) [Cmnd 8697].
2. *Broadcasting Committee: Report* (Sykes Report, 1923). [Cmnd 1951], X, 13, para. 21.
3. *Report of the Broadcasting Committee* (Crawford Report, 1926) [Cmnd 2599], VIII, 327, para. 49.
4. *Report of the Broadcasting Committee* (Ullswater Report, 1936) [Cmnd 5091], VII, 617, para. 7.
5. *Report of the Broadcasting Committee* (Beveridge Report, 1951) [Cmnd 8116], IX, 1, para. 217.
6. *Report of the Committee on Broadcasting* (Pilkington Report, 1960) [Cmnd 1755], IV, 259, para. 23.

7. *Report of the Committee on the Future of Broadcasting* (Annan Report, 1977) [Cmnd 6753], XVI, para. 311.
8. *Report of the Committee on Financing the BBC* (Peacock Report, 1986) [Cmnd 9824], II, para. 636.
9. S. Brittan, 'The fight for freedom in broadcasting', *Political Quarterly*, 58, 1 (March 1987).
10. C. Heller, *Broadcasters and Accountability*, BFI Television Monograph 3 (London, British Film Institute, 1978), p. 39.
11. ACCT report, quoted in C. Heller, *Broadcasters and Accountability*, BFI Television Monograph 3 (London, British Film Institute, 1978), p. 50.
12. M. Tracey, *The Production of Political Television* (London, Routledge & Kegan Paul, 1978), p. 13.
13. T. Burns, *The BBC: Public Institution and Private World* (London, Macmillan, 1977), p. 137.
14. N. Garnham, *Structures of Television*, BFI Television Monograph 1 (London, British Film Institute, 1973), p. 21.
15. K. Kumar, 'Holding the middle ground: The BBC, the public and the professional broadcaster' in J. Curran, M. Gurevitch, and J. Woollacott (eds), *Mass Communication and Society* (London, Edward Arnold/Open University, 1977), p. 232.
16. A. D. Smith, *The Shadow in the Cave* (London, Allen & Unwin, 1973), p. 85.
17. C. Seymour-Ure in O. Boyd-Barrett, C. Seymour-Ure, and J. Tunstall (eds), *Studies on the Press*, Royal Commission on the Press 1974–7, Working Paper 3 (London, HMSO, 1977), p. 196.

Part IV

Politics of the media

18

Contradictions in public policy

In some ways official attitudes towards the media have changed remarkably little over the last sixty years. One recurrent theme has been the emphasis on greater efficiency. Thus in 1949 the Gater Report on the British Film Industry called for more effective financial planning, while the second (1962) Press Commission urged that better machinery for negotiation should be established, a point also stressed by the Prices and Incomes Board Report on the press in 1967. In the same way the Annan Report (1977) concluded that 'clear lines of decision making, fewer chieftains, better communications' were the most important remedies, and the Peacock Report on the BBC (1986) argued that 'the assessment of efficiency is one of our Committee's chief aims'. Such comments, few of which have ever had any significant effect, have become part of the ritual of official investigation.

Most government reports have also taken an optimistic view of the independence of journalists and programme-makers, and their capacity for autonomous reform. Thus two Royal Commissions have stressed in identical words that 'On the quality of the individual journalist depends not only the status of the whole profession of journalism but the possibility of bridging the gap between what society needs from the press and what the press is at present giving it.' Similarly the Annan Report has argued that 'The strength of British Broadcasting lies in the creativity of people who make programmes.'

Hence successive reports have suggested better recruitment policies, improved training and education, and greater integrity and responsibility amongst communicators as the best ways to improve the media. Annan proposed an Open Broadcasting Authority which would show programmes made by 'small independent production groups', a term which is reminiscent of the 'small independent producer' which film policy has been unsuccessfully trying to help since the Moyne Report in 1936. In the same way, three Royal Commissions have attempted to secure a more varied press by encouraging individual entrepreneurs.

This emphasis on individuals – as opposed to structures – has led to a neglect of the role of financial limitations. Thus for over thirty years public money has been used in an attempt to finance independent film producers. Yet, because there has been no reform of the organization of film distribution and exhibition, this money has merely increased the profits of the large production companies. Public finance has reinforced those monopolistic tendencies within the film industry which it had been intended to mitigate. Similarly the Annan Committee proposed an Open Broadcasting Authority to introduce more adventurous minority programmes, yet failed to suggest how the finance of the new authority could be arranged to protect it from the economic pressures which inhibited experimental programming on the other channels. Indeed the Peacock Committee, appointed by a government hostile to the BBC, nevertheless made an important contribution to the survival of public service broadcasting precisely because for the first time its main object was to consider the financial structures that underlay the cultural considerations.

Thus, Channel 4's success in assisting the renaissance in the British film industry has been more a result of regularizing the product than of providing the finances. By giving individual, one-off, British art movies a predictable audience on television, systematizing their careers through the art movie theatres and making it possible to present each film as part of a successful series, the channel has immensely facilitated independent producers' capacity to raise film finance. Whether this development will survive the decline in cinema attendance, or the new commercial pressures of video, remains to be seen.

Thus government reports retained a number of basic assumptions over the years, glossing over or ignoring problems which their recommendations failed to solve. Yet the essential conservatism of official policy was less important than its contradictions. Good policy is not necessarily consistent policy, but one of the most curious features of government relations with the media has been the way in which reports on the press, broadcasting, and film industries have often conflicted sharply with one another.

The state as a threat

A common feature of many major inquiries into the workings of the media has been a liberal suspicion of the state and a determination to reject state intervention. The most recent Royal Commission on the Press (1977) formulated two principles concerning the limitation of state power:

We are strongly against any scheme which would make the press, or any section of it, dependent on government through reliance on continuing subsidies from public funds. We are also opposed absolutely to the establishment of any public body which could, or might have to, discriminate among publications in such a way as to amount to censorship in the sense of preferring to support some publications and not others.

The MacGregor Commission, like its predecessors, rejected any form of public support that was either selective or which led to economic dependence on the state. These principles were invoked in opposition to proposals for financial reform of the press. In addition, it was believed that they would forestall any further discussion of economic intervention. 'Suggestions [for financial reform of the press] were put to the two previous Royal Commissions', stated the 1977 report, 'and, although rejected, have continued to be advocated. We hope, perhaps optimistically, that ... we may have finally laid them to rest.'

The two principles have been expressed in technical arguments. On the one hand most schemes for subsidizing newspapers involved providing aid for small or insecure publications; since this meant a 'selective' award, they have always been rejected. On the other hand, schemes that did not discriminate in favour of the weaker publications have been rejected because they were ineffective. As the second Press Commission put it, 'If the subsidy were available to all newspapers, it would leave their respective competitive positions unchanged. If it were discriminatory it would involve in an obvious way the dangers of government interference in the press.'

Practical proposals for press reform have therefore been seen as politically unacceptable, while politically acceptable ones have turned out to be impractical. Consequently any interventions in the economic conditions of the press have been dismissed.

Yet the principle of selectivity, which the Royal Commission found so dangerous, has been central to much public policy on communications. 'No public body', argued the third Press Commission, 'should ever be put in a position of discriminating like a censor between one applicant and another.' However, this is exactly what the Independent Broadcasting Authority has always done when awarding radio and television franchises. The same has been true of the National Film Finance Corporation when granting loans to production companies, and of the Arts Council when making grants (including some to small press publications). Channel 4 has 'commissioning editors' who discriminate between projects and companies often on political grounds. Indeed the Economic and Social Research and Science Research Councils have also always discriminated among research projects, including politically sensitive ones, in awarding grants. It may be that the discrimination exercised by these bodies has been politically acceptable because they have not been concerned with news. However, it is increasingly difficult to separate 'news' from information, research, and opinion – the production of which several of these organizations are involved in.

Moreover, previous examples of economic intervention by the state in the press have not even been examined by Royal Commissions. Yet there is little evidence that economic regulation of the British press during the Second World War, or press subsidies in other democratic countries, have led to covert political censorship. At the same time the state continues to intervene in the market for newspapers. Newspapers receive a considerable government subsidy in the form of zero-rating for VAT, which makes a number of marginal publications dependent on government for their continued existence. Also, a number of local government authorities provide funds for small community papers. This is a form of selective aid that contravenes the Commission's principles. Indeed it might well be argued that selective aid given directly by any level of government to its potential critics, unmediated by any independent agency, is liable to abuse. Yet the Commission accepted both these subsidies without complaint. Its position seems to have been that schemes which contravene its guidelines are acceptable, provided they are established practice. They are unacceptable in principle if they are being proposed for the future.

The negative view of the state held by successive Royal Commissions contrasts with their positive view of the market. Having rejected selective public subsidies because they might be open to political manipulation, the Commissions did not apply the same criteria to advertising. Thus advertising subsidies are discretionary, keep alive some publications, and favour right-wing rather than left-wing newspapers. Similarly the political consequences of the exorbitant expense of launching a newspaper were not recognized. These have, of course, been reduced by new technology. However, the market tended to be seen as natural, inevitable, and politically neutral: public intervention on the other hand was always seen as politically biased.

The benign state

In contrast public reports on broadcasting reveal a positive image of the state. Conservative paternalism and an Arnoldian concern with moral and cultural values have contributed to this view. A corporatist tradition has also played a part, equating central planning with the rational and scientific use of resources, and so has a radical belief in the redistribution of power and wealth through state intervention. In addition, broadcasting has been seen as so powerful a political instrument that the state has been unwilling to abandon a close relationship with it. Thus the evolution of broadcasting policy has been shaped by a variety of justifications for close involvement by the state.

All of the nine major reports on British broadcasting have argued that a publicly appointed agency could act in the public interest, because it could be independent of all sectional interests, including that of the government. As the Crawford Committee put it, 'The actual commission should be persons of judgement and independence, free of commitments, and ... they will inspire confidence by having no other interests to promote than those of public service.'

Broadcasting has been repeatedly presented in reports as serving the public interest by being subject to regulations framed for the public good and controlled by people committed to the best interests of the entire community. The BBC at least was to be financed from licence revenue and therefore, in the words of the Pilkington Report (1960), was under 'no obligation, express or implied, to pursue any other objective other than that of public service'. Public regulation was seen as both necessary and desirable even after the introduction of commercial television.

This conception of public service has depended on a number of principles. First, that broadcasting services should all be made available to everyone in the UK, and not merely developed in areas where it was easy or cheap to do so, or restricted to those who could pay for them. Secondly, that public service broadcasting should produce a wide variety of high quality programmes because it would not be so subject to the pressures that make for low standards and uniformity. Lastly, that public regulation should ensure broadcasters' accountability through the relationship of the authority with parliament.

Reports on broadcasting have also been hostile to the effects of the market. The Crawford Committee (1926) argued that 'No company or body constituted on trade lines for profit ... can be regarded as adequate, in view of the broader considerations which now begin to emerge.' The Ullswater Committee (1936) regarded commercial advertising as incompatible with 'the intellectual and ethical integrity which the broadcasting system in this country has attained'. Much of this opposition has been based on the belief that what the Beveridge Committee (1951) called 'competition for numbers' results in standardized programming. This view has been justified by references to the deplorable condition of commercial broadcasting in the USA. 'Experience in other countries', concluded the Pilkington Report, 'is that this kind of competition, so far from promoting the purposes of broadcasting, or extending the range of programmes, or helping to realize the potential of the medium, serves rather to restrict them.'

Despite increasing anxiety about the nature of the relationship between the government and party politicians in general with broadcasters, the necessity of state regulation has never been questioned until 1986 in public reports on television or radio. State control has long been portrayed as the best way of guaranteeing that broadcasting does not become an instrument of narrow sectional interests.

The notion of a 'public good' implies a commonly accepted consensus of opinion within society. Thus the Annan Report introduced a variety of reforms with the intention of encouraging a more sensitive balance. Annan remained committed to the notions of 'common interest', 'impartiality', and 'balance' on which public service broadcasting is based.

However, the belief that publicly regulated broadcasting could 'maintain cultural standards' arose in a period when values were more secure than they are now. As the Annan Report commented, 'The ideals of middle-class culture, so felicitously expressed by Matthew Arnold a century ago ... found it ever more difficult to accommodate the new expression of life in the sixties.' The Annan Committee found it harder to define what good broadcasting was than did Pilkington. Nevertheless, Annan did make qualitative judgements, finding the BBC's output, on balance, superior to that of ITV. Annan was opposed to the unrestricted commercial control of broadcasting, and saw the fact that ITV made 'some programmes which both stimulate and entertain, and are not concocted in order to drug their audience into an uncritical stupor' as a product of public regulation. However, even the Peacock Report turned out to be a surprisingly staunch supporter of public service ideals. Regulated broadcasting, it argued, had led to a 'mixed diet' of programmes at 'a low cost', and it was particularly concerned to protect 'the interweaving of information, education and entertainment that has broadened the horizon of a great number of viewers'.

Thus there had been an unresolved contradiction between the approaches adopted in press and broadcasting reports. The idea that government should give money to a publishing corporation, even one with a publicly appointed managing authority, would have been opposed by all the Royal Commissions on the Press. Yet this is precisely what the Annan Committee proposed when it suggested that a government grant could be given to start an Open Broadcasting Authority. Moreover, this is precisely what the Conservative government in effect did when Channel 4 was launched.

The Conservative administration of the 1980s intended to resolve this contradiction permanently, by making broadcasting subject to market forces – just like the press. Incidentally it also no doubt sought through financial reorganization to rid itself of what it perceived as a political irritant in the BBC. The Peacock Committee was established to consider substituting advertising revenue for the BBC's licence fee, and to look into the further 'deregulation' of broadcasting. With considerable ingenuity, the report in fact produced a defence of 'public service broadcasting' on the impeccable grounds that it had most perfectly promoted the aims of a monetarist policy. 'Public service institutions', the report commented,

> have been necessary to provide the viewer and listener with what he or she wants as a consumer. The BBC and the regulated ITV system had done far better in mimicking the effects of a true consumer market than any purely *laissez-faire* system financed by advertising could have done.

Peacock argued that there was an important category of programme, not merely of minority interest, and not restricted to narrow political and cultural ghettos in content, that consumers as voters and citizens had a significant interest in seeing preserved. These programmes, however, would be destroyed by exposure to market forces. 'More than that,' the report went on to argue, 'we are clear that the component in consumer welfare which represents exposure to programmes which expand their range of tastes and preferences is of major importance'. Public service broadcasting for the Peacock Committee, in a classic definition entirely consistent with the traditional British view of the role of broadcasting, is about 'knowledge, culture, criticism, and experiment'. In the past the attitude of broadcasting reports to pay TV has revealed a fundamental hostility to market pressures. It is technically feasible, by linking a cable television service to a pay-as-you-watch scheme, to establish a market-based system of broadcasting use which would be comparable to the press and film industries. Such a system has already been introduced in the USA and Canada. Its advocates argue its merits in much the same terms as the advocates of the capitalist press. Cable-based pay TV, they argue, guarantees independence from state control and offers a wide diversity of programmes to choose from. Thus it is suggested that it forces programme-makers to respond to the interests and needs of consumers who pay only for what they want to see.

Previous Committees of Inquiry into broadcasting have rejected these arguments. Rather, they point out, pay TV would increase the cost of broadcasting to the consumer. It would discriminate against those who could not afford it and for whom it would not be profitable for pay TV operators to cater. Above all, it would impoverish public service broadcasting. Not only would it divert revenue from existing services and increase their costs, but also it would result in a reduction in programme choice, for pay TV operators would merely compete to attract the largest number of subscribers. They would have no obligation to consider programme standards. The whole basis of balanced programming and public service broadcasting would be undermined.

The Peacock Report, while suggesting that some more direct form of finance will be necessary to protect public service broadcasting by the end of the century, also rejects 'pay TV' in its crude form. Rather, it argues, people should subscribe to a 'channel' of programmes, buying not individual programmes but rather a mixed diet of programmes for a fixed period. Most consumers, it suggests, would find this more convenient. But crucially this form of protection would support the continuing opportunity for broadcasters to provide the audience programmes which would not survive the pressure of market forces.

Recent government policy has sought to increase the influence of market pressures on broadcasting by the way in which it has advocated the introduction of cable television. Nevertheless, policy has been influenced by a continuing commitment to protect broadcasting from the full effects of unregulated market competition. Thus cable services are largely to be paid for by subscription, and not on a programme-by-programme basis. In addition, unlike the American system, the cable stations will be obliged to relay all BBC and ITV programmes; are prohibited from interfering with the networks' schedules; and will not be allowed to buy up the exclusive rights to televising major public events. Finally, the cable stations will have to maintain the standards of 'taste' and 'decency', and follow the regulations governing advertising content laid down by the BBC and ITV. In seeking to control some of the effects of pay TV and to consider the economic conditions for the production of public service broadcasting, public reports have thus continued to reject in part the market-based rationale for information that has determined policy towards the press, and have argued instead that public service regulation at the moment makes the market in broadcasting more perfect.

The government and lame ducks

Finally, government intervention has been justified as an exceptional measure that will make subsequent interference unnecessary and restore a stable and competitive market. Thus in 1927 a Board of Trade inquiry into the film industry had advocated special measures to deal with 'unfair, devious and improper trading' by American competitors. This report resulted in the Cinematograph Act, 1927, which banned block booking (when good films were sold only in a 'package' with a number of less desirable Hollywood products) and obliged distributors and exhibitors to purchase and show quotas of British films. But the ban was intended to be only a short-term measure, to promote 'free and equitable trade'. In 1948 the National Film Finance Corporation was set up to provide loans for film production. It was seen as a response to a temporary inability of British film producers to obtain private investment capital. The Eady Levy, introduced during the same period, was also designed to promote national film production through a tax on box office takings which was supposed to fall most heavily on successful foreign imports. Similarly the last Royal Commission on the press recommended that newspapers should be offered cheap loans in order to pay for the introduction of new printing technology during a period of financial crisis. The proposal was seen as a unique measure.

Yet schemes initially proposed as short-term expediencies have tended to become permanent. The 'temporary' measures to control the import of films, introduced in 1927, were strengthened in 1938, further added to during the 1940s, and abandoned only in 1983. Similarly the National Film Finance Corporation was forced to write off many loans and so became a continuing source of state finance for the film industry. The Eady Levy survived until 1984, even though it reinforced American domination of the British film industry by subsidizing American-backed films which were only nominally British. The rationale for the levy changed, and it came to be seen as a way of maintaining employment in the British film industry. All these one-off interventions have led to a more permanent government involvement in the industries than had been originally intended.

The variety in policy goals

British communications policy has pursued contradictory goals. Thus the IBA Act, 1973, required that 'a proper proportion' of the programmes shown should be made in Britain, which led to a rule that no more than 14 per cent of commercial broadcasts should be foreign (excluding Commonwealth countries). Foreign was subsequently defined to apply to countries outside the EEC in the Broadcasting Act, 1981. The BBC in turn voluntarily adopted this quota. In addition the IBA has prevented foreign, and in particular American, investment from controlling too large a share of British commercial television. The Annan Committee supported this protectionist policy, and added that: 'Foreign holdings in television companies should be severely limited.' Indeed the

Committee criticized the IBA for its permissive attitude towards
Commonwealth investment in local radio.

Yet unregulated foreign investment in the newspaper industry has
been accepted by successive Royal Commissions (admittedly because of
the unwillingness of others to invest in such a marginally profitable area).
Public reports on the press, however, have expressed little concern for
the potential political implications of this development. Furthermore,
foreign investment, particularly by Americans, has been encouraged in
the British film industry. As the 1968 review of film legislation suggested,
the National Film Finance Corporation should be maintained, 'as it
constitutes a real attraction for American investment'.

Many regulations exist to maintain standards in broadcasting. Thus
the IBA attempts to mitigate the effects of 'competing for numbers'.
Backed with the sanction of withholding licences, the IBA ensures that
some of the advertising revenue generated by programmes reaching
large audiences is invested in programmes for smaller audiences.
However, the same principle did not apply in the allocation of film funds
through the Eady Levy. This tax on cinema takings was paid to
production companies in proportion to the box office revenue for their
films. It constituted a bounty distributed according to market demand,
rather than quality. 'The levy', concluded the 1968 Board of Trade
review, 'should not be used to breed indifference to economic reality.'
This seems to imply that the consideration of cultural or qualitative
standards would be economically harmful.

Many public reports have argued that the media are not like other
industries, and should be treated as special cases. As the Palache
Committee (1944) put it, 'A cinematograph film represents something
more than a mere commodity to be bartered.' Nevertheless, there is little
discussion about how the traditional economic goal of maintaining full
employment should be balanced against the wider objectives raised by
the media's special role. In the case of film policy, priority has been given
to the support of employment in the industry. In the case of the press,
however, the main concern of Royal Commissions has been to maintain
the diversity of the press.

The politics of information and the politics of entertainment

Policy reports have also differed in the way in which they have
approached the media. Royal Commissions on the Press have been
almost exclusively concerned with the current affairs content of newspapers, and policy proposals have dealt largely with the political function

of the press. In contrast, broadcasting committees have considered the whole range of broadcasting. They have discussed the role of television and radio in wider social and cultural terms, and their recommendations have been intended to improve the general quality of programmes.

This difference of approach may have arisen when current affairs reporting in broadcasting was severely limited. Until the Second World War the press, anxious about competition from the BBC, attempted to restrict the range of news that could be broadcast. In addition the Corporation, wishing to avoid charges of political bias, was also very cautious about political comment or opinion. Thus broadcasting came to be seen as a medium of entertainment for which 'cultural' and not 'political' standards were appropriate.

However, this has led to a confusion in public policy. On the one hand, it is felt to be important that politicians' control over information and news is very restricted, not only because politicians might use any such power to further their own ends, but also because the news media may help to control politicians. On the other hand, there has been little concern about political control over entertainment, leisure, and culture. Indeed public policy towards these areas has largely been concerned to secure a variety of cultural expression reflecting national life.

Yet the distinction between the media of 'information' and those of 'entertainment' has now almost completely broken down. Hence the different political approaches which have developed to deal with broadcasting and the press are no longer adequate.

Recently there has been a reduction in the amount of current affairs and political news carried in the press. Moreover, the proportion of broadcasting time devoted to news and information has increased (between 1962 and 1974 current affairs coverage trebled on the BBC). BBC radio and television both now carry more current affairs content, as a proportion of total output, than does the popular press.

In many ways, however, the 'cultural' focus in reports on broadcasting has allowed them to consider the wider social and political consequences of the media. Thus in 1960 the Pilkington Committee recommended a ban on television advertisements 'appealing to human weakness'. Yet two years later, in 1962, the Royal Commission on the Press did not even consider the content of newspaper and magazine advertising, let alone recommend its reform. Similarly the Annan Committee recommended that the joint ownership of commercial broadcasting companies and record or music publishing companies be banned, on the grounds that there was bound to be a conflict of interest between them. The third Royal Commission on the Press, reporting in the same year, made no such recommendation in relation to the musical press and record production.

Pressure groups and policy

Public inquiries have also been exposed to different pressure groups and economic interests in each of the media. In the absence of an integrated approach to communications policy (or even comparable terms of reference for media inquiries), this has inevitably resulted in contradictory recommendations. The last two Press Commissions, for example, influenced by a powerful press lobby, supported the principle that one company could own several media industries, and subsidize the more vulnerable enterprise from the profits of the other. Thus the Press Commissions approved of limited press holdings in profitable television and radio franchises. Similarly the Prime Minister's Working Party on the Film Industry (1977), closely influenced by the views of the industry, also proposed that television should finance film-making. On the other hand, the Annan Committee was exposed to a broadcasting lobby which was hostile to the idea that broadcasting should subsidize less profitable media industries. The Annan Report consequently opposed the view that 'Like an aged parent, the film industry has a right to look to television to support it in its old age.' It therefore rejected the proposal (which had already been accepted by the Working Party on the Film Industry) for an allowance for film investment to be made out of the television levy.

The uncoordinated way in which policy for the media is formulated has meant that reforms have been proposed and implemented for one industry, which have then had unforeseen effects on the other media. Thus the decision to introduce commercial television had important repercussions for the press, many of which are still being worked out. Many of the major advertising agencies informed the 1962 Press Commission that commercial television had diverted advertising funds away from the press (and, in particular, the general magazine press). It is difficult to assess the precise impact of commercial television on the advertising revenue of the press, as some losses may have been offset by the influence which television may have had in raising the total amount that was spent on advertising. On the other hand, the increase in advertising expenditure may have been caused not by television but by the ending of newsprint rationing and the general economic growth which characterized the period. However, it is clear that, since 1961, the amount of television advertising has grown much faster than display advertising in the press. Moreover, the competition from commercial television caused newspaper managements, for a long time, to keep the increase in advertising rates below the rise in costs. Newspaper profits from advertising were thus steadily eroded.

However, despite this experience, the Annan Committee proposed to start a second television channel dependent on advertising revenue, without considering its consequences for newspapers. It seems to have been assumed that the new channel would compete mainly with quality newspapers and specialist magazines for advertising revenues. In turn the Peacock Report considered the extension of advertising to the BBC. Yet the implications of such a proposal for the press were hardly considered by the reports.

Thus while the third Press Commission was considering how to help unprofitable quality papers, the Annan Committee was simultaneously proposing to make them even more vulnerable. The Hunt Committee took the process even further, for its recommendations about the finance of cable television pose a serious threat to the local press. Yet all these inquiries were merely acting within the terms of reference imposed on them by government.

The need for an integrated approach

Of course, a degree of variation in approach to the different media could reasonably be justified in terms of the contrasting characteristics of the media themselves. However, in practice, the conflicts and contradictions which have been described are the product, not of rational differentiation, but of the piecemeal way in which communications policy has emerged.

Some thirty public bodies are involved in formulating and carrying out British media policy. In practice this proliferation of responsibility has led, at times, to its unacknowledged concentration – in the hands of the Prime Minister. This has not resulted in any greater co-ordination, but rather in the erratic pursuit of narrowly defined political objectives with little reference to their overall effect on the media.

Since the late 1970s media policy, and particularly that governing the introduction of new technologies, has been determined by narrow and unthought-out commercial considerations. The view of broadcasting as providing a national service for the nation's good has not merely been attacked, it has been abandoned. The justification for this destruction has been commercial expediency. Yet there are few signs of the new, British industrial revolution that, for example, cable television was supposed to introduce.

The need for a coherent news, information, and communications policy is now critical. For many of the principles on which media policy has traditionally been based are being undermined by new technological developments.

Thus British broadcasting has been obliged to maintain cultural standards, properly balanced programming, and equality of access. Yet there is no way of controlling video-recording according to these principles. Similarly the IBA is obliged to control advertising standards and to regulate the quality of commercial broadcasting. But no effective method has been agreed for regulating broadcasting beamed directly by satellite to individual households.

In the same way, the development of teletext (the transmission of printed material of a great variety on to television screens) would intensify the competition for classified advertising. This would have dramatic effects on the advertising revenues of local newspapers and specialist magazines, which have largely been insulated from the effects of television. In turn, the way in which teletext is developed will have important implications for the future of broadcasting, and change the nature of the postal and telephone communications services. This blurring of traditional demarcations between the media provides new opportunities. But it also poses problems for communications policy, which seem hardly to have been considered.

Indeed the development of schemes which link computers to satellites and which are capable of transmitting unprecedented amounts of commercial, political, and industrial information internationally, make any kind of national regulation increasingly difficult. Such schemes are being developed by multinational corporations like IBM, which are concerned with information as a commodity, not with its political implications. Just as 'freedom of speech' was invoked in the 1950s by American film exporters during their expansion into a world market, so 'freedom of information' is now being used to facilitate American domination of the market for facts. The only way in which these developments can be properly monitored, let alone regulated, is through the development of a comprehensive policy for communications. Indeed a national communications policy, sensitive to the commercial and political implications of information, is a prerequisite for the development of any international policy. It is also needed to ensure that British media industries take proper advantage of their commercial opportunities.

A unified policy for communications

A single Ministry of Arts, Communications, and Entertainments (ACE) needs to be created. This would be responsible not only for the mass media, but also for the post, telephone, and the emerging technologies of information, It would thus be able to oversee and control the entire commercial development of these critical industries. The ministry would also deal with the interrelated areas of the arts, public libraries, publishing, sports, and recreations. This reorganization would entail the merging of responsibilities now dispersed between the Cabinet Office, the Home Office, and the Department of Trade and Industry, as well as the Department of Education and Science.

This rationalization would facilitate the development of an integrated policy, committed to more clearly defined goals, that could properly consider the political and economic implications of developments (including the increased concentration of economic power across all the media by a few large companies) in the information industries. The creation of the proposed ministry would also be a recognition of the role which the media, information, arts, and sport have in contemporary society. It is a role which is likely to increase in the future. Predictions made after the Second World War of a great increase in the amount of time available for leisure, have proved false in Britain, as in other developed societies. Nevertheless, the development of new technology is already creating enforced leisure through loss of jobs, and it seems likely to cause a revolution in habits comparable to the marked reduction in working hours which occurred in the latter part of the last century.

19

Alternative approaches to media reform

When the first edition of this book appeared in 1981, relatively little had been published on media reform outside government-sponsored reports. This has changed as a consequence of the increasing politicization of the media as an 'issue'. There is now a growing public debate about how the media can be made to reflect a wider range of minority tastes and opinions, yet remain responsive to majority demands. Another focus of discussion is how to render the media more accountable to the public without making it dependent on the state. This is linked to a further debate about how media power can be more widely diffused in society.

While none of these concerns is new, what is new is the practical bent that recent debate has taken. Five distinctive reform strategies (summarized in Table 9) have emerged, although these sometimes overlap with one another. This chapter will selectively summarize each of these. It is intended as a convenient guide to what is being argued in a bewildering plethora of articles, pamphlets, policy papers, reports, speeches, and books.

Traditional public service approach

Although the public service tradition has been discussed already, it may be helpful to summarize its main arguments here. Its central credo is that broadcasting should be publicly owned or regulated so that it serves the public good rather than private gain. Only in this way, it is argued, can broadcasting be prevented from becoming subservient to the commercial forces that make for low quality, cultural uniformity, and right-wing bias.

Traditionalists believe that the ideals of public service broadcasting have been successfully realized in the British system. Although the BBC competes with ITV for viewers, the two do not compete for the same source of revenue. This has produced supposedly a delicate balance of pressures encouraging both creativity and audience responsiveness. The BBC must attract viewers and listeners from the commercial system in order to justify the licence fee: it has thus been forced to shed some of its Reithian paternalism. At the same time, the standards of ITV have been raised by its need to compete in quality against the BBC as well as by being regulated by a public service body, the IBA.

As a consequence we have, according to traditionalists, the best broadcasting system in the world. This is allegedly manifested in a cheap, universally available service that does not discriminate against the poor or against inaccessible areas; high quality programmes for both minorities and mass audiences; news coverage that is balanced and unsensational by comparison with the bingo-jingo, popular press; cultural provision that reflects the diversity of British society rather than a bland transatlantic culture; and a flourishing television industry that creates much-needed employment.

They also argue that public service broadcasting performs vital functions for society which go far beyond neo-liberals' narrow concern with gratifying consumer demand. It promotes social cohesion at a time of increasing fragmentation; its balanced and informative coverage of news enables people to participate responsibly in a healthy democracy; and its mixed programming extends and enriches the nation's tastes.

But some traditionalists have come round to the conclusion that certain changes are needed in order to maintain the excellence of British broadcasting. Their first concern is that public licence fee funding of the BBC – in their view, the cornerstone of the Corporation's political independence and public service commitment – may be subverted by the combined clamour of left- and right-wing critics. These have argued variously that the licence fee is a regressive poll tax; that it is too high due to the embargo on BBC advertising; that it makes the BBC vulnerable to political pressure from governments which alone have the power to authorize licence fee increases; and that it has resulted in a growing gap between the funding of public and commercial broadcasting (with ITV spending an estimated 62 per cent more on television services than the BBC in 1985).

Some traditionalists have responded to these criticisms by proposing modifications to the licence fee system. Old age pensioners and those on long-term benefit, they argue, could be exempted from paying and the money made up by a Treasury grant. An independent review body could be appointed to advise the government about licence fee increases and so act as a buffer against political pressure. Alternatively the BBC could be insulated from inflation by indexing the licence to the growth of national earnings (but not the retail price index which does not keep up with the

Table 9 Alternative approaches to media reform: A selective survey[a]

	Traditional public service	Radical public service	Free market	Radical market	Radical libertarian
Broadcasting Ownership	Preserve BBC and ITV	Subdivide BBC	Privatize TV and radio	Private enterprise and Public Service Broadcasting Council	Lease publicly owned broadcasting facilities
Funding	Licence fee and advertising	Pooled public and advertising finance	Subscriptions and advertising	Pay TV	Lease payments
Interim reform	Independent review body for licence fee	Elected or nominated authorities/new guidelines/ recruitment quotas	Auction franchises (incl. BBC)/ fifth TV channel	Independent TV production quota/ two commercial national radio channels	Democratize broadcasting structures/reduce legal restrictions
New TV industries	Strengthen Cable TV Authority	Pan-European regulation of DBS/ Expand publicly owned cable TV	Minimum regulation	Monopoly controls/ national cable grid	—

Press

Ownership	IPA franchise newspapers and public service daily	IPA franchise press groups	Private enterprise	Private enterprise and state-aided small publishers	Lease publicly owned printing facilities
Regulation	Statutory Press Council/legal right of reply	——	Opposed to regulation	Publishers' right to be distributed	Reduce legal restrictions
Reform	Newspaper ownership confined to British or EEC citizens	——	Opposed to all reforms	Anti-monopoly law/ Media Enterprise Board/Launch Fund/grants	Democratize press managements

Note: [a] Some proposals listed under each approach are mutually exclusive.

rise of broadcasting costs). It has also been suggested that an additional levy could be imposed on the ITV companies and the proceeds redistributed to the BBC.[1]

Traditionalists' second main concern is that the growth of cable and satellite television may undermine public service broadcasting by diverting audiences away from the BBC and ITV. If this were to happen, the BBC would find it more difficult to justify licence fee increases, while ITV's share of advertising could decline. The result could be a serious drop in revenue, and loss of programme quality.

Declining audiences could also undermine commitment to public service goals. The BBC and ITV might be tempted to produce more formula-based, entertainment programmes at the expense of minority provision in a bid to claw back lost viewers. And in an effort to offset a contraction in the home market, both organizations would probably seek to sell more programmes abroad. This could result in more co-productions, more made-for-TV programmes instead of single plays, more costume drama instead of contemporary fiction, in short more programmes geared to the global market at the expense of catering for the varied interests and experiences of the domestic TV audience.

Pessimists also argue that British television could be heading eventually towards the sort of economic crisis that has bedevilled the British film industry. At present, British television production is buoyant partly because it is heavily protected. BBC and ITV allow no more than 14 per cent of their transmission time (with some exemptions) to be taken up by programmes made outside the EEC. But cable and satellite television could potentially undermine this protectionist wall by broadcasting mainly American programmes. This would be likely to happen in a deregulated, commercial system, since USA-made programmes are available in Britain for as little as one-tenth the price of domestically produced equivalents (and at a fraction of their production cost in the USA).

Traditionalists' favoured solution is to regulate the new television industries so that they become an extension of public service broadcasting. They wanted the BBC or the broadcasting duopoly to develop satellite television and now argue that the remaining, unallocated channels should go eventually to the BBC and ITV. Some also advocate tougher regulation of cable television (including a set limit on imported programmes).

Yet even if British satellite and cable television is extensively regulated, this still does not protect public service broadcasting from the winds of change. In the next decade, there could be between twenty and thirty satellite television channels. Some of these will have a 'footprint' over

Britain but will be controlled from outside this country. All the indications are that a number of them will draw heavily upon the stockpile of cheap American programmes. To forestall this threat to a protectionist, national tradition of public service broadcasting, some conservationists are now calling for a European framework of broadcasting regulation.

Although the traditional public service approach is increasingly attacked by critics on both left and right, it is still a powerful influence on reformers. Indeed one strategy favoured by a number of left-wing Labour politicians is to transplant wholesale the key institutions of public service broadcasting to the press. Michael Meacher has argued, for instance, that newspaper publishing should be franchised in the same way as commercial broadcasting. Under his scheme, all newspapers would be franchised by an Independent Press Authority, modelled on the IBA, which would require them to adhere to an ethical code of conduct and maintain 'a reasonable balance' in the presentation of news and opinion. These franchises would be subject to periodic review as in the case of ITV. Similarly Tony Benn has proposed that *The Times* should be established as a public corporation on the model of the BBC, while Stuart Holland has urged the creation of a publicly owned press distribution agency in much the way that broadcasting transmitters are publicly owned. This would assist, he argues, the proper distribution of minority magazines which sometimes encounter censorship from newsagents and wholesalers.

Underlying this approach is a belief that British broadcasting is, despite its shortcomings, far superior to the British press. However, the two media are very different and some surgery is needed before a transplant will 'take'. For Meacher's scheme to work, a substitute would have to be found for the corporate cross-subsidies that keep alive some loss-making papers. Otherwise a revocation of their franchise could result in their closure. And although the monopoly position of some papers effectively debars new market entrants, the press is not physically constrained like over-the-air broadcasting by the availability of spectrum frequencies. This weakens the political justification for franchising, particularly in relation to new newspapers.

An alternative approach, preferred by some in the public service tradition, is to reform the press by taking small skin grafts from the broadcasting system and applying them to 'infected' areas. The Broadcasting Act, 1981, restricts control of ITV companies to individuals and companies in the EEC. Since becoming Labour's leader, Neil Kinnock has suggested that the same regulations could apply to the press on the grounds that global concentrations of power ought to be limited. This would have the effect of impaling Murdoch on the legislative equivalent of Morton's fork. Murdoch has recently acquired American citizenship in order to get round the Federal Communications Commission's prohibition of foreign ownership of American television stations. Kinnock's proposal would thus force him to choose between his American television and British press interests. It could also lead to the eviction of the new Canadian proprietor of the Telegraph group, the forced sale of the largest local daily combine controlled by the Canadian-based International Thomson Group, and cause problems for Robert Maxwell, whose holding company controlling his press interests is registered in Liechtenstein.

Similarly some public service reformers have proposed that the Press Council – a private body funded mainly by proprietors – should be reconstituted along the lines of the Broadcasting Complaints Commission, set up in 1981. This would transform the Press Council into a publicly funded institution, with the legal authority to call for evidence and require publication of its judgements in offending publications. Others have urged a still more far-reaching role for a reformed Press Council, including the enforcement of an ethical code of conduct, with the power to impose fines.

Another variant of this approach derives from the public service tradition of the medical profession. It has been suggested that journalists should be registered by an equivalent body to the British Medical Council which would have the power to 'strike off' individuals found guilty of unprofessional conduct. This would revive the seventeenth-century tradition of licensing and withdraw the fundamental right of freedom of expression from a minority of journalists.

A less restrictive reform, based on the principle of retrospective redress, is a legal right of reply. This could be a legal right to correct 'distortions' as proposed in Frank Allaun's celebrated private member's bill or this right could be defined more narrowly to counter-statements correcting demonstrable errors of fact. It could be administered either through the courts or through a press 'ombudsman' with the power to determine the form in which corrections are published.

It has also been argued that a legal right of privacy should be established to protect people from press intrusions that are not justified by the public interest. This would be enforceable in the courts, which could award damages. Critics argue, however, that most people are not financially in a position to sue newspapers, and that privacy cases could compound the original wrong by generating further, unwelcome publicity.

A more ambitious approach, rooted in the public service tradition, seeks to elevate editors into trustees of the public interest by reinforcing their autonomy and authority. Thus Tom Baistow argues that editors should be legally protected against improper pressure from proprietors, advertisers, trade unions, and other organizations. In addition, editors of national newspapers, under his scheme, could be appointed or dismissed only with the agreement of independent directors. This proposal leaves unclear how 'independent' directors would be appointed – whether by government, boards of directors, staff, or other interests. It also allows considerable scope, in practice, for proprietors to exercise 'proper' control over editors through the allocation of editorial budgets. His scheme could also be criticized for championing the integrity of editors but not that of others employed on newspapers. However, a conscience clause could be inserted into journalists' and production workers' contracts of employment which would entitle them to appeal against unfair dismissal if they refused to act in a way that was contrary to a reformed Press Council's code of conduct.

Radical public service

There is a heterogeneous group of reformers who broadly accept the core assumptions of the public service approach but who think that the ideals of public service cannot be equated with the flawed institutions of British broadcasting.

Some of these reformers complain that both the BBC and ITV construct news and current affairs coverage from a narrow range of perspectives roughly corresponding to those of the leadership of the parliamentary parties. They point to broadcasting coverage of Northern Ireland which, they claim, has tended to define the crisis as being essentially one of maintaining law and order against criminals and terrorists, to the exclusion of other interpretations. This is merely an extreme instance, they maintain, of the way in which broadcasting generally marginalizes or ignores perspectives that are outside a narrow band of consensus.

Another (though partly overlapping) group of critics advances broadly the same argument in 'cultural' terms. Although public service rhetoric sometimes stresses innovation and experiment, in practice British broadcasting provides, they allege, mainly safe and formulaic programmes. ITV is, in their opinion, a highly centralized system which is geared to satisfying the lowest common denominator of mass viewing. At the same time, the BBC has allegedly surrendered its former high standards in favour of a shallow professionalism defined by market values. It is also berated for being steeped in the culture of London and the Home Counties.

These criticisms have led to increasingly wide-ranging demands for reorganizing broadcasting. Some argue that reform should begin at the top and that the present system of government appointment of broadcasting authorities should come to an end. This has resulted, they complain, in over-recruitment from a small, unrepresentative élite. In early 1985 seven of the twelve BBC Governors were educated in Oxford or Cambridge. Similarly nine out of twelve IBA members were graduates and, of the remaining non-graduates, one was a university Vice-Chancellor.

Critics also argue that direct government appointments to broadcasting authorities have caused broadcasting to become too closely aligned to the state. Recent developments, they contend, underline the dangers inherent in the present system. The Thatcher administration has departed from the tradition of bipartisan appointments and imposed two known Conservatives, both brothers-in-law of government ministers, as successive chairmen of the BBC. The BBC board of governors sought to suppress a controversial *Real Lives* programme about Northern Ireland in response to pressure from the Home Secretary – and relented only after an unprecedented strike by BBC staff. It also emerged in 1985 that the state security service, MI5, had been routinely involved in vetting recruits to the Corporation (though this practice has since been confined to a small number of appointments).

Various alternatives to the present system have been advanced. One proposal is for an independent review body to advise the government whom to appoint. Another is for broadcasting authorities to consist of nominees of national representative organizations and broadcasting workers. A variant of this proposal involves establishing an electoral college, composed of representatives from national organizations and broadcasting employees, which would elect people to the broadcasting authorities. The rationale for this last proposal is that elected representatives would be answerable to a national constituency rather than exclusively to corporate or special interests, and the annual meetings of the electoral college would become a national forum for publicly debating broadcasting issues. The overriding purpose of the reform would be to make broadcasters accountable to the community but not beholden to governments.

An alternative scheme, advanced by the Glasgow University Media Group, is direct elections to newly created local and regional broadcasting authorities: these would send delegates, in turn, to a national conference which would be the sovereign broadcasting body. However, political parties are the only organizations geared to mobilizing large numbers of people to the polls. This could result in the same political party controlling both government and the supreme broadcasting body, which would frustrate the purpose of the reform.

Another approach favoured by some in the radical public service tradition is to change the official guidelines of broadcasting organizations. At present both the BBC and ITV (the latter by specific injunction) are expected to maintain due impartiality and balance in the treatment of controversial subjects. However, some critics contend that this is an unrealizable objective since there is no neutral perspective from which events can be reported or neutral point either side of which opposing views can be balanced. In practice, they argue, the difficulties inherent in the broadcasters' remit are resolved through 'the homogeneous social, educational and economic background of the individuals who control and operate the BBC and ITV'.

The Changing Television Group argues that the self-deluding conventions of impartiality and balance should be abandoned; and that, instead, an obligation should be imposed on broadcasters to 'represent fairly and accurately the differences within society, and ... produce programmes from the different perspectives in society'. This can be achieved best, in their view, by having openly partisan, clearly authored programmes 'given always the requirement to report with accuracy'. They counter the argument that this would give predominantly male, white, middle-class broadcasters a licence to express their personal prejudices by saying that recruitment policies should be changed. Quotas for women and ethnic minorities should be introduced, and formal educational and technical requirements should be waived in favour of special training programmes for recruits drawn from all social classes.

Some critics are in favour of going only half-way down this road. They accept the need for more openly partisan programmes and a fuller representation of dissensus and conflict as a way of extending the pluralism of the broadcasting system. But they still want to retain an obligation on the broadcasting system to maintain an overall balance across the full output of programmes because they believe that, in the absence of massive redundancies, broadcasters will long continue to be socially and politically unrepresentative. They also fear that big business control of commercial broadcasting will cause it to lurch to the right in the absence of restraining guidelines.

Another proposal that surfaces from time to time is for new duties to be imposed on broadcasters, requiring them to 'combat racism, sexism, and class bias'. This would deliberately constrain the range of values that could be expressed on the airwaves into an anti-right-wing framework. Critics of this proposal point out that there are already laws that lay down acceptable limits of racial intolerance, defamation, obscenity, and so on.

Tightening these further would restrict freedom of expression. It would also invite a retributive revision of broadcasting guidelines when the political pendulum swung the other way, perhaps leading to an escalating spiral of censorship.

Indeed other critics coming from a different part of the radical public service tradition, argue ironically for less television regulation. In particular, they propose that the IBA should be stripped of its power to veto ideas, programmes, and scenes because it has allegedly misused this power to constrain ITV's current affairs coverage into an overly consensual strait-jacket. Instead the IBA should publicly criticize contractors after items it deemed offensive had been broadcast. Advocates of this proposal counter the argument that this would effectively remove public service regulation of ITV by saying that no ITV company would want to offend repeatedly for fear of losing their franchise.

All these proposals entail modifying existing broadcasting organizations by changing their guidelines, management, or intake of new personnel. An alternative, although not necessarily mutually exclusive, approach is to inject new blood into the broadcasting system by creating new broadcasting structures. This was the rationale for the creation of Channel 4 as a new kind of broadcasting body: a 'publisher' of programmes, drawing extensively on independent companies.

The critical success of Channel 4 has encouraged reformers to advocate new ways of opening up broadcasting to a wider range of experiences and inputs. A recurrent, modest proposal has been for more better-funded access programmes in which outside groups have editorial control. Some have also argued that a duty should be placed on the IBA to allocate at least some franchises to non-profit-making trusts and genuinely regionally based consortia in the next round of franchise awards.

Others have urged that both the BBC and ITV should be required to transmit a set quota of programmes made by production companies which are registered in the UK but which are not controlled by the BBC, ITV, or any international media company or foreign franchise holder. This is a proposal which has gained increasing support. But whereas it is advocated by some neo-liberals as a way of reducing costs and getting British broadcasting into training for the new era of international television competition, it is canvassed by radicals in the public service tradition principally as a way of injecting new ideas and perspectives into the oversocialized and overcontrolled environment of the broadcasting duopoly. However, it is a proposal which is strongly resisted by the broadcasting trade unions on the grounds that it would make some people redundant and lead to the casualization of the broadcasting industry.

The desire to extend broadcasting diversity also lies behind the campaign for the franchising of new, low-powered radio stations serving small, localized areas. Some argue that these should be allowed to operate in a new way, with the freedom to be partisan. Others argue – in a replay of the television impartiality debate – that a balance should be maintained either in the overall output of each new community radio station or of the new local radio network as a whole.

Another approach within the radical public service tradition goes beyond merely modifying existing broadcasting structures or facilitating the emergence of new programme providers. It seeks to break up the BBC principally on the grounds that it is over large (with more than 20,000 employees), hierarchical, and bureaucratic.

The most modest of these proposals, advocated by a minority on the Annan Committee, is a simple subdivision of the BBC into radio and television corporations. However, some reformers advocate the creation of two competing, publicly owned television corporations, one of which would have a decentralized, regionally based structure. The two new television corporations would receive a set percentage of licence fee revenue in order to discourage them from competing head-on with each other, as well as ITV, for mass audience ratings.

The subdivision of BBC radio has also been advocated in a variety of ways. One proposal is for four competing national radio networks, two of which would have a decentralized structure. They would be financed by a radio licence and a tax on new car radios. Again, each corporation would have a set share of public radio funding in order to encourage them to cater for differentiated publics rather than all compete for the mass market.

Some reformers also suggest that BBC local radio should be hived off and developed in conjunction with commercial local radio, and new localized community radio stations, under a Local Radio Authority. According to one scheme, the authority could draw upon two sources of revenue – a set share of the radio licence revenue and a levy on the profits of the commercially successful, quasi-regional radio stations. This money would be used to fund publicly owned radio stations and subsidize community radio enterprises run by groups with limited resources.

The Labour Party has proposed a more fundamental restructuring of broadcasting that would do away with both the BBC and ITV in its present form. It suggested to the Annan Committee that programme-making should be carried out 'by a wide variety of dispersed programme units reflecting the creative talent of all parts of the UK', organized through two television and two radio corporations. These would be funded by the pooled proceeds of advertising and a rolling quinquennial grant awarded by parliament. Finance would be allocated by a Public Broadcasting Commission (PBC) which would also oversee general scheduling problems and administer guidelines for broadcasting practice.

The Annan Committee objected to this plan on the grounds that it would lead to overcentralized control of broadcasting. However, this objection could be met if the role of the PBC was shrunk to merely collecting revenue and maintaining transmission facilities. The key co-ordinating functions for the broadcasting system as a whole could be carried out by a federal body composed of representatives from the different broadcasting organizations.

But perhaps the most pressing question for the future is how cable and satellite television should be developed. Radical public service reformers are divided on this issue. One group wants British Telecom (in which the community would once again be the majority shareholder) to develop on a subsidized basis a national grid connecting each household with fibre optic cable. This grid would be a 'common carrier' for a multitude of franchised channels, and make possible the development of interactive services. A more modest variant of this proposal entails taking into social ownership the existing, broadband cable television network and gradually extending it over time as the local telephone network is replaced with fibre optic cable.

Enthusiasts justify subsidizing cable television on the grounds that it would both create much needed employment and revitalize public service broadcasting since its indefinite channel capacity would enable the introduction of specialized television channels. This would strengthen the popular appeal of public service broadcasting in the 1990s when what they see as 'space invaders' – foreign controlled satellite television channels beamed direct to Britain – will mount their attack on the British television audience. Some reformers also favour imposing a levy on the domestic reception of foreign-controlled commercial satellite television channels as a way of increasing their consumer cost and raising additional revenue for British public service broadcasting.

Another group believes that cable television will never take off in this country. In their view, the rapid diffusion of video-recorders in Britain (with the highest take-up rate in the world) has greatly reduced the cable television market; and satellites now provide a cheaper and more efficient delivery system than digging up roads. Consequently they maintain that public subsidies for cabling up Britain would be a waste of resources. Instead they argue that cable television should be brought more firmly under public control even if this restricts its expansion. Operators should be obliged to provide reasonable access to community programming, and observe a set limit on imported programmes under the aegis of a strengthened Cable Authority.

Direct satellite broadcasting (DBS) is, in their view, the formative force of the future. The new generation of high-powered satellites will make it possible to receive programmes on cheap, small dishes well within the budgets of most households, while advertising on satellite television (if allowed) will bring down subscription costs. Like traditionalists, this group of public service radicals wants to develop DBS within a public service mould by establishing a pan-European agreement which would lay down quotas on advertising and imported programmes, and a set of broadcasting guidelines. These would be enforced by national satellite television authorities in the different countries of Europe in order to stop the broadcasting of excessively violent or pornographic films, and prevent programme-making in Europe from being undermined by the import of cheap programmes from the USA.

However, some sceptics question whether all western European countries – and, in particular, Luxembourg, Eire, and (under a Conservative government) Britain – will ever agree to an effective framework of public service regulation. They argue, therefore, that the most realistic defence of public service broadcasting in a global free market is for European public service broadcasting organizations to sell programmes to each other at discounted prices and undertake more co-productions in a bid to match the resources and economies of scale of American television. Some also contend that the increasing disaggregation of the American television industry, with the growth of independent television stations, the expansion of cable television, and the emergence of a fourth television network, have created new opportunities for public service broadcasting institutions in Europe to export successfully to the USA.

It is also questioned whether DBS will have the impact that is widely anticipated. Some experts argue that the prior development of low-powered satellite systems feeding cable television, the diffusion of video, and the cheapness of over-the-air television will reduce the demand for new direct broadcasting by satellite channels. If they are right, DBS will not prove a major threat to established networks and the regimes of public service regulation that underpin them.

The diffusion of video-recorders (VCRs) has provoked relatively little discussion among reformers. However, Golding and Murdock have suggested that VCRs could be developed more fully as a distribution system for films and programmes that are blocked by oligopolistic control of television and cinema circuits. For instance video shops which undertake to add the full range of local and alternative production could be subsidized, and alternative video material could be shown in public libraries.

There are few radical public service proposals for reforming the press. One exception to this is a proposal from Chris Mullin (former editor of Tribune) for restructuring the press through a radical variant of Meacher's Independent Press Authority. The authority would create profitable group franchises by matchmaking profitable with loss-making papers. These would be tendered for competitive bids, with preference being given (1) to companies without vested commercial interests; (2) to staff consortia; and (3) to forms of ownership in which the interests of all staff are represented. Mullin argues that since these franchises would be profitable, successful applicants with limited resources would be able to raise the necessary finance from the city to buy out existing owners on a compulsory purchase basis. The authority would be required to provide outlets for a wide variety of views in its allocation of franchises but newspapers would not be obliged to provide balanced news coverage. However, they would be expected to adhere to a code of ethical conduct and to allocate not less than a specified proportion of editorial content to news and current affairs.

This proposal would transform the character of the press. It would also get round the problem, in the short term, of what to do with established but loss-making papers since these would be incorporated into profitable group franchises. But like all schemes for the commercial franchising of the press, Mullin's ingenious plan would encounter considerable difficulty in gaining political acceptance.

Free market approach

The starting-point of the free market approach is that consumers are the best judges of what is in their interests. The overriding objective of media policy, according to neo-liberals, should be therefore to maximize freedom of consumer choice by creating the conditions in which a large number of different media concerns can market their wares, free of restrictions. This will produce, in their view, a mixed output of information and entertainment; a 'discovery mechanism' by which consumers can extend their tastes and interests by shopping around; and a media system which is responsive to audience demand, yet independent of the state.

Since the press is organized on free market principles, most neo-liberals see no need for reform. When confronted with evidence that some sectors of the press market are 'imperfect' in terms of the theory to which they subscribe, they usually argue that new technology and a reduction of print union power will reform these markets by revitalizing competition. In any case, the threat to press freedom posed by state intervention is, most neo-liberals argue, more to be feared than any current shortcoming of the press.

Although generally complacent about the press, a growing number of free market radicals are sharply critical of the broadcasting system. Its three main defects, they maintain, is that it does not give people what they want; it is too vulnerable to government pressure; and its costs are too high because it is a victim of trade union blackmail. Some also argue that the BBC – like education – is a protected haven for radicals. This is in marked contrast to the competitive environment of the press where the consumer is sovereign and unpopular, radical views get short shrift.

The short-term answer to these problems, according to the Adam Smith Institute, is to 'deregulate' the broadcasting system. The BBC should be broken up into 'an association of independent and separately financed stations' funded by subscription, advertising, and sponsorship; the IBA should become 'more flexible and more commercially aware'; controls requiring political balance should be relaxed or removed altogether; and community radio stations should be established on vacant frequencies.

Less uncompromising neo-liberals are currently advocating interim measures which will expose the broadcasting duopoly to new competition. Some want Channel 4 to seek its own advertising rather than rely upon subscription income from the ITV companies. The effect of this would be almost certainly to orientate Channel 4 away from minority audiences to a mass market. Others want a fifth TV channel, on the UHF frequency, funded by advertising and run commercially either by a new network of local TV companies or by a national TV company.

But most neo-liberals look to the new television industries as a way of reconstituting broadcasting along free market lines. One plan, eloquently advocated by Peter Jay, is for a system of 'electronic publishing' secured through the expansion of cable television and the installation of a national cable grid. Programme-makers would have the right to have whatever programme they wanted transmitted on cable television on payment of a transmission fee, while viewers could call up any programme they fancied by dialling the right code and paying a programme charge.

However, some neo-liberals believe that the much vaunted, entertainment-led boom in cable television will never materialize, and look to satellite television as a way of generating increased competition. They argue that since each country in Europe has been allocated five satellite television channels, and these could all potentially have supra-national 'footprints', a combination of satellite and conventional broadcasting could potentially provide the requisite number of channels to constitute a genuinely competitive market. The important thing, they believe, is that governments should encourage entrepreneurs to invest by minimizing bureaucratic interference in the development of satellite television.

The benefits claimed for this approach are that unfettered competition would transfer control of television from an unrepresentative élite to the general public; it would break the power of the broadcasting trade unions by creating organizations without a union tradition; and it would distance broadcasting from the state. As to whether British broadcasting will flourish in a global free market, only the customer will – and should – decide.

Radical market approach

Reformers in the radical market tradition broadly endorse the core assumptions of the free market approach. Where they differ from traditional neo-liberals is in thinking that public intervention is sometimes needed in order to release the coiled springs of competition. The more interventionist among them also argue that a policy of *laissez-faire* is inherently incapable of producing, in certain circumstances, the range of choice that free market theory promises.

This approach has been more fully developed in relation to the press than to broadcasting. Some reformers argue that the introduction of new print technology and greater industrial flexibility will not so reduce costs that it will become possible for groups with limited resources to launch new publications in most sectors of the press. The modest lowering of costs, according to this viewpoint, has reinforced rather than undermined the case for making it easier to launch new publications through public intervention.

One way of doing this, favoured by some, is to establish a National Printing Corporation which would make available modern print facilities, at subsidized prices, to under-resourced groups. But this would not give them access to the very substantial capital needed to research and develop a new publication, and cover its initial trading losses. An alternative approach, advocated by others in the radical market tradition, is to set up a Launch Fund to aid the launch of new publications through development grants, low interest loans, and management advice.

Others argue that a Media Enterprise Board (MEB) should be established with a wider remit, not confined to the press, since high entry costs are a major obstacle to new launches in most sectors of the media. However, the MEB's advocates usually argue that it should be required to support only those media projects which appear, on the basis of professional assessment, to have a reasonable chance of success. Its terms of reference could also specify that it give priority to projects mounted by groups (1) without other media interests; (2) with a demonstrable need for public venture capital; (3) which have some form of democratic decision-making; (4) which would extend media diversity; and (5) which would create a significant number of new jobs. Thus the MEB would be an enabling body, not a regulatory agency like the IBA or Cable Authority. It would be funded by the Treasury but its establishment could be accompanied by the introduction of a 2 per cent levy on all media advertising, yielding a gross annual revenue of over £90 million.

The MEB would be answerable to parliament. It could be composed of members elected by media industry organizations (including both employers and trade unions) and important national organizations (such as local government, churches, teachers, Consumer Association, etc.) to ensure its independence from government. Competition could also be encouraged by enacting the press equivalent of a 'common carrier' policy. A legal obligation could be placed on wholesalers and newsagents to handle and display lawful publications whenever they were requested to do so by publishers. The commercial interests of the wholesale trade could be safeguarded, reformers claim, if a regulated administration charge was imposed on unsold copies and legal privilege granted to the distribution trade in relation to defamation cases.

The main thrust of the radical market approach has been to assist financially the launch of new publications. However, some critics also argue that competition and consumer choice should be extended through tougher anti-monopoly legislation. They claim that the chains' domination of the press threatens freedom of expression by creating centralized control over what is published; and that their market domination and large resources make it more difficult and costly for new publications to become established.

One approach would be to strengthen the Fair Trading Act which has had a poor record in terms of preventing the growth of the press chains. Some argue that the onus should be placed on press groups to show that their acquisition of newspapers is *not* contrary to the public interest rather than the other way round; that the Act should be extended to the smaller regional chains; and that the criteria for referring cases to the Monopolies Commission should be made more stringent.

Other reformers want to carry the anti-monopoly approach further and limit the market share or number of titles that any one proprietor or group can control. One proposal, for example, would restrict overweight press groups to no more than three national newspapers, ten local dailies, and fifty local weeklies (paid-for and freesheet). The effect of this 'diet plan' would be to force Murdoch's News International to shed one national paper, the Thomson Organization to lose two local dailies, and the Pearson, Reed, United Newspapers, Thomson, Guardian, and BET and Eastern County Newspaper Groups to sell off over two hundred local weeklies. An alternative proposal is to limit all press groups to controlling no more than a specified share of national and local newspaper markets.

The reasoning behind this more radical approach is that purely preventative measures against future mergers are insufficient since press concentration is more advanced in Britain than in any other country in the western world. Some pessimists also argue that the Fair Trading Act, even when strengthened, is likely to be ineffectual since governments, regardless of their political complexion, will allow most mergers to go ahead rather than risk titles going to the wall.

However, one difficulty with limiting press groups to a specified number of titles is that some press chains will offload marginal or loss-making papers. These papers will be placed in immediate jeopardy unless a Media Enterprise Board is already functioning and is willing to finance a rescue operation. The alternative proposal of imposing a limit on market shares is also not an easy option. Expanding press groups would be tempted to stay within the stipulated limit by reducing their distribution in high-cost outlying areas.

One way of getting round these difficulties would be to limit multiple ownership of national papers to no more than one national daily and Sunday paper. This would lead to the divestment of profitable papers since the national press is now booming. Under this scheme, Murdoch would have to sell two national newspapers, and Lord Stevens and Robert Maxwell would each have to sell one.

The alternative reform advocated by Neil Kinnock – the imposition of a national citizenship requirement on newspaper ownership – would also have the effect of releasing highly profitable papers (as well as some unprofitable ones). But Kinnock's proposal, like all anti-monopoly measures taken in isolation, would result merely in a game of musical chairs in which millionaire proprietors would change places. In this instance American and Canadian millionaires would be replaced by British ones.

But one way of strengthening anti-monopoly legislation would be to introduce a statutory option period of three months in which sales of divested papers could be made only to employees or to independent consortia with no holdings in newspapers. This could be organized in the form of an auction, with an independent market valuation establishing a reserve price. Bidders would be able to raise most of the money from private sources but could apply also to a Media Enterprise Board, providing they could demonstrate the need for public venture capital. In this way, anti-monopoly legislation would modify the capitalist character of the press and allow genuinely new voices to be heard.

Another anti-monopoly approach, advocated by Bruce Page, is for the ownership of the Press Association to be divorced from the press chains. In this way, he argues, a much used agency service would have the opportunity to develop alternative news values and inject new diversity into the press.

Others (including the Labour Party) have urged that joint control of television, radio, and newspapers should be prohibited in order to make them more independent of each other. If control was defined in terms of collective press interests rather than individual titles, this proposal would have significant consequnces. In early 1985 the combined press share amounted to a 'controlling interest' (as defined by the Monopolies Commission) in ten radio stations and four ITV companies.

An alternative, radical market strategy for fostering press diversity is to provide subsidies to small circulation papers. These subsidies are usually proposed in the form of grants allocated according to impersonal, automatically functioning criteria, irrespective of the editorial contents of papers, in order to prevent public funds being diverted only to pro-government publications.

This approach has been inspired by the example of other European countries where a conscious attempt has been made to sustain small circulation, political papers in the face of competition from mass market, entertainment papers. This has taken the form either of providing selective aid to ailing papers or, more usually, of providing an expensive subsidy cushion for the press industry as a whole. While these strategies have been relatively successful and confounded fears that it would lead to covert government control, some radical market reformers question their relevance for Britain. Most minority, political daily and Sunday papers (save for those which reach élite audiences and are well-endowed with advertising) have long since closed down in this country.

Others argue, however, that selective subsidies should be seen as complementing the introduction of a Media Enterprise Board. They point out that large circulation papers have an unfair competitive advantage over their smaller rivals. Successful papers generally have lower unit costs due to the importance of scale economies in the publishing industry; they also obtain usually more advertising per reader by comparison with smaller, comparable papers and more sales revenue with which to outspend their rivals. Some critics consequently maintain that unless these advantages are offset by selective subsidies for minority papers, the Media Enterprise Board could become a convalescent home for lame ducks.

Subsidies are usually discussed in relation to the biggest cost item in newspaper budgets – newsprint. One self-financing proposal is for a levy to be imposed on the newsprint production of each newspaper. Its proceeds would be distributed on a sliding scale that was fixed in relation to the volume of editorial newsprint published. This scheme would ensure that large circulation newspapers funded small ones and, to a lesser extent, that large advertising papers helped their low advertising rivals. A variety of selective newsprint subsidies funded by the Exchequer have also been proposed. Most of these would give the greatest help to low circulation papers and those with the smallest editorial paging.

An alternative approach, advocated by some radical market reformers, is for advertising revenue to be redistributed from strong to weak papers. However, many of the proposed redistributive schemes have technical flaws. The most efficient and politically feasible of these is for a levy to be imposed, on a rising scale, on net newspaper revenues and for its proceeds to be redistributed as a differential subsidy. But even this proposal is not without difficulties since some strong papers would raise their advertising rates in order to offset the levy, and this might divert advertising away from their weaker rivals. Conceivably rate increases might also divert some advertising away from the press to other media. This said, the net effect of a progressive levy would be to redistribute revenue from strong to weak papers and assist the latter to survive.

However, one generic difficulty with the redistributive subsidy approach is that it assumes a sufficiently high level of profitability among 'strong' papers for them to be able to carry weak ones. This may be valid for the national press but it is more questionable in relation to the regional press where many once highly profitable papers are suffering from the rise of the freesheets.

This has prompted some reformers to advocate a more narrowly selective approach geared to realizing small, readily attainable objectives. Thus one plan (adapted from a scheme pioneered in France) has been proposed which is designed to make middle-market or down-market papers viable with a circulation as small as that of the *Guardian* or *Sunday Telegraph*. Any newspaper which obtained less than 40 per cent of its revenue from advertising and devoted over 20 per cent of its editorial space to current affairs would be eligible for a cash bounty for every additional 1,000 copies it sold over 20,000 until it reached 750,000, at which point its subsidy would taper off to zero when it reached 1 million. No newspaper would currently qualify for this grant but its existence would encourage the launch of non-élite, minority papers.

The advantage of this targeted approach, according to its advocates, is that it costs much less money than an industry-wide subsidy. It also sidesteps the principal pitfall of self-financing, selective subsidies: the sheer difficulty involved in devising a scheme which is both automatically functioning and which does not, in a few instances, result in funds being diverted from loss-making to profitable papers – the reverse of what is intended. A more narrowly selective approach is also much simpler and less cumbersome to administer.

The radical market approach to broadcasting has come into being largely as a reaction against recent free market proposals for transforming broadcasting. Typical of this approach is the Conservative government's 1987 Green Paper on radio. Its starting-point is that 'there continues to be a case for services of quality, wide range and assured geographical coverage in accordance with the traditions of public service broadcasting'. The Green Paper proposed, however, two key changes: the reassignment of two national frequencies from BBC radio to allow for the development of two commercial, national radio services; and the lighter regulation of independent local radio under either a new radio authority or an enlarged Cable TV Authority.

But the seminal document expounding the radical market approach in broadcasting is the much misrepresented Peacock Committee Report on *Financing the BBC* (1986). The report's central contention is that 'collective provision and regulation of programmes does provide *a better simulation of a market designed to reflect consumer preferences* than a policy of *laissez-faire*' (emphasis added) in a broadcasting system where the number of competing channels is limited by spectrum shortage. This view was influenced by comparative research, undertaken from the Leeds University Centre for TV Research, which indicated that commercially funded broadcasting systems offer a much narrower range of programme choice than the UK's broadcasting system mainly because lucrative entertainment programmes, pulling in large audiences, tended to crowd out information and cultural programmes. This led the Committee to conclude that the replacement of the licence fee with advertising and sponsorship might result in the banishment of arts, documentary, and current affairs programmes to off-peak periods and, in some cases, their complete withdrawal from the schedules. It could also lead, they feared, to the colouration of programmes by advertising and the suppression of abrasive satire, drama, and documentaries that ran counter to received opinion.

Consequently the committee favoured a gradual phasing-in of a free market system, at a pace determined largely by the rate of expansion in the number of competing channels. In the first phase, they recommended more independently produced programmes on ITV and the

BBC, rising to 40 per cent of output over ten years; competitive auctioning of ITV franchises, with some safeguards; and the option of privatizing BBC radio 1, 2, and local radio as advertising funded channels. Anything more, at this stage, could seriously impair, in their view, the current broadcasting system which has given 'good value for money'.

They proposed in the second phase (roughly the mid-1980s) that the BBC's licence should be replaced by voluntary subscriptions. Almost certainly fewer people would take out a subscription than currently pay the licence fee since the change-over would occur when there would be a wider choice of television channels. This would raise the consumer cost of subscriptions, which would further depress the level of take-up. But the committee judged the change desirable since it would reduce political pressure on the Corporation.

In the final phase, broadcasting regulations would be phased out, and a broadcasting free market would be secured through competition between over-the-air, cable, and satellite television channels funded mainly by pay TV.

The committee was thus determined to remodel ultimately broadcasting on *laissez-faire* lines. However, its free market commitment was qualified in three ways. It wanted to compel either the individual consumer or the general public to subsidize the manufacture of a cheat-proof pay TV system. It favoured tough anti-monopoly measures particularly in relation to the independent television sector and satellite television. Perhaps most significant of all, it wanted to introduce a Public Service Broadcasting Council (PSBC), funded by ITV or a television tax, once the transition to a competitive free market had been completed. The function of the PSBC would be to provide a regular supply of 'programmes of a more demanding kind with a high content of knowledge, culture, education and experiment (including entertainment)' which might not be forthcoming from a wholly commercial system. This residual ghost from public service broadcasting was justified principally on the grounds that it would widen consumer choice and give viewers an opportunity to develop new preferences.

Radical market criticism of these proposals has usually focused on the committee's proposals that a quota of 40 per cent of independent television productions should be shown on the main networks which would destroy, in effect, the basic institutions of public service broadcasting. Another criticism is that a competitive auctioning of ITV franchises would lead to a lowering of standards, particularly at a time of growing channel competition. Critics also argue that the committee has failed to take into account the very heavy costs that would be involved in publicizing television programmes and channels within a fully competitive free market situation. Public funds would be needed, in their view, to assist the emergence of new television enterprises, if commercial broadcasting was not to be dominated by the communication conglomerates.

Andrew Ehrenburg has also attacked the committee's commitment to pay TV from a radical market perspective. He points out that pay TV would greatly increase consumer costs since it would require new television equipment, additional administration charges, and probably the competitive auctioning of sporting and other popular events that are currently covered at no premium charge. Its justification, he claims, is also spurious since it would not provide a direct expression of consumer demand: payments averaging about two pence a programme would be debited in monthly, cumulative bills or else packaged in the form of channel subscriptions. This would provide, in his opinion, no more sensitive a gauge of market demand, and of the intensity of demand, than information about what people watch, whether they watched to the end, and what they thought of programmes, which can be obtained through survey research.

Radical libertarian approaches

Radical libertarians are a heterogeneous group, drawn from a variety of political traditions. But they are worth considering as a single group despite their differences, because they have in common a desire to reduce restrictions on communicators' freedom of expression. Liberty, as George Orwell once powerfully argued, means allowing people freely to say things that you do not want to hear. It is a definition of freedom which many libertarians believe should be a foundation stone of our media system.

The most prominent group among the libertarians are those who have been campaigning for changes in media law. Their central argument is that greater weight should be given to the public's right to know the basis upon which all decisions which affect the common good are made, and to the fundamental right of freedom of expression, at the expense of other rights and interests that are overprotected by law.

Their principal target is the Official Secrets Act. They argue that it is a bad piece of legislation, rushed through parliament in a single day in 1911 during a period of moral panic. It makes unlawful the unauthorized disclosure of state information over a wide area not directly connected with national security. As the head of MI5 told the Franks Committee, 'it is an official secret if it is in an official file'. This has enabled successive governments to prevent the release of information which damages their credibility rather than endangers the nation, and to seek judicial revenge on whistle-blowers from Jonathan Aitken to Sarah Tisdall who have caused them political embarrassment.

The Act should be revised, in their view, so that it applies only to the betrayal of secrets to a national enemy. They also argue that this reform should be accompanied by the introduction of a Freedom of Information Act which would give a legal right of access to documents in all government departments, with a High Court judge determining government claims to privilege. They claim that the experience of other countries which have introduced a Freedom of Information law refutes the arguments based on cost and efficiency that have been advanced against it.

The demand for increased access to information has usually focused on government. But some radicals also argue that business corporations should be obliged to disclose information about their activities and that exemptions should be granted only in relation to information which would seriously damage their competitive position.

Calls have also been made for the abolition of restrictive laws which make it illegal 'to stir up enmity between different classes of Her Majesty's subjects', to encourage members of the armed forces or the police to disobey orders, or for aliens to cause disaffection. The libertarian case for abolition is that politically repressive laws should not remain on the statute book even if they have fallen into disuse since they could be reactivated in a different climate of opinion. This argument acquired some force when, during the worsening of the Northern Ireland crisis during the mid-1970s, Pat Arrowsmith was charged and jailed under the 'dormant' Incitement to Disaffection Act for distributing a leaflet to members of the armed forces urging them not to serve in Ulster.

Libertarians also argue that the laws which make investigative journalism difficult in Britain should be modified. They contend that the laws of confidence and copyright are being manipulated to prevent the media's legitimate use of information leaked from organizations; that defamation laws deter critical probing of the activities of élites while failing to provide adequate protection for the general public (since freedom from unjustified defamation is the only important civil right not covered by legal aid); and that the laws of contempt prevent the disclosure of some information relating to matters pending litigation that should be publicly available.

A number of radical lawyers and journalists argue therefore that greater weight needs to be given in the courts to public interest justifications for breaching copyright and confidence laws. Contempt law needs to be abolished, some also argue, in cases not tried by juries since judges should be capable of reaching proper judgments on the basis of detailed evidence and legal advocacy in the court-room, uninfluenced by media reporting. Some reformers also contend that most libel cases (other than criminal libel) should be taken over by a media 'ombudsman' with the power to authorize retractions and award damages. Their contention is that this would reduce the costs arising from defamation disputes and thus encourage media organizations to pursue legitimate investigations, while at the same time making public redress speedier, cheaper, and more widely available.

Some lawyers insist that it is not enough merely to modify media laws. A major obstacle to investigative journalism is, they argue, the readiness with which High Court judges issue injunctions if it is suggested that a forthcoming article or programme is based on confidential information, copyrighted documents, or else passes comment on pending litigation. The granting of injunctions amounts, in their view, to a form of pre-censorship since it frequently delays publication until the information, and the story on which it is based, has become out of date. It also makes for bad journalism since reporters are sometimes reluctant to crosscheck their stories with the people they criticize for fear of provoking a gagging injunction. Some lawyers argue, therefore, that there should be no prior restraint by court injunction except in relation to information which damages the national interest or prejudices criminal proceedings. The only remedy for breach of confidence and copyright (other than patents) would thus be money damages assessed after publication or transmission.

Some libertarians also argue that obscenity laws should be revised. Their views influenced the Williams Committee (1979) which proposed, to no effect, that all obscenity and indecency laws should be replaced by new, more permissive legislation. The committee argued that legal restraint should be formally lifted from all explicit writing in publications where there is no offensive illustration. But it also suggested that pictorial pornography featuring under age or sadistic sex should remain subject to specific prohibition, and that the sale of pornography 'whose unrestricted availability is offensive to reasonable people' should be restricted to persons over the age of 18.

The government has since strengthened rather than relaxed obscenity law by introducing, with some exemptions, compulsory censorship of videos which feature sex or violence. Some critics argue that 'video nasties' – the main target of the Video Recordings Act – could be dealt with more satisfactorily by enabling the British Board of Film Censors to respond to complaints from the police or public about specific video-cassettes and, where desirable, prohibit their public sale. This would be preferable, they suggest, to the present unprecedented apparatus of pre-censorship covering thousands of videos.

Reforming the law is viewed by libertarians as only one way of unshackling the media. Another libertarian approach emphasizes the restrictions on communicators' freedom of expression arising from the present pattern of media ownership, and the economic structures that underlie it. Its main thrust is to restructure the ownership and control of the media so that all significant interests and views can find expression over the airwaves and in print.

In Britain it currently costs up to £2 million to establish a profitable, local radio station; well over £10 million to set up and run in a new national daily; about £30 million to develop a cable television station; and £300 million to £400 million to launch a satellite television channel. According to socialist critics, these high entry costs restrict ownership of most commercial media to the capitalist class. They argue, therefore, that the state must intervene if control over mass communications is to be extended to other classes and groups.

While this much is agreed by most socialists, libertarians among them are strongly opposed to the way in which this reasoning can become a rationale for illiberal media regimes. Communists in the Soviet tradition argue that workers' organizations and the state should monopolize control of the media since they alone represent the interests of the masses. Although this permits considerable media differentiation in terms of provision for ethnic minorities, age, and special interest groups, it does not result in ideological diversity. All Soviet media broadly follow the political line laid down by the Communist Party leadership, although guidelines are less rigid than they were, due to the introduction of *glasnost*.

However, libertarian socialists argue that a genuinely socialist media system should enable competing definitions of the public interest to be articulated, and should reflect the different values and perspectives of contending groups and political parties. Some libertarians propose therefore that all media should be publicly owned and leased out to the principal interests and political groupings in the community. Others seek to inscribe diversity into the media system through a varied pattern of ownership in the form of public trusts, self-managing collectives, public corporations with elected authorities, joint stock companies, consortia launched with the help of public grants, and so on.

An example of the first model is provided by a plan for reorganizing the British media advanced by Militant, a Trotskyist group within the Labour Party. It proposes that *editorial* control over both newspapers and broadcasting should be vested in the political parties in proportion to the votes that they win at general elections, and that specialist publications should be controlled by scientific, technical, and professional groups and organizations. However, this plan is only superficially libertarian since fascist political parties and specialist organizations without democratic structures would be excluded, in the Militant scheme, from having a stake in the media.

A more pluralist version of the same model is afforded by the Dutch broadcasting system. This allocates both airtime and publicly owned production facilities, with technical staff, to different groups on the basis of their membership, usually linked to the sales of their programme guides. As a result, a variety of organizations from the commercial enterprise, TROS, to political-cultural groupings like VARA (with close links to the Labour Party) and NCVR (a conservative, Protestant organization) all provide a comprehensive package of services, with smaller organizations also being responsible for a limited quota of broadcasting hours each year.

The second model of a mixed pattern of public and private media ownership is implicit in at least some of the radical market and radical public service plans that have been discussed already. Lurking behind them is the hope that these will evolve over time into a libertarian media system in which all important groups and interests will have a stake.

Discussion about alternative forms of ownership is part of a wider debate about how the media should be managed. Most libertarians favour structures that give communicators considerable freedom from hierarchical control. Indeed some argue that media organizations should be controlled exclusively by the people who work in them. However, others advocate that outside interests should be represented on management structures on the grounds that media workers are not properly representative of the community.

This debate is complicated by the fact that workers' control or participation is sometimes advocated on grounds that are only partly connected with libertarian ideas. Some favour participation as a way of increasing job satisfaction or fostering editorial responsibility. Others argue for participation as a way of making it more difficult for governments or proprietors to suborn newspapers' editorial independence.

These different motivations have given rise to a variety of proposals. These are in ascending order of significance: access to information about advance corporate plans; the right to be consulted about major decisions; participation in making senior appointments; the election and reselection at regular intervals of senior personnel; representation on editorial committees, boards of management, or supervisory boards (like the BBC board of governors); full control over all decision-making bodies within media organizations.

In some plans, control over media organizations is also subdivided, on the Yugoslav model, between production and editorial 'spheres'. In others, control is shared jointly by media workers and external representatives. Sometimes these two approaches are fused, as for example in the Militant blueprint which proposes that the production sphere of media organizations should be controlled by a management committee composed equally of representatives of media production workers, TUC, and government.

Reformers also differ in terms of how they propose democratizing measures should be implemented. Some advocate a gradualist approach in which the terms of reference of franchise and grant giving bodies are changed to favour applications from consortia with democratic structures. Others argue that industrial democracy should be pioneered in publicly owned media, notably the BBC. A further group contends that workers should be given rights of representation by statute in all enterprises (including media organizations) where the majority of workers vote in favour of acquiring them.

Epilogue

The main aim of this chapter has been to summarize the policy options that are on offer, and provide a general orientation to the issues raised by media reform. However, it may be helpful to conclude with our own personal set of preferences, culled eclectically from different research approaches. This will be done without repeating the rationale for each proposal.

The overriding objectives of reform should be to conserve the existing strengths of the British media; increase its independence from both government and the expanding communications conglomerates; and extend the media's political and cultural diversity so that it is more representative of the different classes and sub-cultures that make up British society.

A Ministry of Arts, Communications, and Entertainment (ACE) should be established to co-ordinate the development of a media, culture, and leisure poiicy. It should be headed by a minister of Cabinet rank. The new minister should seek a European agreement for regulating the development of satellite television (including a quota on imported programmes and advertising). This is the only effective way of preserving the strengths of British broadcasting in the new era of global competition.

Steps should also be taken to inject greater diversity into the British media by promoting the growth of a vigorous, independent sector which is controlled neither by powerful public agencies nor by the communications combines. This could be achieved by the following:

1. Require the BBC, ITV, and British satellite television channels to carry a specified quota of programmes made by independent UK production companies.
2. Franchise new local community radio stations.
3. *Either* restrict ownership of newspapers to EEC citizens and registered companies *or* limit joint ownership of national papers to only one national daily and Sunday paper. This should be accompanied by a statutory option period of three months in which the sale of divested publications is limited to employees and independent consortia with no newspaper holdings.
4. Introduce grants for low advertising, low circulation national newspapers on the model pioneered in France.
5. Establish a Media Enterprise Board to aid the launch of new media companies and fund alternative ownership of divested media.

Of these five proposals, the last perhaps is the most important. The strategy of promoting the development of an independent media sector could amount to merely encouraging the growth of small businesses and, at worst, to encouraging the casualization of the media industry in a way that would threaten the security and living standards of people working in broadcasting. But it could also lead to a major enfranchisement of interests under-represented in the media *providing* a Media Enterprise Board is established to assist groups with limited capital to start media enterprises and buy up existing ones.

The introduction of an independent programme quota makes unnecessary a restructuring of the BBC and ITV since it encourages both networks to draw upon new inputs and experiences. However, a duty to 'present fairly and accurately important differences of interest and outlook within society' should be written into the terms of reference of both organizations. This would not supersede the requirement to maintain an overall balance in programme output but it would underwrite an obligation on both networks to reflect a wider range of opinions and value systems than they do at present.

The media should also be distanced from the state. All members of broadcasting authorities should be elected through an electoral college instead of being appointed by government. The Official Secrets Act should be reformed to cover only the betrayal of national security to a foreign power, and this should be accompanied by the introduction of a Freedom of Information Act.

Among the many other desirable legal reforms that have been proposed, the legal right of reply stands out as a measure which has extensive support across the political spectrum. It should be confined to corrections of factual misrepresentation, and cover both the press and broadcasting (thereby superseding the unsatisfactory Broadcasting Complaints Commission).

The programme above has been restricted to twelve proposals since any more would be indigestible. This self-imposed limitation has resulted in some valuable proposals being excluded. Our choice is also based on what is politically feasible as well as desirable. No proposal has been included which does not have a serious chance of securing the political support necessary for it to be placed on the statute book in the next decade.[2]

These proposals would not establish a fully democratic media system. But taken together, they would go some way towards creating media with power *and* responsibility – to the public rather than to proprietors and governments.

Notes

1. The heat has been temporarily taken out of this debate by the government's decision to link increases of the license fee to the retail price index for three years from April 1988. This will make the BBC's revenue fall still further behind that of ITV, and probably below the rate of inflation of broadcasting costs.
2. Indeed a number of these proposals were included in the 1987 general election manifestos of the major political parties. The Conservative Party promised to introduce a 25 per cent quota of independent programmes on both the BBC and ITV. Both the Alliance and Labour Parties proposed a unified ministry for the media and the arts, the reform of the Official Secrets Act, and a Freedom of Information Act. The Labour Party also pledged 'a launch fund to assist new publications' (corresponding to a Media Enterprise Board with a narrow remit) and new legislation 'to ensure that ownership and control of the press and broadcasting are retained by citizens of Britain and to place limits on the concentration of ownership'. The word 'retained' implies a significant abridgement of Kinnock's original proposal.

Bibliography

Public reports and papers

Broadcasting

Broadcasting Committee: Report (Sykes Report, 1923) [Cmd 1951].
Report of the Broadcasting Committee (Crawford Report, 1926) [Cmd 2599].
Report of the Television Committee (Selsdon Report, 1935) [Cmd 3703].
Report of the Broadcasting Committee (Ullswater Report, 1936) [Cmd 5091].
Report of the Television Committee (Hankey Report, 1944) (Privy Council Office).
Broadcasting Policy (1946) [Cmd 6852].
Report of the Broadcasting Committee (Beveridge Report, 1951) [Cmd 8116].
Report of the Broadcasting Committee 1949 (1951/2) [Cmd 8117].
Broadcasting, Memorandum on the Report of the Broadcasting Committee (1951) [Cmd 8291].
Broadcasting, Memorandum on the Report of the Broadcasting Committee, 1949 (1952) [Cmd 8550].
The Television Act 1954, 2 & 3 Eliz. II, c. 55.
Report of the Committee on Broadcasting (Pilkington Report, 1962) [Cmnd 1753].
The Television Act 1964, 12 & 13 Eliz. II, c. 21.
The University of the Air (1966) [Cmnd 2992].
An Alternative Service of Radio Broadcasting (1971) [Cmnd 4636].
Sound Broadcasting Act 1972, 19 & 20 Eliz. II, c. 31.
Session 1971–2 Independent Broadcasting Authority, Sub-Committee B, House of Commons Paper 465 (1972).
Observations on the Second Report of the Select Committee of the Nationalized Industries (1973) [Cmnd 5244].
Report of the Committee on the Future of Broadcasting (Annan Report, 1977) [Cmnd 6753].
Radio Choices and Opportunities (1982) [Cm 92].
Report of the Committee on Financing the BBC (Peacock Report, 1986) [Cmnd 9824].

The press

Monopolies Commission (1965–6). *The Times Newspaper and Sunday Times* (London, HMSO, 1966).

Monopolies Commission (1967–8), *Thomson Newspapers and Crusha and Son Ltd*, House of Commons Paper 66 (London, HMSO, 1968).

Monopolies Commission (1969–70), *George Outram and Company Ltd and Hamilton Advertiser Ltd and Baird and Hamilton Ltd*, House of Commons Paper 76 (London, HMSO, 1970).

Monopolies Commission (1971–2), *The Berrows Organisation Ltd and the County Express Group*, House of Commons Paper 224 (London, HMSO, 1972).

Monopolies Commission (1972–3), *Westminster Press Ltd and Kentish Times Ltd, Gravesend and Dartford Reporter Ltd and F.J. Parsons Ltd, Subsidiaries of Morgan-Grampian Ltd*, House of Commons Paper 460 (London, HMSO, 1973).

Monopolies Commission (1973–4), *Courier Printing and Publishing Company Ltd and Associated Newspapers Group Ltd*, House of Commons Paper 108 (London, HMSO, 1974).

Monopolies Commission (1974–5), *G. and A.N. Scott Ltd and The Guardian and Manchester Evening News Ltd*, House of Commons Paper 349 (London, HMSO, 1975).

Monopolies and Mergers Commission, *The Observer and George Outram* (London, HMSO, 1981).

Monopolies and Mergers Commission, *Wholesaling of Newspapers and Periodicals* (London, HMSO, 1978).

National Board for Prices and Incomes, *Wages, Costs and Prices in the Printing Industry* (1965) [Cmnd 2750].

National Board for Prices and Incomes, *Costs and Revenue of National Daily Newspapers* (1967) [Cmnd 3435].

National Board for Prices and Incomes, *Journalists' Pay* (1969) [Cmnd 4077].

National Board for Prices and Incomes, *Costs and Revenue of National Newspapers* (1970) [Cmnd 4277].

Report of the Committee on Contempt of Court (1975) [Cmnd 5794].

Report of the Committee on Data Protection (Lindop Committee, 1978) [Cmnd 7341].

Report of the Committee on Defamation (Faulks Committee, 1975) [Cmnd 5571].

Report of the Committee on the Official Secrets Act (1972) [Cmnd 7140].

Report of a Court of Inquiry into the Problems Caused by the Introduction of Web-offset Machines (1967) [Cmnd 3184].

Royal Commission on the Press 1947–9 Report (1949) [Cmnd 7700].

Royal Commission on the Press 1961–2 Report (1962) [Cmnd 1811].

Royal Commission on the Press Interim Report (1976) [Cmnd 6553].

Royal Commission on the Press 1974–7 Final Report (1977) [Cmnd 6810].

Royal Commission on the Press Final Report Appendices (1977) [Cmnd 6810–1–6].
Select Committee of the House of Commons on Newspaper Stamps, *Parliamentary Papers, xvii* (1851).

Film

Cinematograph Films Act (1927) [Cmnd 2053].
Report of the Committee appointed by the Board of Trade (Moyne Report, 1936) [Cmnd 2053].
Report on Tendencies to Monopoly in the Cinematograph Film Industry (Palache Report, 1944) [Cmnd 4059].
Report of the Working Party on Film Production Costs (Gater Report, 1949) [Cmnd 7837].
Report of the Committee on the Distribution and Exhibition of Cinematograph Films (Plant Report, 1949) [Cmnd 7837].
Cinematograph Films Council, Distribution and Exhibition of Cinematograph Films (London, HMSO, Board of Trade, 1950).
Cinematograph Films Bill 1960, 8 & 9 Eliz. II.
The Films Act, House of Commons Paper 206 (1960).
Board of Trade Review of Films Legislation (1968) [Cmnd 3584].
The Prime Minister's Working Party on the Future of the Film Industry (Wilson Report, 1976) [Cmnd 6372].

Miscellaneous public reports referred to in the book

Machinery of Government Report (1918) [Cmnd 9230].
Board of Education, *Inspectors' Report* (1932) [Cmnd 4068].
Board of Education Consultative Committee on Secondary Education (Spens Report, 1938), 10/119.
Report of the Department Committee on Curriculum and Examinations in Secondary Schools (Norwood Report, 1943).
The Nation's Schools: their Plans and Purposes, Ministry of Education Pamphlet 1 (London, HMSO, 1945).
Royal Commission on Local Government (1969) (Redcliffe Maud Report), Research Paper 9, *Community Attitudes Survey* [Cmnd 3409].
Report of the Committee on Privacy (1972) [Cmnd 5012].
Royal Commission on the Distribution of Income and Wealth, Report 4, (1976) [Cmnd 6626].
Report of the Committee on Film Finance (1985) [Cmnd 7610].

The press

General historical perspectives

R. D. Altick, *The English Common Reader* (Chicago, Ill., University of Chicago Press, 1957; London, Phoenix, 1963).

A. Andrews, *History of British Journalism*, 2 vols (London, Richard Bentley, 1859).

G. Boyce, 'The fourth estate: the reappraisal of a concept' in G. Boyce, J. Curran, and P. Wingate (eds), *Newspaper History* (London, Constable, 1978).

P. Brendon, *The Life and Death of the Press Barons* (London, Secker & Warburg, 1982).

C.J. Bundock, *The National Union of Journalists: A Jubilee History, 1907–1957* (London, Oxford University Press, 1957).

D. Chaney, *Processes of Mass Communication* (London, Macmillan, 1972).

G. A. Cranfield, *The Press and Society* (Harlow, Longman, 1978).

J. Curran, 'Capitalism and control of the press 1800–1975' in J. Curran, M. Gurevitch, and J. Woollacott (eds), *Mass Communication and Society* (London, Edward Arnold/Open University, 1977).

—— 'The press as an agency of social control: an historical perspective' in G. Boyce, J. Curran, and P. Wingate (eds), *Newspaper History* (London, Constable, 1978).

—— 'Communications, power and social order' in T. Bennett, J. Curran, M. Gurevitch, and J. Woollacott (eds), *Culture, Media and Society* (London, Methuen, 1981).

H. R. Fox Bourne, *English Newspapers* (London, Chatto & Windus, 1887; London, Russell & Russell, 1966).

J. Grant, *The Newspaper Press*, 3 vols (London, Tinsley Brothers, 1871–2).

M. Harris and A. Lee (eds), *The Press in English Society from the Seventeenth to Nineteenth Centuries* (London and Toronto, Associated University Presses, 1986).

R. Harrison, G. Woolven, and R. Duncan, *The Warwick Guide to British Labour Periodicals 1790–1970* (Brighton, Harvester, 1977).

S. Harrison, *Poor Men's Guardians: A Record of the Struggles for a Democratic Newspaper Press 1763–1973* (London, Lawrence & Wishart, 1974).

H. Herd, *The March of Journalism* (London, Allen & Unwin, 1952).

F. Knight Hunt, *The Fourth Estate* (London, David Bogue, 1850).

P. Knightley, *The First Casualty: The War Correspondent as Hero, Propagandist and Myth Maker from the Crimea to Vietnam* (London, Deutsch, 1975).

S. Koss, *The Rise and Fall of the Political Press in Britain*, vols 1–2 (London, Hamish Hamilton, 1981 and 1984).

A. Marshall, *Changing the Word: The Printing Industry in Transition* (London, Comedia, 1983).

M. Milne, *Newspapers of Northumberland and Durham* (Newcastle, Frank Graham, 1972).

S. Morison, *The English Newspaper* (Cambridge, Cambridge University Press, 1932).

A. E. Musson, *The Typographical Association: Origins and History up to 1949* (London, Oxford University Press, 1954).

C. Pebody, *English Journalism* (London, Cassell, Petter & Galpin, 1882).

G. Scott, *Reporters Anonymous: The Story of the Press Association* (London, Hutchinson, 1968).

F. S. Siebert, T. Peterson, and W. Schramm, *Four Theories of the Press* (Urbana, Ill., University of Illinois Press, 1956; New York, Books for Libraries Press, 1973).

A. Smith, *The Newspaper: An International History* (London, Thames & Hudson, 1979).

—— 'Technology and control: the interactive dimensions of journalism' in J. Curran, M. Gurevitch, and J. Woollacott (eds), *Mass Communication and Society* (London, Edward Arnold/Open University, 1977).

G. Storey, *Reuter's Century 1851–1951* (London, Parrish, 1951).

K. von Stutterheim, *The Press in England* (London, Allen & Unwin, 1934).

H. A. Taylor, *The British Press* (London, Arthur Barker, 1961).

J. Tunstall, 'Editorial sovereignty in the British press: its past and present' in *Studies on the Press*, Royal Commission on the Press 1974–7 Working Paper 3 (London, HMSO, 1977).

A. P. Wadsworth, 'Newspaper circulations 1800–1954', *Transactions of the Manchester Statistical Society*, iv (1955).

C. White, *Women's Magazines, 1693–1968* (London, Michael Joseph, 1970).

F. Williams, *Dangerous Estate* (Harlow, Longman Green, 1959; London, Arrow, 1959).

R. Williams, *The Long Revolution* (London, Chatto & Windus, 1961).

—— 'The press and popular culture: an historical perspective' in G. Boyce, J. Curran, and P. Wingate (eds), *Newspaper History* (London, Constable, 1978).

C. Wilson, *First with the News: The History of W.H. Smith 1792–1972* (London, Cape, 1985).

Newspaper histories

Anon, *The History of the Times*, vols 1–5 (1935–58).

D. Ayerst, *The Guardian: Biography of a Newspaper* (London, Collins, 1971).

Lord Burnham, *Peterborough Court: Story of the Daily Telegraph* (London, Cassell, 1955).

A. Christiansen, *Headlines All My Life* (London, Heinemann, 1961).

P. Cockburn, *The Years of the Week* (Harmondsworth, Penguin, 1971).

H. Cudlipp, *Publish and be Damned* (London, Andrew Dakers, 1953).

M. Edelman, *The Mirror – A Political History* (London, Hamish Hamilton, 1966).

W. Fienburgh, *25 Momentous Years: A 25th Anniversary in the History of the Daily Herald* (London, Odhams, 1955).

G. Fraser and K. Peters, *The Northern Lights* (London, Hamish Hamilton, 1978).

M. A. Gibb and F. Beckwith, *The Yorkshire Post: Two Centuries* (Leeds, Yorkshire Conservative Newspaper Co., 1954).

P. M. Handover, *History of the London Gazette, 1665–1965* (London, HMSO, 1965).

A. Hetherington, *Guardian Years* (London, Chatto & Windus, 1981).

D. Hill, *Tribune 40* (London, Quartet, 1977).

W. Hindle, *The Morning Post, 1772–1937* (London, Routledge & Kegan Paul, 1937).

H. Hobson, P. Knightley, and L. Russell, *The Pearl of Days: An Intimate Memoir of the Sunday Times*, 1822–1972 (London, Hamish Hamilton, 1972).

R. J. Lucas, *Lord Glenesk and the Morning Post* (London, Alston Rivers, 1910).

I. McDonald, *History of the Times 1939–66*, vol. 5 (London, Times Books, 1984).

R. McKay and B. Barr, *The Story of the Scottish Daily News* (Edinburgh, Canongate, 1976).

J. W. Robertson Scott, *The Story of the Pall Mall Gazette* (London, Oxford University Press, 1950).

H. R. G. Whates, *The Birmingham Post, 1857–1957* (Birmingham Post and Mail, 1957).

O. Woods and J. Bishop, *The Story of the Times* (London, Michael Joseph, 1983).

Nineteenth-century press history

W. E. Adams, *Memoirs of a Social Atom*, 2 vols (London, Hutchinson, 1903).

Anon, *Guide to Advertisers* (London, 1851).

A. Aspinall, 'Statistical accounts of London newspapers 1800–36', *English Historical Review, lxv* (1950).

——*Politics and the Press, 1780–1850* (London, Home & Van Thal, 1949; Brighton, Harvester, 1973).

I. Asquith, 'Advertising and the press in the late eighteenth and early nineteenth centuries: James Perry and the *Morning Chronicle*, 1790–1821', *Historical Journal*, xvii (1975).

P. Bailey, *Leisure and Class in Victorian England* (London, Routledge & Kegan Paul, 1978).

V. Berridge, 'Popular Sunday papers and mid-Victorian society' in G. Boyce, J. Curran, and P. Wingate (eds), *Newspaper History* (London, Constable, 1978).

L. Brown, *Victorian News and Newspapers* (Oxford, Clarendon, 1985).

T. Catling, *My Life's Pilgrimage* (London, John Murray, 1911).

I. R. Christie, 'British newspapers in the late Georgian age' in *Myth and Reality in Late 18th Century British Politics* (London, Macmillan, 1970).

C. D. Collet, *History of the Taxes on Knowledge* (London, T. Fisher Unwin, 1899).

S. Coltham, 'The *Bee-Hive* newspaper: its origins and early struggle' in A. Briggs and J. Saville (eds), *Essays in Labour History* (London, Macmillan, 1960).

—— 'The British working-class press in 1867', *Bulletin for the Society for the Study of Labour History* (autumn 1967).

F. Dilnot, *Adventures of a Newspaper Man* (London, Smith, Elder, 1913).

J. A. Epstein, 'Feargus O'Connor and the *Morning Star*', *International Review of Social History*, xxi (1976).

T. H. S. Escott, *Masters of English Journalism* (London, T. Fisher Unwin, 1911).

J. Foster, *Class Struggle and the Industrial Revolution: Early Industrial Capitalism in Three English Towns* (London, Weidenfeld & Nicolson, 1974).

M. D. George, *English Political Caricature, 1792–1832* (London, Oxford University Press, 1959).

E. Glasgow, 'The establishment of the *Northern Star* newspaper', *History*, xxxix (1954).

B. Harrison, 'A world of which we had no conception: liberalism and the temperance press, 1830–1872', *Victorian Studies*, xiii (December 1969).

J. Hatton, *Journalistic London* (London, Sampson, Low, 1882).

A. F. Havighurst, *Radical Journalist: H. W. Massingham* (Cambridge, Cambridge University Press, 1974).

P. Hollis, *The Pauper Press* (London, Oxford University Press, 1970).

D. Hopkin, 'The socialist press in Britain 1890–1910' in G. Boyce, J. Curran, and P. Wingate (eds), *Newspaper History* (London, Constable, 1978).

D. Hudson, *Thomas Barnes of the Times* (Cambridge, Cambridge University Press, 1943).

L. James (ed.), *Print and the People, 1819–1851* (London, Allen Lane, 1976).

E. E. Kellett, 'The press' in G. M. Young (ed.), *Early Victorian England* (London, Oxford University Press, 1934).

C. Kent, 'Higher journalism and the mid-Victorian clerisy', *Victorian Studies*, xiii (December 1969).

S. Koss, *Fleet Street Radical: A. G. Gardiner and the Daily News* (London, Allen Lane, 1973).

A. J. Lee, 'The management of a Victorian local newspaper: the *Manchester City News*, 1864–1900', *Business History*, xv (1973).

—— 'The radical press' in A. Morris (ed.), *Edwardian Radicalism, 1900–1914* (London, Routledge & Kegan Paul, 1974).

—— *The Origins of the Popular Press, 1855–1914* (London, Croom Helm, 1976).

J. R. McCulloch, *Dictionary of Commerce and Commercial Navigation* (London, Longman, Brown, & Green, 1854).

Mitchell's Newspaper Press Directory (Mitchell).

P. Mountjoy, 'The working-class press and working-class conservatism' in G. Boyce, J. Curran, and P. Wingate (eds), *Newspaper History* (London, Constable, 1978).

A. E. Musson, 'Newspaper printing in the Industrial Revolution', *Economic History Review*, x, 2nd series (1957–8).

V. Neuberg, 'The literature of the streets' in H. J. Dyos and M. Wolff (eds), *The Victorian City* (London, Routledge & Kegan Paul, 1973).

T. Nevett, 'Advertising and editorial integrity in the nineteenth century' in M. Harris and A. Lee, *op. cit.*, 1987.

L. O'Boyle, 'The image of the journalist in England, France and Germany, 1815–1848', *Comparative Studies in Society and History*, x (1968).

P. O'Malley, 'Capital accumulation and press freedom, 1800–1850', *Media, Culture and Society*, 3, 1 (1981).

H. J. Perkin, 'The origins of the popular press', *History Today*, vii (1957).

R. Pound and G. Harmsworth, *Northcliffe* (London, Cassell, 1959).

R. Price, *An Imperial War and the British Working Class: Working-class Attitudes and Reactions to the Boer War 1899–1902* (London, Routledge & Kegan Paul, 1972).

D. Read, *Press and People 1790–1850* (London, Edward Arnold, 1961).

J. Roach, 'Education and public opinion' in C. Crawley (ed.), *War and Peace in an Age of Upheaval* (Cambridge, Cambridge University Press, 1965).

F. G. Salmon, 'What the working class read', *Nineteenth Century*, cxiii (1886).

M. Sanderson, 'Literacy and social mobility in the Industrial Revolution', *Past and Present*, 5, 6 (1972).

A. R. Schoyen, *The Chartist Challenge: A Portrait of George Julian Harney* (London, Heinemann, 1956).

J. Shattock and M. Wolff (eds), *The Victorian Periodical Press: Samplings and Soundings* (Leicester, University of Leicester Press, 1982).

H. Simonis, *The Street of Ink* (London, Cassell, 1917).

J. A. Spender, *Life, Journalism and Politics*, 2 vols (London, Cassell, 1927).

J. F. Stephen, 'Journalism', *Cornhill Magazine*, 6 (1862).

L. Stone, 'Literacy and education in England 1640–1900', *Past and Present*, 42 (1969).

J. D. Symon, *The Press and its Story* (London, Seeley Service, 1914).

T. Tholfsen, *Working-Class Radicalism in Mid-Victorian Britain* (London, Croom Helm, 1976).

D. Thompson, *The Chartists* (London, Maurice Temple Smith, 1984).

E. P. Thompson, *The Making of the English Working Class* (London, Gollancz, 1963).

R. K. Webb, *The British Working-Class Reader, 1790–1848* (London, Allen & Unwin, 1955).

W. H. Wickwar, *The Struggle for the Freedom of the Press, 1819–1832* (London, Allen & Unwin, 1928).

J. H. Wiener, *The War of the Unstamped* (New York, Cornell University Press, 1969).

Twentieth-century press history

R. Adams, *Media Planning* (London, Business Books, 1971).

A. Angell, *The Press and the Organisation of Society* (London, Labour Publishing Co., 1922).

D. Ayerst, *Garvin of the Observer* (London, Croom Helm, 1985).

Lord Beaverbrook, *Men and Power* (London, Hutchinson, 1956).

W. Belson, *The British Press* (London, London Press Exchange, 1959).

R. Boston (ed.), *The Press We Deserve* (London, Routledge & Kegan Paul, 1970).

O. Boyd-Barrett, C. Seymour-Ure, and J. Tunstall, *Studies on the Press*, Royal Commission on the Press, Working Paper 3 (London, HMSO, 1977).

R. Braddon, *Roy Thomson* (London, Fontana, 1968).

P. Brendon, *Eminent Edwardians* (London, Secker & Warburg, 1979).

T. B. Browne, *Advertisers' ABC* (Browne).

A. Calder, *The People's War* (London, Panther, 1971).

S. Chibnall, *Law-and-Order News* (London, Tavistock, 1977).

C. Chisholm, *Marketing and Merchandising* (London, Modern Business Institute, 1924).

H. Christian (ed.), *The Sociology of Journalism and the Press*, Sociological Review Monograph 29 (Keele, University of Keele, 1980).

A. Christiansen, *Headlines All My Life* (London, Harper, 1961).

T. Clarke, *My Northcliffe Diary* (London, Gollancz, 1931).

—— *Northcliffe in History* (London, Hutchinson, 1950).

G. Cleverley, *The Fleet Street Disaster* (London, Constable, 1976).

C. Cockburn, *Brothers: Male Dominance and Technological Change* (London, Pluto, 1983).

M. Cockerell, P. Hennessy, and D. Walker, *Sources Close to the Prime Minister* (London, Macmillan, 1984).

S. Cohen and J. Young, *The Manufacture of News* (London, Constable, 1973).

H. Cox and D. Morgan, *City Politics and the Press* (Cambridge, Cambridge University Press, 1973).

R. A. Critchley, *UK Advertising Statistics* (London, Advertising Association, nd).

H. Cudlipp, *At Your Peril* (London, Weidenfeld & Nicolson, 1962).

—— *Walking on the Water* (London, Bodley Head, 1976).

J. Curran, 'The impact of TV on the audience for national newspapers, 1945–68' in J. Tunstall (ed.), *Media Sociology* (London, Constable, 1970).

—— (ed.), *The British Press: A Manifesto* (London, Macmillan, 1978).

—— 'Advertising and the press' in J. Curran (ed.), *The British Press: A Manifesto* (London, Macmillan, 1978).

T. Driberg, *Beaverbrook* (London, Weidenfeld & Nicolson, 1956).

H. W. Eley, *Advertising Media* (London, Butterworth, 1932).

H. Evans, *Good Times, Bad Times* (London, Weidenfeld & Nicolson, 1983).

B. Falk, *He Laughed in Fleet Street* (London, Hutchinson, 1933).

M. Ferguson, *Forever Feminine* (London, Heinemann Educational, 1983).

P. Ferris, *The House of Northcliffe* (London, Weidenfeld & Nicolson, 1971).

C. Freer, *The Inner Side of Advertising: A Practical Handbook for Advertisers* (London, Library Press, 1921).

H. Fyfe, *Sixty Years of Fleet Street* (London, W. H. Allen, 1949).

F. R. Gannon, *The British Press and Germany, 1936–1939* (London, Oxford University Press, 1971).

J. E. Gerald, *The British Press under Government Economic Controls* (Minneapolis, University of Minnesota Press, 1956).

P. Gibbs, *Adventures in Journalism* (London, Harper, 1923).

F. Giles, *Sundry Times* (London, Murray, 1986).

G. Glenton and William Pattinson, *The Last Chronicle of Bouverie Street* (London, Allen & Unwin, 1963).

P. Golding and S. Middleton, *Images of Welfare* (Oxford, Martin Robertson, 1982).

D. Goodhart and P. Wintour, *Eddie Shah and the Newspaper Revolution* (London, Coronet, 1986).

S. Hall, 'The social eye of *Picture Post*', *Cultural Studies*, ii (1971).

—— 'Deviancy, politics and the media' in M. McIntosh and P. Rock (eds), *Deviancy and Social Control* (London, Tavistock, 1973).

S. Hall, C. Critcher, T. Jefferson, J. Clarke, and B. Roberts, *Policing the Crisis: Mugging, the State, and Law and Order* (London, Macmillan, 1978).

J. Halloran, P. Elliott, and G. Murdock (eds), *Demonstrations and Communication* (Harmondsworth, Penguin, 1970).

D. Hamilton, *Who is to Own the British Press?* (London, Birkbeck College, 1976).

J. A. Hammerston, *With Northcliffe in Fleet Street: A Personal Record* (London, Hutchinson, 1932).

R. Harris, *Gotcha: The Media, The Government and The Falklands War* (London, Faber, 1983).

W. Harris, *J. A. Spender* (London, Cassell, 1946).

G. Harrison and F. C. Mitchell, *The Home Market: A Handbook of Statistics* (London, Allen & Unwin, 1936).

N. Hartley, P. Gudgeon, and R. Crafts, *Concentration of Ownership in the Provincial Press*, Royal Commission on the Press 1974–7, Research Series 5 (London, HMSO, 1977).

P. Hartmann, 'Industrial relations in the news media', *Industrial Relations Journal*, 6, 4 (1975/6).

—— 'News and public perceptions of industrial relations', *Media, Culture and Society*, 1, 3 (1979).

P. Hartmann and C. Husband, *Racism and the Mass Media* (London, Davis-Poynter, 1974).

J. Harvey (ed.), *The War Diaries of Oliver Harvey 1941–5* (London, Collins, 1978).

H. Henry (ed.), *Behind the Headlines* (London, Associated Business Press, 1978).

—— *The Dynamics of the British Press 1961–1984* (London, Advertising Association, 1986).

A. Hetherington, *News, Newspapers and Television* (London, Macmillan, 1985).

C. Higham, *Advertising* (London, Williams & Norgate, 1925).

F. Hirsch and D. Gordon, *Newspaper Money: Fleet Street and the Search for the Affluent Reader* (London, Hutchinson, 1975).

P. Hoch, *The Newspaper Game* (London, Calder & Boyars, 1974).

R. Hoggart (ed.), *Your Sunday Paper* (London, University of London Press, 1967).

M. Hollingsworth, *The Press and Political Dissent* (London, Pluto, 1986).

D. Hubback, *No Ordinary Press Baron* (London, Weidenfeld & Nicolson, 1985).

Hulton Readership Surveys (London, Hulton, 1947–55).

N. Hunter, *Advertising Through the Press* (London, Pitman, 1925).

Institute of Incorporated Practitioners in Advertising, *An Analysis of Press Circulations 1934* (London, IIPA, 1934).

—— *Survey of Press Readership* (London, IIPA, 1939).

—— *National Readership Surveys* (London, IIPA, 1956–67).

—— *Joint Industry Committee for National Readership Surveys* (London, IIPA, 1968–84).

S. Inwood, 'The press in the First World War, 1914–1916', unpublished PhD thesis (University of Oxford, 1971).

I. Jackson, *The Provincial Press and the Community* (Manchester, Manchester University Press, 1971).

S. Jenkins, *Market for Glory* (London, Faber, 1986).

N. Kaldor and R. Silverman, *A Statistical Analysis of Advertising Expenditure and of the Revenue of the Press* (Cambridge, Cambridge University Press, 1948).

P. Kimble, *Newspaper Reading in the Third Year of the War* (London, Allen & Unwin, 1942).

C. King, *The Future of the Press* (London, MacGibbon & Kee, 1967).

—— *Strictly Personal* (London, Weidenfeld & Nicolson, 1969).

—— *With Malice Towards None: A War Diary* (ed. W. Armstrong) (London, Sidgwick & Jackson, 1970).

—— *Without Fear or Favour* (London, Sidgwick & Jackson, 1971).

—— *The Cecil King Diary 1965–70* (London, Cape, 1972).

S. Koss, *Fleet Street Radical: A. G. Gardiner and the Daily News* (London, Allen Lane, 1973).

G. Lansbury, *The Miracle of Fleet Street* (London, Victoria House, 1925).

J. Lawrenson and L. Barber, *The Price of Truth* (London, Sphere, 1986).

M. Leapman, *Barefaced Cheek* (London, Hodder & Stoughton, 1983).

H. P. Levy, *The Press Council* (London, Macmillan, 1967).

London Research Bureau, *Press Circulations Analysed 1928* (London Research Bureau, 1928).

A. G. Lyall, *Market Research: A Practical Handbook* (London Research Bureau 1933).

D. McLachlan, *In the Chair, Barrington-Ward of The Times, 1927–48* (London, Weidenfeld & Nicolson, 1971).

I. McLaine, *Ministry of Morale* (London, Allen & Unwin, 1979).

D. McQuail, *Analysis of Newspaper Content*, Royal Commission on the Press 1974–7, Research Series 4 (London, HMSO, 1977).

Mass Observation, *The Press and its Readers* (London, Art & Technics, 1949).

T. S. Mathews, *The Sugar Pill: An Essay on Newspapers* (London, Gollancz, 1957).

R. J. Minney, *Viscount Southwood* (London, Odhams, 1954).

S. Mulvern, *The End of the Street* (London, Methuen, 1986).

G. Munster, *Rupert Murdoch* (Victoria, Viking, 1985).

G. Murdoch, 'Class, power and the press: problems of conceptualisation and evidence' in H. Christian (ed.), *The Sociology of Journalism and the Press*, Sociological Review Monograph 29 (Keele, University of Keele, 1981).

D. Murphy, *The Silent Watchdog: the Press in Local Politics* (London, Constable, 1976).

News Chronicle, A Survey of Reader Interest (1934).

H. Nicolson, *Diaries and Letters* (London, Collins, 1967).

Lord Northcliffe, *Newspapers and their Millionaires* (London, Associated Newspapers, 1922).

L. Owen, *Northcliffe: The Facts* (privately published, 1931).

Periodicals and the Alternative Press, Royal Commission on the Press 1974–7, Research Series 6 (London, HMSO, 1977).

F. Pethick-Lawrence, *Fate Has Been Kind* (London, Hutchinson, 1943).

H. Porter, *Lies, Damned Lies and Some Exclusives* (London, Chatto & Windus, 1984).

R. Pound and G. Harmsworth, *Northcliffe* (London, Cassell, 1959).

A. Rappaport, *The British Press and Wilsonian Neutrality* (London, Oxford University Press, 1951).

Report on the British Press (London, Political & Economic Planning, 1938).

G. Robertson, *People Against the Press* (London, Quartet, 1983).

T. Russell, *Commercial Advertising* (London, Putnam, 1919).

A. P. Ryan, *Lord Northcliffe* (London, Collins, 1953).

C. Seymour-Ure, *The Press, Politics and the Public* (London, Methuen, 1968).

—— 'Policy-making in the press', *Government and Opposition*, iv, 4 (1969).

—— *The Political Impact of the Mass Media* (London, Constable, 1974).

—— 'The press and the party system between the wars' in G. Peele and C. Cook (eds), *The Politics of Reappraisal, 1918–1939* (London, Macmillan, 1976).

A. Sharf, *The British Press and Jews Under Nazi Rule* (London, Oxford University Press, 1964).

K. Sisson, *Industrial Relations in Fleet Street* (Oxford, Blackwell, 1975).

A. Smith, *The British Press Since the War* (Newton Abbot, David & Charles, 1974).

A. C. H. Smith, E. Immirzi, and T. Blackwell, *Paper Voices: The Popular Press and Social Change, 1933–1965* (London, Chatto & Windus, 1975).

Social and Community Planning, *Attitudes to the Press*, Royal Commission on the Press 1974–7, Research Series 3 (London, HMSO, 1977).

J. A. Spender, *Life, Journalism and Politics* (London, Cassell, 1927).

R. Stannard, *With the Dictators of Fleet Street* (London, Hutchinson, 1934).

Survey of the National Newspaper Industry (London, Economist Intelligence Unit, 1965).

A. J. P. Taylor, *English History 1914–1945* (Harmondsworth, Pelican, 1970).

—— *Beaverbrook* (London, Hamish Hamilton, 1972).

—— (ed.), *Off the Record: W. P. Crozier, Political Interviews, 1933–1943* (London, Hutchinson, 1973).

Lord Thomson of Fleet, *After I Was Sixty* (London, Hamish Hamilton, 1975).

The Times, The History of The Times, iv: The 150th Anniversary and Beyond, 1912–1948, 2 vols (London, The Times Publishing Co., 1952).

J. Tunstall, *The Westminster Lobby Correspondents* (London, Routledge & Kegan Paul, 1970).

—— *Journalists at Work* (London, Constable, 1971).

—— 'The problem of industrial relations news in the press' in *Studies on the Press*, Royal Commission on The Press 1974–7 Working Paper 3 (London, HMSO,1977).

—— *The Media in Britain* (London, Constable, 1983).

J. Whale, *Journalism and Government* (London, Macmillan, 1972).

C. White, *The Women's Periodical Press in Britain, 1946–1976,* Royal Commission on the Press, Working Paper 4 (London, HMSO, 1977).

H. Wickham Steed, *The Press* (Harmondsworth, Penguin, 1938).

T. Wilson (ed.), *The Political Diaries of C. P. Scott* (London, Collins, 1970).

R. Winsbury, *New Technology and the Press*, Royal Commission on the Press and Acton Society Press Group (London, HMSO, 1975).

C. Wintour, *Pressures on the Press: An Editor looks at Fleet Street* (London, Deutsch, 1972).

J. E. Wrench, *Geoffrey Dawson and our Times* (London, Hutchinson, 1955).

Broadcasting

Memoirs and biographies

R. Baker, *Here is the News* (London, Leslie Frewin, 1966).

G. Beadle, *Television, A Critical Review* (London, Allen & Unwin, 1963).

A. Boyle, *Only the Wind Will Listen: Reith of the BBC* (London, Hutchinson, 1972).

C. Brewer, *The Spice of Variety* (London, Muller, 1948).

D. G. Bridson, *Prospero and Ariel: The Rise and Fall of Radio* (London, Gollancz, 1971).

H. Brittain, *The ABC of the BBC* (London, Pearson, 1932).

J. C. Cassell, *In Town Tonight* (London, Harrap, 1935).

S. Chesmore, *Behind the Microphone* (London, Nelson, 1935).

Sir Kenneth Clark, *The Other Half: A Self-Portrait* (London, Murray, 1977).

Sir Alfred D. Cooper, *Old Men Forget* (London, Hart-Davis, 1953).

N. Davenport, *Memoirs of a City Radical* (London, Methuen, 1959).

R. Day, *Television – A Personal Report* (London, Hutchinson, 1961).

—— *Day by Day* (London, William Kimber, 1975).

B. Deane, *Seven Ages, An Autobiography, 1927–72* (London, Hutchinson, 1973).

J. Dimbleby, *Richard Dimbleby: A Biography* (London, Hodder & Stoughton, 1975).

R. Dimbleby, *The Waiting Year* (London, Hodder & Stoughton, 1944).

P. P. Eckersley, *The Power Behind the Microphone* (London, Cape, 1941).

R. Eckersley, *The BBC and All That* (London, Sampson, Low, Marston, 1946).

L. Fielden, *The Natural Bent* (London, Deutsch, 1960).

V. Gielgud, *Years of the Locust* (London, Nicholson & Watson, 1947).

G. W. Goldie, *Facing the Nation: Television and Politics, 1936–76* (London, Bodley Head, 1977).

M. Gorham, *Sound and Fury* (London, Percival-Maskell, 1948).

F. Grisewood, *The World Goes By* (London, Secker & Warburg, 1952).

—— *Years in the Mirror* (London, Gollancz, 1967).

H. Grisewood, *One Thing at a Time* (London, Hutchinson, 1968).

H. Hall, *Here's to the Next Time* (London, Deutsch, 1935).

L. Henry, *My Laugh Story* (Edinburgh, Simon Paul, 1937).

A. S. Hibberd, *This is London* (Plymouth, Macdonald & Evans, 1950).

Lord Hill of Luton (C. Hill), *Both Sides of the Hill* (London, Heinemann, 1967).

—— *Behind the Screen* (London, Sidgwick & Jackson, 1974).

J. Hilton, *This and That* (London, Allen & Unwin, 1938).

P. J. Kavanagh, *The Itma Years* (London, Heinemann, 1974).

T. Kavanagh, *Tommy Handley* (London, Hodder & Stoughton, 1949).

R. S. Lambert, *Ariel and All his Quality* (London, Gollancz, 1940).

C. A. Lewis, *Broadcasting from Within* (London, George Newnes, 1924).

E. Maschwitz, *No Chip on My Shoulder* (London, Jenkins, 1957).

S. A. Mosely, *Broadcasting in my Time* (London, Rich & Cowan, 1935).

—— *Private Diaries* (London, Parrish, 1960).

E. Nixon, *John Hilton* (London, Allen & Unwin, 1946).

J. Payne, *This is Jack Payne* (London, Marston, 1932).

—— *Signature Tune* (Edinburgh, Simon Paul, 1947).

W. Pickles, *Between You and Me* (London, Heinemann, 1949).

J. B. Priestley, *Margin Released* (London, Mercury, 1966).

J. C. W. Reith, *Into the Wind* (London, Hodder & Stoughton, 1949).

R. Silvey, *Who's Listening?* (London, Allen & Unwin, 1974).

C. Stuart, *The Reith Diaries* (London, Collins, 1975).

Sir Stephen Tallents, *Man and Boy* (London, Faber, 1943).

H. Thomas, *With an Independent Air* (London, Weidenfeld & Nicolson, 1977).

M. Tracey, *A Variety of Lives: A Biography of Sir Hugh Greene* (London, Bodley Head, 1982).

M. Whitehouse, *Who Does She Think She Is?* (London, New English Library, 1971).

The history of broadcasting

M. Abrams, *Granada Viewership Survey* (1959).

R. Alston, *Taking the Air* (London, Hodder & Stoughton, 1951).

G. L. Archer, *A History of Broadcasting to 1926* (London, Allen & Unwin, 1938).

J. Bakewell and N. Garnham, *The New Priesthood: British Television Today* (Harmondsworth, Allen Lane, 1970).

E. Barnouw, *A Tower in Babel: The History of Broadcasting in the United States* (London, Oxford University Press, 1966).

BBC Handbook (London, BBC, annually).

BBC, 'Comparative European programming', *BBC Handbook* (London, BBC, 1934).

—— *The Third Programme: Plans for October–December 1944* (London, BBC, 1944).

—— *The Public and their Programmes* (London, BBC, 1959).

J. Bennett, *British Broadcasting and the Danish Resistance Movement 1940–1945* (Cambridge, Cambridge University Press, 1965).

P. Black, *The Biggest Aspidistra in the World* (London, BBC, 1972).

—— *The Mirror in the Corner* (London, Hutchinson, 1972).

P. Bloomfield, *BBC* (London, Eyre & Spottiswoode, 1941).

A. Briggs, *The History of Broadcasting in the United Kingdom*: vol. I, *The Birth of Broadcasting*; vol. II, *The Golden Age of Wireless;* vol. III, *The War of Words*; vol. IV, *Sound and Vision* (London, Oxford University Press, 1961, 1965, 1970, and 1979).

—— 'The rise of the mass entertainment industry' (Fisher Lecture, 1961).

—— *The BBC Governors* (London, BBC, 1979).

P. J. Brown, 'Broadcasting in Britain', *London Quarterly Review*, 145, 1 (January 1926).

A. R. Burrows, *The Story of Broadcasting* (London, Cassell, 1924).

Sir Cyril Burt, 'The psychology of listeners', *BBC Quarterly*, iv, 2 (April 1949).

H. L. Childs and J. B. Whitton (eds), *Propaganda by Shortwave* (London, Oxford University Press, 1943).

J. A. Cole, *Lord Haw Haw — and William Joyce* (London, Collins, 1964).

C. A. R. Crosland, 'The mass media', *Encounter* (November 1962).

R. H. S. Crossman, 'The politics of viewing', *New Statesman* (25 October 1968).

—— 'The BBC, Labour and the public', *New Statesman* (17 July 1971).

C. Curran, *Code or Conscience* (London, BBC, 1970).

—— *A Maturing Democracy* (London, BBC, 1973).

—— *The Seamless Robe* (London, Bodley Head, 1979).

R. Day, 'Troubled reflections of a TV journalist', *Encounter* (May 1970).

B. Deane, *The Theatre At War* (London, Harrap, 1956).

S. Delmer, *Black Boomerang* (London, Secker & Warburg, 1962).

L. W. Doob, 'Goebbels' principles of propaganda', *Public Opinion Quarterly*, 21, 2 (1950).

P. P. Eckersley, *Captain Eckersley Explains* (London, Hodder & Stoughton, 1924).

—— *All About your Microphone* (London, BBC Broadcast Library, 1925).

—— *The Power Behind the Microphone* (London, Cape, 1941).

H. Fairlie, 'The BBC' in H. S. Thomas (ed.), *The Establishment: A Symposium* (London, New English Library, 1962).

—— 'TV, idiot box', *Encounter* (August 1959).

Sir Robert Fraser, *The Coming of Independent Television* (London, Hutchinson, 1955).

—— *ITA Notes* (October 1970).

V. Gielgud, *British Radio Drama 1922–1956* (London, Harrap, 1957).

G. W. Goldie, 'The new attraction', *Listener* (26 December 1940).

—— 'TV report', *Listener* (23 October 1968).

—— *Facing the Nation: Television and Politics 1936–1976* (London, Bodley Head, 1977).

M. Gorham, *Broadcasting and Television Since 1900* (London, Collins, 1952).

T. Green, *The Universal Eye: World Television in the Seventies* (London, Bodley Head, 1972).

—— 'The Future of Broadcasting in Britain', Granada Guildhall Lecture (1972).

H. C. Greene, 'The BBC since 1958', *BBC Handbook* (1969).

—— *The Third Floor Front: A View of Broadcasting in the Sixties* (London, Bodley Head, 1969)

T. Harrisson, 'War books', *Horizon* (December 1941).

D. Hawkins and D. Boyd (eds), *BBC War Report* (London, Oxford University Press, 1946).

Sir William Hayley, *The Central Problem of Broadcasting* (London, BBC, 1948).

IBA, *Annual Reports*.

ITV, *The Annan Report:An ITV View* (London, ITV, 1977).

E. T. Lean, *Voices in the Darkness* (London, Allen & Unwin, 1943).

D. McLachlan, *Room 39* (London, Weidenfeld & Nicolson, 1968).

Mass Observation, *The War Begins at Home* (London, Chatto & Windus, 1940).

H. Matheson, *Broadcasting* (London, Butterworth, 1933).

—— 'Listener research in broadcasting', *Sociological Review*, xxvii, 3 (1935).

A. Mitchell, 'The decline of current affairs television', *Political Quarterly*, 44, 1 (1973).

H. Nicolson, *The Third Programme: A Symposium of Opinions and Plans* (London, BBC, 1947).

S. Orwell and I. Angus (eds), *The Collected Essays, Letters and Journalism of George Orwell* (Harmondsworth, Penguin, 1971).

B. Paulu, *British Broadcasting: Radio and Television in the United Kingdom* (Oxford, Oxford University Press, 1957).

G. Pedrich, *Battledress Broadcasters* (London, Marston, 1964).

R. Postgate, *What to Do with the BBC?* (London, Hogarth, 1935).

J. B. Priestley, *Postscripts* (London, Heinemann, 1940).

J. C. W. Reith, *Broadcast over Britain* (London, Hodder & Stoughton, 1924).

N. Riley, *999* (London, Gollancz, 1943).

C. J. Rolo, *Radio Goes to War* (London, Hutchinson, 1943).

G. Ross, *T.V. Jubilee* (London, W. H. Allen, 1961).

P. Rotha (ed.), *Television in the Making* (London, Bodley Head, 1956).

P. Scannell, 'The social eye of television, 1946–1955', *Media, Culture, and Society*, 1, 1 (1979).

P. Scannell and D. Cardiff, 'The social foundations of British Broadcasting' in J. Curran, M. Gurevitch, and J. Woollacott (eds) *Mass Communication and Society* (London, Edward Arnold/Open University, 1977).

J. Seaton, 'The BBC and the Holocaust', *European Journal of Communication*, vol. 2, 1 (1987).

G. Seldes, *The Great Audience* (London, Oxford University Press, 1950).

R. Silvey, 'Some recent trends in listening', *BBC Handbook* (London, BBC, 1946).

—— 'TV viewing in Britain', *Public Opinion Quarterly*, 25, 2 (1950).

—— *Whose Listening?* (London, Bodley Head, 1974).

Lord Simon of Wythenshawe, *The BBC from Within* (London, Gollancz, 1953).

A. Smith, *The Shadow in the Cave* (London, Allen & Unwin, 1973).

—— *British Broadcasting* (Newton Abbot, David & Charles, 1974).

S. W. Smithers, *Broadcasting from Within* (London, Pitmans, 1938).

N. Swallow, *Factual Television* (London, Focal, 1966).

J. Swift, *Adventures in Vision* (London, Lehmann, 1950).

I. Thomas, *Warfare By Words* (London, Gollancz, 1942).

The Times, special broadcasting number (14 August 1934).

P. Todd, 'Scarcity of TV time', *Campaign* (26 January 1979).

M. Tracey, *Whitehouse* (London, Constable, 1979).

R. West, *The Meaning of Treason* (London, Macmillan, 1948).

H. Wheldon, 'Competition in television', Address to the Royal Society of Arts (1971).

—— *Tastes and Standards in BBC Programmes* (London, BBC, 1973).

H. H. Wilson, *Pressure Group* (London, Secker & Warburg, 1961).

F. Worsley, *ITMA* (London, Collins, 1948).

The background to broadcasting

M. Abrams, 'Advertising', *Listener* (15 December 1956).

—— 'Motivation research', *Advertising Quarterly* (November 1959).

P. Addison, *The Road to 1945* (London, Cape, 1975).

K. Allsop, *The Angry Decade* (London, Owen, 1958).

N. Annan, 'Love among the moralists', *Encounter* (February 1960).

D. Bell, 'Advertising: is it worth it?' *Listener* (13 December 1956).

W. H. Beveridge, *Unemployment: A Problem of Industry* (London, Longman Green, 1910).

—— *Public Service in War and Peace* (London, Constable, 1920).

—— *Constructive Democracy* (London, Allen & Unwin, 1937).

—— *Power and Influence* (London, Hodder & Stoughton, 1953).

V. Bogdanor and R. Skidelsky, *The Age of Affluence* (Harmondsworth, Penguin, 1970).

E. Bowen, *The Heart of the Matter* (London, Faber, 1944).

V. Brittain, *Testament of Friendship* (London, Macmillan, 1940).

G. Bruntz, *Allied Propaganda and the Collapse of the German Empire in 1918* (Stanford, Calif., Stanford University Press, 1938).

Sir Cyril Burt, *The Distribution and Relations of Educational Abilities* (London, London County Council, 1917).

—— 'The measurement of mental capacities', Henderson Trust Lecture 7, Edinburgh, (1927).

—— (ed.), *How The Mind Works* (London, Allen & Unwin, 1933).

—— *Intelligence and Fertility* (London, Cassell, 1952).

D. Butler and R. Rose, *The British General Election of 1959* (London, Macmillan, 1960).

Lord Butler, *The Education Act of 1944 and After*, First Noel Buxton Lecture, University of Essex (Harlow, Longman, 1965).

—— *The Art of the Possible* (London, Hamish Hamilton, 1971).

A. Calder, *The People's War: Britain 1939–45* (London, Cape, 1969).

H. Cantril, *Public Opinion 1935–46* (Princeton, NJ, Princeton University Press, 1951).

C. Cockburn, *I Claud* (Harmondsworth, Penguin, 1967).

C. A. R. Crosland, *The Future of Socialism* (London, Cape, 1956).

R. H. S. Crossman, 'Psychological warfare', *Journal of the Royal United Services Institution* (August 1952).

—— 'The lessons of 1945' in P. Anderson and R. Blackburn (eds), *Towards Socialism* (London, Fontana, 1965).

H. Dalton, 'The "popular front"', *Political Quarterly*, 4, 7 (1936).

M. E. Dimmock, *British Public Utilities and National Development* (London, Allen & Unwin, 1933).

C. H. Dobinson (ed.), *Education in a Changing World* (Oxford, Oxford University Press, 1951).

T. Driberg, *The Best of Both Worlds* (Phoenix House, 1958).

M. R. D. Foot, *Resistance: An Analysis of European Resistance to Fascism* (London, Methuen, 1976).

P. Foot, *The Politics of Harold Wilson* (Harmondsworth, Penguin, 1968).

Fougasse (pseud. C. K. Bird), *The Changing Face of Britain* (London, Methuen, 1950).

M. Gilbert, *Churchill*, vol. 5 (London, Heinemann, 1976).

M. Gilbert and R. Gott, *The Appeasers* (London, Weidenfeld & Nicolson, 1963).

D. Gordan, 'Ten points about the crisis in the British film industry', *Sight and Sound*, 43, 2 (1974).

L. Gorden, *The Public Corporation in Great Britain* (Oxford, Oxford University Press, 1938).

P. H. J. H. Gosden, *Education in the Second World War* (London, Methuen, 1972).

J. Harris, *William Beveridge* (Oxford, Clarendon, 1977).

N. Harris, *Competition and the Corporate State*, (London, Methuen, 1972).

R. Harris, *Politics Without Prejudice* (Tonbridge, Staples, 1956).

T. Harrisson, 'Who'll win?', *Political Quarterly*, 15, 4 (1944).

—— *Living Through the Blitz* (Harmondsworth, Penguin, 1978).

J. A. Hodson, *Somewhere in France. . . . B.E.F.* (London, Whithey Grove, 1940).

—— *War Diary* (London, Gollancz, 1941).

—— *The Home Front* (London, Gollancz, 1944).

L. J. Kamin, *The Science and Politics of IQ* (Harmondsworth, Penguin, 1977).

Labour Party, *Twelve Wasted Years* (London, Labour Party, 1963).

D. Low, *Low's Autobiography* (London, Michael Joseph, 1956).

R. Low, *The History of the British Film*, vol. 1 (London, Allen & Unwin, 1948).

I. McLaine, *The Ministry of Morale* (London, Allen & Unwin, 1978).

—— 'The Ministry of Information', unpublished DPhil thesis (University of Oxford, 1976).

F. Marquis (ed.), *The Memoirs of the Rt Hon. the Earl of Woolton* (London, Cassell, 1959).

A. Marwick, 'Middle opinion in the thirties', *English Historical Review*, lxxix 2 (1964).

Mass Observation, *The War Begins at Home* (London, Chatto & Windus, 1940).

—— *Home Propaganda* (London, Chatto & Windus, 1941).

—— *War Factory* (London, Gollancz, 1943).

—— *The Journey Home* (London, Murray, 1944).

—— *The Press and Its Readers* (London, Art & Technics, 1949).

Ministry of Pensions, *Neuroses in War Time* (London, HMSO, 1940).

J. Montgomery, *The Fifties* (London, Collins, 1965).

H. Morrison, *Socialization and Transport* (London, Constable, 1933).

H. Nicolson, *Diaries and Letters* (London, Collins, 1967).

T. H. O'Brien, *British Experiments in Public Ownership and Control* (London, Allen & Unwin, 1937).

F. Owen, 'This war', *Horizon* (February 1940).

V. Packard, *The Hidden Persuaders* (London, Longman, 1957).

H. Pelling, *Britain and the Second World War* (London, Collins, 1970).

B. Pimlott, *Labour and the Left in the 1930s* (Cambridge, Cambridge University Press, 1977).

—— *Hugh Dalton* (London, Cape, 1985).

J. W. C. Reith, *Personality and Career* (London, George Newnes, 1925).

—— *Winning Spurs* (London, Hutchinson, 1966).

P. Renshaw, *The General Strike* (London, Methuen, 1975).

W. A. Robson, *Public Enterprise* (London, New Fabian Research Bureau, 1937).

—— *Nationalized Industry and Public Ownership* (London, Allen & Unwin, 1960).

R. J. W. Selleck, 'The scientific educationalist', *British Journal of Educational Studies*, xv, 3 (June 1967).

B. Simon, *Education and the Labour Movement, 1870–1920* (London, Lawrence & Wishart, 1965).

—— *The Politics of Educational Reform, 1920–1940* (London, Lawrence & Wishart, 1971).

—— *Intelligence, Psychology and Education* (London, Lawrence & Wishart, 1978).

P. Sissons and R. French (eds), *The Age of Austerity* (Harmondsworth, Penguin, 1962).

R. Skidelsky, *Politicians and the Slump* (London, Macmillan, 196 ̄).

—— 'Keynes and the reconstruction of liberalism', *Encounter* (April 1979).

J. Strachey, *Post D* (London, Gollancz, 1940).

B. Sweet-Escott, *Baker Street Irregular* (London, Collins, 1966).

J. Symons, *The General Strike* (London, Cressett, 1957).

S. Tallents, *The Projection of England* (London, Empire Marketing Board, 1932).

A. J. P. Taylor, *English History 1914–1945* (London, Allen & Unwin, 1965).

—— *Beaverbrook* (London, Hamish Hamilton, 1972).

R. Titmuss, *Problems of Social Policy* (London, Longman/HMSO, 1950).

Sir Robert Vansittart, *Black Record: Germans Past and Present* (London, Hamish Hamilton, 1941).

P. E. Vernon and J. B. Barry, *Personnel Selection in the British Forces* (London, University of London Press, 1949).

Beatrice Webb's Diaries, 1924–32, ed. M. Cole (London, Longman Green, 1956).

N. S. Wilson, *Education in the Forces, 1939–1946: The Civilian Contribution* (London, Allen & Unwin, 1949).

S. W. L. Woodward, *British Foreign Policy in the Second World War* (London, HMSO, 1970/1).

Sociology

T. W. Adorno, *Prisms* (Sudbury, Spearman, 1967).

—— *The Jargon of Authenticity* (London, Routledge & Kegan Paul, 1973).

T. W. Adorno, E. F. Brunswick, D. J. Levinson, and R. N. Sandford, *The Authoritarian Personality* (London, Harper & Row, 1950).

M. Alvarado and E. Buscombe, *Hazell: The Making of a Television Series* (London, British Film Institute, 1978).

H. Arendt, *The Burden of Our Time* (London, Secker & Warburg, 1950).

—— *The Life of the Mind*, vol. 2, *Thinking* (London, Secker & Warburg, 1978).

C. Aubrey, *Autonomy, Control and Communication* (London, Comedia, 1983).

S. H. Bagdikian, *The Information Machines, Their Impact on Man and the Media* (New York, Harper & Row, 1971).

P. Becker and M. McCombs, 'The development of political cognition' in S. H. Chaffee (ed.), *Political Communication: Issues and Strategies* (Beverly Hills, Calif., Sage, 1975).

B. Berelson, 'The state of communication research', *Public Opinion Quarterly*, 31, 2 (1959).

S. Blanchard, *What's This Channel Four?* (London, Comedia, 1983).

J. G. Blumler, 'The audience', in *The Political Effects of Mass Communication* (Milton Keynes, Open University Press, DE 353, 1977).

—— 'The intervention of television in British politics', *Report of the Committee on the Future of Broadcasting* (Annan Report) (1977) [Cmnd 6753, Appendix E].

—— 'An overview of recent research into the impact of broadcasting in democratic politics' in M. J. Clark (ed.), *Politics and the Media* (Oxford, Pergamon, 1979).

J. G. Blumler and M. Gurevitch, 'Towards a comparative framework for political communication' in S. H. Chaffee (ed.), *Political Communication: Issues and Strategies* (London, Sage, 1975).

J. G. Blumler and D. McQuail, *Television in Politics: Its Uses and Influences* (London, Faber, 1968).

J. G. Blumler and J. Madge, *Citizenship and Television* (London, Political & Economic Planning, 1965).

D. Boorstin, *The Image, Or What Happened to the American Dream* (Harmondsworth, Penguin, 1963).

P. Bourdieu, *Outline of a Theory of Practice* (Cambridge, Cambridge University Press, 1977).

O. Boyd-Barrett, D. Seymour-Ure, and J. Tunstall, *Studies on the Press*, Royal Commission on the Press 1974–7, Working Paper 3 (London, HMSO, 1977).

B. Brown, 'An interview with the film censor', *Screen*, 23, 5 (1982).

―― 'Pornography: some modest proposals', *M/F* (January 1982).

M. Bulmer, *Working-Class Images of Society* (London, Routledge & Kegan Paul, 1975).

T. Burns, *The BBC, Public Institutions and Private World* (London, Macmillan, 1977).

H. Cantril, *The Invasion From Mars: A Study in the Psychology of Panic* (Princeton, NJ, Princeton University Press, 1940).

D. Chaney, *Processes of Mass Communication* (London, Macmillan, 1972).

M. Cockerell, P. Hennessy, and D. Walker, *Sources Close to the Prime Minister* (London, Macmillan, 1984).

S. Cohen, *Images of Deviance* (Harmondsworth, Penguin, 1971).

S. Cohen and J. Young (eds), *The Manufacture of News* (London, Constable, 1973).

I. Connell, 'Commercial broadcasting and the British left', *Screen*, 24, 6 (1983).

Conference of Socialist Economics Microelectronics Group, *Microelectronics: Capitalist Technology and the Working Class* (CSE Books, 1980).

J. Dearlove, 'The BBC and politicians', *Index*, 6, 1 (1974).

R. Dyer, *Light Entertainment*, BFI Television Monograph 2 (London, British Film Institute, 1973).

M. Edelmann, *The Symbolic Uses of Politics* (Urbana, Ill., University of Illinois Press, 1964).

P. Elliot, *The Making of a Television Series* (London, Constable 1972).

―― 'Intellectuals and "The information society" and the disappearance of the public sphere', *Media, Culture and Society*, 6, 4 (1982).

P. Elliot, G. Murdoch, and P. Schlesinger, *Televising Terrorism* (London, Comedia, 1984).

―― 'Terrorism and the state: a case study in the discourse of television', *Media, Culture and Society*, 5, 2 (1983).

J. Ellis, *Visible Fiction: Cinema, TV, Video* (London, Routledge & Kegan Paul, 1982).

E. J. Epstein, *News from Nowhere* (New York, Random House, 1973).

S. Frith, *The Sociology of Rock* (London, Constable, 1979).

P. Fussell, *The Great War in Modern Memory* (London, Oxford University Press, 1975).

N. Garnham, *Structures of Television*, BFI Television Monograph 1 (London, British Film Institute, 1973).

—— 'Contribution to a political economy of mass communications', *Media, Culture and Society*, 1, 2 (April 1979).

—— 'Public service versus the market', *Screen*, 24, 1 (1983).

T. Gitlin, 'Prime time ideology: the hegemonic process in television entertainment', *Social Problems*, 26, 3 (1979).

—— *The Whole World is Watching* (Berkeley, Calif., University of California Press, 1982).

Glasgow University Media Group, *Bad News* (London, Routledge & Kegan Paul, 1976).

—— *More Bad News* (London, Routledge & Kegan Paul, 1980).

P. Golding, *The Mass Media* (Harlow, Longman, 1974).

P. Golding and P. Elliot, *Making the News* (Harlow, Longman, 1979).

P. Golding and S. Middleton, *Images of Welfare* (London, Macmillan, 1980).

J. H. Goldthorpe and D. Lockwood, *The Affluent Worker: Political Attitudes and Behaviour* (Cambridge, Cambridge University Press, 1968).

S. Hall, 'The external/internal dialectic on broadcasting', *4th Symposium on British Broadcasting Policy*, February 1972.

—— 'The determination of news photographs' in S. Cohen and J. Young (eds), *The Manufacture of News* (London, Constable, 1973).

—— 'The hinterland of science: ideology' in Centre for Contemporary Cultural Studies, *On Ideology* (London, Hutchinson, 1977).

—— 'Culture, the media, and the ideological effect' in J. Curran, M. Gurevitch, and J. Woollacott (eds), *Mass Communication and Society*, (London, Edward Arnold/Open University, 1977).

—— 'Newspapers, parties and classes', in J. Curran (ed.), *The British Press: A Manifesto* (London, Macmillan, 1978).

S. Hall, C. Critcher, T. Jefferson, J. Clarke, and B. Roberts, *Policing the Crisis: Mugging, the State, and Law and Order* (London, Macmillan, 1978).

S. Hall, C. Curtis, and I. Connell, 'The unity of current events TV' in Centre for Contemporary Cultural Studies, *Working Papers in Cultural Studies* 9, (Spring 1976).

J. D. Halloran, *The Effects of Television* (St Albans, Panther, 1970).

J. D. Halloran and G. Murdoch, *Demonstrations and Communications* (Harmondsworth, Penguin, 1970).

P. Halmos (ed.), *Sociology of Mass Media Communicators*, Sociological Review Monograph 13 (Keele, University of Keele, 1969).

R. Harris, *Gotcha! The Media and the Falklands War* (London, Faber, 1983).

M. Harrop, 'Can Labour recover?', *Political Quarterly*, 54, 1 (1983).

M. Harrop, 'Voters and the media' in J. Seaton and B. Pimlott (eds), *The Media in British Politics* (Aldershot, Gower, 1987).

M. Harrop and R. Worcester (eds), *Political Communication: The 1979 General Election* (London, Macmillan, 1981).

P. Hartmann and C. Husband, *Racism and the Mass Media* (London, Davis-Poynter, 1973).

F. Hayek, *The Road to Serfdom* (London, Routledge & Kegan Paul, 1944).

C. Heller, *Broadcasters and Accountability*, BFI Television Monograph 3 (London, British Film Institute, 1978).

P. M. Hirsch, 'Processing fads and fashions', *American Journal of Sociology*, xxlvi, 1 (1977).

D. Hobson, *Crossroads* (London, Methuen, 1983).

P. Hoch, *The Newspaper Game* (London, Calder & Boyars, 1974).

R. Hoggart, *The Uses of Literacy* (London, Chatto & Windus, 1957).

S. Hood, *The Mass Media* (London, Macmillan, 1972).

A. Hooper, *The Military and the Media* (London, Routledge & Kegan Paul, 1981).

M. Horkheimer, *The Eclipse of Reason* (Oxford, Oxford University Press, 1947).

C. I. Hovland, *Experiments in Mass Communication* (Princeton, NJ, Princeton University Press, 1949).

—— 'Reconciling conflicting results derived from experimental and survey studies of attitude change', *American Psychologist*, 14, 3 (1959).

J. Howkins, *New Technologies, New Policies* (London, British Film Institute, 1982).

G. A. Huaco, *The Sociology of Film Art* (New York, Basic Books, 1965).

C. Husband (ed.), *White Media and Black Britain* (London, Routledge & Kegan Paul, 1962).

B. Jackson and D. Marsden, *Education and the Working Class* (London, Routledge & Kegan Paul, 1962).

M. Jay, *The Dialectical Imagination* (London, Heinemann, 1973).

E. Katz and P. Lazarsfeld, *Personal Influence: The Part Played by People in the Flow of Mass Communication* (West Drayton, Free Press, 1955).

T. Klapper, *The Effects of Mass Communication* (West Drayton, Free Press, 1960).

F. G. Kline and P. J. Tichenor, *Current Perspectives in Mass Communications Research* (London, Sage, 1972).

W. Kornhauser, *The Politics of Mass Society* (London, Routledge & Kegan Paul, 1959).

R. Kuhn, 'Government broadcasting in the 1980s: cross channel perspective', *Political Quarterly*, 53, 4 (1982).

—— 'Ballot box', *Stills* (May–June 1983).

K. Kumar, *Policy and Progress* (Harmondsworth, Penguin, 1978).

—— 'Holding the middle ground: the BBC, the public, and the professional broadcaster' in J. Curran, M. Gurevitch, and J. Woollacott (eds), *Mass Communication and Society* (London, Edward Arnold/Open University, 1977).

S. Lambert, *Channel 4* (London, British Film Institute, 1982).

K. Lang, 'Images of society, media research in Germany', *Public Opinion Quarterly*, xxii, 3 (1974).

K. Lang and G. Lang, *Politics and Television* (New York, Quadrangle, 1968).

—— *The Battle For Public Opinion: Watergate and the Media* (Westport, Conn., Greenwood, 1982).

H. D. Lasswell, *Psychopathology and Politics* (Chicago, Ill., University of Chicago Press, 1930).

—— 'The garrison state', *American Journal of Sociology*, 46, 2 (1941).

P. Lazarsfeld, B. Berelson, and H. Gaudet, *The People's Choice* (New York, Columbia University Press, 1944).

P. Lazarsfeld and R. Merton, 'Mass communication, popular taste and organised social action' in B. Rosenberg and D. White (eds), *Mass Culture* (West Drayton, Free Press, 1957).

P. Lazarsfeld and F. Stanton, *Radio Research 1942–3* (Boston, Mass., Duell Sloan Pearce, 1944).

M. Leapman, *Treachery? The Power Struggle at TUAH*, (London, Allen & Unwin, 1984).

F. R. Leavis, *Mass Civilisation and Minority Culture* (London, Minority Press, 1930).

—— *The Common Pursuit* (London, Chatto & Windus, 1952).

—— *Scrutiny: A Retrospect* (Cambridge, Cambridge University Press, 1962).

—— *A Selection From Scrutiny*, 2 vols (Cambridge, Cambridge University Press, 1968).

F. R. Leavis and D. Thompson, *Culture and Environment* (London, Chatto & Windus, 1933).

Q. D. Leavis, *Fiction and the Reading Public* (London, Chatto & Windus, 1932).

T. Lovell, 'Sociology of aesthetic structures' in D. McQuail (ed.), *Sociology of Mass Communications* (Harmondsworth, Penguin, 1972).

L. Lowenthal, *Prophets of Deceit* (New York, Harper & Row, 1949).

R. S. Lynd and H. M. Lynd, *Middletown: A Study on Contemporary American Culture* (London, Constable, 1929).

—— *Middletown: In Transition* (London, Constable, 1935).

A. McBarnett, 'The North Sea oil story', *Scottish Journal of Sociology*, 3, 1 (1977).

M. McCombs, *The Emergence of American Political Issues* (St Pauls, Minn., West, 1979).

J. Mcleod, L. Becker, and J. Byrnes, 'Another look at the agenda setting function of the press', *Communications Research*, 11, 3 (1974).

D. McQuail, *Towards a Sociology of Mass Communication* (West Drayton, Collier Macmillan, 1969).

—— *Sociology of Mass Communications* (Harmondsworth, Penguin, 1972).

—— 'Review of sociological writings on the press', Royal Commission on the Press 1974–7 Working Paper 2 (London, HMSO, 1977).

—— *Mass Communication Theory: An Introduction*, second edition (London, Sage, 1987).

H. Marcuse, *'The End of Utopia', Five Lectures* (Harmondsworth, Allen Lane, 1970).

—— *One Dimensional Man* (London, Routledge & Kegan Paul, 1974).

M. Mendelsohn and I. Crespi, *Polls, Television and the New Politics* (New York, Harper & Row, 1970).

R. K. Merton, *Social Theory and Social Structure* (West Drayton, Free Press, 1957).

F. Mulhearn, *The Moment of Scrutiny* (London, New Left Books, 1979).

T. Pateman, *Television and the February 1974 General Election* (London, British Film Institute, 1976).

—— *Language, Truth and Politics* (Brighton, Southern Books, 1974).

J. A. R. Pimlott, *Public Relations and American Democracy* (Princeton, NJ, Princeton University Press, 1951; repr. 1974).

A. Ray and K. Rowan (eds), *Inside Information: British Government and the Media* (London, Constable, 1982).

D. Reisman, *The Lonely Crowd* (New Haven, Conn., Yale University Press, 1950).

J. P. Robinson, 'The press as king-maker', *Journalism Quarterly*, 41, 4 (1974).

B. Rosenberg and D. White (eds), *Mass Culture,* (West Drayton, Free Press, 1957).

P. Schlessinger, *Putting 'Reality' Together* (London, Constable, 1974).

J. Seaton, 'The image of trade unions in the media' in B. Pimlott and C. Cook (eds), *Trade Unions in British Politics* (Harlow, Longman, 1982).

—— 'The media and the politics of unemployment' in S. Allen, S. Waton, and S. Wood (eds), *Unemployment* (London, Macmillan, 1985).

—— 'Politics and the media in Britain', *Journal of Western European Politics*, special broadcasting issue (London, summer 1985).

J. Seaton and B. Pimlott, 'The role of the media in the Portuguese Revolution' in A. Smith (ed.), *Newspapers and Democracy* (Cambridge, Mass. MIT Press, 1980).

—— 'The Portuguese media in transition' in K. Maxwell (ed.), *The Press and the Rebirth of Iberian Democracy* (Westport, Conn., Greenwood, 1983).

—— 'Political power and the Portuguese media' in L. Graham (ed.), *In Search of Modern Portugal: The Revolution and its Consequences* (Wisconsin, University of Wisconsin Press, 1983).

C. Seymour-Ure, *The Press, Politics and Public* (London, Methuen, 1968).

—— *The Political Impact of the Mass Media* (London, Constable, 1974).

—— *The American President: Power and Communication* (London, Macmillan, 1982).

—— 'The SDP and the media', *Political Quarterly*, 53, 4 (1982).

E. Shils, *The Intellectuals and the Powers* (Chicago, Ill., University of Chicago Press, 1972).

E. Shils and M. Janowitz, 'Cohesion and disintegration in the Wehrmacht in World War II', *Public Opinion Quarterly*, xii, 3 (London, 1948).

P. Siegelhart (ed.), *Chips with Everything* (London, Comedia, 1982).

P. Slater, *The Origin and Significance of the Frankfurt School* (London, Routledge & Kegan Paul, 1977).

A. Smith, *The Shadow in the Cave* (London, Allen & Unwin, 1973).

—— *The Politics of Information* (London, Macmillan, 1968).

—— (ed.), *Television and Political Life* (London, Macmillan, 1979).

—— 'The fading of the industrial age', *Political Quarterly*, 53, 3 (June 1983).

B. L. Smith, H. D Lasswell, and R. Casey, *Propaganda Communication and Public Opinion* (Princeton, NJ, Princeton University Press, 1946).

A. Swingewood, *The Myth of Mass Culture* (London, Macmillan, 1977).

M. Tracey, *The Production of Political Television* (London, Routledge & Kegan Paul, 1978).

J. Trenaman, *Communications and Comprehension* (London, Collins, 1967).

J. Trenaman and D. McQuail, *Television and the Political Image* (London, Methuen, 1961).

G. Tuchman, 'Making news by doing work', *American Journal of Sociology*, 79, 1 (1973).

—— (ed.), *The TV Establishment* (New York, Random House, 1975).

J. Tunstall, *Advertising Man* (London, Constable, 1969).

—— *The Westminster Lobby Correspondents* (London, Routledge & Kegan Paul, 1970).

—— *The Media in Britain* (London, Constable, 1983).

—— *Journalists at Work* (London, Constable, 1971).

E. G. Wedell, *Broadcasting and Public Policy* (London, Michael Joseph, 1968).

—— *Structures of Broadcasting* (Manchester, Manchester University Press, 1970).

J. Whale, *The Half Shut Eye* (London, Macmillan, 1969).

—— *The Politics of the Media* (London, Fontana, 1977).

R. Williams, *The Long Revolution* (Harmondsworth, Pelican, 1965).

—— *Communications* (London, Chatto & Windus, 1966).

—— *Television: Technology and Cultural Form* (London, Fontana, 1974).

—— *Drama from Ibsen to Brecht* (Harmondsworth, Penguin, 1976).

—— *Keywords* (London, Fontana, 1976).

—— *Marxism and Literature* (Oxford, Oxford University Press, 1977).

—— *Politics and Letters: Interviews with the New Left Review* (London, New Left Books, 1979).

P. Willis, *Learning to Labour* (Farnborough, Saxon House, 1977).

—— *Sacred and Profane Culture* (London, Routledge & Kegan Paul, 1978).

P. Willmott and M. D. Young, *Family and Class in a London Suburb* (London, Routledge & Kegan Paul, 1960).

—— *The Symmetrical Family* (London, Routledge & Kegan Paul, 1973).

Mass communications readers

S. Ball-Rokeach and M. Cantor (eds), *Media, Audience and Social Structure* (Beverly Hills, Calif., Sage, 1986).

B. Berelson and M. Janowitz, *Reader in Public Opinion and Communication* (Glencoe, Free Press, 1966).

R. Collins, J. Curran, N. Gamham, P. Scannell, P. Schlesinger, and C. Sparks, *Media, Culture and Society: A Critical Reader* (London, Sage, 1986).

J. Curran, M. Gurevitch, and J. Woollacott (eds), *Mass Communication and Society* (London, Edward Arnold/Open University, 1977).

L. F. Dexter and D. M. White, *People, Society and Mass Communications* (Glencoe, Free Press, 1964).

M. Gurevitch, T. Bennett, J. Curran, and J. Woollacott (eds), *Culture, Society and the Media* (London, Methuen, 1982).

J. Halloran, *The Effects of Television* (London, Panther, 1970).

P. Halmos (ed.), *Sociology of Mass Media Communicators*, Sociological Review Monograph 13 (Keele, University of Keele, 1969).

D. McQuail, *Sociology of Mass Communication: Selected Reading* (Harmondsworth, Penguin, 1972).

B. Rosenberg and D. M. White, *Mass Culture and the Popular Arts in America* (Glencoe, Free Press, 1956).

W. Schramm, *Mass Communication: A Book of Readings* (Urbana, Ill., University of Illinois Press, 1960).

W. Schramm and D. Roberts, *The Process and Effects of Mass Communication* (Urbana, Ill., University of Illinois, 1971).

G. Tuchman, *The TV Establishment* (Englewood Cliffs, NJ, Prentice Hall, 1974).

J. Tunstall, *Media Sociology* (London, Constable, 1970).

Economic approaches to the media

T. P. Barwise, A. S. C. Ehrenberg, and G. J. Goodhart, 'Audience appreciation and audience size', *Journal of the Market Research Society*, 21, 4 (October 1979).

O. Boyd-Barrett, *Mass Communications in Cross Cultural Contexts: The Case of the Third World* Mass Communications and Society DE 353, Unit 5 (Milton Keynes, Open University, 1977).

L. Brown, *Television: The Business Behind the Box* (New York, Harcourt Brace Jovanovich, 1971).

R. H. Coase, *British Broadcasting: A Study in Monopoly* (London, Longman Green, 1950).

—— 'The market for goods and the market for ideas', *American Economic Review* (1974). p. 384.

J. Curran, 'Advertising and the press' in J. Curran (ed.) *The British Press: A Manifesto* (London, Macmillan, 1978).

—— 'Press freedom as a property right', *Media, Culture and Society*, 1. 1 (1979).

—— 'Advertising as a patronage system', *Sociological Review Monograph* 29 (1980).

—— 'The impact of advertising on the British mass media' in R. Collins *et al* (eds), *Media Culture and Society: A Critical Reader* (London, Sage, 1986).

J. Curran, A. Douglas, and G. Whannel, 'The political economy of the human interest story' in A. Smith (ed.), *Newspapers and Democracy* (Cambridge, Mass., MIT Press, 1981).

E. Epstein, *Broadcast Journalism. The Ratings Game* (Vintage, 1975).

J. E. Gerald, *The British Press under Government Economic Controls* (Minneapolis, University of Minnesota Press, 1956).

T. Gitlin, *Inside Prime Time* (New York, Pantheon, 1983).

G. J. Goodhart, A. S. C. Ehrenberg, and M. A. Collins, *The Television Audience: Patterns of Viewing* (Farnborough, Saxon House, 1975).

T. H. Gubach, *The International Film Industry* (Indiana, University of Indiana Press, 1971).

F. Hirsch and D. Gordan, *Newspaper Money* (London, Hutchinson, 1975).

P. M. Hirsch, 'Processing fads and fashions', *American Journal of Sociology*, 77 (1972).

S. Hoyer, S. Hadenius, and I. Weibull, *The Politics and Economics of the Press: A Developmental Perspective* (Beverly Hills, Calif., Sage, 1975).

R. E. Jackson, 'Satellite business systems and the concept of the dispersed enterprise', *Media, Culture and Society*, 1, 3 (1979).

F. D. Klingender and S. Legg, *Money behind the Screen* (London, Lawrence & Wishart, 1937).

A. Mattelart (trans. M. Chanon), *Multinational Corporations and the Control of Culture* (Brighton, Harvester, 1979).

G. Murdoch and P. Golding, 'For a political economy of mass communication' in J. Saville and R. Milliband (eds), *The Socialist Register 1973* (London, Merlin, 1974).

—— 'Capitalism, communication and class relations' in J. Curran, M. Gurevitch, and J. Woollacott (eds), *Mass Communication and Society* (London, Edward Arnold/Open University, 1977).

Political and Economic Planning, *The British Press* (London, Political & Economic Planning, 1938).

—— *The Factual Film* (London, Arts Enquiry, PEP, 1947).

—— *The British Film Industry* (London, PEP, 1952).

K. Robins and F. Webster, 'Mass communications and information technology' in R. Milliband and J. Saville (eds), *The Socialist Register 1979* (London, Merlin, 1979).

H. Schiller, *Who Knows: Information in the Age of Fortune 500* (New Jersey, Ablex, 1981).

A. Smith, 'Subsidies and the press in europe', *Political and Economic Planning*, xliii, 569 (1977).

—— *The Geopolitics of Information* (London, Faber, 1980).

—— *Goodbye Gutenburg: The Newspaper Revolution of the 1980s* (London, Oxford University Press, 1980).

S. G. Sturmey, *The Economic Development of Radio* (London, Duckworth, 1958).

J. Tunstall, *The Media are American* (London, Constable, 1977).

T. Varis, 'The international flow of television programmes', *Journal of Communication*, 34 (1984).

F. Wolf, *Television Programming for News and Current Affairs* (New York, Praeger, 1972).

Politics of British mass media

Adam Smith Institute, *Omega Report: Communications Policy* (London, Adam Smith Institute, 1984).

—— *Funding the BBC* (London, Adam Smith Institute, 1985).

N. Ascherson, 'Newspapers and internal democracy' in J. Curran (ed.), *The British Press: A Manifesto* (London, Macmillan, 1978).

T. Baistow, *Fourth-Rate Estate* (London, Comedia, 1985).

D. Berry, L. Cooper, and C. Landry, *Where is the Other News?* (London, Comedia, 1980).

Broadcasting Research Unit, *The Public Service Idea* (London, Broadcasting Research Unit, 1985).

R. Collins, 'Broadband Black Death cuts queues: the information society and the UK' in R. Collins *et al*, *Media, Culture and Society: A Critical Reader* (London, Sage, 1986).

L. Cooper, C. Landry, and D. Berry, *The Other Secret Service* (London, Comedia, 1980).

J. Curran (ed.), *The British Press: A Manifesto* (London, Macmillan, 1978).

—— 'Reconstructing the mass media' in J. Curran (ed.), *The Future of the Left*, (London, Polity, 1984).

J. Curran, J. Eccleston, G. Oakley, and A. Richardson (eds), *Bending Reality: The State of the Media* (London, Pluto, 1986).

C. Dunkley, *Television Today and Tomorrow* (Harmondsworth, Penguin, 1985).

M. Ferguson, *New Communication Technologies and the Public Interest* (London, Sage, 1986).

N. Garnham, 'Telecommunications policy in the United Kingdom', *Media, Culture and Society*, 7, 1 (1985).

C. Gardiner and J. Sheppard, 'Transforming TV: the limits of left policy', *Screen*, 25, 2 (1984).

N. Garnham, 'Public service versus the market', *Screen*, 24, 1 (1983).

Glasgow University Media Group, *Really Bad News* (London, Writers & Readers, 1982).

P. Golding and G. Murdock, 'Confronting the market: public intervention and press diversity' in J. Curran (ed.), *The British Press: A Manifesto* (London, Macmillan, 1978).

—— 'The new communications revolution' in J. Curran, J. Ecclestone, G. Oakley, and A. Richardson (eds), *Bending Reality : The State of the Media* (London, Pluto, 1986).

S. Hearst, 'The development of cable systems and services', *Political Quarterly*, 54, 3 (1983).

P. Hennessy, D. Walker, and M. Cockerell, *Sources Close to the Prime Minister* (London, Macmillan, 1985).

S. Holland, 'Countervailing press power' in J. Curran (ed.), *The British Press: A Manifesto* (London, Macmillan, 1978).

Labour Party, *People and the Media*, (London, Labour Party, 1974).

C. Landry, D. Morley, R. Southwood, and P. Write, *What a Way to Run a Railroad*, (London, Comedia, 1985).

C. MacCabe and Olivia Stewart (eds), *The BBC and Public Service Broadcasting* (Manchester, Manchester University Press, 1986).

D. McQuail and K. Siane (eds), *New Media Politics* (London, Sage, 1986).

Militant, *What We Stand For* (London, Militant, 1985).

E. Moonman (ed.), *The Press: A Case for Commitment* (London, Fabian Society Trust, 391, 1969).

G. Mulgan and K. Worpole, *Saturday Night or Sunday Morning* (London, Comedia, 1986).

G. Robertson, *People Against the Press* (London, Quartet, 1983).

G. Robertson and A. Nicol, *Media Law* (London, Sage, 1985).

J. Seaton, 'Government policy and the mass media' in J. Curran (ed.), *The British Press: A Manifesto* (London, Macmillan, 1978).

—— 'Broadcasting and politics in Britain' in R. Kuhn (ed.), *Broadcasting and Politics in Western Europe* (London, Sage, 1985).

—— 'The media and politics in Britain', *Journal of Western European Politics*, 6, 3 (June 1985).

—— 'Pornography annoys' in J. Curran (ed.), *Bending Reality: The State of the Media* (London, Pluto, 1986).

—— 'The media and the politics of unemployment' in S. Allen (ed.), *The Experience of Unemployment*, (London, Macmillan, 1986).

—— 'Atrocities and the media', *International Journal of Communications*, 2, 1 (January 1987).

—— 'The Holocaust: a case study of atrocities and the media' in J. Seaton and B. Pimlott (eds), *The Media in British Politics* (Aldershot, Gower, 1987).

J. Seaton and B. Pimlott, 'The struggle for balance: the BBC and the politicians 1926–1945' in J. Seaton and B. Pimlott (eds), *The Media in British Politics* (Aldershot, Gower, 1987).

P. Schlesinger, 'From public service to commodity: the political economy of teletext in the UK', *Media, Culture and Society*, 7, 4 (1984).

C. Seymour-Ure, 'Leaders and the media' in J. Seaton and B. Pimlott (eds), *The Media in British Politics* (Aldershot, Gower, 1987).

A. Smith, *Subsidies and the Press in Europe* (London, Political & Economic Planning, 1977).

J. Whale, *The Politics of the Media* (London, Fontana, 1980).

P. Whitehead, 'Reconstructing broadcasting' in J. Curran, J. Ecclestone, G. Oakley, and A. Richardson (eds), *Bending Reality: The State of the Media* (London, Pluto, 1986).

Index

Sub-entries are arranged in chronological order where significant. All others are in alphabetical order.

the Repeal of the Taxes on Knowledge, 26
Astor, D., 79
Astor, Lord J.J., 49
Atlantic Richfield, 91, 92
Attlee, C., 69, 76, 132, 154
ATV Showbook, 178, 181
audience: discovering (BBC), 117–19; knowledge, 232–4; mass media, 227–32, 237; television, 177–9, 185–210, 269, 286, 313; *see also* listeners
Audience Appreciation Index, 201–2
Audience Research Department, 140
Audit Bureau of Circulation, 60
austerity (BBC), 172–4
Austin, Sir H., 131
autonomy: broadcasting, 239, 243, 249, 272; commercial television, 198; editors, 299; *see also* independence (broadcasting)

Baistow, T., 299
Baldwin, S., 46, 56, 57, 62, 120
Barnett, A., 240
barons, press (era of), 46–64; empire creation, 47–9; proprietorial control and, 49–52; profits and politics, 52–4; rise of fourth estate, 54–7; social order and, 57–9; modified economic controls, 59–63
Barry (psychologist), 166
Bartholomew (editor), 62
Battle of Britian, 142, 148
BBC: accountability, 267–8; expansion in 1960s, 191–2; finances, 8, 313; news, 138, 146, 150–2, 154–8, 160, 238, 287; public policy, 277, 282–5, 287; public service ideal, 263–7, 269; radio separate from television, 303; social reforms, 161–4, 167–9; television, 172, 175–84,

193, 197, 203, 207–8; *see also* BBC (fall); BBC (origins and growth); BBC reforms; World War II (BBC in)
BBC (fall), 172–84; austerity, monopoly and Beveridge, 172–4; commercial television and, 174–84; monopoly ends, 183–4; *see also* BBC; BBC (origins and growth); BBC reform
BBC (origins and growth), 117–35; audience, 117–19; first Director General, *see* Reith, J.; as public corporation, 119–24; political independence, 124–6, 134; and General Strike, 126–8, 152; and government in 1930s, 128–30; society and programme, 130–2; and journalism, 133; and appeasement, 133–4; *see also* BBC; BBC (fall); BBC reforms; World War II (BBC in)
BBC reforms (alternative approaches), 292–4, 296–7, 299–303, 307, 313–14, 320–1
Beadle, G., 175
Beavan, J., 98
Beaverbrook, Lord W.M.A., 34, 46, 48, 49–51, 52, 54, 55–6, 69, 79
Becker, P., 230, 233
Beckett-Denison, E., 42
Beehive, 34
Bell, A., 41
Bell, D., 188, 211
Bellenger, F., 72, 74
Benjamin, W., 226
Benn, A.W., 297
Bennett, T., 155
Berelson, B., 230
Bernstein, S., 209
Berridge, V., 31
Berry brothers, *see* Camrose; Kemsley
BET, 309